Popularizing
Pennsylvania

Shoemaker at Restless Oaks, 1913, posing with two of his great loves—books and animals. He is holding "Ramsden Rex," his English-bred Russian wolfhound. (Juniata College Archives)

Simon J. Bronner

Popularizing Pennsylvania

Henry W. Shoemaker and the Progressive Uses of Folklore and History

The Pennsylvania State University Press
University Park, Pennsylvania

Library of Congress Cataloging-in-Publication Data

Bronner, Simon J.
   Popularizing Pennsylvania : Henry W. Shoemaker and the progressive
uses of folklore and history / Simon J. Bronner.

      p.   cm.
   Includes bibliographical references and index.
   ISBN 0-271-01486-5 (cloth : alk. paper)
   ISBN 0-271-01487-3 (paperbk : alk. paper)
   1. Shoemaker, Henry W. (Henry Wharton), b. 1880.   2. Folklorists—
Pennsylvania—Biography.   3. Folklore—Pennsylvania.
4. Pennsylvania—Social life and customs.   I. Title.
GR55.S53B76   1996
398′.092—dc20
[B]   95-15354
                                        CIP

It is the policy of The Pennsylvania State University Press to use acid-free paper for the
first printing of all clothbound books. Publications on uncoated stock satisfy the minimum
requirements of American National Standard for Information Sciences—Permanence of
Paper for Printed Library Materials, ANSI Z39.48-1992.

For Ken and Ann Marie Thigpen

Contents

List of Illustrations

Acknowledgments

This book combines oral history with archival research and folkloristic and historical analysis. It complements my previous book *American Folklore Studies: An Intellectual History* (1986), which is largely devoted to the academy. After completing that book, I realized that the public realms of America's promoters of American tradition have yet to be properly chronicled for consideration by historians, folklorists, and American Studies scholars. My hope is that this biographical study makes a contribution to that effort, and also appeals to the residents on whom Henry W. Shoemaker had such a large impact.

The largest collection of Shoemaker's papers and photographs is in private hands, and I am fortunate to be the first researcher to have had access to the material. Another major collection is at the Pennsylvania State University, University Park campus, in its Historical Collections and Labor Archives and in its Rare Book Room. The State Archives of Pennsylvania has substantial holdings that pick up Shoemaker's trail after World War II. I also benefited from other holdings at Juniata College, the Lycoming County Historical Society, the Huntingdon County Historical Society, the Blair County Historical Society, the Clinton County Historical Society, Millersville University, the State Library of Pennsylvania, Bucknell University, Franklin and Marshall College, the Annie Halenbake Ross Library in Lock Haven, and the *Lock Haven Express*. I thank the many directors, archivists, and curators that helped me in my research, including Sara Briggs, Donald Durnbaugh, Charles Mann, Linda Ries, Nancy Shedd, and Jonathan Stayer.

A project such as this entails exploring many libraries for information on subjects that seem at first disparate—history, geography, nature, folklore, politics, and literature. Just tracking down Shoemaker's tremendous output of publications covering these subjects and more was in itself a task. To document my searches and make suggestions for your future reading or study, I've given probably more than the usual space to bibliography. At the Heindel Library at Penn State Harrisburg, Ruth Runion Slear deserves praise for attending to interlibrary loans, and Alan Mays and Henry Koretzky looked out for my interests in periodicals. Darrell Peterson lent his photographic expertise, and Donna Horley and Sue Etter gave assistance in the office. Kenneth Patrick at the Center for Pennsylvania Culture Studies, Penn State Harrisburg, was an outstanding research assistant. My colleagues in American Studies—Michael Barton, Alison Hirsch, John Patterson, and Irwin Richman—offered welcome encouragement and advice. I especially appreciate the support of Howard Sachs, Office of Research and Graduate Studies, and William Mahar, Humanities Division, Penn State Harrisburg, for their support of the project.

Outside the archives, several people assisted my field research. Lisa Rusnak has my fondest gratitude for her caring and interest in the project. Related to some of Shoemaker's key informants, she generously guided me through mountain trails that Shoemaker followed to gather his stories. I also owe special thanks to Kim Yarnell, who helped me find my way around Shoemaker's haunts in Lock Haven and aided me in numerous other ways. I also appreciate the time that acquaintances of Shoemaker spared toward my oral history: Samuel Bayard, Dolores Coffey, Robert Crist, Frank Hoffmann, Autumn Leonard, Robert Maguire, Martha Simonetti, William Wewer, John Witthoft, Sybil Jane Worden, and Don Yoder. In addition, my thinking benefited from discussions with historians, geographers, and folklorists: William Aspinall, Ronald Baker, Jan Harold Brunvand, Angus Gillespie, Henry Glassie, Harvey Green, David Hufford, Michael Owen Jones, Bill McNeil, Jay Mechling, Thomas Schlereth, Linda Shopes, Robert Weible, David Wilson, and Wilbur Zelinsky. Not least, I gained insights from talking with Pennsylvanians about their image of the state and its sources. The list is long, but I trust they know who they are, and I hope they recognize my gratitude.

Professors Kenneth Thigpen and Ann Marie Thigpen of Penn State University have been my gracious hosts, colleagues, and friends since I arrived in Pennsylvania. They have taught me much about the life and lore of the region and have had much to offer during conversations that lasted through the night. They too have followed Shoemaker's trails and understand the need for this book. To them, to their example, I dedicate this work.

Introduction

If you've heard about the Pennsylvania mountains as a storied getaway, you can thank Henry Wharton Shoemaker. If you've ever enjoyed a state park or forest in Pennsylvania, give him some credit. If you've ever noticed a historical marker, you may be reading his words. Those Lions, Panthers, and Eagles you cheer on the field may have gained much of their association with Pennsylvania because of his efforts. The museum you visit, the memorial you honor, and the vista you admire may all have been touched by Henry Shoemaker's creative hand. That Pennsylvania legend you hear may just be the work of his imagination, and the curious place-name that grabs your attention could well have been his idea.

Few regions have had as energetic and influential a promoter as Henry Shoemaker. His campaign to popularize Pennsylvania and conserve its resources arose with a flurry during the Progressive Era, and he continued his unrelenting support through the New Deal and the post–World War II period. Proud of the "Progressive" label, and sounding some of its keywords of utility, efficiency, and public good, he made his mark within the Progressive movement by mobilizing private organizations and state programs for the "public use" of folklore, history, and nature to preserve America's cultural and natural heritage. The ways that this heritage became defined for ensuing generations, and the manner in which government became involved in the management of regional folklore, history, and environment, deserve attention in the ongoing discussion of American identity.

My exploration of Henry Shoemaker's life and career reveals how American and Pennsylvanian traditions were shaped and packaged to inspirit the land, provide a hedge against rapid industrialization, and instill civic values and regional pride. Drenched with religious symbolism, Shoemaker's campaign for conservation of folklore, history, and nature advanced America as a unified nation based on the principles of its founding in the wilderness. The cause encouraged patriotism, he claimed, and its literature underscored loyalty to the land by being imbued with a romantic regionalism that expressed the glory of the frontier and its common, hardy folk. The spiritual reverence Shoemaker and his supporters gave to the rustic past signaled a realization that the times had changed dramatically—and not all for the better—as a result of industrialization and immigration. Alarmed at the threat to the pristine land and the lore he adored, Shoemaker's answer was to promote Pennsylvania's image as the bucolic wonderland, to "see America first."

Beyond this intellectual concern, Henry Shoemaker's life story contains high drama worth recounting. He was born into one of America's wealthiest families in an exclusive area of New York City, and yet he came to champion the outdoor life of Pennsylvania's highlands. Mingling in the city's upper crust with Vanderbilts, Rockefellers, and Astors, he took to wandering off by himself on foot and horseback through treacherous backcountry trails, in addition to joining safaris in Africa and jaunts to Europe to meet royalty. He was already publishing his writing by the time he was eighteen, and began amassing collections of art and historical artifacts. He broke into Wall Street as one of its youngest brokers, and created a stir around town with his reported daredevil feats of mountain-climbing, ballooning, and airplaning. When he married, he enjoyed the most expensive wedding gift ever reported in America. A short time later, he suffered scandal in the front pages of the leading New York newspapers as his marriage disintegrated. Around the same time, he faced the tragic death of his young brother and business partner. Henry Shoemaker served his country abroad as a diplomat and soldier, then returned to Pennsylvania to become a prominent newspaper publisher known for espousing Progressive Republican causes. He gained renown as an ardent conservationist and used his wealth to save forestland and threatened animals across the state of Pennsylvania. The romantic writer and the dedicated historian, he was also the urban sophisticate and backcountry roamer. He lost his family fortune and went to work for the state, again making his mark, becoming the nation's first State Folklorist. He died amid controversy over his use of folklore and history, but he left a lasting legacy of work for Pennsylvania's heartland.

It was my interest in the heartland's image and reality that led me to Henry Shoemaker's story. I consumed the popular image of Penn's Woods: farms, forests, and folk. I remember taking in those nationally broadcast Penn State games in "Nittany Valley," and I thrilled along with gazing millions when the blimp panned the gorgeous mountain vista. (And I wasn't alone in wondering, Exactly what is a Nittany lion?) Despite lingering industrial memories of coal mines and rust-belt mills, Central Pennsylvania— the "heart" and "highlands" of the state—carries the mystique of a place where hunters and fishermen enjoy nature's bounty. It is a storied place with countless small towns, ethnic varieties, and legends at every turn.

Think of the region's fame for hosting Amish, Mennonite, Jewish, French, Italian, Irish, and countless other ethnic-religious communities, and you see an epitome of tradition and tolerance. Standing squarely between distinct regions of New England and the South, Pennsylvania has a character— indeed, a mystique—all its own.

From one end of America to the other, even on foreign shores, people told me about Pennsylvania. Statements such as "The mountains are beautiful there," "That's where the Amish are," and "You have lots of folklore there" resounded in countless conversations. More than a state, the place appeared to be a cultural region unto itself. The longer I lived in Pennsylvania, the more I realized that this image, this mystique, is both fact and fiction. The state is not as unified, or as diverse, as the image suggests. The landscape is wilderness in spots, pastoral in others, scenic and stunning to be sure, but it is equally industrial and modern. In Lancaster County, the "garden spot" where so many tourists come attracted by Amish farmlands, commercial strips multiply, and in the mountains and the Black Forest region of Central Pennsylvania, the woods struggle to return to their pre-logging splendor. Many languages can be heard in the state, and residents are fiercely proud of their ethnic heritage, but in many communities tradition waits for revival as young people leaving for more prosperous pastures break the links of the generations.

As a resident of the state, as well as a cultural historian, I wanted to explain this romantic image. The narratives of rustic Pennsylvania abounded around me, and one especially seemed to capture the essence of this image. Tellers pointed to Mount Nittany, one of Pennsylvania's majestic picturesque peaks smack in the middle of the state, and began relating the saga of "the Indian Princess Nita-nee." She ran off for love with a French trapper, I was told, but her brothers caught up with the couple at the ledge over Penn's Cave and threw the Frenchman into the murky waters below. Since then, one could hear the sound of "Nita-nee" echoing through the area.

If I didn't perk up my ears for stories about "Nita-nee," I could read her story on postcards, advertisements, and promotions. Every summer it welcomes many thousands of visitors to Penn's Cave and is a favorite of generations of Penn State students studying in the shadow of Mount Nittany and walking by the famed Nittany Lion "shrine." And there were other similar stories, mystifying the mountains and streams of the mid-state. Often glorifying the original Indian inhabitants living in commune with nature, the romantic stories are complemented by countless Pennsylvania place names, such as Indian Grave Hill, Warrior Trail, and Picture Rocks. The stories might dwell on the ghosts of Indians past or recount incidents that bring pioneers in battle with nature, and adventurers in search of treasure,

or tell of workcamp intrigue in the isolated mountains and forests. The
imposing landscape of the mid-state lends an air of wonder and mystery that
probably fostered tales of shifty ghosts and strange characters.

Romantic place-names, the "Nita-nee" story, and the romance of the
Pennsylvania mountain lion were the work of Henry Shoemaker, who lived
from 1880 to 1958. His own life was the stuff of legend as people talked
about his immense wealth, his connections with royalty and power, his
dramatic financial successes and failures, his daredevil cave explorations and
mountain climbs, his brushes with death in the claws of wild animals, his
eccentric hobbies, and above all, his consuming passion for conserving and
promoting Pennsylvania's wildlife, mountains, and common folk. He was an
intriguing character, who simultaneously gained renown and enjoyed obscurity.

Shoemaker led a "Progressive" campaign in the twentieth century to
restore Penn's Woods and preserve the state as a cherished home to wildlife
as well as folklife. Touting rugged frontier figures of Daniel Boone and Davy
Crockett as the new American pantheon born of the wilderness, replacing
the Old World classical heroes, Shoemaker and his Progressive cronies in
the Boone & Crockett Club in New York City (led by Theodore Roosevelt
and George Bird Grinnell) set out to explore and save the wilderness. By
saving a source of American distinction and wonder, they believed, they
could help recover a sense of American nationhood and spirituality at a time
of rapid industrialization, immigration, and urbanization.

Shoemaker and his Progressive friends used their imaginations and their
pens to promote a unified vision of America's genuine landscape and legend.
It was a patriotic movement, Shoemaker often declared, to preserve the
roots of America in the forested wilderness—and where better than in the
only state with forests, or "sylvan," in its name? Not born in the state, he
nonetheless trumpeted Pennsylvania as "God's Chosen wonderland," the
"mystic region," a "wooded paradise," and a "glorious land of romance."
His campaign is significant, because while he was glorifying the abundance
of the Pennsylvania wilderness his adopted state represented the heights of
industrial transformation. After 1870, railroad, coal, oil, iron, steel, and
lumber industries laid their claim to the state's land and people in dramatic
fashion. As Pennsylvania's image went—rustic or industrial—so it seemed
the nation's image would go.

At the forefront of conservation efforts during the Progressive Era,
Shoemaker fell in with national leaders such as President Theodore Roosevelt, Governor Gifford Pinchot, Ernest Thompson Seton, Horace McFarland, Joseph Illick, and George Bird Grinnell, who encouraged American
Victorians to commune with nature and appreciate its history and legend for
future use. They believed that nature and related folk cultures held vitalizing,

even spiritual, powers for a modern age. Roosevelt and Pinchot chimed the keyword "conservation" over the more passive "preservation," and Shoemaker energetically joined in, adding the spiritual resources of "history" and "folklore" to the list of endangered species meant for protection and use. In his newspaper editorials, in his books and many addresses, in his many organizations and state commissions, he lobbied for restoring the balance of nature, and the harmonious life and values it fostered. His special stand in this movement was somewhat ironic, for his wealth and power derived largely from the industrial boom of the late nineteenth century.

Henry Shoemaker took up the conservationist cause in Pennsylvania, where his family had derived a fortune from coal mining, banking, and railroading. His campaign was to convince Pennsylvanians to appreciate the beauty, heritage, and spirit of their natural surroundings, and consequently to prevent the kinds of development, industrial and materialistic, that threatened both the environment and the traditional social values associated with life in the wilderness. He spread this message in countless editorials, speeches, and writings carried all around the state, and in his official state duties on various commissions and boards. The publisher of newspapers in Reading, Altoona, Jersey Shore, and Bradford, he was also active in state and national politics, eventually becoming minister to Bulgaria. And as a prolific writer, he was the author of hundreds of pamphlets and books on nature, history, and folklore, and, counting his articles, columns, and addresses, his output probably ran into the thousands. He established and led numerous organizations designed to "sell Pennsylvania to Pennsylvanians," including the Pennsylvania Alpine Club, the Pennsylvania Folklore Society, the Pennsylvania Federation of Historical Societies and Museums, and the Pennsylvania Conservation Association.

An unabashed romantic and popularizer of legends and history, Shoemaker endured criticism and gained admiration for his version of Pennsylvania's heritage. He struggled to court scholarly bolstering for his endeavors, including support from Cornell's Harold Thompson, who dubbed him "Mr. Pennsylvania." His main allies, however, were fellow newspaper publishers who spread the mystique to their daily readers and to politicos who backed his efforts to involve state government in the promotion of Pennsylvania as a special—indeed hallowed—place.

Residing only doors from the Governor's Mansion, Shoemaker hobnobbed with politicians, bishops, and countless homespun "mountaineers." He represented the state as State Archivist, director of the State Museum, chairman of the State Historical Commission, and a member of the State Geographic Board and State Forest Commission. Politically, he received great notoriety from his appointment as minister to Bulgaria during the Hoover administration, but his crowning glory toward his goal of promoting

Pennsylvania tradition was the distinction of being America's first official State Folklorist, a position that now exists in almost every state of the union. It was also the source of his greatest anguish as he battled for acceptance in his declining years. It is the development of cultural conservation and of the State Folklorist position that deserves special attention in any evaluation of the popularization of Pennsylvania, and I try to give it its due here.

For Henry Shoemaker, folklore represented the realm between history and fiction, nature and culture, and it got everyday people talking about themselves, their past, and their preindustrial surroundings. To him, folklore came from the spirited age of romance before "modern civilization" took over, and it reflected America's roots as the "glorious land of romance." With his booster spirit and popular goals, he found himself at odds with folklorists over what folklore was and how it should be presented. If he failed to woo scholars, he convinced his pals in government that promoting folklore perpetuated what Pennsylvania was all about—a modern-day Eldorado—and it became a centerpiece of a conservation and tourist program that jumped ahead of other industries of steel, coal, oil, and lumbering.

Eldorado. Legends of wealth in the wilderness. Henry Shoemaker claimed to have found the mythical kingdom sought after by sixteenth-century adventurers in the New World. His Eldorado lay in Central Pennsylvania between Philadelphia and Pittsburgh. Indeed, in Shoemaker's kingdom, urbanized and industrialized Philadelphia and Pittsburgh had little to do with Pennsylvania. The spiritual essence of Pennsylvania rested in the Pennsylvania highlands, and it had something of the Appalachian mystique for preserving its past and rusticity. But it had more cultures mixing in its midst, and it fed into, rather than borrowing from, southern Appalachian life. Pennsylvania was, Shoemaker wrote, "the final frontier of the modern complex civilization." Pennsylvania's Eldorado was a hunter's paradise filled with the charming powers of "natural wonders and historic spots," the spirits of ancient Indian wanderers, and the romance of legend filling every awe-inspiring mountain, stream, and forest.

The American "age of romance" that Shoemaker wanted to promote served to allay fears that America would be built over by a pernicious version of industrial capitalism. He worried that money and materialism were goals that overshadowed traditional values of civility and community. He saw the cities and their new residents that commanded the artificial light of industrialization as threats to America's unity and heritage. Like many other leaders who traced their roots to colonial immigration, Shoemaker was startled by the flood tide of immigrants from eastern and southern Europe sparked by turn-of-the-century industrialization. In the mythology of Shoemaker's wilderness, not only Pennsylvania, but also old Protestant

America itself, was being promoted. Pennsylvania held the wilderness, the "frontier," that epitomized the original American consciousness of the invitation extended by the New World's fertile Eden. Shoemaker was hardly alone in believing that in such a place democratic principles and civil values thrived and that assimilation, or "Americanization," would be realized. In rhetoric that dripped old-time religion and evolutionary natural history, one could hear that from the mix of many pilgrim groups coming to the American Promised Land emerged a unique American type, a new Adam born of the Edenic wilderness. Shoemaker's distinction was his promoter's—some even said preacher's—zeal for spreading the good news in the marketing revolution brought by newspapers and periodicals around the turn of the century. Building a reverence for an imagined past that translated into Pennsylvania's special mystique, Shoemaker used his newspapers as his pulpit and his stories as testament for a modern era.

Giving Pennsylvania this mystique was no mean feat. Henry Shoemaker began his campaign in the early twentieth century, when Americans felt more of a romantic inclination toward the frontier West or old New England. Pennsylvania was at that time America's industrial giant, and new factories, railroads, mines, and logging operations sprouted everywhere, so it seemed. Pennsylvania was America's future, it appeared, and new Roman Catholic, Eastern Orthodox, and Jewish immigrants from eastern and southern Europe flocked to its industries to supply an expanding America. Forests and mountains, and old traditions, were giving way before the allure of industrial profits. In this era of invention, Shoemaker and his cohorts fabricated a popular bucolic image to preserve the legendary spirit of Pennsylvania and to assimilate the state's new residents.

How successful, or desirable, was this campaign? That is a provocative question, and one that any account of Henry W. Shoemaker's life and work should address. Pennsylvania certainly draws people to visit its landscape and to consume its legends, but its image still lacks the regional recognition of the South and New England. Pennsylvania has had a mixed record of protecting its environment, and debates still rage about the privilege of industry and protecting folk cultures in the region. Signs of memorializing history and culture abound, and yet many residents question the effects of historical and cultural tourism. Shoemaker constantly advocated state management of history and culture much as government-administered parks or forests. He helped usher in the state's Historical Commission, and later the Pennsylvania Historical and Museum Commission—a groundbreaking agency in the nation's public history movement. Indeed, state government still takes great responsibility for protecting Pennsylvania's history and folklore, melded into "heritage," as natural resources. With the rise of multiculturalism as an educational concept, however, there is resistance to the promotion of an exceptional "state" heritage. One hears more today of a need for the state to return control of historical sites, and especially cultural property, to communities. At stake is the power to interpret, and control, a group's destiny as well as its past.

And what of Shoemaker's Progressive call for the public "management" of the wild? What of his belief that preserving the woods will foster a benevolent morality drawn from life in awe of nature? Pennsylvania usually leads the nation in number of hunting and fishing licenses issued, and it is among the nation's leaders in state park and forest acreage. Just as notable is that the state is the main arena for clashes between city and country values in little towns like Hegins, now known nationally for its annual pigeon shoot (Shoemaker edited a book on the protection of pigeons), and between industry and the region in such places, and symbols, as Three Mile Island. Can it be said that the state's conflicts epitomize the nation's struggles?

Henry W. Shoemaker's vision for Pennsylvania has undergone much alteration. The major one was the addition—some even say the dominance—of the Amish and their farmlands in Lancaster County to the drawing spirit of Pennsylvania. Another Shoemaker, Alfred L., helped bring this legacy to public attention. At first Alfred was an ally, but he became Henry's bitter enemy, and that saga of their affection and disaffection is part of the drama surrounding the popularization of Pennsylvania. Moving beyond Henry Shoemaker's conservationist vision of Pennsylvania for Pennsylvanians, the "Dutchland" brought non-Pennsylvanians to gaze on a variant of the Pennsylvania mystique. To Henry's chagrin in his last days, the "Dutchland" invited more development rather than less.

Another addition has been occurring as Pennsylvania's heavy industries become "history." The National Park Service, which first responded to Henry Shoemaker's conservationist campaign to protect the environment, now seeks to create what are called "Heritage Parks" revolving around industries in different regions of the state, such as oil, lumber, and coal. Designed for the purposes of economic development and supported by the state, the Heritage Parks program is intended to enhance "community, regional, and state-wide awareness and pride of Pennsylvania's historical and cultural legacy through the preservation, adaptive reuse, or restoration of historic sites and properties."[1] The machine has entered Shoemaker's garden.

My accounting of Pennsylvania's popularization thus essentially involves the colorful life and pioneering work of Henry W. Shoemaker, the state's greatest promoter. I look at his ideas, sources, associates, and contributions. I especially cover his collection and fabrication of folklore because Shoemaker himself called it his "real life's work," and it provides a focus for analysis of the cultural conservationist cause that had national implications.

Room still remains for analysis of Henry Shoemaker's contributions in the context of other intellectual concerns, but I believe that his use of folklore provides the most prominent point of departure for consideration of twentieth-century movements to define cultural tradition for a modern age. In the romantic promotion of folk tradition's connection to nature is found a new kind of spirituality that is still being explored, and exploited, today.

My chronicle begins with Henry W. Shoemaker's early life and endeavors and moves on to his championing of folklore and history as a way to build an appreciation for the natural Pennsylvania environment. My chapter titles are borrowed from quotations by and about Shoemaker from his early to later life. His journey begins as a Victorian gentleman dabbling in the protection of nature while pursuing business, writing, and travel, and ends focused on the conservation of culture. "A Rich and Colorful Life" covers his early multiple activities stretched between New York and Pennsylvania. I offer context for his efforts in the high society of which he was a part and the Progressive Era in which he came into his own.

In "Along the Line of Popularizing the Old Legends" I analyze his renown, especially after 1920, for collecting and promoting Pennsylvania folklore, and discuss specific stories that drew the attention of the public, the styles of writing he used, and the impact of his prose. The Appendix provides some of his best-known stories. If you haven't read Shoemaker's work before, you might want to read "Nita-nee" and the other legends in the Appendix and elsewhere, before beginning my chronicle. In Chapter 2, I also delve into the effects of various organizations of which Shoemaker was a part. "Of Service to the Public" examines his efforts at building cultural conservation into the structure of state government. I particularly follow his tenure as the first State Folklorist and discuss the praise and criticism he received for his organization of historical and cultural conservation in state government. I close with a reflection on his influence on today's public history and folklore movements. Taken together, these chapters form the conclusion that whether fact or fiction or both, the romantic image that Shoemaker helped popularize endures as part of America's regional consciousness.

My attention to the power of enduring stories and symbols in Henry Shoemaker's popularization of Pennsylvania connects this study to other works in American studies that seek to comprehend the ways that Americans have defined their purposes through images and narratives brought together as a kind of driving, unstated myth. Indeed, William A. Clebsch has underscored the narration of American identities by suggesting the word "mythique" as a name for those "complexes of legendary or mythical stories and meanings," such as Shoemaker's, used to denote "tales that tell us where we are going and who we are who are going wherever we are

going."[2] What Shoemaker had in mind were tales for Pennsylvania that trace
a broad national mission to preserve the founding wonder of settlers facing
the wilderness. He also gave a more localized story of a region hanging on
to a heritage that is worthy of appreciation and conservation. Shoemaker
often used the word "mystical" and "mythical" for his account of the past. It
might be fair to say that he was more interested in a sense of the past than
in the science of history. To him, folklore was "unwritten history," and
history was the stuff of legend. His influence has had an effect on perceptions
of, and reverence for, Pennsylvania's heritage, environment, and traditions
by Pennsylvanians today.

It may seem surprising that an intellectual and cultural history of his
influence has taken this long to appear, especially considering the growing
national interest in "history-making" and public folklore. It is less surprising,
though, if one realizes that popularization by character appears "natural"
and unattributable to human invention. As books such as *The Invention of
Tradition,* edited by Eric Hobsbawm and Terence Ranger (1983), *The
Conservation of Culture,* edited by Burt Feintuch (1988), and *Public Folklore,*
edited by Robert Baron and Nicholas R. Spitzer (1992), show, we know
much more about the programs for promoting tradition that have developed
than we do about their intellectual sources, the promoters and their ideolo-
gies. Henry Shoemaker's story deserves special attention because Pennsylvania's programs in public recreation, history, and folklore became a model
for many other states in the Union. It is also an engaging drama of a
crusading visionary who battled himself, as well as the times in which he
lived, and not always successfully. As he espoused a political ideology and
sought a romantic mystique that would combine nature and culture in a
harmonious balance, so he struggled with both the country mountain man
and the city businessman in himself, and in his writings he wavered between
the facts in his newspaper stories and the romance of his books. A private
man with a large public presence, Henry Wharton Shoemaker was beloved
and despised, celebrated and dismissed. And the achievements of his legacy
have received equally mixed reviews, raising questions about the images we
continue to invent.

1

"A Rich and Colorful Life"

Imagine a life that includes safaris to Africa, climbs to the world's highest peaks, time on the front lines of war, and audiences with European royalty. Envision huge fortunes gained and lost. Think about efforts going into bringing lions, wolves, elk, and other wild game into a private forest preserve stretching for 4,000 acres. From there you can help initiate and name a vast system of state forests, parks, camps, and trails. Amass barns full of museum-quality remnants of pioneer life—wagons, canoes, spinning wheels, guns, and much, much, more. While you're at it, write more than 200 books and pamphlets, address thousands of groups, prepare a daily column, and manage four newspapers. Venture into the backwoods and collect ancient stories from the lips of old frontiersmen. From them create an elaborate mythology for a region that speaks for a nation and crusades for its redemption. Construct a social calendar that boasts visits from governors and senators and poor mountaineers with an old tale to tell. If you can imagine all that, you have an idea of the enormity of Henry Shoemaker's life.

Testimonies to Henry Wharton Shoemaker's contributions often refer to a "rich and colorful" past. "Col. Henry W. Shoemaker," one salute in the Harrisburg newspaper began, "has packed enough occupations and avocations into his life to provide sufficient material for a novel. As a banker, soldier, diplomat, publisher, historian and industrialist he may well be considered to have led a rich and colorful life."[1] Sensitive about references to his wealth, he preferred to say he had a "long and prolific career" and often emphasized that his folklore-collecting from common people emerged from his early endeavors as his gritty "real life's work."[2] At one point, he was described as "the greatest American reporter and the foremost living compiler of oral traditions in the United States."[3] Beginning in business and diplomacy, he shifted to publishing and journalism while maintaining interests in local history, nature conservancy, and state politics. In his final position as State Folklorist, he combined previous work as archivist, journalist, government official, and, perhaps most significant, historian and conservationist.

Roots and Early Life

Henry Wharton Shoemaker traced his history to the beginnings of colonial Pennsylvania. He claimed as his first American ancestor Peter Shoenmaker, a Quaker arriving at Germantown, Pennsylvania, in 1685 from Holland, but with roots like many other emigrants to Pennsylvania, in the Palatinate region of what is now Germany. This ancestor became prominent in the administration of Philadelphia and, like family members that followed, became active in public life. John Wise Shoemaker (Henry Wharton Shoemaker's grandfather) had the foresight to invest in the budding anthracite coal industry in Schuylkill County in the early nineteenth century. John Wise Shoemaker's wife was Mary A. Brock, daughter of a coal operator of English and Scots-Irish descent. Their son Henry Francis was born in 1843 (died in 1918) and attended Genesee Seminary, later to become Syracuse University, where he graduated in 1861. In order to see action in the Civil War as first lieutenant in the Western Army, he declined an appointment to the Naval Academy that Harrisburg political boss Simon Cameron had arranged with President Lincoln. He was engaged in several battles, most notably at Shiloh and Gettysburg.

After John Wise Shoemaker died in 1863, Henry Francis took over the management of coal mines owned by the family. During the 1870s he expanded the family interests to railroads and banks. In 1874 he married Blanche Quiggle (1853–1928), who also came from a well-off family with roots deep in Pennsylvania. She traced her lineage back to Richard Buffington (1654–1747), an agent for William Penn, who came to Pennsylvania from England in 1675. The ethnic ties of her lineage were mostly to English, Scots-Irish, and Huguenot ancestors. Well-traveled and educated in Philadelphia and Europe, Blanche was the daughter of James W. Quiggle (1820–78), former state senator from Clinton County and foreign diplomat, and Cordelia (Mayer) Quiggle (1828–1914), a creative and religious woman (a minister's daughter) with a fondness for poetry and song.

Henry Francis made the move to America's commercial capital of New York City in 1878 to expand his financial interests in railroading and banking, which were booming at the time. Expand and profit he did, especially from his ownership of the Cincinnati, Hamilton & Dayton Railroad, controlling interest in the Cleveland, Lorain & Wheeling Railway Company, the directorship of the Texas Pacific Railroad and the North American Trust Company, and presidency of the Mineral Range Railroad Company. The Shoemakers represented new wealth born of America's industrial boom, and they settled north of the "old money" of Astors and Roosevelts to join other newcomers, like the Rockefellers and the Huntingtons.[4] The Shoemakers made a name for themselves within New York City high society and were regularly mentioned on New York newspaper society pages as appearing at such events as the annual ball at the Waldorf-Astoria and at Metropolitan Opera House performances, along with the Goulds, the Havemeyers, and the Vanderbilts. The five-story Shoemaker home at 21 West Fifty-third Street, called Villa D'Este, adjoined the residence of John D. Rockefeller's family and, according to the *New York Times* "was a favorite rendezvous of persons well known in the social world."[5] Besides nurturing John D. Rockefeller Jr., who became a conservationist of nature and history in his own right, the neighborhood near Central Park sported numerous mansions as the turn of the century neared, including those of railroad magnate William K. Vanderbilt, Senator Chauncey Depew, and department-store founder Benjamin Altman. During the 1880s, Rockefeller recalled, the area was "far more like the country than the city. . . . In the beginning the houses were scattered. There were ledges of rock between them and trees were plentiful."[6]

Amid this New York City environment in 1880, Henry Wharton was the first child born to Henry and Blanche Shoemaker.[7] One year later, William Brock was born, followed by the arrival of Blanche in 1886. The parents apparently spoke of Pennsylvania as the beloved "old country" to the children. Henry Francis, a lifelong member of the Pennsylvania Society of New York City (in 1902 he became its vice-president), filled the children with a fondness for the old home state.[8] As Henry Wharton (or "Harry," as he was affectionately called) said of himself, "As a boy he loved to listen to his father tell tales of old Orwigsburg, of Regina Hartman, the Indian captive, but later in school days there was danger of that romance being shattered in the maelstrom of 'higher historical criticism.'"[9]

The Shoemakers spent summers at the Quiggle family estate called "Restless Oaks" in McElhattan, Pennsylvania, near Lock Haven, and at an opulent Victorian residence called "Cedar Cliff" in Riverside, Connecticut. A two-and-a-half-story country house near the West Branch of the Susquehanna River and the Bald Eagle Mountains, Restless Oaks (in Cordelia Quiggle's day it was known as "Villa Vista"), stood beside extensive forestland. It was young Henry's favorite, and all the more so because of the romantic history it offered. An ancestor, Michael Quigley, "descendant of the Waldensian martyrs in the Piedmontese Alps of Europe," first settled there in 1768.[10] His grandmother Cordelia, who died at the age of eighty-six in 1914, regaled the boy with stories of the family and the region stretching back into the eighteenth century. She also entertained him with folk songs, accompanying herself on the piano, and her grandson remembered those songs well many years later.[11] She also nurtured his interest in literature and the outdoors by reserving a room at Restless Oaks for his use, and she arranged for him to inherit the estate. Recalling his summer days of boyhood at Restless Oaks, Shoemaker wrote: "Those early impressions decided my whole life and I have been ever a loyal son of Pennsylvania."[12]

At Restless Oaks, young Henry learned to explore the woods and hunt, and heard many a legend from older mountaineers while observing the dramatic effects of lumbering, coal, and railroading on life in the wilderness. It was also Restless Oaks that his often sickly mother sought for rest and the popular Victorian "wilderness cure" for ailments ranging from rheumatism to "nervousness."[13] His uncle James Quiggle watched over Restless Oaks and invited young Henry to leave his city ways: "I believe if I had resided in a city under the same conditions I would have been broken down physically and that my living in the country in this pine mountain air has lended to keep me youthful in appearance and added to my longevity."[14] Uncle Jim implied that Restless Oaks held natural curative powers: "Regarding your mother's nervous breakdown I have emphasized in letters to Grandma that the road to "Well ville" lies via McElhattan. Years ago when she was brought here from Philadelphia—so weak she had to be carried out of the cars—she rapidly improved. . . . The plan is to live naturally—not artificially."[15]

Besides receiving the lessons of living "naturally" at Restless Oaks, young Henry acquired his early education from private tutors, and then attended the prestigious Dr. E. D. Lyons Classical School. At Lyons from 1889 to 1896, he came under the tutelage of William Edgar Plumley, originally from Lackawanna County in Pennsylvania, who instilled in his pupils a reverence for natural history. A remembrance of Plumley pasted into one of Henry Shoemaker's scrapbooks read: "Nature possessed a most remarkable charm for him. It was his delight to wander among the fields and woods and to commune with nature when at her loveliest. There was not a flower, shrub or plant that grew in Lackwanna county with which he was not familiar, and his facile pen was frequently employed in describing the wild beauty of our hills and valley and the heavy forests with which the Pocono and Moosic mountains abound."[16] A Presbyterian preacher, Plumley emphasized the spiritual experience of nature as manifestation of the divine.

The Lyons School prided itself on developing students' skills in prose and poetry, music performance, and especially by immersion in the classics. As a schoolboy, Henry Shoemaker became enthralled with Greek myths and French literature, and wondered why American history was so neglected. He visited Paris, admired the French romanticism of Jean Jacques Rousseau, and wrote: "Chivalry had developed in France more rapidly and more brilliantly than elsewhere."[17] He later offered that the country deserved credit for championing "intellectual understanding" and "primitive art."[18] Among his studies were the writings of the English nationalist and reformer John Ruskin, an enthusiast for art and natural history, and an opponent of industrial abuses, who discussed "field work, in the interpretation of myths relating to natural phenomena."[19] In his study of Greek myths, Ruskin called for the "masters of modern science" who have artificially "divided the elements" to give him back his romantic view of "Athena out of your vials, and seal, if it may be, once more, Asmodeus therein."[20] Shoemaker appreciated his reference to the spiritual inspiration of the pure snowy Alps, standing antithetically to industrial "languid coils of smoke, belched from worse than volcanic fires."[21] Through time and across cultures, Shoemaker learned, humans found a spiritualism present in nature that forced them to respect and preserve it. Their myths and tales revealed their reverence and became great literature for future generations to appreciate. The mythical age was a wondrous epoch of romance and mystery.[22]

While Henry's brother seemed preoccupied with athletics and business, his sister Blanche also pursued classical studies and took to writing, later becoming an accomplished poet.[23] She also had major achievements in golfing, fishing, hunting, aviation, and motorcycling (she claimed to be the first woman motorcyclist in New York State and served as chair of the National League of Women's Service during World War I).[24] "We are shy, shrinking beings," Blanche wrote her brother, and she kidded him that their "naturally sensitive and neurotic nature" probably derived "from defective glandular systems of our parents." She blamed "over developed sex-hormones" for their "exaggerated romanticism, and imagination—but not the *force* to sell" themselves.[25]

As a youth, Henry Shoemaker was a model of physical strenuosity in the great outdoors and of intellectual bookishness in the Victorian library. His father wrote him: "I have adapted your plan in part and am taking lots of exercise in the open air. I walk and drive over and around the mountains, and barring horseback riding, am doing about what you would do if you were here. I am very sorry you could not accompany me as it is the kind of life and amusement that you are fond of."[26] The senior Shoemaker seemed more at ease on his yacht or in his roadster than hiking or reading in the woods.

The books the younger Shoemaker loved covered literature or local-color writing, natural history, Pennsylvania local history, and American history. He leaned toward the contemplation of art and environment as he devoured the popular nature-writing or American "poetic rambles" of Ernest Thompson Seton, George Bird Grinnell, and Theodore Roosevelt. An avid reader, romantic, and dreamer, so his sister remembered, Henry also reveled in the oral tradition of the mountains and forests around Restless Oaks.[27] With the developed instincts of a Victorian naturalist "field-collecting" specimens that reveal a hidden past, he gathered in the details of what he saw and heard.[28] Referring to himself in the third person, Henry later recalled:

> The collecting began when he was a small boy, on ostensible hunting and fishing trips, with certain old hunters in Clinton County, and it came to pass that he enjoyed their story-telling more than the game-slaying, and took more pleasure writing the stories than any other form of "compositions" in school and at college. Living mostly in a large city at the time, and born with an insistent longing for the woods and mountains, probably a heritage from some Indian ancestor, the quest for quaint stories of the long ago grew with the years, until it is now his favorite form of "hunting" (there is an open season twelve months in the year), with no "bag" limit, working in beautifully with his activities in forestry organization and the Pennsylvania Alpine Club.[29]

In a school paper he edited in prep school, Shoemaker included some of the old legends he bagged, but by his account "they were sorry attempts, and the work was abandoned."[30] Nonetheless, he recalled, "Folk-lore always had a deeper spell over me than researches into the vanishing fauna of Central Pennsylvania."[31]

A Rage for Collecting

Henry Shoemaker's natural-history enthusiasm for collecting specimens of flora, fauna, and folklore extended to material reminders of the past. In boyhood, he expressed an enthusiasm for acquiring historical and artistic Currier and Ives prints, "beginning a collectors' enthusiasm which is widely-shared."[32] That "collectors'" enthusiasm for prints later grew to include stallions, wild animals (e.g., wolves, elk, buffalo, bears), exotic trees, horses, carriages, wagons, spinning wheels and other domestic craft items, guns, paintings, stamps, and rare books.[33] His collecting was more than the usual hobbyist's, however. As he filled barns, zoos, and later, many books with his specimens, newspapers covered his searches and discussed his taste for rare Americana. Henry Shoemaker followed the late Victorian emphasis on the assumedly creative act of forming an assemblage of exotic items that could be arranged into a pattern, a style Lynn Merrill calls an aesthetic "mosaic of discrete pieces." Victorians filled "cabinets of curiosities" and found "object lessons" from ordering the specimens on the parlor as well as on a museum shelf.[34] Collecting things, natural and crafted, was a way to save a past that Victorians felt was either well hidden or disappearing. As Victorians became more and more "worldly," they ventured out on collecting trips and reported them to a reading public. "Victorian natural history writing," Merrill has pointed out, "was not goal oriented but rather discursive—a gathering up, or collection, of disparate observations acquired on rambles or jaunts."[35] Victorians believed that their collections revealed wondrous hidden worlds that opened up a lengthy, forgotten past for contemplation of human origin and development.

The influence of natural history in the wake of Darwin's explosive evolutionary theories was felt in a range of writing, both academic and popular. Natural history at the time worshiped a version of science that rewarded a new faith in knowable, minute facts—"links," as one writer explained, "in a great chain" of development from primitive to advanced forms.[36] Reacting to religious reliance on the unknowable, natural history offered keywords stressing observable objectivity: specimens, collections, cabinets. It used positivistic classification and arrangement of specific facts shaped by humans into an ordered whole emphasizing advancement through time. "The nineteenth century made the mistake of worshipping the Muse of History as a goddess," Noel Annan reflected. "Truth, they believed, was revealed in History, not in the Bible—but like every revelation it required interpretation."[37]

Truth was based on empirically verifiable facts, but faith could still be interpreted from sentimental virtues of nature, lore, and literature. Indeed, in a secularizing and industrializing age, nature and lore held a special spiritual appeal for a growing middle class to temper the "nervousness"—the popular term for a kind of anxiety over change—engendered by the new cult of business and science.[38] "Try to shake off the nervousness," Henry's grandmother Cordelia Quiggle wrote him. "You cannot improve unless your mind is more at rest from matters of the city and you can be active here among the trees."[39] In the perception of the period, nature and lore—"the old log cabins, shady groves, giant trees, old fords, ferries, beaver dams, and reed-grown pools" and "the legends, the folklore, the ghosts that lingered about these survivals"—represented "a simpler and happier day" that had been left behind because of the inevitable march of civilization.[40] Shoemaker added to this view that "no one can be truly happy who does not live in an atmosphere of the past, whether it be mental or actual. The mechanical world may pile up bank accounts mountain high for the few, but it brings monotony, dreariness, empty pleasures, short life for the many."[41] Engaging nature, listening to lore, was a kind of therapy providing "that wonderful sense of being born anew," particularly in the mountains and the wilderness.[42] For an exhilarating sense of power, Victorians traveled great distances to remote summits to take in glorious "vistas." The Victorians saw these climbs as spiritual and earthly. They offered a godly glimpse of natural wonder, opportunities to collect specimens of that wonder and therapeutic strenuous activity in the healthy out-of-doors.

Closer to home, Victorians prescribed healthy doses of fantasy, some "collected" and many more concocted. Building on the collections of the Brothers Grimm, Victorian writers anthologized and created new fairy tales of enchanted forests and magical animals.[43] European folklore, especially, was popularly collected and presented to satisfy the public hunger for fantasy and mysticism, and even nationalism, while a small circle of "scientific men and women" insisted on keeping the study of folklore on "sound" evolutionary principles.[44] In fact, the very term "folklore" was invented for English usage by antiquarian William John Thoms in Victorian England in 1846. Thoms proposed it as a "good Saxon compound" for "the Lore of the People" and enlisted aid in "garnering the few ears which are remaining, scattered over that field from which our forefathers might have gathered a goodly crop."[45] Calling it "curious and interesting," associating it with a past romantic age, Thoms hoped that the collecting "folklore" of England's past could do for the country's pride and nationalism what the Grimms's *Deutsche Mythologie* did for Germany. No less a political figure than Theodore Roosevelt urged the collection from the folkloric "treasure-house of literature . . . of a buried past" in the United States to stir nationalism.[46] He especially praised the "expressions of that valor of soul" as the wellspring of a serious national art and literature found in the national folklore in Ireland. Citing the collecting of Ireland's Lady Gregory, he wished for an American effort to represent the country's uniqueness through "all the local features of our composite nationality."[47] "American work must smack of our own soil, mental and moral, no less than physical, or it will have little of permanent value," he emphasized.[48] Answering the call were such volumes as the popular *Myths and Legends of Our Own Land* by Charles Skinner (1896), and also his *American Myths and Legends* (1903).[49] Even earlier, in 1888, an American Folklore Society was formed, giving organizational impetus for "the collection of the fast-vanishing remains of Folk-Lore in America," such as old English ballads and American Indian myths and tales.[50]

Evolutionary thought had an influence on the early development of folklore collection, since a basic anthropological premise especially after the 1870s was that modern-day folklore revealed survivals of lower primitive levels of "savage" and "barbaric" customs. The characterization of these lower levels had strong racial overtones; varied "savage" races gave way as cultural evolution progressed to the unity of modern white civilization. By scientifically comparing the survivals much as biological specimens might be classified and arranged, Victorian evolutionists imagined constructing a "natural history of civilization."

A similar trend balancing science and romance emerged with regard to the use of nature, both as a subject of positivistic study and as a setting for spiritual and artistic contemplation.[51] Great natural-history museums invited visitors to see the glory as well as the order of nature. They displayed masses of specimens in cabinets to match the power of art galleries. Natural history combining travelogue and mystery writing became a popular type of literature. Writers offered Victorians what Lynn Merrill called "the hybrid pleasures of natural history—part scientific exactitude, part emotional pleasure."[52] Victorians read of these hybrid pleasures in accounts of escapes in nearby country rambles or exotic adventures in the name of natural history and geography, generously sprinkled with ethnology, such as the *Journal of the Discovery of the Source of the Nile* by John Hanning Speke (1863) and *Wanderings in West Africa* by Richard Francis Burton (1863).[53] It was the period when mountain-climbing became a sport and "natural selection" was a popular social as well as scientific phrase, when doctors prescribed camping in the outdoors for many ailments and painters witnessed God in their depictions of glorious wilderness landscapes.

School Days

Looking through Henry Wharton Shoemaker's scrapbooks of his school days, one would think that he spent little time in class. His clippings recount outings for track, football, boating, golf, and camping excursions into the wild. Sport and the great outdoors were also the subjects of his first publishing effort while still in prep school. In 1896 he edited, and his brother William managed, the *Argyle News,* a monthly devoted to schoolboy athletics. The inaugural issue opened with Henry's interview of an Adirondack hunter from Yonkers, New York. It was essentially a plaint about the crowding of hunters from the city that had invaded the Adirondacks, and it called for "stringent measures" to remedy the situation.[54] Henry's editorializing also included an attack on control of New York politics by Tammany bosses and support for the Spanish-American War. To the announcements of club football, biking, and racing, he added romantic poetry and "mystery" stories. In "The Porter's Tale," for example, he introduced an oral narrator who related a tale of mysteriously changing from white skin to black.[55]

Henry W. Shoemaker attended Columbia College, near his New York City residence, in 1897, intending to take up commercial art (owing to his admiration for Currier and Ives prints). Soon, however, he turned to literary interests, including classical studies—when he was not vigorously engaged in sports, including track, golf, and boating. He also had a fascination for motoring and became the first president of the university automobile club, which sponsored intercollegiate races. The auto club was a recent innovation on the collegiate scene, and Henry followed by forming the first Aero Club chapter, devoted to aviation on a college campus. His brother joined him at Columbia a year later and became vice-president of the Columbia Automobile Club in addition to managing the college's football and hockey teams. Henry, meanwhile, managed track, directed the Tennis Club, and was editor and assistant manager for the *Columbia Spectator,* and also became manager and staff writer for the *Columbia Jester.* And while he was doing all this, he volunteered his press services to the Republican County Committee. Henry Shoemaker was voted class treasurer by his classmates in 1900, and gave a toast at the class dinner on "How to Become Famous."

If Henry Shoemaker intended to become famous, it already appeared by the turn of the century that he intended his renown to be literary. In 1898 he suggested that the appropriate prop for him for a photograph would be a "pen or roll of manuscript," while his brother should be shown "clutching rolls of bills" in his "energetic fingers."[56] At the tender age of eighteen, Henry published a volume of poetry drawn from his work for the *Argyle News* (1898), and two years later he published his first book of prose, *From Lancaster to Clearfield, or Scenes on the By-ways of Pennsylvania* (1900), in a small run of 150 copies. Recalling its inspiration, Henry stated: "I travelled over hilly, winding back roads where I enjoyed meeting interesting people and visiting strange, out-of-the-way places."[57] Combining his interests in Pennsylvania's "national survivals" of "mixed races" and natural environment, the "travel tale" recounted a historian's experiences on the way to the "lost colony" of New Judea (now Schaefferstown, Lebanon County) to study the early Jewish pioneers of Pennsylvania. Along the way, the historian records accounts of Swedes, French Huguenots, Germans, Scots-Irish, and English Quakers, set against the backdrop of detailed geographical descriptions of the region's flora and fauna.[58]

His prose apparently held more promise than his poetry. He continued to publish poetry until he entered the armed services during World War I, but he left poetic efforts in the family largely to his sister, Blanche. Still, he later often received letters detecting, or requesting, the "poetic" in his prose, he was a lifelong member of the Pennsylvania Poetry Society, and he encouraged poets to call on the muses of local history and folklore. His poetry is interesting in that it identified early the romantic allure of history, folklore, and nature associated with bygone days. In *Elizabethan Days* (1912), for example, his titles, many dating from 1898, included "False Love," "The Mountain," "Cassie George's Ghost," and "The Country Church." "The Mountain" was among his earliest poems, and his lines showed the reverence that echoed later in many of his stories:

> Fearlessly jutting into the sky,
> Into the sky (not the above)
> Clad in a dress of darkest green,
>   Which to the west wind's call doth move,
> Whose eyelets are torrents brash
>   (Verily, less eyeless than orbs),
> In whose far reaching pathway
> Hillside and valley absorbs;
> Adding a luster unmeant,
> As if by chance 'twere sent.[59]

The mountain comes up again in "The Country Church," in which

> And as the freshening mountain breeze
> Blows through the open windows wide
> And sincere songs of praise ring out
> I always feel that God was close beside![60]

As prosaic a work as *Extinct Pennsylvania Animals* (1917) even featured Henry Shoemaker's "Ode to a Stuffed Panther," in which he opened his heart to the image of a dead Pennsylvania mountain lion on a museum shelf in such lines as:

> But as your race declines, so dwindles man
> The painted cheek replaces coat of tan
> And marble halls, and beds of cloth of gold
> Succeed the log-cabins of the days of old;
> When the last panther falls then woe betide,
> Nature's retributive cataclysm is at our side,
> Our boasted civilization then will be no more,
> Fresh forms must come from out the Celestial Store.[61]

The implication for Shoemaker was that the animals had to be restored to life, conserving nature's balance, not preserved for the museum shelf.

Henry credited a Columbia professor for turning his focus toward folklore. In his junior year at college, he took a composition course for which the rhetoric professor, George R. Carpenter, required a "daily theme" paper. "For want of subjects," Shoemaker recalled, "the old Pennsylvania stories were drawn out, and to the writer's surprise they were praised by the Professor. 'Go on with them,' he said; 'you have found an original field.' "[62] These themes were about "his tramps in the Clinton County woods," and "his first effort of this kind was an account of the capture of a bear at the Hostrander cabin on Pine Creek; his second was about the Swedenborgian colony once established at the top of the mountain near North Bend. They aroused the interest of his teacher, who encouraged him to continue his folklore studies."[63] An early folklore study of his, published in the *Columbia Jester,* is an essay entitled "John Q. Dice, The Pennsylvania Mountaineer." Dyce (sometimes spelled Dice by Shoemaker) was a real-life figure, and the story, delivered in dialect, is a hunting tall tale about a wrestling match between buck and hunter after the ammunition is gone. Set against the backdrop of John Dyce's rustic cabin, the tale-teller spins his yarn: "Ez he cum past me, I med a grab an' cot him be th' tail, an' aay we went, crawst th' crick, over lawgpiles, an' stumps, until I calklated thet uz ter be meh last day. Ez we were clearin' er bresh-heap, I jerked up with meh legs, an' braced meself agin th' buck, and pult. Something' hed teh give, an' it wuz th' buck, I turnt er summerset er two, but I pult out thet buck's tail an' er saddle of venison come with it thet leasted me fer three days."[64] Shoemaker underscores the traditional quality of the story by introducing "Lying Bill" Williams, who interjects: "You he'rd thet stawry frum ole' Jawsh Sykes, an you know it."

"I have made quite a study of the old legends and natural history of Pennsylvania," Shoemaker wrote a college classmate, but he regretted not applying himself "more diligently" to his coursework. "It would have been a great help to me in journalistic and literary work if I could have had the solid training which only a college course can give," he admitted.[65] Recurrent topics in his writing during his college days included wildlife, conservation issues, and Indian legendry and song recalled from visits to the Pennsylvania countryside. Getting away from the city, he went out on his own, exploring the isolated mountains and forests of rural Central Pennsylvania on foot and horseback. Seeking more than scenery, Henry Shoemaker enjoyed listening to "the old pioneers and hunters, as well as a few of the Indians" tell their stories of "outlaws, of witches, ghosts, lumbermen, wild beasts and birds, that must inhabit this wilderness."[66] He tied these regional stories to the founding wilderness myths of the nation involving "rugged individual" characters who were connected to nature and who boasted an invigorating, even redeeming, integrity and spirituality.

Taking Up the Progressive Cause

While Henry was at Columbia, his father made plans to shift his base of operations to Ohio as chairman of the board of the Cincinnati, Hamilton & Dayton Railroad. When the move came, the son came along as his father's private secretary. While in his father's employ, he traveled through Ohio and Kentucky and was fascinated by the folk speech and legends he heard. "The desire came to write," the younger Henry recalled, "and write he did, on the trains, in the evenings, at any spare time."[67] He reflected on the strong connections between the lore of this region and that of his favored Pennsylvania mountains. He read popular romantic writings steeped in Appalachian folklife by such authors as James Lane Allen (1849–1925) and John Fox Jr. (1863–1919).[68] Praising the "primitive strength and romantic chivalry" of the people from whom this folklore came, Henry bemoaned the loss of "simplicity, sincerity and romance" as the "train of modernization," for which he worked, sliced through the mountains of Kentucky. "Big mining towns now flourish," he wrote, "in the most out-of-the-way valleys, railroads penetrate everywhere, old customs are being put to the test, will simplicity outlast the thirst for ease and prosperity?"[69]

Shoemaker turned away from his father's railroad business to the Progressive politics of conservation, and in 1904 he was a delegate to the Republican Party convention and got swept up by Roosevelt fever. Shoemaker wrote that Theodore Roosevelt "possessed a remarkably clear understanding of the problem created by the abuse of wealth. Like David of old, he set out after the Goliath of ill-diverted wealth and privilege."[70] Roosevelt appeared to be a man of action who called for reform in the name of restoring the glory of the national character. In his first annual message to Congress, in 1901, President Roosevelt called for the regulation of monopolies to offer "a resolute and practical effort" to correct the economic and social "evils" of concentrated wealth and to "subserve the public good."[71] Although many political applications of Darwin's evolutionary doctrine suggested a climb from small to big and from nature to industry as progressive, Roosevelt's progressivism that came to be known as the "New Nationalism" emphasized the rationality of regulation to ensure economic progress and democratic principles. Invoking Darwinian metaphors for his cause, Roosevelt declared: "The progress has been done by evolution, not by revolution."[72]

If Theodore Roosevelt was in his restraint of industrial development more moderate than Henry W. Shoemaker would have liked, Henry agreed wholeheartedly with Roosevelt's assertion that "the conservation of our natural resources and their proper use constitute the fundamental problem which underlies almost every other problem of our national life."[73] Calling for practical management, and invoking "forward-thinking," or "progressivism," Roosevelt explained that "the government has been endeavoring to get our people to look ahead and to substitute a planned and orderly development of our resources in place of a haphazard striving for immediate profit."[74] His goal was to increase the "usefulness," rather than exploitation, of the land to ensure prosperity. He promised that, with regulation, he could promote industrial growth while protecting the precious American landscape.

A keyword that Henry W. Shoemaker borrowed heavily from Theodore Roosevelt was "use."[75] "I appeal to you from the standpoint of use," Roosevelt told an audience at Stanford in 1903. "A few big trees, of unusual size and beauty, should be preserved for their own sake; but the forests as a whole should be used for business purposes, only they should be used in a way that will preserve them as permanent sources of national wealth."[76] Roosevelt harped on government's role of allowing for business initiative while correcting its "evils." Government sought to ensure the use of natural resources for the "public good." Again, Shoemaker took a more activist stand than Roosevelt by advocating more stringent protection of natural resources from private development, but he unswervingly praised Roosevelt's "progressive" principles.

Those progressive principles deserve some explanation, since "Progressivism," as historian Richard Hofstadter has pointed out, is a not altogether cohesive or consistent movement.[77] By most accounts, Progressivism reached its height around 1912, but marked the national "Progressive Era" from Roosevelt to Wilson between 1901 and 1917, although its offshoots continued well into the 1930s, especially at the state level.[78] Henry W. Shoemaker joined in the broad impulses of the early twentieth century toward criticism and change. He chimed the theme of restoring economic individualism and political democracy associated with an earlier American tradition crushed by monopolized heavy industries and corrupt political machines. Led by Roosevelt ally Gifford Pinchot in Pennsylvania, for example, the Progressives took on the name of the Washington Party to represent the ideals of George Washington, especially the model of "exalted justice and benevolence."[79] The Washington label also emphasized Progressivism as a nationalist American approach to industrial problems, as separate from supposedly "un-American" socialist or other "European" ideas.

Conservation was important to this Progressive view because it protected the resources of the early American tradition and represented the control of industries for the public good.[80] The rhetoric of "conservation" carried the implication of allowing for use of natural resources and also had the ring of a "conservative" rather than radical approach to reform. Some critics have translated this concern for the public good as the self-interest of professionals and businessmen in a rising urban middle-class. "But for all the Progressives' talk of a new era of popular rule," historian Daniel Rodgers argued, few of them were comfortable with the open, ramshackle, decentralized structure of elective offices they had inherited from the nineteenth-century champions of popular government."[81] While they railed against concentration of wealth, authority was consolidated in "fewer, more visible hands, farther from the partisan, log-rolling considerations of elections and popularity."[82]

The attack on the concentration of wealth suggested allowance for more competition that promoted the development of smaller companies rather than iterating earlier Populist rhetoric about the rights of workers. Shoemaker criticized William Jennings Bryan's Populism as "impracticable" and radical. "If able to carry out his plans," Shoemaker wrote, "the financial structure of the country would have been upset, and among the chief sufferers would have been the great 'common people,' whom he professed to love so well."[83] He trumpeted a conservative warning about the "un-American radicalism of workers" but recognized their right to bargain collectively.[84] Roosevelt may not have gone far enough in his reforms, Shoemaker believed, but "he was not a re-actionary, a revolutionary, or an unstabilizer of business."[85] His aims "were of the constructive order," Shoemaker commented, "but they required time to work out and that precious time was not given," and they were also bogged down by machine politics.[86]

Shoemaker's Progressivism tended to follow Republican Party lines, although he expressed "much faith in Wilson and on his past record" and supported Gifford Pinchot who bucked the Republican Party to run for Senator of Pennsylvania as a Progressive in 1914.[87] He criticized Republican William Howard Taft and "the chaos" of his administration for trying to "please everyone" but "pleasing no one."[88] Like other professionals who shared Republican convictions, Shoemaker feared a national transformation that rapid industrialization and unrestricted immigration from eastern and southern Europe brought. They believed in an American tradition of pre-industrial "morality and civic purity," as Hofstadter called it, but touted a new era of reform activism and efficient management, which they would lead after the turn of the century.

If there were two camps of Progressives—those who promoted reforms in government and business on the grounds of efficiency, and those who supported humanitarian policies—as historian Sean Dennis Cashman has pointed out, Shoemaker dwelled in each. Calling for attention to the "struggle for humanity," he contributed to organizations for the welfare of children, women, immigrants, and blacks. He was equally a vocal advocate of reducing government waste and corruption.[89] In 1912, Episcopal Bishop James Henry Darlington noted in a letter to Shoemaker that "you are working [through editorials and philanthropy] most efficiently for all three of your worthy objects. Saving the wild, protecting the colored people and trying to drive out White Slavery."[90] Believing in the therapeutic qualities of athletics, Shoemaker helped fund a parish gymnasium in Manhattan. John Wesley Johnson, from the parish, complimented him for his "progressivism" and added: "It is easy to interest New Yorkers in the Negro in Alabama or Georgia: but the rub is to make our wealthy men see that there is an increasing Negro Problem at our very door."[91] Yet there may have been some subtle criticism of Progressive reliance on assistance for facilities, rather than social change, when Johnson commented on Shoemaker's hiring of blacks in his office, "It is cheaper in the end to treat Negroes humanely and encourage him along right lines than it is to take care of him in hospitals, jails, etc. This is the sort of work that for the last 2 years you have helped me to do among the good colored people in my neighborhood."[92]

Summarizing his Progressive "convictions," Shoemaker sent a list of editorial stands to his newspapers. First on his mind was "ridding out the last vestiges of Penrosism, bossism, and old-guard machine politics in Pennsylvania, and all alliances between politicians, corporations, liquor and crime." He wanted government control of anthracite coal, expansion of the state highway construction, a reorganization of veterans' hospitals, and reform of basic education. He advocated legal restrictions on immigration, "better treatment of the Indians and their enfranchisement as American citizens," and "stringent laws against lynching of Negroes." He opposed "the reckless granting of the Nation's natural resources in the West or Alaska to political favorites, corporations, or other insiders" and insisted that "the National Parks should belong to the people, not be run and exploited by private favored enterprises." He supported the "protection and preservation" of "forests, game, and fish" along with "historic spots, historic trees," and he opposed "the blasting and destroying of mountains in view of railroads or highways for a few dollars of passing gain." "The most serious menace now facing this country," Shoemaker concluded, was the "automatic drift of all the increment of the nation into the hands of the few." He called for "a deeper sense of individualism" and the use of wealth to solve social problems and to make government efficient.

Shoemaker's name for his brand of Progressivism is "Prosperity."[93] Echoing Roosevelt's view that "public welfare depends upon general public prosperity, and the reformer whose reforms interfere with the general prosperity will accomplish little,"[94] he therefore supported the growth of America as a business nation, an "economic democracy" or "consciousness that all the world is free and competing on an equal basis."[95]

The Shoemaker family were frequent guests at the Roosevelt White House, especially because Vice-President Charles Fairbanks, formerly a U.S. Senator from Indiana, was the senior Shoemaker's chief counsel and family friend. Henry Wharton offered his services for a diplomatic post associated with the legacy of his mother's family, and with the assistance of Fairbanks, he became secretary of American legations in Costa Rica and Portugal, and then held the post of third secretary of the American embassy in Berlin. After five months in Berlin, however, Henry Shoemaker wrote his mother to say he had all he wanted—"namely the prestige and the experience"—and he was tempted by an offer from his brother William for a partnership on Wall Street. "I am in dead earnest about starting in business," Shoemaker continued, and he feared that "unless I return the matter may lapse, or else be settled in some way which would not suit me exactly."[96] Despite President Roosevelt's request that he stay on, Henry W. Shoemaker returned to the United States in 1905.[97]

Business, Marriage, and Scandal

With his brother and a college classmate, Henry W. Shoemaker organized the brokerage firm of Shoemaker, Bates & Company in 1905. His young partners had worked on Wall Street since leaving Columbia College, and set up shop in a prominent location in the Blair Building at 24 Broad Street. In addition to working in the firm, Shoemaker purchased the *Daily Record* in Bradford, Pennsylvania, and entered the National Guard. While his brother focused his attention on the success of the firm, Henry seemed to have his focus elsewhere. His many-sided interests attracted attention in the financial world; one clipping touted the "Young Broker" who was also "Editor, Athlete, Soldier, Horseman, Balloonist and Was in Diplomatic Service."[98]

Shoemaker enjoyed being reunited with his brother, who by all accounts had a mind for organization and business detail, but tragedy struck shortly after the enterprise began. Stepping out of the elevator in the Blair Building on his way to the office, William got his leg caught between the car and the gate. He died shortly thereafter, reportedly from shock and internal injuries. "I lost interest in Wall Street," Henry recalled, "and devoted more and more of my time to my newspapers and literary work."[99] His father, who noticed that Henry seemed easily distracted by his outside interests, warned him: "Be careful not to mix up your *individual* transactions with those of the *corporation*."[100] He feuded with his remaining partner, and in 1910 the firm's manager reported: "We are managing to eke out an existence of expenses and little more besides."[101] Shoemaker remained a senior partner until 1911, when he dissolved the firm.

While in the firm, Henry W. Shoemaker had a roller-coaster courtship, marriage, and divorce. He met Beatrice Barclay, the daughter of a prominent and wealthy Cameron County family in the lumbering industry, on one of his summer getaways at Restless Oaks. The couple married in 1907 and a year later had a child, whom they named Henry Francis. Shortly after the birth, however, his wife left with the infant for Seattle to stay with her father, and in 1910 she obtained a divorce decree on the grounds of abandonment and was granted custody of the child. Subsequently, Beatrice married Dr. Richard Perry and remained in Seattle. Then, apparently to prevent any relationship from forming with the boy's natural father, she arranged with her new husband to adopt the child and change his name to Henry Barclay Perry, without notifying the natural father.

When Shoemaker learned of the change, he fought back and sought an annulment of the adoption. At that point his own father, for whom the child was originally named, stepped in, offering to set aside an inheritance of $2 million for the boy if the court retained his original name. Prominent newspapers picked up the story, and on May 24, 1913, the *New York Times* featured the scandal on the front page. Shoemaker issued a statement criticizing the adoption for causing "a lifetime of injustice to the boy because it would deprive him of the love and protection of his paternal relatives of his rightful inheritance." Although he won a victory in court, Shoemaker suffered from the publicity. Readers soaked up the story of a self-righteous Progressive advocating social welfare but not attending to his own child. Newspaper reports of divorce among high society often implicated the individuals involved with a failure of morality. "It does not seem to be brought out in any of the papers that I had supported the child up to the time of the divorce," Shoemaker complained to his lawyer. "I did my duty to the child."[102] Newspaper coverage of divorce tended to be negative and was often set against the background of a dramatic Progressive Era increase in the divorce rate in America and a debate over divorce-law reform. In that debate, Shoemaker's Episcopal church in New York took a hard line against divorce.[103] Shoemaker's cousin Lillie Crawford wrote him to assure him that he would not be stigmatized by the divorce:

> Do not worry about your divorce. I happen to know that few if any people condemn you on that account. Only a few weeks ago I was conversing with a noble woman in Lock Haven—her husband was, I believe, accounted one of the wealthiest men in Central Pa., as well as one of the most prominent politically and she said some *beautiful* things about you. She mentioned your divorce and said she was sure that one engaged in the work for struggling humanity as you are could not have been to blame. She has been watching your interesting

career and has great faith in you. I told her how you had helped me in my literary work and she said "I hear nothing but *praise* of him" and then she went on to tell me how her husband was once divorced before she married him and when she told me about the woman with whom he had been unable to live happily, I wondered if she were not like your wife.[104]

Newspapers reporting the Shoemaker family squabble dwelled on the intrigue of big money's power to sway decisions, but Shoemaker's lawyer insisted that the senior Shoemaker's offer was a "rightful," "natural" inheritance that showed the adoption and name change to be "contrary to the interests of the child." Shoemaker's ex-wife resisted. The *Times* reported: "While little Henry was unconscious of the heartburns his change of name has caused his father, grandfather, and grandmother, and knew nothing of the fortune at stake, or the reasons for his new name, his mother had announced that he would be amply provided for under his new name." Explaining the reason for Shoemaker's apparent "desertion," as the papers claimed, his lawyer offered: "He never sought possession of the boy because of his age when he and his wife were separated. The child was only a year or so old, and, of course, the proper place for him was with his mother. But he did intend to provide for Henry's maintenance and education and ultimately intended to ask the court for his guardianship. He loved the little fellow and was waiting for him to get older before asserting any natural right to his companionship."

Although Shoemaker's petition claimed that he was unlikely to remarry and produce another "scion of his stock," he was enjoying a four-month European honeymoon with his new bride when the news of the annulment proceedings broke. He had married Mabelle Ruth Ord of San Francisco on May 10, 1913, in a quiet ceremony in New Rochelle, New York. Coming from a military family, Mabelle had spent most of her life in California and Mexico, and met Henry in New York City after one of his safari trips to Africa. It is true that Shoemaker did not have another child, but he and Mabelle Ruth Ord—"Tia," as she was known—had custody of Allen West Shaw Jr., born June 7, 1918, the son of Mabelle's niece Marion Shaw Gardner. Unlike his sister and brother, who chose spouses from within New York's select families, Shoemaker appeared to be disdainful of the city's high society. "That Henry Shoemaker, Junior, has chosen a bride far outside his family's social circle, is no surprise," the *Club Fellow* of New York City commented, for "Henry has always scoffed at the New York girl."[105]

The most eventful aspect of the wedding, according to the New York papers, was the wedding gift given to the couple by Shoemaker's parents. They gave their son a five-story house at 21 West Fifty-third Street, close to their home at number 26 and that of Blanche Shoemaker and her husband at number 24. The house was valued at $250,000, and the *New York Times* reported it was the "largest wedding gift of New York real estate that has been made."[106] The papers took notice of the gift as a sign of competitiveness among the wealthy families of New York. The Shoemakers had just outdone George Gould, who had given his son and Annie Douglass Graham a house on Fifth Avenue and previously bestowed another elegant home to his daughter Marjorie and Anthony Drexel. Other arenas for the competitiveness included the round of debutante balls and dog shows at Madison Square Garden, where Blanche Shoemaker vied with Havemeyers and Roosevelts for pure-bred prizes.[107]

Henry Shoemaker wanted to avoid the New York society scene, but he found himself enmeshed in city circles because of the family business. At the time he was feeling more trapped by the city, his writing expressed a longing for the Pennsylvania highlands: "All my literary work centers about that section of [Central] Pennsylvania and I feel more at home there than anywhere else."[108] With his father's health failing (he had a stroke and suffered from heart disease) and his business-minded brother dead, the family looked to him to manage its affairs. After 1912, the Shoemaker interests suffered, and a family adviser warned about "the fortune disappearing too rapidly or being dissipated."[109] Shoemaker pointed to an economic downturn and the burden of meeting the growing financial demands of the family. But the adviser diplomatically questioned his abilities to protect the family's investments: "It seems to me your gifts are pronounced as a writer along literary lines," he wrote with concern. "Your tastes are not for figures and statements of account. You do not inherit the business traits of your father."[110] Shoemaker agreed, but felt obliged to tend to his father's needs. "Were it not for my business interests which I must have to keep things going, but which take so much of my time, I would have been able to have written more of Pennsylvania history and perhaps done something really worth while," he wrote.[111]

Shoemaker laid the groundwork for establishing himself in Central Pennsylvania by purchasing the *Altoona Tribune* and, soon after, papers in Jersey Shore and Reading, Pennsylvania, and in Bridgeport, Connecticut. "His desire to aid the down-trodden urged him to become a newspaper man," the *Altoona Tribune* reported beneath the headline "Millionaire Has Written Legends of Susquehanna." "Without fear Shoemaker has fought corruption and wrongdoing, even turning his pen against his own political faith when those who controlled 'went wrong' according to his conception of what is wrong with state and national affairs."[112] In addition to news of current industrial events, and editorials strongly espousing nature conservation and controls on industrialization, he insisted on including columns that explored the local history and folklore of the preindustrial past. Such columns had long been a staple of "local interest" in American journalism, especially in the form of literary folktales in sportsmen's weeklies, regional almanacs, and rustic dailies.[113] Much of Shoemaker's considerable energy after 1913 went into managing his newspapers and writing political editorials, wildlife accounts, local history chronicles, and literary folktales. Throughout his writings, the *Altoona Tribune* observed, "runs a steady advocacy of the conservation of animal life, forests and all that tends to make the State more interesting and beautiful."[114]

Shoemaker's correspondence during the time he was in New York often showed frustration about being away from Pennsylvania. He wrote a business associate in Altoona: "I confess that it is very hard for me to be living in New York and trying to build up a newspaper in Altoona. I ought to be on the ground all the time. My wife would be willing to live in Altoona, but I cannot leave here on account of my invalid father whose many business affairs were left in an unsettled state when he was stricken with paralysis."[115] Henry Francis finally succumbed on July 3, 1918, while his son was in Europe in military service. Notices of the death drew attention to his millionaire status and his generosity to his family. According to the details of the will, his surviving son and daughter received bequests of $200,000 and annuities of $15,000 each. His son was executor of the estate and to the family interests added investments in the Rocky River Coal & Lumber Company in Tennessee (1913–27), Madison Trust Company in New Jersey (1910–20), and the Lock Haven Trust Company (1920–30). Shoemaker concerns included interests in banking, paper pulp, lumber, cemetery, and real-estate enterprises.[116]

Shoemaker did not hide his wealth, but he often criticized the life of high society and "the abuse of wealth" in addresses. Speaking to the Ministerial Association of Williamsport, he railed against "the perfectly good smug person, who possesses wealth, yet leads an aimless, self-centered life, or spends his days re-investing his income regardless of the sufferings of others. . . . Never in the world's history has there been a time when wealth can be used to better advantage than now. There is a stricken, bleeding world calling for help."[117] Following Carnegie's "gospel of wealth," he believed in maintaining a strong work and service ethic, rather than a life of leisure, and applying personally gained wealth for the public good. One columnist remarked that Shoemaker had "an unconcealed contempt for the idle rich, the flippant youth, and the impressive Professors who know so much that isn't so."[118] Shoemaker was quoted as saying that "a name matters very little where there is accomplishment—it is only useful with society people who do nothing, and need a name to prop them a brief period on the ragged edge of inevitable oblivion."[119] Described as "healthy, vigorous [with a] . . . great capacity for work," he believed in the virtues of diligent labor and "the strenuous life."[120] Often concerned with the damaging moral effects of money and materialism, he claimed that his success came from "heredity, environment and training properly availed of" rather than from his inheritance.[121]

The Strenuous Life

While engaging in business, Henry Shoemaker did not give up his mountain-climbing and big-game pursuits.[122] He admired the strenuous, active life of Theodore Roosevelt, who he called "the most constructive American of the present day," and joined the Boone & Crockett Club, a big-game hunting club Roosevelt organized before he became U.S. President.[123] The club's name glorified the legends of Daniel Boone and Davy Crockett, demigods of an imagined American heroic age rivaling that of Europe's Roland and King Arthur.[124] These rugged legendary American heroes—"ringtailed roarers," as they were sometimes called—penetrated the mysterious wilderness, where they wrestled huge wild animals and outwitted hostile tribes in the name of the common people. They epitomized the democratic national spirit of the frontier and the romantic ideals it raised.[125] Shoemaker often pointed out that the heroic pair had Pennsylvania roots and were symbols of the protection of the frontier,[126] and he built up other Pennsylvania pathfinders to the West, such as buffalo hunter Daniel Ott and keelboatman Mike Fink.[127]

Henry Shoemaker was also, with Roosevelt, a member of the Ends of the Earth Club in New York City, which promoted exploration and exotic travel. And like Roosevelt as well, he went on five safaris to Africa, traveled out West, and engaged in outdoor sports, including football, baseball, golf, track, yachting, and swimming[128]—leading a strenuous life well into middle age. Operations during the 1920s for hernia, appendicitis, adhesions of the intestines, and mastoiditis slowed him down, but he bounced back to scale mountains again.[129] When he reached the age of forty, the strain of his activities caused concern among his friends. Cyrus Fox, secretary of the Historical Society of Berks County, wrote him: "Please be careful in regard to your mountain climbing, as there is a possibility of your overdoing yourself."[130] Despite Fox's concern, at the age of forty-eight the 5-foot, 8-inch, red-haired Shoemaker easily passed a physical exam for his military appointment, weighing in at 185 pounds with a 36-inch waist, a 38-inch chest, and 20/20 eyesight.

Shoemaker's self-image as a strenuous, patriotic American also depended on having military rank. He entered the New York National Guard in 1906 and became lieutenant-colonel in the Pennsylvania National Guard in 1915, serving on Governor Martin Brumbaugh's staff. His grandfather James Quiggle had such a post during the nineteenth century. Shoemaker's newspapers had supported Brumbaugh in the election of 1914, and Senator-Elect Snyder recommended him for the honorary position. The governor was a naturalist and educator, as well as a religious man, from the Juniata Valley not far from Altoona.[131] Although not in sympathy with much of Roosevelt's Progressivism, Brumbaugh was apparently influenced by Shoemaker's suggestions for social and conservationist legislation. In 1916 the governor wrote him a confidential note: "You are in a strategic position to sense the public mind and to determine what is best for the great Commonwealth we love. Will you be good enough to write me what in your judgment would be a constructive legislative program for the coming session?"[132] Governor Brumbaugh eventually signed child-labor and worker-compensation laws and enlarged state forest lands. Throughout his life, Shoemaker remained loyal to Brumbaugh, and after the governor's death in 1930 he led annual pilgrimages to his grave.

Conservationist and fellow publisher J. Horace McFarland was especially delighted that Henry Shoemaker was in a position of influence. McFarland was president of the American Civic Association and vice-president of the Pennsylvania Conservation Association in 1915. "It is a fine thing that a man with your sentiments should be in so influential a relation to public opinion as you undoubtedly are."[133] McFarland made an appeal to Shoemaker to argue for conservation on the basis of practicality. Citing "the real value to them as business men, in the economic way," McFarland wrote: "We are not after beauty in the abstract, or for itself. We are after beauty as an incident to usefulness."[134] McFarland joined Shoemaker in a call for a state park system, and in a letter to McFarland Shoemaker framed the argument as a matter of social reform: "The people of many Pennsylvania cities do not realize that better parks and better surroundings produce better citizens. There are lots of people in the world occupying mediocre positions that might have amounted to something had their early environments and impressions been uplifting."[135]

When World War I broke out, Henry Shoemaker went on active duty in France as a military intelligence officer, serving on the general staff of the U.S. Army. After the war he returned to Europe as historian of the Pennsylvania Battlefields Memorial Commission in France, and in 1933 he rose to the rank of full colonel. This especially pleased him because he attained the same rank as his hero Colonel Theodore Roosevelt. Although he did not have a San Juan Hill to charge, he boasted that he had climbed "every noted mountain in Pennsylvania and Mus-Allah (God's Throne), the highest peak in the Balkans" and "as former president of the Pennsylvania Cave Men's Club, he had explored all the known caves of Pennsylvania."[136]

With every exploration, Shoemaker took notes on the stories he heard about the natural sites and their wildlife inhabitants. He subsequently published books prodigiously from the early 1900s through the 1920s, giving the history and folklore of Pennsylvania's caves and mountains, wild animals, forests, and great hunters. Wolves, eagles, and panthers were particularly fascinating to him, and at his Pennsylvania home he raised wolves as well as pure-bred stallions. Shoemaker admired the fierceness of his wolves and the beauty of his horses. Invoking the evolutionary doctrine of "survival of the fittest," he revered the speed and strength of wolves, eagles, and panthers as the reigning predators in the Pennsylvania wilderness, and resented the industrial forces that threatened to upset the balance.[137] Shoemaker agreed with the plaint of a Professor Lavizzari, which he emblazoned on the frontispiece of one of his publications: "With the passing of the Wolfish race will vanish much of the folk-lore and romance of our mountain communities."[138] "You are indeed a fortunate man to have heard the panther cry," in 1913 he wrote the "father of Pennsylvania forestry," J. T. Rothrock (1839–1922), "I was born too late for this, but my spirit lives in the picturesque and primitive days gone by."[139] Besides keeping wild animals at his estate, Shoemaker contributed to and established several zoos in Pennsylvania. Describing his work with animals, one article offered that "by kindness he has exercised an unusual influence over animals and birds, training, riding, and driving all kinds of wild horses. His timber wolves, now at the Washington Zoo, fondled him like pet dogs, and once in the Balkans he carried a golden eagle on his lap on a one-hundred-mile motor trip to Sofia."[140]

Shoemaker had what was perhaps his most active period of writing stories about the mountains of Pennsylvania in the period after his brokerage firm was dissolved. He defended the coverage of folklore in his newspapers by claiming that "it is more than a pastime; it is a spiritual necessity. It is the inner life's history of the Pennsylvania frontier people. It is interesting to collect and valuable to preserve."[141] It would inspire, he hoped, an authentic American artistry based on the soul of the folk in the wilderness that Theodore Roosevelt called for. For Shoemaker, folklore identified a "source of a new spiritual renaissance in Pennsylvania," a reminder of an American tradition steeped in community and nature.[142] As an officer of several historical and conservation groups, he encouraged the recording of local legends as the intersection of history, literature, and nature study.[143] "In a humble way I want to be able to preserve the old traditions, which are fast passing away," he explained to the Rev. George P. Donehoo, a local historian in his own right. "Out of the actual traditions will come a genuine literature."[144] Anxious to awaken folkloristic interest in younger generations where it had been lost because of industrial changes, Shoemaker's newspaper offered a prize at Lock Haven High School in 1913 for the best original story with a local setting collected from students' parents and grandparents, and he arranged for a primary school in McElhattan to engage in folklore-collecting.[145]

Newspaper Man

Newspapers and periodicals had an essential communicative role at the start of the twentieth century. As historian Robert H. Walker has observed, "Benefiting from technological advances and from the growth of population and literacy, magazines and newspapers played an irreplaceable role in a crucial marketing revolution while they entertained, informed, aroused, and abused a population confronted with many kinds of turbulence." In this "age of the periodical," newspapers and magazines "enjoyed a period of unrivaled influence and exhibited an exuberant vitality as exciting as it was unsteady."[146] Newspapers grew in size and prominence; they were the voice of independent-minded editors and publishers who gained stature as voices for the public's "common good."

In Pennsylvania, Henry W. Shoemaker's ally Edwin A. Van Valkenberg, editor of the *Philadelphia North American,* instigated the creation of an independent state and national Progressive Party organization.[147] He and a growing number of Progressive publishers encouraged muckraking journalists to reveal poor working conditions in the factories and the graft of the corporate "Interests." In their editorials they took on corruption and championed reform, and in their expanded sections and Sunday editions they featured new "human-interest" and "local color" columns that suggested a preindustrial American tradition of rustic harmony and civic purity.[148]

Shoemaker's newspapers became major Progressive sounding boards in Central Pennsylvania, and Shoemaker consolidated his position as the premier newspaper publisher in the highlands by buying out what he called the "radical" *Altoona Gazette* and *Altoona Times* and merging them into his *Tribune* operation. Altoona was an industrial town in the midst of Pennsylvania's former wilderness. Shoemaker wrote a fellow publisher that Altoona "is surely the ugliest city in the state of Pennsylvania," and he complained that "there is much civic indifference which in a way brings about a certain kind of misgovernment." He saw his work in the city as a Progressive crusade to make government efficient and the surroundings beautiful. "I would rather be in a city where there is work to do than in one which approaches your and my idea of Utopia," he wrote.[149] At least once a week his editorials called for the need for conservation and "beautifying their neighborhoods" to ensure a better, "progressive" future.[150]

As much as Henry Shoemaker's publications elaborated on the changeful future, many columns reflected on the natural and pioneer past, especially after America's centennial. Shoemaker's favorite journalist for this kind of reporting was Walker Lewis Stephen (1860–1929), who wrote for his *Reading Eagle*. Familiar with Pennsylvania-German and fond of Indian lore, Stephen collected historical legends and information on folk medicine and crafts. Shoemaker admired the way his "researches are always clothed in an atmosphere of rare charm and mysticism."[151] "To follow the Doctor's writing in the local papers," he added, "is like reading after a contemporaneous Sir Walter Scott, for he has evolved from the real life, of our days of long ago, a cycle of heroes and heroines, red and white, who make our blood tingle in the imagery of their stirring achievements."[152] Giving the chairman's report for the Pennsylvania Historical Commission in 1926, Henry Shoemaker praised Stephen "as the greatest of all Pennsylvania folklorists by his quaint tales of long ago."[153] Although Stephen restricted his writing mostly to the local newspaper, he was recognized by Vassar professor Martha Beckwith in *Folklore in America* (1931) as "the man who knew most about the old lore" in Pennsylvania-German tradition.[154] Locally renowned, Stephen's work would probably not be known to scholars today at all if Shoemaker had not insisted on publishing his glossary of Pennsylvania-German crafts as the first publication of the Pennsylvania Folklore Society in 1925.[155]

The newspaper connection went well beyond Stephen's contributions. Several editors and publishers joined Shoemaker's campaign. They saw one another regularly at Associated Press meetings and many were members of the Alpine Club. The Alpine Club, which Shoemaker founded in 1917, made climbs (fifty-three in 1924 alone) to Pennsylvania peaks and published folklore and history associated with the mountains they explored. Newspaper editors publicized their climbs and conservation efforts and often gave "photo opportunities" to politicians who came along. The organization grew rapidly, and by 1924 it claimed 2,500 members and seventeen chapters. J. Herbert Walker, the secretary of the Alpine Club, was editor of the *Lewisburg Journal* and the *Altoona Tribune*. Thomas W. Lloyd, also a founding member of the Alpine Club, was editor of the *Williamsport Gazette and Bulletin;* George W. Wagonseller was editor of the *Middleburg Post;* and E. A. Van Valkenberg was publisher and William Shearer was editor of the *Philadelphia North American*.

In League with Pinchot and the Conservationists

As a prominent Pennsylvania newspaper publisher and editorial writer, Henry Shoemaker was sought out by politicians for their causes. With his

backing of Roosevelt's conservation policies, he came to be linked in
Pennsylvania with Gifford Pinchot (1865–1946). Roosevelt's protégé Pinchot
was recognized as America's first professionally trained forester and was a
leading Progressive politician as governor of Pennsylvania and a senatorial
candidate. In 1898 he was appointed chief of the U.S. Division of Forestry
until he was dismissed by President Taft after a much publicized dispute in
1910 about the industrial development of government forestland, which
Pinchot opposed, but not before acreage of national forests increased from
51 million acres to 175 million.[156] Pinchot's crusade for conservation became
a platform to fight the industrial "special interests" and power monopolies
that were vying for control of natural resources.[157] Pinchot organized the
National Conservation Association and used his conservation efforts to
catapult him to become governor of Pennsylvania for two terms (1923–27,
1931–35). Social cries such as "Equality of opportunity," "A square deal for
every man," and "The protection of the citizen against the great concentra-
tions of capital, the intelligent use of laws and institutions for the public good"
rang from his conservation platform.[158] Shoemaker agreed and applauded
Pinchot's nationalism expressed in *The Fight for Conservation* (1910), which
invoked the idea of national character springing from America's historic and
legendary attachment to the soil. "That is the principal spring of his
steadiness," Pinchot wrote of the archetypal American, and he venerated
the "simplicity and directness" of that archetype, "and many of his other
desirable qualities."[159]

Pinchot promoted himself as the champion of the "little man" against
the "privileged classes." Sometimes accused of socialist radicalism, he
nonetheless offered to build an individualistic "nation of homes" in which
every American could own property and in which the government would
work on behalf of the "common man" against the evil trusts and robber
barons, who would gobble up irreplaceable natural resources for excessive
profits.[160] Conservation of America's heritage in the soil, for the cause of
public welfare in the present and to benefit future generations, was the key,
the "largest single task which now confronts the Nation," Pinchot proclaimed
with Shoemaker at his side.[161] Pinchot and Shoemaker had contrasting
styles. The charismatic Pinchot sought center stage, while the literary
Shoemaker worked behind the curtain. Their alliance joined Pinchot the
public man with Shoemaker the publicist, and both benefited politically from
the relationship.

Pinchot shared with Shoemaker a love of the outdoors and a fondness for
a good story,[162] and Shoemaker featured this aspect of his personality as
well as his political views in his widely circulated biography *Gifford Pinchot:
The Man Who Made Good* (1922).[163] "Pinchot was one of the best shots we
had, and is a sportsman and a gentleman," he wrote. According to Shoe-

maker, the outdoor life bestowed on him the wholesome character traits of simplicity, fairness, and humility. Although rural in his orientation, Pinchot in Shoemaker's argument would be the first "Labor Governor" because "he is not 'stuck up' with pride of place and power." Pinchot more successfully advocated for prohibition and conservation than for labor reform after the election, and he carried the Progressive Republican banner in the state after Theodore Roosevelt's death.[164] It was important for Shoemaker to include in his campaign biography of Pinchot that "the shadow of Col. Roosevelt was always by his side."[165] He compared their fights for Prohibition in heroic terms: "Colonel Roosevelt, by superhuman effort, once made New York City as dry as the Sahara Desert with the oases drained; Gifford Pinchot can do the same thing in Pennsylvania, if the people give him their backing."[166] Shoemaker quoted Roosevelt as saying that Pinchot was "the most useful man in public life in my time."[167]

Besides the Roosevelt connection to Pinchot, the tie to the President surfaces again in Henry Shoemaker's friendship with George Bird Grinnell (1849–1938), editor of *Forest and Stream* magazine. Based in New York City, where he organized the Boone & Crockett Club with Roosevelt, Grinnell shared Shoemaker's passion for combining natural conservation with cultural conservation. Grinnell was associated with the New York City branch of the American Folklore Society, and Shoemaker devoured his writing on the frontier in both folklore and nature journals. In addition to founding the Audubon Society of New York and serving as president of the National Parks Association, Grinnell published several significant volumes on the folklore of Blackfoot, Cheyenne, and Pawnee tribes in the West.[168] Grinnell was impressed with the youthful Shoemaker's writings on the lore of bison, elk, and other "extinct animals" in Pennsylvania, and complimented him on making it possible for the state "to have gone ahead in game protection much faster than any other state."[169] Grinnell attempted to temper Shoemaker's antimodernism by cautioning him:

> I haven't the slightest sympathy with men who ask to have nature's balance restored. They might as well ask to have all the brick houses swept off the continent of North America. You have your civilized man here, and he has so effectively destroyed nature's balance that it never can be brought back. The best we can do is to bring about a lot of artificial changes by which small tracts of territory may be made to simulate things as they used to be. Neither you nor I, I suspect, would like to have the whole western country swept bare again and the buffalo and the antelope restored to their old range. That is something that the Indians may talk about but that we can never see.[170]

Shoemaker replied that he too had given up on restoring the "balance of nature." "But I would like to see *all forms* of Wild Life allowed to work out their destinies in restricted areas. I have never seen any examples where artificial protective measures, like a complete destruction of so-called vermin, have brought back the Game, as it increases up to a certain point in a deteriorated form and then disease wipes it off the map, and then nature tries to come back and do it her own way."[171]

Other older conservationists who influenced Henry Shoemaker's combination of natural and cultural conservation were Ernest Thompson Seton (1860–1946) and Charles M. Skinner (1852–1907). Seton is best known as co-founder of the Boy Scouts of America, and he was a prolific author of books that combined folklore and natural science about animals and American Indians. Shoemaker wrote him to say that his "books were a constant inspiration to me during my boyhood days."[172] Like Seton, he applied the wolf and the lion as a kind of emblem, and also used romanticized animal stories to "stop the extermination of harmless wild animals" and as an impetus to the collection of nature lore.[173] Indeed, he wrote Seton that "those of us who love nature are hoping that in some mysterious way the panther and the wolf will come back when the forest is restored."[174] To Shoemaker, the wild panther and the wolf epitomized a romantic, golden age of harmony in the world. They were examples of animals that had lived in relative peace, maintaining nature's balance through their predatory ways, until white settlers forced their extinction, to the detriment of modern civilization. In the special surroundings of Pennsylvania, they became a distinctive breed and epitomized the ruggedness and romance of the highlands. Along with Seton, Shoemaker bemoaned the extinction of wildlife in a volume entitled *North American Big Game*.[175] Shoemaker's chapter on "Vanished Game" opened with this plaint: "The title 'Vanished Game' may not mean much to coming generations but it pictures a lack, a void, and an absence to those who have seen, even in decreased numbers, the grand game that is no more."[176] Adding his romantic touch, Shoemaker commented: "The Vanished Game leave ghosts behind in the form of very vivid memories, and for years after, whenever the brush cracks, their former hunters seem to note their once familiar forms in the shadows."[177] In the fight between expansive industry and the wildlife in its way, he wrote Seton, "there are only a few of us who take the side of the animals, but I am glad that we are all trying to do the best we can to save them for the edification of future generations."[178] Saddened by deforestation, animal extinction, and military devastation in Europe, Seton and Shoemaker both hoped, and wrote, for redemption in America.

In the growing rift between Europe and America that fostered a cultural and historical self-discovery of America after its centennial celebration in

1876, Charles Skinner helped make the case for the uniqueness of the United States. Like Shoemaker, Skinner was a journalist who reconstructed folklore from a variety of sources to reach a popular audience. From his newspaper and magazine base in New York City, Skinner's early contribution was to recognize the significance of American legendry.[179] Although America did not have a marvelous fairy-tale tradition akin to the popular European variety, he argued that American Indian mythology and pioneer legendry were the roots of a romantic American nationalism. In volumes such as *Myths and Legends of Our Own Land* (1896) and *American Myths and Legends* (1903), he built up the importance of the mythology surrounding American landscape and locality. He emphasized the garden-like wonder of the New World evident in the stories Americans tell. Whereas Europe had a long national history, America had a long *natural* history, and consequently a diverse legendry of place. The attachment to community and home-grown values comes through in stories from "Mississippi's Crooked Mountain" to "Pike's Peak."[180]

An avid reader of Skinner's works, Shoemaker used his notes on *Myths and Legends of Flowers, Trees, Fruits, and Plants* (1911) in many naturalist tracts. Skinner espoused the view that in "a material, dull age," folklore stands for "imagination and sheer loveliness."[181] To Skinner, "scientific" treatment of history that lauds industrial progress is lacking in the spiritual depth provided by rural American traditions. As Skinner wrote in the preface to his *American Myths and Legends,* "the immortality of the spirit which is betokened in these stories is more illuminative, as to certain phases of thought, than are volumes given to the recounting of merely material happenings instructive as to mankind's moral advancement."[182] His was also a Ruskian perspective that used legend, open as it was to literary rendering, to give the United States a mythological past of high moral character and national distinction.[183] More ingrained in the common people and presented more with a ring of folk authenticity than, let's say, Parson Weems and his dubious cherry-tree legend of Washington, it planted an American spirit firmly in its own soil. It was Skinner's structure of presenting legends as discrete literary stories, elaborated narratives without sources, that Shoemaker followed in his first collections of "Pennsylvania Mountain Stories."

Shoemaker often spoke of "wild life conservation," the protection and even restoration of game animals to the forests, yet he was not against hunting as a means of controlling numbers of deer and bears. Crucial to the protection of living animals, he believed, was the protection of their environments in the forests and the recognition of the special spirit that wildlife and their habitats held. That spirit, of course, could be revealed through the legends that local residents and respectful hunters knew well.

Shoemaker wrote one animal lover: "I am anxious to do all in my power to protect all kinds of wild life until such time as it may become plentiful and its presence will amuse and interest and also afford pleasure to those who care to hunt. As matters stand now all manner of game is rapidly diminishing, especially in Eastern Pennsylvania."[184] Shoemaker rejected the idea of wild-game preserves because of the cost and dependence on humans and supported increasing state forest lands and eliminating bounties for game kills.[185] "The existence of all the necessary attributes such as natural cover," he argued, "working for the common good in perfect unison, must be provided, else the game will languish, like gold fish in a sandless globe."[186] Thus, in addition to keeping game on his property, Shoemaker held more than 4,000 acres of posted forest lands near his estate in McElhattan.

In 1913, Shoemaker joined the advisory board of the Pennsylvania Conservation Association with his friends the Rev. James Henry Darlington, Gifford Pinchot, and Horace McFarland. Accepting the appointment, he wrote: "I will do all in my power through my newspaper and personal effort to further the cause of conservation of the Pennsylvania animals and birds, natural scenery and water power."[187] Indeed he did, getting his friend Governor Pinchot to ban pigeon shoots on Capitol Hill and eliminate market hunting, and setting up one of the nation's most extensive state forest and park systems.[188] He was against importation of game or artificial breeding, preferring to ensure the "purity" of remaining wildlife by preserving their wilderness habitats. "Not only must we strive to prevent the yellow blot of vanished game from extending over the sporting map of the continent," he declared, "but we must try to conserve in type and race what remains to us in its fine purity."[189]

Henry Shoemaker's concern for the conservation of animals extended to the American Indians—who had been forced out of Pennsylvania, he felt, like wild game. In his editorials on game conservation, he intentionally laid blame for the extinction of precious wildlife, such as the panther, elk, and passenger pigeon, at the feet of despoiling "white hunters." He wrote the editor of the *Altoona Tribune:* "I felt very badly to read of a fresh Indian outbreak, as it seems that there is no peace for the Red men while they remain on this earth. They will be hunted like the panthers were in Central Pennsylvania."[190] Shoemaker admired the way that Pennsylvania's Senecas "read from the Book of Nature and translated it into the language of God in their hearts."[191] "The entire Indian race was in closer tune with the Infinite than was any of the white races," he told a columnist, and added, "Many may have progressed financially, mechanically, physically, but he has deteriorated spiritually."[192] Speaking toward the end of World War I at a meeting of the Young Men's Christian Association that included Governor Brumbaugh in the audience, he offered: "The Senecas were Patriotic, they all worked for

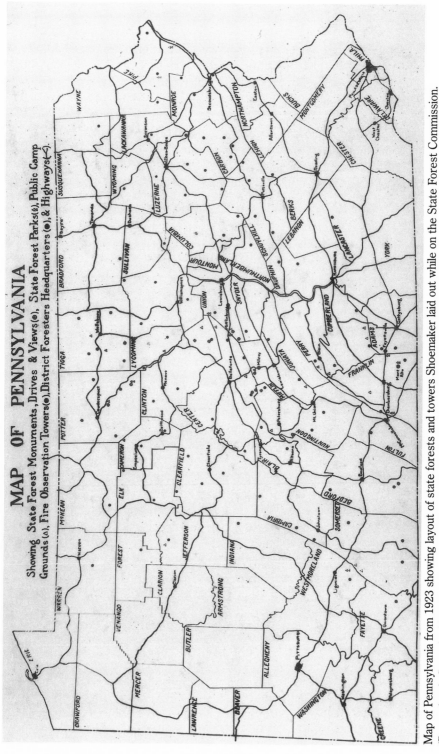

Map of Pennsylvania from 1923 showing layout of state forests and towers Shoemaker laid out while on the State Forest Commission. (Pennsylvania State Archives)

the common good; their Patriotism, like ours must be, was born from unselfishness."[193] Even in a secularizing age such as the present one, Shoemaker (a practicing Episcopalian) called "a love of Nature . . . a step towards reaching Religion, Faith," and said, "Religion is nature translated into language, and Nature is the clothing of God." Learning from Seneca philosophy about commune with nature, he warned that "there must not be too much 'speeding up' industrially, to try and catch up with the days lost by the war. We must not exercise superenergy, and exhaust life, by trying to get the last ounce out of it. We must move slowly, decorously, as preached and practiced by the Seneca philosophy."[194]

When he was not invoking the example of Pennsylvania's Indians in the wilderness, Henry Shoemaker used the Progressive rhetoric of "the greatest good to the greatest number." After penning one stinging antitrust editorial, he wrote: "I suppose some of the Altoona bankers will not appreciate my editorial on the Currency bill, but I am writing from the viewpoint of the greatest good to the greatest number. . . . The one hundred men who make up the interlocking boards of the Money Trust enterprises have become inordinately rich—but what of the rest?"[195] As a "newspaper man," Shoemaker claimed to speak independently for the conscience of the region's people, and he supported social legislation to curb child labor and begin worker compensation, but as an upper-class gentleman he had a hard time understanding the "submission" of backwoods families to industry. He implied that it was not only the power that industry abused, but also a lack of will, maybe even a loss of traditional values, on the part of the region's people. Most notably, he decried the emerging irreverence for the past, a failure to "show faith" in the regional heritage of wilderness lore and frontier history. If locals had this faith, they surely would preserve their natural surroundings and halt the ruthless march of mass industry, he reasoned. Some of the basis of Shoemaker's support for antimonopoly legislation was his belief that modern industrialism, which grew without responsibility to a community, fostered dangerous greed. He also believed that government needed to intervene because the people might not know what is good for them. On similar grounds, government had a directive to promote and initiate heritage education programs for the public.

As a prominent public figure in the Progressive movement and a noted writer and publisher, Henry Shoemaker received public recognition as a man to watch. He obtained honorary doctoral degrees from Juniata College in 1917 and from Franklin and Marshall College in 1924—Pennsylvania colleges with connections to his family—and in 1918 his old boss, Governor Brumbaugh, appointed him to the Pennsylvania State Forest Commission, which organized a massive system of parks in the state (totaling 114 areas) and initiated a conservation plan for state forests, streams, and fields.[196]

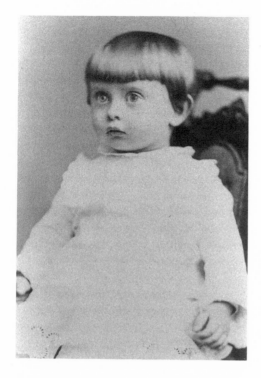

Henry W. Shoemaker, 20 months old, October 24, 1881. Photo by S. A. Thomas, New York City. (Private collection)

The Shoemaker children, William, Blanche, and Henry, c. 1888. Photo by W. Kurtz, New York City. (Private collection)

Henry F. Shoemaker Sr., c. 1900.
Photo by Davis & Sanford, New
York City. (Private collection)

Three generations of Quiggle women: Blanche Shoemaker, Blanche (Quiggle) Shoemaker, Cordelia (Mayer) Quiggle, c. 1900. Photo by Hargrave Portraits, New York City.
(Private collection)

The Shoemaker summer estate in Riverside, Connecticut, 1905. (Private collection)

Henry W. Shoemaker, after attending Columbia University, Photo by Rockwood Photographers, New York City. (Private collection)

Top: Restless Oaks, McElhattan, Pennsylvania, early twentieth century. *Bottom:* Interior of Henry Shoemaker's study at Restless Oaks, located on the first floor of the house. Shoemaker spent evenings working in this room on his books and other publications. From his desk, Shoemaker looked out toward the mountains and forest on his estate. In addition to a reference library, the room contained several of his emblems of Pennsylvania drawn from the once vibrant Central Pennsylvania animal kingdom. Note the lion and eagle on top of the bookcase and the bearskin on the floor. (Private collection)

Henry Shoemaker at the time he was lieutenant-colonel on Governor Brumbaugh's staff. Pennsylvania National Guard, c. 1915. (Historical Collections and Labor Archives, Pennsylvania State University)

Mabelle Ord Shoemaker, Henry Shoemaker's second wife, 1920. (Private collection)

Henry W. Shoemaker posing in a studio with his mother, c. 1915. The prop relates to Henry Shoemaker's participation in the Aero Club. The photo was used on a postcard. (Private collection)

Shoemaker as Minister to Bulgaria, c. 1930, passing the Russian church, Sofia, on the way back from an audience with King Boris. (Pennsylvania State Archives, John S. Fisher Collection)

Henry Shoemaker with the "Dauphin Sycamore" (near Linglestown, Pennsylvania, October 1920), one of the many "mighty monarchs," as he called the old trees, he worked to save. The inscription reads: "It is said that this tree stands as a memorial to John Goodway, the last of the friendly Indians. Colonel W. Shoemaker is standing upon the spot where the Indian is believed to be buried. Nominated for the hall of fame for trees. Spread of 135 feet, 125 feet high, with trunk about 25 feet in circumference and 7 feet in diameter." Photo by Joseph Illick. (Pennsylvania State Archives, Department of Forestry Photo Collection)

Dedication of Captain John Brady marker in East Lewisburg, September 22, 1928. Shoemaker stands to the left of the boulder. Left of him is Chief Strong Wolf. Congressman Clyde Kelly of Braddock, whose wife was a descendant of Brady, is standing with folded arms third from the left. The children standing with their parents are also Brady's descendants. Other dignitaries include the state librarian and members of the Pennsylvania Historical Commission. (Historical Collections and Labor Archives, Pennsylvania State University)

Shoemaker designed the reorganization of the Forestry Department into the Department of Forests and Waters and became a director of the American Forestry Association. He especially lobbied for support of Pennsylvania's first forestry school at Mont Alto, expressing the belief that "forestry has represented the highest ideal of the state, and is the spiritual side of commercial development," adding, "The forester has been the high priest of clean manhood and the outdoor life."[197] He also greatly increased the visibility of the commission and the ideals of the state when he arranged for Gifford Pinchot, the chief priest of forestry, to come on board after his rift with President Taft.

Pinchot recognized Shoemaker's instrumental role in bringing him onto the commission, and Shoemaker credited Pinchot with giving him free rein to put his conservation ideas into practice. "As a result," Shoemaker recalled, "the system of State Forests, State Forest Monuments, Parks, Views, Campsites and trails were developed, incomplete through lack of funds, but a definite step forward with the chief's backing."[198] In 1920, Shoemaker and Pinchot visited all the forestlands of Pennsylvania and developed an ambitious plan for naming the state forests and their subdivisions, and for a system of state forest monuments, parks, drives, views and campsites. Shoemaker went even further to identify and photograph "historic" trees throughout the state that were in need of protection, and he collaborated with Joseph Illick on a guide to the state forests for the public.[199] Pinchot sprang from the commission to run a successful campaign for governor in 1922, despite Shoemaker's advice to stay on the commission and concentrate on forestry work. "I felt I had a right to try to keep him where he had started a great work," Shoemaker commented to his friend Governor John Fisher in 1930.[200]

Making His Mark on the Historical Commission

When he took office as governor of Pennsylvania in 1923, Pinchot appointed Shoemaker chairman of the Pennsylvania Historical Commission, at which time Shoemaker announced his intention to have the commission achieve "its greatest usefulness and efficiency."[201] In this post, Shoemaker directed an extensive program for marking historical sites and undertaking archaeological excavations of American Indian and frontier sites,[202] and claimed to have written more than 4,000 markers himself.[203] He had been funding the dedication of historical monuments since at least 1912, when he paid for the marker at Fort Horn, near his home in McElhattan. Several others followed. It was his hope that marked sites would increase appreciation among Pennsylvanians for local contributions to national history, instill a regional sense of pride, and help protect historic locations from industrial development.

As chairman of the Pennsylvania Historical Commission, Henry Shoemaker had the opportunity to turn his private philanthropy into state policy. In the early years of the commission the members were not particularly active, so he wrote the secretary of the commission and complained that markers had not gone up and that the commission "is merely a bunch of people with official titles": "I think we should get busy at once and put across our projects for markers."[204]

Shortly after Shoemaker became chair of the commission, more than one hundred markers went up, with the cooperation of local historical and patriotic societies. The markers were usually affixed to large natural boulders and often set in recreational areas. By 1933, however, new commission members complained that the markers "were not easy reading in an increasingly fast-paced automobile age." So the erection of new markers ceased.[205] When the program was revived after World War II, the commission oriented plain two-dimensional markers to roadsides and city streets and recognized modern historic figures, many from urban areas. In keeping with the building of a Pennsylvania mythology, however, most of the earlier markers commemorated ancient Indian sites and frontier events, many of which had entered oral tradition. In 1924, for example, Shoemaker dedicated the site of the frontier home of Captain John Hanson Steelman (1655–1749), ten miles southwest of Gettysburg. Steelman, the stone explained, was an "Indian trader and Interpreter of Maryland and Pennsylvania" and the "First Permanent White Settler in Pennsylvania West of Susquehanna River." The "tall, native, weathered stone, to which is attached an inscribed bronze tablet, . . . is picturesquely located on a slight elevation of primitive woodland at a public cross-roads, overlooking the vale in which lies Steelman's land." Following Shoemaker's introduction at the dedication and to underscore the American Indian connection, Ojibwa Chief Strong Wolf from Philadelphia delivered the "Invocation to the Great Spirit."[206]

Other sites equally carried a sense of mystery as well as history. In 1925, Henry Shoemaker presided over markers for legendary as well as historical figures, such as "Indian Hannah, The Last of the Lenni-Lenape or Delaware Indians in Chester County" and "The Famous Indian Walk of a Day and a Half From Wrightstown, Bucks County to Near the Present Mauch Chunk, Carbon County As Performed for the Penn Proprietors of Pennsylvania, September 19–20, 1737 by The Fleet-Footed Youth Edward Marshall and His Associates." And near Lewisburg he dedicated an inscribed boulder for Captain John Brady, frontier-fighter and something of a folk hero claiming a cycle of legends.[207] In one four-month period of 1924, the Historical Commission erected ten markers under Shoemaker's direction. Four were

for extinct Indian settlements, three were for frontier forts or homes of
white pioneers among the Indians, and others were for historic houses,
including sites associated with William Penn and the "cave or dugout of
Francis Daniel Pastorius," founder of Germantown.

Ever mindful of his conservationist mission, Shoemaker especially delighted in marking historic sites around trees, mountains, and paths, such as
the Tiadaghton Elm in Clinton County, where the "Fair Play" settlers
supposedly declared independence before hearing the news of action from
the Congress at Philadelphia, and the Shamokin Path, a "much-traveled
Indian path; followed north shore of Susquehanna from present Sunbury to
Great Island near Lock Haven."[208] This site was especially important to
him, not only because it was near his home at Restless Oaks, but because it
was an example of an oral tradition, or "unrecorded history," that preserved
a significant nationalistic event.[209] At ceremonies for the 175th anniversary
of the event at the tree on Independence Day, he used the occasion to point
out the multiple ethnic roots of the Fair Play settlers who composed the
declaration and their subsequent transformation into Americans.

Unlike the more famous Philadelphia, "almost purely Anglo-Saxon," declaration that came after the Pine Creek announcement, the multiethnic one
under the Tiadaghton Elm "came from the soil, from the hearts of sturdy
frontiersmen, who worked with their hands, pathfinders, woodsmen, boatmen, toilers." Shoemaker implied that the birth of the nation rested in the
multiethnic Central Pennsylvania wilderness, not in the elite and narrowly
defined urban surroundings of Philadelphia. He invoked one of Theodore
Roosevelt's favorite themes: "The immigrant of to-day can learn much from
the experience of the immigrants of the past, who came to America prior to
the Revolutionary War." Already a people of "mixed blood," Roosevelt
asserted, they achieved success because "they became American in speech,
conviction, and thought."[210]

For Shoemaker, the declaration under the Tiadaghton Elm "showed
conclusively the wide scope of the demand for freedom by the colonists,
how these settlers of different races and creeds got together, framed a
document and signed it—the greatest document in all of the history of the
Revolution yet still to be rescued from the realms of tradition and folklore
and confirmed by markers put up by Governor Fine's Pennsylvania Historical
and Museum Commission."[211] In addition to marking the spot, the commission preserved the tree. "As long as the tree stands," Shoemaker reminded
his audience, "it is the symbol of human liberty, peace and equality." He
closed with his frequent projection of the spirituality in nature and the
necessity of its preservation when he exclaimed: "We commemorate, we
consecrate, we acclaim, this sacred tree today as a foundation shrine, not

to the memory of a patriotic happening, but as a living and ever present symbol of human liberty in its highest and most distinguished form."[212]

Some of the preoccupation with marking historical sites for public consumption stemmed from a feeling that Pennsylvania lacked the historical cachet of Old New England. For example, Shoemaker had heard from the state's auditor-general: "The neglect of the history of Pennsylvania by our forefathers is tragic. If we would have had a few New England vagabonds in Pennsylvania, history would record it as the greatest principality under the skies. Much that is recorded of its history is due to your industry, ability and love of our Commonwealth."[213] Penn State Professor Frederic Lewis Pattee underscored this feeling when he wrote Shoemaker regarding his collections of historical legends: "I have often thought that Pennsylvania is peculiarly rich in such lore and if she had been a state in New England she would long ago have made this material classic."[214] Shoemaker and Governors Brumbaugh and Pinchot realized that New England attracted the lion's share of tourists in the "See America First" campaign in the wake of war tensions in Europe. Thus Shoemaker proclaimed: " 'See America First' is a slogan we hear many times a day, but where to begin, and how to do it is the question. Let these perplexities be answered in the language of Pennsylvania's Governor, Dr. Martin G. Brumbaugh, 'See Pennsylvania first; there is no state like the 'Old Keystone.' "[215] Shoemaker kept up the "See Pennsylvania First" theme through the 1920s and 1930s, when he frequently went on radio using local folklore and history to "sell Pennsylvania to Pennsylvanians."[216]

Wilderness and American Mythology

Henry Shoemaker urged Pennsylvanians to appreciate "a pleasure-land lying at one's doors"—the Central Pennsylvania highlands, which he majestically dubbed "Eldorado Found."[217] Appealing to the late Victorian fondness for great escapes from modernity into the "primitive" outdoors, he prepared a tourist's survey inviting Pennsylvanians to hike on foot and ride on horseback through a secluded region "where all the charms of the old world and the new will be found blended in artistic harmony."[218] "There is no better place for tired bodies, weary minds, and depressed souls than a sylvan retreat with a gala garment of green," he wrote passionately. "There one finds quiet and rest. There the heart is lightened, the mind eased, the vitality restored. The out-of-doors lifts us up and casts away our burdens."[219] With the mythical reference to Eldorado (especially prevalent during the sixteenth century), Shoemaker evoked images of New World adventurers seeking wealth and beauty in the forested wilderness. The omnipresence of forests distinguished the American landscape from Europe, and Shoemaker and many others mythologized its promise of a moral, democratic separation from the aristocracy of Europe and a sense of national abundance and harmony. The myth suggested American (particularly New England) visions of nationalistic glory in a landscape dominated by "virgin" forests, and indeed he often displayed special reverence for "original" stands of "pure" or "virgin" timber in his books.

The tradition of the American wilderness or virgin forest strengthening character was especially prevalent in popular figures that Shoemaker admired, such as James Fenimore Cooper's Leatherstocking and Davy Crockett during the nationalistic period of the 1840s.[220] Shoemaker actively lobbied for setting aside a "primitive area . . . where all nature is left undisturbed, and future generations can see the forest primeval as the first settlers found it."[221] After all, he reflected, Pennsylvania is "the only State that embodies the word 'forest' [sylvan] in its name,"[222] and Pennsylvania held the essence, the mystique, of America at its natural core. "The responsibility rests upon us," he added, "to see that some unaltered samples of native character and natural beauty are left for the recreation and inspiration of generations to come."[223]

Shoemaker built on the wilderness myth when he wrote of the highland residents as national ancestors of the highest moral virtue. In an address on the Pennsylvania mountaineers, he preached:

> In the humblest cabins in the South Mountains, or the Seven Mountains or the Blue Mountains, in the hills about Keating, or in the former Black Forest you may happen upon a single oil painting of some elegant man or woman of the long ago, all that survived the vicissitudes of crossing seas, penetrating trackless forests, fires, movings, misfortunes, that one link with the far-distant period of gentility that elicits our respect, and ever commands our attention. . . . The Pennsylvania Mountaineer has always been essentially American. His ancestors were mostly officers in all of our earlier wars, he preserves the finest and purest traditions of the struggle for independence. In that respect he is a contemporary ancestor."[224]

These mountaineers were "as strong and solid, and unsullied as the 'imperishable hills' among which they live."[225] In conveying the ruggedness and independent spirit of life in the wilderness, Shoemaker sketched the wilderness not as a barrier to settlement but an invitation to human use. Constructing a historic shrine in the Buchanan State Forest—named after President James Buchanan who was born in what is now Franklin County, Pennsylvania—Shoemaker wrote that the site "shows from what a humble sylvan retreat a great man can rise to the pinnacle of eminence."[226]

The successor to the glorified nationalistic image of the wilderness was the garden myth, the conversion to a pastoral paradise by industrious plowmen.[227] As a version of the garden myth popularized to justify "manifest destiny" might be narrated, the trees were cut, the cabins built, the fields cleared, the crops planted, the family fed from their bounty, and a nation expanded and advanced. Yet any examination of Shoemaker's rhetoric reveals time and again his insistence on the spiritual quality that the wilderness over the garden gave to the roots of the new American experience. And sometimes Shoemaker felt uneasy about relating the story of white settlers who forced the Indian off the untamed land. His stories often had a strong theme of mysterious revenge exacted on the descendants of the despoilers of the wilderness and its original peoples. For example, in his story "The Original," a white hunter shoots a black moose, reverently called "The Original" by the Indians because it was the parent of all the deer families. Shoemaker narrates, "With a sound like a falling pine the Original crashed to the earth, lying dead among the ferns and hazel brushes, his wide-spreading palmated antlers stretching out on either side like the knives of a reaper." An Indian named Young Jacob sees the act and, expecting that the shooting was for some utility, asks the hunter what he intends to do with the animal. "Why, of course, leave it," he says. On hearing that, the Indian criticizes the senselessness of the shooting of the Original, and the hunter responds: "You say you Indians only kill when you have to. You are damn fools. We white men kill when we want to, and intend to kill everything before we get through." When he raises his rifle threateningly at Jacob, the Indian defensively shoots the hunter. Young Jacob consoles him, but still the hunter has no remorse. Jacob finally mutters, "Now you know how it feels to be in the moose's place." In "The White Deer," a Bohemian immigrant who abandons his sweetheart in Europe to work furiously in the Pennsylvania lumber industry is startled one day by the sight of a ghostly white deer in the forest. The deer appeared, he discovers later, on the very day his sweetheart died, and he exclaims: "The white deer was her fading spirit. Like one struck on the head I staggered from the office. I saw no more of the white deer: but I made myself an old man slaving in the lumber camps."[228] In "The Indian's Twilight," timber-cutters who proudly vanquish a tree later suffer horrible, unexplained consequences.[229]

After illustrating the glories of the once-mighty wilderness in *Black Forest Souvenirs*, Shoemaker closed the book with a photograph of a farmer at his plow surrounded by family and pets and sternly captioned "New Order of Things." Wilderness Pennsylvania struck Shoemaker as "God's chosen region," "a mystic region," "a Glorious Land of Romance where the sun was

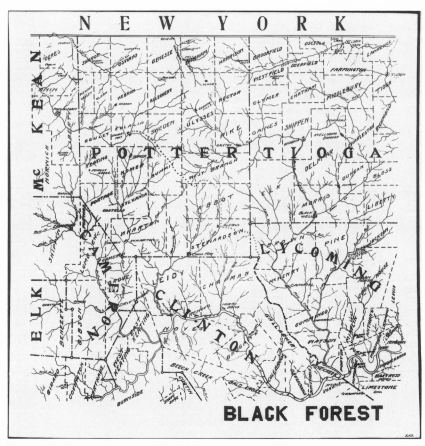

Map of Northcentral Pennsylvania area known as the "Black Forest" of Pennsylvania. This is the region where much of Pennsylvania's lumber industry was based in the late nineteenth century. Shoemaker's home "Restless Oaks" was in McElhattan, Wayne Township, near the West Branch of the Susquehanna River, at the lower right. Shoemaker celebrated the region in stories he collected in the book *Black Forest Souvenirs* (1914). (Pennsylvania State Archives)

always shining and people were always smiling."[230] It needed protection, and in the state forest preserves of the wilderness one could still find intact an invigorating "woodland paradise" containing "birds, wild flowers, and rare ferns."[231] "The State forests of Pennsylvania are the people's property," he wrote. The aim of the State Department of Forests and Waters is to handle them so that they will produce continuous crops of forest products and bring a full measure of other benefits to the citizens of the State." These areas became favorite picturesque "play-places," with "plentiful supplies" of "pure" water. Much as trails pushed into the wilderness brought America toward greatness, many miles of paths "push far into the forest depths."[232]

The garden myth implied that the New World environment promised fertility and abundance, and American industriousness and technology could turn even desert into fertile ground.[233] Shoemaker was ambivalent about narrating the past according to the garden myth because it could be interpreted to support the exploitation of land by American industrialism. He lobbied for government controls and for providing parks for the enjoyment of the public, so that the garden myth could be made into a frontier heritage ideal. Shoemaker's work for the development of state parks, and later the allure of Amish farmlands, depended on the garden myth. Parks protected a pastoral image of America, and Shoemaker proposed to make each one based on historical events that suggested the source of American heritage in frontier settlement, battle, and reconstruction.

Henry Shoemaker was especially active in the development of the Conrad Weiser Homestead site and Bushy Run Battlefield. The marker for Weiser describes him as a "pioneer, Indian interpreter, treaty maker from 1732–1760. The Indians called him the 'Holder of the Heavens.' "[234] Surrounding his home in Berks County, a state park preserves a pastoral setting. At Bushy Run in Westmoreland County, the site of an Indian defeat in 1763 opened the gateway for settlement of the West, so the site's interpretation goes, and a state park turns this battleground into a pleasure ground.[235] An executive of the Pennsylvania Parks Association, Shoemaker went to Europe to "study the course of forest destruction, stream depletion, and its resultant misfortunes to mankind."[236] He became one more voice pointing to America's opportunity to redeem itself by taking up conservation, and thereby to separate itself from Europe.[237]

By extolling the virtues of the wilderness and mountain life, Shoemaker hoped to reverse the growing national image of industry representing wealth, a "short-cut to Eldorado"; in his survey, nature held heavenly power and glory.[238] The wilderness is owed mystical reverence, not indifference or exploitation. "This is an age of hurry," he wrote, and too many residents "must tell the number of miles traversed on their excursions, not what they saw. To fully appreciate every vista, every cloud, every bird, every butterfly, every lofty pine, the pedestrian method is supreme."[239] This appreciation invoked a kind of Puritan symbolism for the environment in which "every natural fact was an emblem of the divine law which governed spirit as well as thing; every object, creature, and event in nature held a moral purpose over and above its scientific or temporal meaning."[240] If the wilderness gave Puritan spiritual inspiration and was not meant to be exploited, it was meant to be used, and conservation offered Progressive protection and earthly practicality.

The conservation movement during the early twentieth century came up against a "peculiarly American belief that the continent contains so much of everything that anything can be infinitely used."[241] It had to convince the public that natural resources could run out and that they had priority over the growth of massive machines and industrial profit. This was not easy, considering that industrialism had been intellectually connected with "progress" and "modern civilization," and nature with the "primitive."[242] In Shoemaker's story "The Vista," included in *More Pennsylvania Mountain Stories* (1912), he contrasted the forest of the fertile past and the desert of the modern present. "It is hard to realize that the woodsman's axe has levelled the entire forest into a desert vista," he wrote. "Evidently regarding nature's prodigality as limitless," the wielder of the axe "demolished . . . the giant virgin white pines" that "stood so thick that the trees which had been cut could not fall."[243]

Conservationists like Shoemaker and Pinchot denied that they wanted to halt industrial progress, and indeed they invoked the Progressive label to underscore that conservation meant advancement by wisely managing resources for future generations. They often spoke of using government to slow down "wasteful and destructive" industrial growth for the good of the populace and to ensure the perpetuity of the wilderness to allow moderns healthful, spiritual escape from the pressures of modern business. Pinchot offered both business and populist metaphors in his Progressive rhetoric for conservation as the "same kind of practical common sense management of this country by the people that every business man stands for in the handling of his own business."[244] Writing *In Penn's Woods* with state forester and national leader of American conservation Joseph Illick, Shoemaker used these Progressive metaphors: "It is the business of government to make it easy for people to do right and hard for them to do wrong. Everywhere in our social life it is becoming evident that the right use of leisure is as vital to our general welfare as the right use of toil. It is as imperative to see that our citizens have proper places to play as it is that they have good working conditions. To develop a citizenry on a sane and safe basis, and to insure the moral strength and physical fitness of our people, we must immediately give thought to the open and full development of our forests."[245]

Mountains and streams, in addition to the forests, are essential to completing the portrayal of paradise. "The mountains seem to be the last stand of primitive life, simple faith, forests, game and old traditions," Shoemaker told one audience, "their aloofness holding together the threads which bind the modern complex existence with a kindlier far-off day."[246] Elsewhere he described the mountains as "pavilions of spiritual refreshment, cool shady nooks, where we may find deep in the moss the faith of our fathers."[247] In equally mystical terms Shoemaker claimed that "it seemed from the start that his lode-star ever carried him towards the Blue Mountains, and he always viewed the great, long level line of those mountains standing bold against the horizon, with the most peculiar feelings of awe and mystery."[248] He was equally taken with ensuring the original "purity" of natural water as well as the "virginity" of timber. His most frequently used illustration for his books showed American Indians gently canoeing down a mountain stream. The mountains (and observation towers Shoemaker built in the forests) offered inspiring vistas to absorb the scenic beauty and harmony of the land, another kind of "mosaic of discrete pieces." Climbs to summits in Shoemaker's world became akin to religious pilgrimages calling for collecting nature's specimens to appreciate the details of those pieces. Once at the top, climbers could gain a vista giving a sense of human wisdom and power as they looked down on their dominion. Eldorado Found had the Seven Mountains at its heart, and by Shoemaker's definition included the sources of the Juniata River and the West Branch of the Susquehanna, the two highest mountains in the state, and the Black Forest. Within its boundaries, animals and people have left a legacy of folklore and history, Shoemaker emphasized, that adds to the region's "mystic" charm and the Keystone State's grandeur.

Mythical wilderness metaphors and more than a hint of nationalism abound in Shoemaker's connection of the vitalizing powers of nature and folklore in relation to history. "Folklore being a part of the soul of the earth and the hills is eternal if it can be rescued from the primeval jungles and inscribed on the tablets of time," he said to the Ohio Valley Historical Association.[249] He told his audience that if they go "out to collect for yourself among the few remaining sages who lived when Indians were less rare than they are today, when the virgin forests stood and the flights of the wild pigeons darkened the sun," then "you will drink from the pure fount of folklore that runs below the solid rock of history, all hard and fast fact, but sometimes deadly uninteresting. It will make you love your country more knowing its beginnings and how its pioneers lived, thought and struggled."[250] He realized the power of this mythology to define what William Clebsch has called the "mythique" of American destiny and identity, for Shoemaker concluded by bringing his audience to a mountaintop, where "perhaps you will find legends that explain the modern crisis in human destiny, truths that will give us an added power to make the world free, for, aided by simplicity, we shall see great, grand, unending vistas."[251] Brought together in that vista, retold, and made part of a national consciousness, Shoemaker's mythical stories of wilderness and simple life in the Pennsylvania heartland directed their audiences to a conservationist view of progress, a nationalist consideration of what makes America distinctive.

Conserving the Past

Henry Shoemaker hoped to give "Old Keystone" distinction as the epitome of American heritage by bestowing picturesque names on Pennsylvania's landscape. The Geographic Board, of which he was a member, actively gave names to mountains, streams, and paths, or officially gave names to localities—usually the older and more charming, the better,[252] for he had complained that modernity was turning its back on names associated with the past: "Every month the senseless shifting is going on, newcomers wresting from the historic past the heritage of honored names. It will be difficult a century hence to follow the course of history in Pennsylvania; even now it is hard to identify the places visited by early travelers like Spangenberg, Ettwein and Col. Weiser, as innovators have changed and re-changed even the names of the streams and mountains that they crossed."[253] Indeed, Shoemaker urged legislation that required permission of the Pennsylvania Historical Commission before any name could be changed in the state.[254] He promoted the use of American Indian names (he claimed that Pennsylvania had discarded fewer Indian names than other states), for "the Indian-named mountains, valleys, lakes, rivers and streams persist and bid fair to defy the ruthlessness of the ages."[255] He gave "Karoondinha," a "distinctive, euphonious Indian name," to a state forest district in Centre County.

Centre County locales seemed to bring out the most romantic legendary associations for Shoemaker. "The tradition of the last Indians in that region," he wrote, "was that the Great Earth Spirit Loved the Evening Star, but she was already enamored of Jupiter, surrounded by its moons, and feeling that his love would never be requited, opened his side and his anguish overflowing, ever ebbing, became the wondrous Karoondinha."[256] Shoemaker fought changing the name Red Panther's Cave to Woodward, calling the latter name an ahistorical and abhorrent "infliction of the Post Office Department."[257]

Although he was unsuccessful in attempts to change the spelling of Pittsburgh back to Pittsburg (he blamed the "misspelling" on the Pennsylvania Railroad) or to restore Funkstown as the name of Mont Alto (which was "ruthlessly and prosaically re-named," by the post office, he wrote), he was responsible for giving many picturesque names to Pennsylvania locations. For example, he wrote Thomas Lloyd: "The Mountain which we located is the culminating peak of the Nittany Range which looks down on Catharine Smith's former home, mill and grave. It was most impressive, and the name 'Catharine's Crown' to my mind is admirable, and I am hoping that it will be adopted at the next meeting of the State Geographic Board at Harrisburg."[258] He even named public campgrounds and observation towers, including "Promised Land" (Pike County), "Laurel Summit" (Westmoreland County), and "Chickaree" (Cambria County). He also used names of Pennsylvania historical figures and prominent conservationists for mountains, forests, and parks, and eventually he had a mountaintop in Union County named for himself. Shoemaker offered Bishop James Henry Darlington's name for one Clinton County peak, and the name of his friend J. T. Rothrock, founder of the Pennsylvania Department of Forestry, for a state forest in Huntingdon County. Shoemaker wrote of his naming program for the state: "Much of history and romance is brought to light through the nomenclature of our State forests, and a perusal of them will open fresh vistas of interest and research. They show the wide range of life and history that belong to the Keystone Commonwealth, and cannot fail but make us more deeply appreciate the privileges of being citizens of this incomparable State founded by the wisdom and benevolence of William Penn."[259]

Shoemaker conceived of his Historical Commission and Geographic Board work as conservation similar to the work he did for the environment, as he stated in the creed of the Pennsylvania Alpine Club. In addition to working for "pure air, pure water, pure manhood and womanhood against the inroads of the modern complex, urban civilization," he dedicated himself to "save the ancient landmarks, and historic old forts and other pioneer structures and memorials, and historic and noteworthy trees and groves," and to the mission "to protect, study and preserve, wherever possible, the history, folk lore, folk songs and proverbs of our mountain people."[260] One columnist predicted that, as a result of this initiative to conserve folklore as well as nature, "Mr. Shoemaker will undoubtedly win progressive fame as the conservator of these legends and traditions."[261] Indeed, Shoemaker claimed that the idea of the Alpine Club he founded was originally to "learn more of Nature in our own state, see Pennsylvania first and gather fragments of history and folklore."[262] The *Reading Eagle* reported the Pennsylvania Folklore Society meeting of 1929 as one in which nature, folklore, and politics came together. Congressman Charles Esterly used the occasion to present Secretary of War James Good to the media. "Pennsylvania folklore was reviewed by the Bishop," the news report read. "He praised Col. Shoemaker for his books, declaring that the Shoemaker publications are an inspiration for good. High tribute was paid to Pennsylvania scenery and natural resources of the state by the speaker."[263] Nature and folklore, history and folklore, were often intertwined—perhaps to their collective detriment, because their separation might have reduced the confusion of sources that usually came from Shoemaker's publications, although at the same time their interconnection continued to build the mystique around Pennsylvania's heritage and promoted the cause of conservation.

To "conserve" meant materially preserving memory and allowing for its future use. The state forests and parks became materialization of memories—properties as much as historic battlefields. One Progressive assumption was that if organizations and governments did not intervene and take over as managed properties the sites of history and nature, the industrial interests would destroy them. Henry Shoemaker's collections of oral traditions responded similarly to material sites of mountains and later highways and houses. When he took the cronies on "expeditions," his itinerary read something like this: "Mother Seaton's Tomb, then to site of Polly Zimmerman kidnap escapade, John Eiker's Museum; have John show us the Indian Rhyolite quarry near Fairfield, Pa., thence to the site of Bard kidnapping and Massacre near Virginia Mills, then to McKesson place about two miles due south of Bard place, where Alex McKesson was carried off by Indians, then back to Cashtown."[264]

Years later, he compiled a booklet entitled *Conserving Pennsylvania's Historic Past* (1939), in which he announced the expansion of the Historical Commission's conservationist mission from erected markers to developing properties. Choosing the active word "development" rather than "preservation," he emphasized the economic and popular benefits of conservation. "Pennsylvania has spent and will continue to spend thousands of dollars to attract the rich tourist trade," he wrote. "No state is better equipped to profit from this natural resource. To fully realize upon this asset it is vital, however, that Pennsylvania intensively develop its scenic and historic treasures."[265] One ramification of this approach was that public history came to be translated largely into sites (and maintained properties for the Historical Commission) to visit.[266]

For depicting the past, Shoemaker's version of history depended greatly on settings and on oral sources, rather than on documents. To be sure, it was concerned with important figures and significant events, such as battles, but it often offered the personal, human side of history steeped in everyday life and natural surroundings. "What makes your histories more interesting than the histories found in schools," one reader wrote, "[is that] you do not quote what part the few Generals and prominent people took in making our country what it is. You give to the mass of people what part their ancestors took in the settlements of our beautiful valleys and hills."[267] "It is the outside, legendary oral form of human annals that lasts longest," Shoemaker proclaimed, and imagined that "it would be truly wonderful . . . if a collection of old-time legends or folk-lore could be collected in the vicinity of every town where there is a library."[268]

Shoemaker's version of national history dwelled on particular locations rather than on the nation as a whole, for it is in locality that the everyday activities of most people take place. Early in his writing career he was encouraged by a letter that told him: "Too much credit cannot be given you for preserving the traditions that otherwise would soon pass from memory for the coming generation has a limited knowledge of local history."[269] Influenced by his local newspaper reporting, Shoemaker presented history by covering not only people but also the familiar natural sights that present barriers and inspirations for inhabitants. In his investigation of legends, he sought to verify them as history, as reports of "true" events that had eluded documentation. But as he collected more traditions of Central Pennsylvania, he became less concerned with finding the "facts" and more concerned with recording memory and re-creating the spirit and romance of a bygone age. "The romance of Pennsylvania history is its folklore and a few partly accepted episodes like Brady's leap, Regina Hartman's captivity, Molly Pitcher and the Jewish Settlement at Schaefferstown," he told the Lycoming County Historical Society in 1929. "Otherwise, many declare it as dull as is to be expected from a history conceived by pious Quakers and narrow Covenanters."[270] Asked to speak on history at Penn State University that same year, Shoemaker explained: "While I am not exactly an historian, but a collector of Folk Lore and Legends, I would be glad to give you a talk on one of the old traditions of Centre County. . . ."[271]

Community Service and Club Fellow

Shoemaker's support for using history and nature studies to build unity is evident in his sponsorship of "community service in Pennsylvania coal fields." He was fund-raising chairman for a program to send teachers to immigrant coal-working communities to teach "Americanization or Citizenship" as well as "Home Sanitation" and "Recreation." The Americanization program included classes on history, manufacture, and natural resources, in addition to instruction on language and government. He claimed that since the program began in 1919 more than thirty communities in eight counties had been served, and wrote prominent businessmen in the region: "The program and method have been developed to the point where definite improvement in conditions is being effected, especially with reference to the assimilation of the foreign-born by the community."[272]

In addition to public education for the purposes of Americanization, Shoemaker also called for special public-health measures in the highlands and the coal regions. He was especially an advocate for government measures in education and health care to halt the spread of tuberculosis and provide for its often indigent victims. Beginning in 1925, he was a director of the Pennsylvania Tuberculosis and Health Society and state chairman for the antituberculosis Christmas seal campaign for twenty-six years. Between his organizational work and column-writing, both of which reached all corners of Pennsylvania, he was becoming known as a spokesman for public welfare and at the same time for business and conservation interests. His high profile in the print media, in social organizational work, and in government service led to his name being mentioned for lieutenant governor and congressman-at-large. An editorial in the *Middleburg Post* on September 16, 1920, offered that Shoemaker "is known over the entire state by his several dozen books on mountain history, folk lore and wild animals." "His unyielding position taken for the preservation of Pennsylvania's forests and his unswerving fidelity to duty," the paper continued, "commends him to the people for a bigger job."

Before 1930, Shoemaker organized or led many groups in Pennsylvania dedicated to conserving history and the environment. He was a founding president of the Pennsylvania Alpine Club (1917–30), a trustee of the Pennsylvania Parks Association, president of the Pennsylvania Federation of Historical Societies (1925–26), president of the Huguenot Society (1919–20), vice-president of the Pennsylvania Waldensian Society (1925–30), vice-president of the Netherlands Society of Philadelphia (1915–29), and fellow of the American Geographical Society. His advancement in these organizations was probably due more to his energy and dedication than to outspokenness. Indeed, testimonials address his quiet commitment and his most sociable and likable personality. His special enthusiasm for donating his time to public and social service may have come from the early influence of Governor Martin Brumbaugh, who made a special plea for extending "the spirit of true Americanism—that greatness lies in service." Accompanying the governor to Valley Forge on July 4, 1915, Shoemaker heard him assert that "the best gift one can give his country is his time, his talent, his service in the advancement, the welfare, the happiness of all his fellows," and he urged "true Americans" to answer that call.[273]

Henry Shoemaker considered the founding and leadership of the Alpine Club a special calling, for it combined many of his driving passions, including mountain-climbing, conservation, public welfare, patriotism, history, and folklore. The idea for the club came about on a trip with fellow newspaper editors J. Herbert Walker and George W. Wagenseller in 1915 to see a legendary buffalo hunter living near the Mahanoy Mountain, who told the group legends about the imposing peak. With mysterious stories fresh in mind, the group climbed the mountain and, in Shoemaker's words, watched "the tempest-tossed old warriors of the mountain soughing as they were today their lament as old as the world." Once at the top, the group unfurled an American flag, "a fit associate of eagles and all that is grand and free in Nature."[274]

At that moment and in this club, nature, society, and folklore seemed, to Shoemaker, to be inexorably intertwined. "Besides the inspiring joy of climbing these lofty mountains," he explained, "the purposes of the club would be to study the history and legends, the fauna, avifauna and flora of the mountains and strive to protect and preserve them for future generations of loyal Pennsylvanians."[275] Invoking Henrik Ibsen's call to "come with me up into the mountains and I will show to you the glory of the world," Shoemaker thought of the club as "a sort of advanced Boy Scout organization where statesmen, bankers and publishers can find surcease of business cares amid the sylvan slopes of the monarchs of our Highlands."[276] It also had an active political role in lobbying for game laws and conservation of wilderness areas, and a social responsibility "to improve the living conditions of the Pennsylvania mountain people, and especially the mountain children."[277]

From the appeal of folklore in the Alpine Club's activities, Shoemaker conceived of an organization devoted specifically to Pennsylvania folklore. At a meeting of the Alpine Club on February 18, 1920, he broached the idea at the home of the Rt. Rev. James Henry Darlington, bishop of the Episcopal Diocese of Harrisburg, who shared his historical and environmental inter-ests.[278] Another clergyman-scholar supporting the idea was the Rev. John Baer Stoudt of Northampton, Pennsylvania, who like Shoemaker had been a member of the Pennsylvania Historical Commission and president of the Pennsylvania Huguenot Society. An experienced local historian and writer on folklore, Stoudt also was president of the Pennsylvania-German Society and, in 1935, a founder of the Pennsylvania-German Folklore Society.[279] Stoudt's support, considering his connections to the active but sometimes parochial interests of the Pennsylvania-German folklorists, was essential to the organization's success.[280] At another Alpine Club meeting on May 23, 1924, the organization was officially organized at Darlington's home.

Shoemaker enrolled the society in the Pennsylvania Federation of Histori-cal Societies (Shoemaker was president-elect of the federation at that time and announced in Harrisburg: "Perhaps the most interesting newcomer into the Federation is the Pennsylvania Folk Lore Society, organized in the classic precincts of the library of Bishop J. H. Darlington, in this city, last spring, and already possessed of a representative membership under the presidency of the versatile and erudite Prelate, whose love of the Nature's

shrines has earned him the name of the 'Outdoor Bishop.' "[281] Journalists J.
Herbert Walker and Harry P. Hays, officers of the Alpine Club, became
secretary and treasurer, respectively, of the folklore society. In addition,
Professor Frank Speck of the University of Pennsylvania represented the
American Folklore Society and Flora Black of the Historical Commission on
the officers' list. After being president of the Alpine Club for thirteen years
before 1930, Shoemaker became president of the Pennsylvania Folklore
Society after 1930 and held the top position of the folklore society for
twenty-seven years.

"Pennsylvania" as it appeared in Shoemaker's organizations appeared to
be more of a country or America-writ-small than a political state. While he
lived in New York City, Shoemaker and his father had belonged to the
Pennsylvania Society, founded in 1899 for the purpose of keeping alive "the
memory of Pennsylvania." The society openly promoted "the good name
and the fair fame of the State" and grew to be the largest state society in
New York City. While his father served on the council and led the publication
committee, Shoemaker chaired the society's library committee, used the
library for some of his research, and participated in the festive banquets,
"whose chief purpose has been to proclaim the glory and fraternal spirit of
the Keystone State."[282] The society's distinguished leadership included
William Guggenheim, Andrew Carnegie, and John Wanamaker. Shoemaker's
early involvement in the society may have influenced his own booster
efforts, and the society praised his "glimpses of the folk-lore of the region"
for their "real and original value, measurably heightened by the fine form in
which Mr. Shoemaker presents them."[283]

Shoemaker was connected to European ancestry primarily through his
leadership of the Huguenot Society of Pennsylvania. To be sure, he was a
member of societies for Holland Dutch and Waldensian (northern Italian)
heritage, but he was most active in promoting French Huguenot pride.[284]
Perhaps he was again driven by a desire to reveal a lost or hidden past, for
unlike other colonial settlers in Central Pennsylvania, such as the Quakers
and Mennonites, the Huguenots did not establish compact communities.
They merged quickly with other ethnic communities, particularly the Germans with whom they mostly emigrated, and usually did not organize their
own churches. French Protestants who fled to the Rhine after being
persecuted by Catholic King Louis XIV, the Huguenots came largely to
Pennsylvania and Georgia.[285] With intermarriage and assimilation in America,
many of them translated or changed their names from the French into
English and German, but family lines for Aurand, Le Fever, and Dupree are
still evident in Pennsylvania. Huguenot immigrants numbered probably no
more than 8,000, although they were prominent as town builders and
promoters of enterprise.[286] Shoemaker claimed that the Huguenots were

largely forgotten in the chronicling of the making of Pennsylvania, and he asserted their original American spirit. In fact, he linked Davy Crockett's ancestry and his wilderness myth to the Huguenots.[287] "The primeval forests they found here were reflected in smooth, calm quiet pools, frequented by the same marine life, just as in Provence, Laguedoc, Oberlin's Steinthal, Neff's Piedmontese valleys, or Franche-Comté, or the beautiful Nivernais," Shoemaker observed. He continued his connection of natural and nationalistic history when he announced in a rhetorical flourish, "Flung abreast the wild sea of life, driven by the force of powerful religious persecution, who can say that these people were not drawn to the new land by a force equally strong—the force perhaps, of creation and evolution. Who can say this blood was not meant to fuse, a rich blood stream for a young, hardy country?"[288] Among these neglected pioneers were his ancestors Copes, Ferrees, and Mayers (originally Lamaire), who had come to Pennsylvania in the late seventeenth century. In 1920 he toured Huguenot source areas in Europe and recognized similarities in the landscapes and settlements of France and Pennsylvania.[289] In the Huguenot Society he was joined by familiar conservationists, such as Governor Gifford Pinchot, Bishop James Henry Darlington, and the Rev. John Baer Stoudt, all of whom served as presidents at one time or another. During Shoemaker's presidency after World War I, he urged the society to lobby for aid to devastated France.[290]

Diplomatic Success, Financial Failure

With so many organizational ties, Henry Shoemaker's name was getting around, and by the late 1920s it was being mentioned by his political cronies for a prestigious diplomatic post. "I would like an appointment as minister to any one of the European countries," he affirmed to the national Republican Party headquarters.[291] He explained that "while the situation of being an 'office-seeker' is hardly a pleasant one, we all have our ambitions, and progress is the order of life. It is within all of us to desire to serve in broader fields."[292] Shoemaker's friend Governor John Fisher had directed Herbert Hoover's successful presidential campaign of 1928 in Pennsylvania, so he was in a good position to work on Shoemaker's behalf. Fisher described Shoemaker as "one of the most prominent citizens of this state," one who "had been so useful, through his newspaper and other connections, in the present campaign."[293] "Have pulled all the wires I know," Fisher wrote Shoemaker in September 1929, and he assured him that "this matter has been presented to the President personally."[294] In January 1930, Hoover named Shoemaker minister to Bulgaria. Shoemaker had hoped for Switzerland and its fabled Alps, and also expressed preferences for Portugal and

Greece, but he was happy for the diplomatic opportunity. Upon arriving in Bulgaria, he drew parallels to the mountains and endangered forests of Pennsylvania and traveled widely in the country, as well as in other diplomatic outposts in Russia, Romania, Turkey, Greece, Switzerland, and Italy. But he maintained close ties to Pennsylvania, publishing several books on highland folklore during his diplomatic tenure, and receiving regular shipments of Pennsylvania pretzels and other foods in his Sofia legation.

Shoemaker befriended Bulgaria's King Boris and advised him particularly on a conservation program for the country's forests.[295] Shoemaker exerted his influence on the king to create a forest preserve system to offset the rapid destruction of forests and wildlife after Turkish dominion ended in 1878. The king launched the conservation program and named one of the preserves in Shoemaker's honor. In keeping with his advocacy for wilderness areas, that preserve was the only one of twelve parks to be kept a primitive area, where all forms of trees, plants, and wildlife were left undisturbed. Shoemaker used his Bulgarian experience to warn Pennsylvanians of the danger of losing its forests. "If one wishes to visualize Pennsylvania fifty years from now," he editorialized, "if forest fires and persistent lumbering continue at the present rate, Bulgaria fits into the picture, a natural forest land, its timber neglected in the past, burned over and over-exploited in the present, a beautiful land of high peaks, rolling hills, and rocky water courses, yet lacking for the most part Nature's supreme gift, trees."[296]

In Bulgaria, Shoemaker was delighted to find animals that had become extinct in Pennsylvania. He perceived that Bulgarian citizens were well attuned to their surroundings and heritage: "The Bulgarians, to my mind, form a splendid example of a healthy, all purposeful living people."[297] He reflected further that "due to existing economic and social factors, the Bulgarian people found their pleasures in their surroundings. Generally they formed hiking parties and picnic or nature groups. Hunting was not a national sport as it is in the United States. Licenses for hunting or fishing were much beyond the means of most Bulgarians. As a result the game known in Pennsylvania sixty years ago still exists there. The wolf, the lynx, the wildcat, the red bear, otter, beaver, the eagle, pelican, wild turkey, swan and others unknown in America survive in that country."[298] Bulgarians brought him animals as gifts, and he established a small zoo in the legation garden.[299]

Shoemaker admired the Bulgarian folk dances and costumes that were regularly a part of national celebrations. Bulgarian farmers "are wearing national costumes," he wrote, "with many hand embroideries and the Queen is wearing one very often too."[300] He romantically proclaimed that "Bulgaria and all the Balkan countries form a refreshing memory, a glimpse back through the centuries when civilization was beautiful and not utilitarian."[301] Bored with his official duties in Sofia, he took to the outdoors in search of forests and common folk. Ever the explorer, Shoemaker put on 100,000 miles in his automobile travels through the Balkans, and boasted that he took the car "over narrow wagon trails, climbed mountain slopes and penetrated to many communities where no automobile had been seen before."[302]

From King Boris, Shoemaker learned of state-sponsored efforts to conserve folklore and community traditions. As early as 1936, he told reporters: "the Bulgarian idea, that the government should subsidize the work of preserving folklore, is worthy of emulation in the United States."[303] He also appreciated government sponsorship of collecting trips and archives for folklore for its conservation of the legacy of the past and its promotion of national spirit[304] and was particularly impressed by the work of the Bulgarian Ministry of Education, which guided Bulgarian teachers in the collection and teaching of folklore and published *Sbornik za narodni umotvoreniia, nauka i knizhnina* [Collection of Folklore, Science, and Literature]. Its purpose was to collect "source materials of Bulgarian culture," such as folk songs, folk tales, legends, and proverbs.[305] Shoemaker contributed to the effort by offering a silver cup prize for the best book on Bulgarian folklife published each year.[306] His interest in folklore research while he was minister resulted in his being awarded honorary membership in the folklore societies of Bulgaria, Romania, and Turkey. Premier Venezelos of Greece even made him a Knight of the Order of the Redeemer in 1930 for collecting the folklore of Greek refugees in Central Pennsylvania.

While Henry Shoemaker was away from America during the first years of the 1930s, his businesses faced ruin as the Great Depression worsened, and ultimately he lost most of his family fortune. Several banks he had invested in failed, and assets from his real-estate and securities holdings shrunk.[307] To keep himself fiscally afloat, he had to borrow heavily against his trust fund. He called 1932 "the most trying one of my life" and continued: "I feel at least a dozen years older. It is an awful feeling. I suppose, however, my case is not individual to me, and that many others have had their series of misfortunes as a result of the crisis. I am hoping for a better and calmer day before I am laid on the shelf."[308] His friend Dolores Coffey said: "The Colonel told me he was not a good businessman but that his father was a genius in money matters. . . . The loss of the Colonel's wealth was a constant topic of conversation by the people who knew him. There was always this question about how many millions. I heard several."[309] Henry's sister reminded him that despite his losses "most people here are much worse off than you are." "Do *not* return here," she advised. She also chastised him for living too high and for not curtailing the spending sprees of his wife. "Relax; hope—struggle on," she added.[310]

Despite his sister's warnings, Shoemaker returned to the States in 1933, probably because the new Democratic administration of Franklin Roosevelt had requested his resignation.[311] The king of Bulgaria expressed his high regard for the departing Shoemaker by awarding him the Grand Cordon of the Order of Civil Merit, four pet Bulgarian wolves, two eagles, and a hand-carved Bulgarian lion sculptured from black oak.[312] His departure caused an outpouring of sentiment from Bulgarian newspapers and citizens, for his many trips into the countryside had made Shoemaker immensely popular. An editorial in *Zname* declared that "only one foreigner, and that after many years, enjoyed such a popularity."[313] "There is something quite significant in the way in which papers announce your withdrawal," friends at the Bulgarian Folk School told Shoemaker.[314] They explained that usually the announcement consisted of a simple statement of transfer, but in Shoe-maker's case the papers devoted long testimonials to his service and expressed regret at his departure. Shoemaker had apparently impressed the Bulgarians with his sympathy for Bulgarian cultural life. "There was not a single manifestation of Bulgarian life in which he was not interested and in which he did not participate personally," *Slovo* reported. "All cultural and humanitarian initiatives had his assistance and encouragement. He had visited a great many places and villages, mountains, caves and sites. By his activities he gave a high example of the activities and approach that a diplomat should have." Another newspaper commented:

> Mr. Shoemaker spent among us about three and half years. During that time he attached himself to our people. From the first day of his sojourn in Bulgaria he manifested a keen interest for the multiform social, economic and cultural life of this country. Diplomacy and politics were not his exclusive occupations. . . . With the interest of a scholar he investigated into the various aspects of our life, particularly cultural progress, peasant life, folklore, fauna and flora, and left lasting marks of his activities. Very sociable and simple in his ways, he entered into relations with the people itself through an uninterrupted personal contact. He was among the people almost every day and was collecting different objects proper to Bulgarian life.[315]

As Shoemaker sailed for home in August 1933, Bulgaria's fond farewells must have cheered him as he faced financial turmoil at home.

Return to Pennsylvania

Upon his return to Pennsylvania, Henry Shoemaker attended to the struggling *Altoona Tribune* and tried to sell off his properties to compensate for reduced income. Unwilling to part with "Restless Oaks"—for "sentimental reasons," he said—he put his New York City house on the market, depressed as it was. While he had been away, John D. Rockefeller had been buying up properties in the area for his Rockefeller Center and other high-rise projects. Rockefeller interests had put the squeeze on Shoemaker to sell them his Fifty-third Street house (near the site of the future Museum of Modern Art), but insisted on paying much less than Shoemaker thought it was worth. Shoemaker's financial manager wrote him: "If you did not sell you would find yourself left out and surrounded without light, etc., with an unrentable house on your hands."[316] Shoemaker gave in to avoid bankruptcy.

Although ever vigilant for the conservation of nature, Shoemaker's last published books reflected a grudging move toward modernity. Whereas his earlier published books reflected on the romantic lore of trees and mountains, his last publications offered the traditions around Pennsylvania roads and houses.[317] And whereas his early work dwelt on Pennsylvania's original inhabitants of animals and Indians, his final volumes gave glimpses of "transplants," or "stories of persons from other lands and states whose lives are interwoven in Pennsylvania mountain folk lore."[318] His stories had caught up with his time. He used himself as one of the "old folks" remembering the way things were.

Shoemaker's attention to Pennsylvania highways was partially in response to Gifford Pinchot's campaign promise to improve automobile roadways in the state. Pinchot's pledge was to "get the farmers out of the mud," and although Shoemaker agreed, he had misgivings about the effects it might have on the environment and on the traditional cultures of the state. He feared that losing the wilderness would be a consequence of "grand highways of the Keystone State" bringing "the centres of modern life and romance closer together."[319] Nevertheless, he told readers that "this writer used to feel that his days as a collector of folklore were ended when the motors drove the horses off the main roads, yet he has been able to secure as many legends, ballads, proverbs, and old words while travelling in a car as in the earlier days when he adventured afoot, in a buggy, or on horseback." Invoking the garden myth, Shoemaker predicted: "The time will come when the concrete highway, too new today to be beautiful, will become a perfect blend with the charm of our matchless countryside."[320]

When the state took over and paved 20,156 miles of township roads, it witnessed the construction of filling stations, restaurants, and "tourist homes," rather than the growth of country charm. Cutting concrete swaths through the landscape increased further when road-building became a major project of the Works Progress Administration, to provide employment during the Depression. A notable initiative in this campaign occurred when construction of the Pennsylvania Turnpike, America's first long-distance superhighway, began in 1938. New roadways began to break down some of the fabled isolation of many Pennsylvania towns, making them accessible to visitors, and tourists, from afar. Shoemaker insisted on preserving the scenery alongside the roads and giving them names from history, folklore, and nature.[321] Successfully lobbying for the creation of "picturesque" roads and elimination of brush-burning and other practices destructive to roadside flora, he wrote one Secretary of Highways that "it seems . . . unnecessary to destroy so many beautiful trees in order to create a State Highway" and reminded him of their importance in providing "beauty and shade" and "protecting the bank."[322] Shoemaker's ally Horace McFarland, president of the American Civic Association, lamented to him: "It seems a pity that outsiders like you and myself are the ones that have to keep after the proper officials to save the scenic aspects, but since such is the case, I feel that neither of us will shirk our duty in the effort to try and save what is left of the natural loveliness of the Pennsylvania highways."[323]

After Pinchot's second term, Democrat George H. Earle III, minister to Austria while Shoemaker had been in Bulgaria, came back to Pennsylvania and ran for governor. When he took office in 1935, Governor Earle invited Shoemaker to come to Harrisburg and work for the new administration. Shoemaker became a member of the Historical Commission in the Department of Public Instruction, and in May 1937 he took on the role of State Archivist, a post he held until 1948, except for the two years he spent as director of the State Museum (1939–40). In Harrisburg, Shoemaker lived down the block from the governor and visited with him frequently. Shoemaker's impressive home sat prominently on Front Street perched between sites representing his love for history and nature. His windows looked out on the scenic Susquehanna River on one side and the historic William Maclay Mansion, home to a member of the first U.S. Senate, who kept a famous journal of its debates, on the other side.

Despite easy access to the seat of government, Shoemaker felt his political influence waning. He wrote local historian Albert Rung: "I don't have much success awakening historical interest as a writer and speaker, it takes political backing I am ashamed to say—when I was Chairman of the Historical Commission with the State Government behind me, I could exert some pressure, now I am a small voice shouting in the wilderness."[324] As Shoemaker settled into life as a civil servant in Harrisburg, he no longer published books, but he wrote columns and gave speeches with amazing frequency. A gifted, if modest, speaker with a flair for dramatic prose, he spoke on Pennsylvania history, forest and wildlife conservation, and especially folklore to nature and science clubs, hiking and climbing clubs, Scouts and other youth groups, men's and women's clubs, animal welfare societies, library associations, ethnic organizations, historical societies and local museums, fraternal and community organizations—in short, to an eclectic array of social and professional groups. In 1939, Governor Earle awarded him the Order of Meritorious Service in recognition of his work for the state, citing particularly his efforts to record the state's history and folklore.

While the award recognized his past efforts, as if his major period of activity was well behind him, Shoemaker was looking ahead to focusing on his "real life's work." Having championed nature conservation in the Progressive Era, he had in mind a new conservation role for state government in the protection of the state's cultural inheritance. The New Deal had created public projects for the collection of folklore under the administration of the Federal Writers Project (FWP), and Shoemaker met with the national FWP editor Benjamin Botkin in 1939 at the State Museum.[325] Known for popularizing regional folklore, Botkin admired Shoemaker's work and included two of his stories in the best-selling *Treasury of American Folklore* (1944). Rather than starting another New Deal project, Shoemaker had in mind an unprecedented permanent office in state government for the conservation of folklore. He worked toward its creation within the archives he directed, but the repository was designed for historic manuscripts and his position did not allow for "outdoors" fieldwork of oral traditions. His efforts were also distracted by World War II, when he devoted time to the Office of War Information broadcasting news to Bulgaria. A new opportunity for cultural conservation, and a new chapter in Shoemaker's life, arose after the war when the Pennsylvania Historical and Museum Commission was organized and responded to renewed public interest by Pennsylvanians for their own cultural heritage.

2

"Along the Line of Popularizing the Old Legends"

Henry Shoemaker found Pennsylvania's spirituality in folklore—and very likely his own too. From his mystical fascination with the legends and customs of Pennsylvania mountaineers, he fashioned a public agenda for the conservation of culture and nature. Bemoaning the changes rapid industrialization brought, he referred to the urgency of collecting folklore to recover the glorious, romantic past and protect the vanishing wilderness. If use of "history" during the early twentieth century suggested the dry bones of the buried past, then folklore for Shoemaker represented the stimulating narrative of past events that often escaped scrutiny. Folklore was not fiction to history's fact; rather, it encapsulated popular memory that held various truths. In Shoemaker's folklore, events took a mysterious and mystical turn that offered lessons for spiritual contemplation and Progressive action. For Shoemaker, folklore built parables out of the historical record.

Shoemaker's association with the promotion of folklore was strong enough during the early twentieth century to merit a headline in one of America's largest dailies. "Pennsylvania Folklore: The Life-Work of Colonel Henry W. Shoemaker" was the news the *Philadelphia North American* blared to its readers in 1920.[1] As the title implied, Pennsylvania's folklorist was Henry Shoemaker's unofficial title before he officially became the State Folklorist.

Making a connection with Shoemaker's touted conservation work, the article's author, William Shearer, pointed out that "the gathering of the folklore of the state and putting it into permanent form has required prodigious effort and considerable personal expense." He emphasized Shoemaker's devotion to ethnographic accuracy rather than artistic license: "He has taken them down as given and reproduced them without embellishment or ornateness. He is but the medium, humble in his own estimation, but none the less diligent in transcribing these tales, quaint songs and other data, which might have been forever lost but for his effort and expenditure of time and money, because the limitations of time will soon be stilled, and the sources of information dried. That is the reason the work is so important and imperative." Reproduced them without embellishment or ornateness? That became an issue that put Shoemaker on the defensive throughout his career as Pennsylvania's pioneer folklorist and public official. He insisted that the folktales he presented "were gathered orally from old people and others, and written down as closely as possible to the verbal accounts," but his hand is nonetheless apparent, for "the direct, simple recitals have been treated in narrative, or short story form, but in every instance the plot is left unchanged—once or twice where it was *too* sordid, it was 'toned down' a trifle, but only then when the ending could be left as he heard it."[2] If he presented such changes as minor, more than one critic recognized that the stories were "fused with his own individuality and pulsating with his own heart-throbs."[3]

The Legend of Penn's Cave and Other Romances

Henry Shoemaker first caused a literary splash with the publication of "The Legend of Penn's Cave," still his best-known story today, which he originally placed in the *Centre County Reporter* in 1902. The tragic romantic legend concerned the sad fate of a French Huguenot by the name of Malachi Boyer who fell in love with an Indian princess, Nita-nee, of the Lenni-Lenapes—the chief's "Diana-like daughter." "But this was all clandestine love," Shoemaker wrote, "for friendly as Indian and white might be in social intercourse, never could a marriage be tolerated, until—there always is a turning point in romance—the black-haired wanderer and the beautiful Nita-nee resolved to spend their lives together, and one moonless night started for the more habitable East."[4] Nita-nee's seven brothers caught up with Boyer and shoved him from the ledge above the mouth of Penn's Cave in Centre County to drown in the "greenish limestone water" below. "And after these years those who have heard this legend declare that on the still summer nights an unaccountable echo rings through the cave, which sounds like 'Nita-nee,' 'Nita-nee.' "[5]

The name "Nita-nee" had a special connection to Central Pennsylvania because of its similarity to the prominent Nittany Mountain. Because Shoemaker placed the date of the Indian princess Nita-nee in the colonial period well after the time that the Nittany Mountain appeared as a mapped place-name, he offered another story about an earlier mythical "Nita-nee" from "the early days of the world" for whom the Nittany Mountain was named.[6] As the legend evolved in popular culture, however, it was the later legend that became attached to the mountain. But place-name guides do not agree with Shoemaker's legendary folk etymology, preferring instead the Indian linguistic sources of *nekti* (single) and *attin* (mountain) for "Nittany."[7] Nevertheless, the legends Shoemaker presented about Penn's Cave enjoyed notoriety because the site was popular with visitors, explorers, and college students from the Pennsylvania State College (later, the Pennsylvania State University, with its "Nittany Lion" as mascot).

Critics kept up their assault on the Penn's Cave legend. The "French" name Malachi Boyer raised doubts among many analysts of the legend, because "Malachi" did not appear in Lancaster County sources of the period.[8] Shoemaker, who admitted to tinkering with names in his stories, probably used ethnic names to draw attention to the "racial mixing" prevalent in Pennsylvania's past.[9] Although supposedly passed down by a Seneca Indian, the story followed the pattern of other legends from the viewpoint of whites, of the "Indian Princess" who leaves her people for the love of a white man. Well after Indians had been removed from the eastern wilderness, mysterious caves became associated in narratives of white settlers with ways of the American Indian.[10] A possible American Indian twist, however, is that the conclusion differs from the usual closing motifs, which would have the Indian princess either rescuing the white man or killing herself. Whether the story was a Seneca Indian legend, a white anecdote, or local-color fiction, Stith Thompson neglected to index Shoemaker's legends and other American regional collections in his standard *Motif-Index of Folk-Literature* (1975).[11] Both the literary tone of the legend, and the fact that natives of Centre County were unfamiliar with the legend, led Don Yoder and Gerard Brault, to name just two later critics, to conclude that the "story was invented out of whole cloth."[12] Calling Shoemaker's tales "local-color fiction" and "romantic fluff, with every sentence flawed by historical inaccuracy," Yoder asserted: "I have always found more of Colonel Shoemaker than of Centre County tradition in his stories."[13]

These condemnations of Shoemaker's "fakelore" notwithstanding, "The Legend of Penn's Cave" enjoyed wide circulation after the publication of his books, and helped introduce the names of Boyer and Nita-nee into retellings of the tale still being turned in to the University Park Penn State folklore archives in Centre County by students. The stories also enjoyed retellings in countless Boy Scout camps and Campfire Girl outings, and Shoemaker himself was active in the Boy Scout movement, serving on its national council and making his land at Camp Shoemaker in Clinton County available for the Scouts. One scoutmaster wrote Shoemaker: "Since Troop One Boy Scouts have returned from their camping trip at Paddy Mountain where I told them the stories or legends of Penn's Cave taken from your fine book, they have asked me for more such stories. I will use the book 'North Mountain Mementos' during the winter months at our scout meetings. Now I know you will be glad to know your books have been put to use, and good use."[14]

Shoemaker's defense of the legend's authenticity was that it had been handed down to him as a boy by Isaac Steele, a "full-blooded Seneca Indian," in 1892. It was at Restless Oaks, he explained, that he "came upon the subject quite by chance or accident." By Shoemaker's account, "One cloudy afternoon in late summer when I was a boy of ten to twelve I came out of my grandmother's front gate and looking down the road saw an aged man seated on the trunk of an old wild apple tree."

> I walked to where the man was seated whittling. He was white haired, yet very brown, and very old, clean shaved as most Indians were who could not grow suitable mustaches or beards. We spoke to one another, and he told me the story of his life, how at 84 years, he was like his relative Chief Cornplanter, making a last visit to scenes in the West Branch Valley he had known so well as a boy, having spent many summers at the Mouth of Tiadaghton, or Pine Creek, where once a trading post was proposed by Governor Mifflin, and had been a headquarters for Indians from the Warren County Grant, as late as 1878. . . . On that afternoon at the old apple log, he went on to tell me the legend of Penn's Cave, where he was a frequent visitor, which made a powerful impression on me. . . . We parted, alas, never to meet, again, but as John Appleseed had planted trees, he sowed the roots of Pennsylvania folklore deeply in my heart.[15]

"Penn's Cave," he wrote, "determined [my] course to collect and preserve, if possible, the dying legends and folk-tales of the Pennsylvania Mountains."[16]

When Shoemaker published the legend in *Penn's Grandest Cavern* (1916), he made a point of adding the subheading "Related by Isaac Steele, an Aged Seneca Indian, in 1892." Although Steele's whereabouts could not be verified, Shoemaker thought he came from a "reservation" in Warren County, Pennsylvania. In reality, however, it was not a reservation, but a grant of land made in 1791 to Cornplanter, a chief of the Seneca nation, and his heirs by the Pennsylvania General Assembly.[17] (The land was eliminated in 1964 when the Kinzua Dam was shut, flooding the area to form the Allegheny Reservoir, thereby submerging the community's physical remains.) After visiting the tract in October 1915, Shoemaker reported: "I inquired for Isaac Steele, the older Indians remembered him well and Jesse Logan showed me his stone-marked grave, he had died about 1903, well over ninety, always highly respected."[18]

Shoemaker cited Steele as a source for at least one other mysterious story besides the legend of Penn's Cave. In *Allegheny Episodes* (1922) he recalled that in the early autumn of 1892 Steele stood beside the "moss-grown stump of the giant 'Grandfather Pine' in Sugar Valley" and "was silent for a long while, then placing his hands over his eyes, uttered these words: 'This is the Indians' Twilight; it explains many things.'" Adding a dramatic touch, he wrote: "Then the venerable Redman turned away, and that same day left the secluded valley, never to return." He explained that the tree was the sacred tree of the Senecas and that myth held that "this great pine reached from heaven to earth, and by its means their ancestors used to climb up and down between the two regions." Lumberman Ario Pardee held little regard for the sacred pine except as one of "millions of logs that would pile up wealth and fame for this modern Croesus" and he began to cut it down. His workers suffered lost eyes and broken legs from the mighty tree, but after two days it finally came down. "The Indians' twilight had come, for now the picked band of warriors and warlocks must forever linger in the star-belt, unless the earth spirit, out of his great love, again heaved such a tree from his inmost creative consciousness." He concluded by noting that the huddled, half-starved Indians, removed from their lands to the West, saw a fearful glow and heard distant cadences beyond Lake Erie. They declared them signals for vengeance of "the Indian braves imprisoned up there in star-land, calling defiance to the white hosts, and inspiration to their own depleted legions, the echo of the day of reckoning, when the red men would come to their own again, and finding their lost people, lead them to a new light, out of the Indians' twilight."[19]

The editor of the *Centre County Reporter* received many requests for reprintings of the Indian legends, and Shoemaker interpreted this outpouring as "showing the call for Pennsylvania folklore in that region." He republished the Penn's Cave story in 1903 in a volume called *Wild Life in Western Pennsylvania*. The title suggested a natural-history tract, but the book contained many oral traditions about animals and their hunters and did not reach the wide regional audience he had in mind. Subsequently, he reprinted the story as the lead narrative in *Pennsylvania Mountain Stories* (1907) and received a greater response. Shoemaker received letters asking him how much of the stories were fiction and how much were factual. One commented, "The little book has its value in preserving the one or two stories which have not previously appeared in print." Shoemaker was offended, he told audiences, by the comments of one young Lebanon writer who stated "that he had been all over the country, and not found any stories at all, how did I do it? I felt sorry at his obtuseness." And one writer, from Lancaster County, "sent a letter to the Lancaster Motorist that I was a fiction writer, but to come to him if they wanted the real history."[20] Later Shoemaker revealed, "I resolved never to write a story until I was certain it had not previously appeared in print."[21]

That put him somewhat at odds with ethnological folklorists of the day who looked for the characteristic story of a group rather than for the unusual or personalized narrative. Shoemaker, who claimed to be well aware of tradition, explained that although the stories he printed were not generally known they were probably circulating back some generations, before modern civilization changed everything—or they were the individual trademarks of marvelous storytellers, a dying breed once essential to the wilderness, who produced mysterious and romantic yarns of a bygone day that he had salvaged from extinction.

Full of previously unrecorded romantic American Indian legends, hunting exploits, and scenic narratives, *Pennsylvania Mountain Stories* received a more favorable reception from the press than *Wild Life in Western Pennsylvania,* and it went into five editions in the next six years. Loosely held together by a connection to the region's natural sights, the book was a literary cabinet of curiosities in its own way. Shoemaker stated that it "was followed by many other books which followed the same dictum, while most editors did not understand my writings they were gradually more favorable in their reviews."[22] If his early work was not at first appealing to reviewers, he nevertheless reached his intended audience in the Pennsylvania highlands. In 1914 he explained to former Governor Samuel Pennypacker that he "brought them out in such style so as to have them within reach of the class of people who hitherto have been their chief readers. I have reason to believe that the more educated class are becoming interested in them, and would like to put something better on the market."[23]

Enlarged in *Penn's Grandest Cavern* (1916) and *Penn's Cave, Pennsylvania's Grandest Cavern* (1930) in numerous editions from 1914 through the 1950s, the Nita-nee legend took on a life of its own in popular circulation. It enjoyed brisk sales at the tourist shop of Penn's Cave and was mentioned in many of the region's newspaper columns. Although no longer bearing Shoemaker's byline, the legend still appears on a board at the entrance to

the cave and in the official brochure produced by Penn's Cave Inc. (1988).
It even appeared in a Wendy's hamburger advertisement in State College
proclaiming the "Hot 'n Juicy Story of the Maiden Nita-nee and Poor Malachi
Boyer." To honor the first "Nittany Lover," Wendy's offered free French
fries to patrons showing ticket stubs from Penn State Nittany Lions football
games.

Although controversy about the legend of Penn's Cave remains, some
Shoemaker stories have been corroborated in other sources. An example is
the buried treasure legend about the pirate Captain Thomas who had a haul
of silver bullion that he buried in Florida at the turn of the nineteenth
century. Thomas escaped Spanish pursuers by settling on the West Branch
of the Susquehanna River in Pennsylvania. Years later, Colonel Noah Parker
purchased the land from Thomas, and in some accounts he found a diary
pinpointing the location of the treasure. Parker set off in search of the loot
but never returned and was presumed killed. Shoemaker referred to the
legend much as it had been reported in local histories as part of "An Antique
Dealer's Romance" in *Some Stories of Old Deserted Houses* (1931).[24]

In 1950, under the headline "Blackbeard's Treasure Cave is McKean
County Mystery," Shoemaker greatly elaborated on the legend, placing the
treasure in a Central Pennsylvania cave and calling Thomas "Blackbeard."
In the story, Noah Parker, described as "the dashing Colonel," marries a
"beautiful young mountain girl" and builds a mansion by the "waters of the
Great Elk Lick." "Every few years," Shoemaker concluded, "a group of
searchers go out, only to be baffled and declare there is 'no such thing.' But
oldtimers, like Uncle Zenas Cowley of Cowley Run, Jame Parmentier and
Eph Hoskins, the pioneers of the Portage, who saw the ox teams passing
up Salt Works Run, refused to be shaken in this story. Thus one of the most
fascinating of Pennsylvania folklore accounts, may well remain folklore, for
the passage of time will but deepen the mystery."[25]

Shoemaker used the word "oldtimers" to lend authenticity to his account,
but his story of Parker's treasure appears to be embellished with literary
flourishes of romance and scenic wonder. This example also points out that
what Shoemaker considered "authentic" were the plots rather than the
tellings of folklore, and often he elaborated his "stories" based on a mere
fragment he had heard. When the story was picked up by newspapers
across the state it became widely known. Later published accounts were
clearly lifted from his version.[26]

Shoemaker occasionally published legends relating to familiar migratory
legends of werewolves, witches, and ghosts, but the bulk of his material
was rooted in local events and scenery. His work was more than just a
Pennsylvania folklore collection, however, because it represented Pennsylvania community and family traditions as well. Shoemaker the journalist

sought narrative "scoops"—stories that usually had not been collected and that were rooted in prominent natural sites or local events. As he said, he had an eye for the "picturesque" and the "unusual."[27] Because of early criticism he received from a newspaper, that he did not offer much that was not already familiar, he had made a vow "to preserve legends that otherwise would be lost, not to rechronicle tales that had been told over and over again by newspaper paragraphers."[28] Thus, his books contain few legends on familiar regional cycles, such as Lewis the Robber, the Paxton Boys, or the Blue-Eyed Six, or ethnic tales, such as those featuring the Pennsylvania-German trickster Eileschpiggel. Shoemaker the writer sought stories that were "novel," mysterious, and surprising to his readers, rather than to present the most representative oral tradition, as folklorists might. Indeed, in some books it is unclear whether he classifies stories as folklore because they are orally transmitted through time, or whether a "folksy" mountaineer related the tale, or whether they had a deceivingly "folkish" feeling.

Yet there is in Shoemaker's books a folklorist's sensitivity to the people for whom narrative was an everyday art. And if his descriptions of settings are to be believed, he equally demonstrated attention to the places, the contexts, in which storytelling thrived. Complaining that his collection of folklore began too late among Central Pennsylvanians to recover the full legacy of what once circulated, he also pointed out that Pennsylvanians did not realize the richness of their everyday traditions, for "people looked upon their individual lives as of little consequence, their deeds as simple duty."[29] Going on to discuss American Indians from whom he recovered legends, he explained:

> As to the Indians or their history, they were regarded with loathing or indifference. We have no one to-day who would collect the annals of English sparrows or Cooper's hawks. Fifty years ago, even, was not too late, as Indians were met with from time to time, and aroused no particular attention; they were tolerated as itinerant basket weavers or harvest-hands. . . . When the present writer came upon the scene 'all was over,' but there were gleams in the embers of romance and folk-lore that showed that they contained life. He was able to learn the legends from a few of the old people, who were boys when there were still borderers and Indians whose talk was interesting enough for them to listen to and remember.

So Shoemaker concluded, "As there seemed to be no one else bent on chronicling and preserving them, the author, with a full realization of his limitations, has 'stuck at it.'"[30]

By his persistence, Shoemaker recorded material that probably is more appreciated by folklorists today than at the time he collected. His attention to local legend as a source of folk imagination was largely overshadowed in the early twentieth century by anthropological studies of myths and by literary analyses of fairy tales and British ballads. The American historical experience had not been explored largely for folklore until the 1930s, when during the "era of the common man" Constance Rourke and Martha Beckwith, among others, drew national attention to the folk legendary roots of an American tradition and opened the way for a comprehensive inquiry into American culture.[31]

Shoemaker's collection from hunting and lumber camps captured a valuable, long-neglected corpus of stories, and his accounts of Indian captivity and community events, for example, invite closer attention by students of American studies.[32] The "Indian Legend"—or, more accurately, white narrative uses of Indian characters and settings—reveals prevalent American images and attitudes. Shoemaker kept his pen poised to record ethnic varieties of stories other than those of the American Indian. He had a special fondness for presenting exploits of French Huguenots, Scots-Irish, Germans, Jews, and Gypsies, and he probably was the first chronicler to discuss African-American hunters in the Pennsylvania highlands.[33] A great many of his accounts preserved what might qualify today as personal narrative or family folklore, although at the time he wrote, these genres were not yet recognized as part of the folklore canon. Much sifting has to be done to recognize his recordings of traditions, however, because he threw together so many different kinds of narratives in his collections— family genealogies, hunting accounts, legendary narratives, literary folktales, and local histories.

The Picturesque in Folklore, History, and Nature

Henry Shoemaker was more concerned about the picturesqueness and the political impact of his material than about whether it qualified as genuine folklore. This scenic quality was reinforced in the design of his books. Publishing his own books allowed him to control production and costs and to reach a regional audience through his newspaper lists (many books were given to subscribers). Revealing his background in commercial art, he designed covers to show the magnificent natural beauties of mountains and streams in need of preservation. Inside, the reader was likely to find romantic quotes from the likes of Longfellow, Shelley, or Rousseau, or Greek and Roman myths, on the title page. In *More Pennsylvania Mountain Stories* (1912) he used Longfellow's nationalistic verse, "Ye who love a nation's legends, / Love the ballads of a people, / That like voices from afar

off, / Call to us to pause and listen." To introduce his premier legends of
Penn's Cave for a 1916 edition of *Penn's Grandest Cavern,* Shoemaker used
lines associated with English romanticism from Percy Shelley's *Prometheus
Unbound* (1820). He did not elaborate on his reasons for giving prominence
to the verse—whether it was intended to show the cave metaphor in a
struggle for social freedom, or the idealistic use of mythology for application
to modern problems and issues. He left less doubt about his use of
Rousseau's sentimental line "Here began the happiness of my life, here
passed the peaceful but rapid moments which gave me the right to say I have
lived" to describe his mountain journeys for *In the Seven Mountains* (1913).

His frontispieces often contained photographs of rustic scenes or figures
or illustrations of Indians in a bucolic setting. A favorite of Shoemaker's, and
the one probably most used, illustrated Indians canoeing a white settler
gently down a stream amid mountain splendor. Other drawings of Indians,
especially Indian princesses and hunting braves, filled blank space at the end
of chapters. Animals held prominent places as well, especially the lion or
panther perched atop a mountainside. The frontispiece to *Black Forest
Souvenirs* (1914) disclosed all that was precious to Shoemaker. It contained
boxed icons of an extinct world, his golden age of romance. To the top and
bottom of his profile was the flight of wild pigeons and a rafting scene down
the Susquehanna River. Moving clockwise from the upper right were a
mountain lion ("our grandest animal"), a buckskin "Nimrod," an "Indian
princess" by the side of a pond, a lonely bison, an elk, an Indian brave, an
old-time logger, and, finally, Shoemaker's beloved wolf.

Shoemaker's zeal for the preserving the natural landscape may have
attracted suspicion about the abundance of legends he had about mountains,
trees, caves, and other parts of the natural environment. "There is no spot
of ground a hundred feet square in the Pennsylvania mountains that has not
its legend," Shoemaker boasted.[34] He wrote elsewhere: "The great value
of legends is that they give to each mountain, valley, rock, lake or waterfall
mentioned a more intimate and lasting charm. 'Here such and such happened' is a happy supplement for 'Oh, what a beautiful sight.' . . . We all
know that the Scotch Highlands, the Irish Lakes, the Rhine Country and the
old castles in Italy are visited annually by millions of people as much on
account of the legends connected with them as for their natural attractions."[35] At times, he seemed so eager to find folklore for every aspect of
the natural environment that he might have been tempted to invent some to
drive home his moral message.[36] In *The Indian Steps and Other Pennsylvania
Mountain Stories* (1912), he explained his narrative selection by stating,
"There are some stories in this book which contain more human interest
than folk-lore, but they are included in order to give romance to certain
places where older legends have not been secured." His goal in that volume

as in others, he told his readers, was "to show the variety and scope of Pennsylvania folk-lore and tradition and through them hopes to give fresh vitality and interest to the localities where they occurred."[37]

The natural wilderness, Shoemaker argued, deserved preservation because every tree and rock potentially had history, folklore, and culture attached to it. And to him they seemed to have more "spirit" as a result than the products of his industrial age (later he bemoaned the advent of the nuclear age). Especially up in the mountains, befitting Christian mythology of wisdom derived from going to isolated mountaintops, one somehow had a clearer vista of life's meaning.[38] In rivers, Shoemaker depicted the constant flow of the past and people who used rivers to explore the wilderness.[39] As for the forests, he said: "It is in the forests that voices were first heard, linking us to the beyond."[40] The forest's folklore helped preserve it, he believed, for "in the dim long ago the forest was a dark hinterland from which evil spirits came to prey." Shoemaker continued: "The frontier children grew up, reasoned themselves out of the witches, and shot the wolves. The forest ceased to be a thing of fear, of veneration, and became a matter of dollars and board feet, a bank account in the rough. It was wantonly cut and criminally devoured by fire. This storehouse of legend, this temple of the race, was in danger of extinction."[41] In *Black Forest Souvenirs* (1914), Shoemaker recounted his trips "into the forest in 1908, 1909 and 1910": "These visits only accentuated the sense of sadness for the arboreal paradise that was no more, which on the wholesale plan, lumbering had swept away. The hand of man had changed the face of nature from green to brown. It was during these latter visits that the writer thought more of the ancient legends which were so easy to hear in 1898, but so difficult to obtain in 1910."[42] The titles of Shoemaker's books, such as *Tales of the Bald Eagle Mountains, In the Seven Mountains, Juniata Memories, Black Forest Souvenirs, Allegheny Episodes,* and *Susquehanna Legends,* thus refer repeatedly to endangered natural sites, particularly mountains, rivers, and forests.

Americans appreciated locality in Europe, Shoemaker complained, but not in their own backyards: "Central Pennsylvania had its folk lore just like the Father and Mother Lands," he wrote. "And it was a good thing that it came to pass thus. It gave an added meaning, an unconscious charm to every mountain, brook, spring, meadow, tarn, or decaying tree. It created that interest of locality which is the reason that Americans loved to travel in Europe—because every rock had its castle brimful of legends, every field was the scene of a battle, every old house had been the birthplace or the abiding place of someone great or notorious, and had its ghost for good measure."[43] Collecting folklore became a "definite form of spiritual activity." "It gives us greater pride of home and birth," Shoemaker reflected. "It enables us to love deeper our native hills and valleys, by feeling that they were once the homes of brave and true men and women, white and red, whose lives were as highly colored as the heroes and heroines of classic antiquity, Theseus and Helen, Orpheus and Eurydice." Believing folklore to be a sign of "the age of romance" before industrialization, Shoemaker called for its conservation as well as its collection to bring back a "reverence for age, of courtesy and gentleness." Folklore, he firmly believed, "is a free field of romance for the enjoyment of us all."[44]

How free with romance was Shoemaker in his writings on folklore and history? One indication is the memoirs of Albert Rung Jr., who recalled trips his father took with Shoemaker to collect material:

> Colonel Shoemaker was a remarkably rosy-cheeked, roly-poly, nervous man, and I had the pleasure of accompanying him and Dad to many historic spots in the surrounding counties. Dad's admiration for the Colonel knew no bounds and, knowing Dad's insistence on the absolutely accurate statement of historical facts, it came as a shock to me to discover the imagination—not to say fiction—which the Colonel injected into his newspaper columns. One hot summer day the three of us had stopped at a weather beaten general store somewhere in the mountains west of Middlesex. The soft drinks we ordered were delivered by what my adolescent eyes informed me was a most unattractive young woman. So I was dumbfounded to read in the Colonel's account of the incident a few days later that this plain woman had been transformed by the Colonel's romantic imagination into a dark haired beauty whose delicate features betrayed her descent from European royalty.[45]

Yet it was also the same Albert Rung to whom Henry Shoemaker showed his ire regarding what he called "crimes of unreliability." Shoemaker attacked pioneer historian Charles A. Hanna, author of *The Scotch-Irish* (1902) and *The Wilderness Trail* (1911), for distorting the ethnic roots of Stephen Franks, an early settler of Central Pennsylvania.[46] He told Rung: "As to Hanna, whether he is alive or dead I regard him as a disgustingly biased and unfair historian. He only wrote to glorify the Scotch-Irish, and knew no more of Pennsylvania than a Finlander. His crimes of unreliability are many, but the Scotch-Irish are rich, and his books sold well. To try to make Stephen Franks, who was a friend of my mother's ancestor into a Scotch-Irishman is shocking, especially after I saw the original manuscripts he distorted."[47]

When history made it into Shoemaker's books, it was not in the style of the annals of his time, such as those by Hanna. The annals rarely had narratives to tell; they were typically multivolume catalogs of documentable, "microscopic" bits of information. They possessed a kind of mechanical scientism that Shoemaker abhorred. If appreciation for the past would prosper, he believed, it needed to reach a popular audience and have literary merit. Bemoaning the lack of imagination in his generation, Shoemaker opined that historians whose narrow concern was a mundane version of "truth" made a mistake in neglecting legendary material that revealed memory and belief. In the absence of archaeological evidence for the extensive presence of bison in Pennsylvania, for example, he offered at least nine stories telling of buffalo herds in Pennsylvania and the exploits of buffalo hunters.[48] Shoemaker also lamented the animal's extinction, and became, in the words of one authority, "the most influential of all authors on this subject, and certainly the most quoted." Yet the same authority was skeptical about the existence of buffalo in the state because of the lack of "real, reliable, confirmable evidence."[49]

Oral traditions often recount historical events, or perspectives, that escape documentation—especially in communities in places such as the highlands, which rely greatly on face-to-face communication. Such oral communications about the past help establish the significance of locality and collective memory as much as they recount events. One scholarly advocate for expanding the study of "oral traditional history," Richard Dorson, has declared: "Oral traditions may well exasperate the historian of a literate, or at least print-glutted society, with their quick-silver quality and chronological slipperiness. But they can be trapped, and they offer the chief available records for the beliefs and concerns and memories of large groups of obscured Americans. The historian can find history alive in the field as well as entombed in the library."[50] For Shoemaker, the legendary status of oral traditional history added to its sense of "mystery" and hence to much of its appeal. In *Allegheny Episodes* (1922), Shoemaker left evaluation up to readers: "Many of the legends or incidents run counter to the accepted course of history, but tradition is preserved for what it is worth, and the reader can draw his own conclusions."[51] Its worth, he insisted, was in recording the past as people heard and retold it.

Historian and educator Homer Rosenberger was impressed with Henry Shoemaker's "extensive knowledge of Pennsylvania's history," but he complained that when Shoemaker "took pen in hand it ran away with him—it seemed that he let fantasy get the better of him when writing." Rosenberger also took issue with the main contents of ghost stories and unfortunate love affairs in Shoemaker's books of Central Pennsylvania life. "The theme seldom varied," Rosenberger wrote, "whereas those books could have given a much more faithful portrayal of the lives of Pennsylvania mountaineers." "Colonel Shoemaker," Rosenberger recalled, "was a peculiar person, who irritated many historians, yet I was fond of him. His voice was somewhat melodious and he could easily be gotten to chat at length about his favorite subjects—folklore, lumbering, forestry, and various aspects of Pennsylvania history."[52]

Collecting and Writing

Aware of skepticism about his historical claims, Shoemaker made a point of addressing his sources and literary embellishments to his stories in the introduction to *Pennsylvania Mountain Stories:*

> As so many of the tales are devoted to subjects of a more or less supernatural order they cannot very well be true; neither are they of the author's invention. The idea for the book came to the writer as the result of college vacation trips through Pennsylvania mountains, on foot, on horseback, or by "buggy," and the stories were told him, mostly after supper, by old settlers at lumber camps, farm houses and backwoods taverns where he stopped. Unfortunately he heard such a lot of stories that numbers of the best were forgotten, or the salient points of others confused; but from the mass of information the contents of this volume were finally knocked into shape.[53]

He fully admitted to changing the "names of persons and places, to transpose localities and dates," but he insisted that "the compiler has endeavored to transcribe the legends exactly as he heard them from the old folks."[54] He had made those changes "reluctantly," he said, so as not to "give offense to persons now living, or descendants of those 'crossed over,'"[55] and asserted that he had been faithful to the tone of the original tellings: "On several occasions he has read the legends to the persons who related them word for word. This fidelity to the original form of the stories has been maintained even to preserving sordid details and unhappy endings, and an entire absence of those fine moral sequels so noticeable in those finest of manufactured folk-tales, 'Young Goodman Brown,' or 'Feathertop,' in Hawthorne's 'Mosses from an Old Manse.'"[56] Shoemaker maintained that his collected stories constituted "tales in the rough, the recitals of plain, untutored persons for the most part, and the writer has not been able or tried to gloss them over with the veneer of a literary style and imagery."[57]

The lengths to which Shoemaker went to reach oral sources cannot be denied. At first venturing forth on vacations on foot and on horseback, he eventually contracted for the construction of a specially built buggy to maneuver around the treacherous mountain roads.[58] "Don't go by automobile," he warned in 1917. "Travel by this deadly, soul destroying machine is fatal to the lover of scenery or the naturalist. It is a pleasure to state that most of the roads in the wilds of Central Pennsylvania are unsuited for automobiles, even Fords, that the writer has traveled for three or four consecutive days without seeing one of these 'scoot wagons,' realizing that Eldorado and the automobile are discordant factors."[59] "You must be close to humanity, close to animate nature, close to the mountains and rivers, to the old trees, the animals and the birds, to be a successful collector of folk lore," he cautioned elsewhere.[60] His advice to would-be collectors confirmed his reliance on key informants. He suggested to Philip Nordell of New York City: "Visit Seth Nelson, the famous old hunter and guide, and cross Sinnemahoning Creek there and go up three Runs to the top of Karthaus Mountain, and visit J. P. McGonigal and J. L. McGonigal, both of whom are well acquainted with the old legends, ballads and proverbs of the Mountain people."[61]

When Shoemaker was not suggesting individual names, he was urging a visit to tradition-bound "localities," such as Karthaus (Clearfield County), Ingleby (Centre County), Schubert (Berks County), Churchtown (Lancaster County), Haneyville (Clinton Country), and Hunter's Run (Adams County).[62] He told Charles Mardt of Philadelphia: "The best way to meet these people would be to go to Lewisburg and take a train there to Coburn and wander out into the Seven Mountains and meet them in their cabin homes; or, go to Lock Haven and walk from there up to Coudersport Pike, in the direction of the former Black Forest, and all along the Pike, clear to Coudersport, you will meet many picturesque characters."[63] He told Professor Harold Thompson of Cornell: "October is the best month to collect folklore, as when the fires are lit the old people seem to be in a more mellow mood."[64] With State Forester J. T. Rothrock, he shared his "secret" of how he was "able to collect these legends when other writers have failed to find them while traveling over the same ground." He wrote: "Whenever I see an aged man or woman, no matter how decrepit or ragged, or generally unattractive, I take the trouble to meet them in a friendly way and, as a reward, they are only too happy to impart their stories of the long ago. I have always followed the principle that every person over sixty years of age, in the Pennsylvania wilderness, has at least one good story to tell."[65]

Because of what he viewed as the loss of "fine stalwart types" of tellers as modern industrial life took its toll on tradition, Shoemaker called for organized folklore-collection as quickly as possible directly from tradition-bearers in the mountains, and for recording songs and legends from American Indians in Warren County, Pennsylvania, where "the gradual lessening of their numbers will automatically cause the disappearance of their songs and legends, unless quickly collected." "To the student of folk-songs, aboriginal music and folk-lore the Pennsylvania Reservation is chiefly interesting by being a practically untouched storehouse of valuable historical material," he told the College Club in Williamsport.[66] Encouraging fieldwork in folklore as part of every school curriculum, every historical society program, every storytelling group's activities, every outdoors club's jaunts, Shoemaker explained to the Ohio Valley Historical Association in Pittsburgh that the tradition-bearers they will meet "will tell you of wolves and wolverenes and panthers, of bison, moose and elks, of wild pigeons, paroquets and cross-bills of Indians, hunters, soldiers, witches, outlaws, sang diggers, lumbermen and traveling preachers, of Jack O'Lanthorns, tokens and ghosts, of the past, the dark, mysterious trackless past, that age of plain living and high thinking that is soothing to ponder over to the spirit which cannot reconcile itself to sky-scrapers and white lights. It will bring you close to the simple life, which is the heart of the world."[67]

Shoemaker wrote down stories from his memory of storytelling sessions, he claimed, and many of the storytellers had been long dead. Nonetheless, in some volumes he made it a point to state that he kept notes on the "sources of information" that gave him the stories, and in *Allegheny Episodes* (1922) he offered to accommodate "persons interested in more intimate details concerning the origins and characters of the various tales."[68] He modestly laid claim to his collecting achievement: "Some old persons were supposed to know old stories," he told one audience, "yet I was able to find rich stories in them. It was having the key to unlock their stories, that key was lacking in others. I try to figure out how I was able to meet so many rich fields of folklore, even when in the mood of thinking I had made from my opportunities, can only say I did the best I could."[69] Shoemaker regretted that before the 1930s "he was never once able to take a trip solely to collect folklore; his visits have always been on some matter of business or of an official nature, and collecting traditional lore has been a 'side issue,' hence he has probably only pricked the surface of the field."[70]

As Shoemaker's interest in folklore grew with the years, his collecting activity—which frequently involved rough camping and rugged climbing—apparently became more intensive. A frequent traveling companion for Shoemaker, J. Herbert Walker, recalled:

By mountain wagon—built especially for travel over the terrible roads far back in the mountains—on horseback, and on foot we traveled thousands of miles in the sparsely-settled hinterland of his beloved Pennsylvania. By candlelight, before fireplaces in hill cabins, by bright daylight at the edge of a clearing—anytime, anywhere—he collected the data for his tales. Frequently we curled up in buffalo robes and spent the night under the stars, far, far back in the woods.

Food for the trips, which covered anywhere from two days to a full
week, was carried in a big willow hamper.[71]

Shoemaker visited noted tale-tellers to seek out stories, but just as often
randomly stopped people on his travels to ask them for lore. He was fond of
taking walks in the country and engaging older residents in conversation
about the way things were. Railroad worker Ben Yarosz recalled seeing him
strolling alongside the track in an isolated section near McElhattan. After
trading greetings, Shoemaker asked whether he knew stories about the
railroad—its characters, accidents, and ghosts. Shoemaker invited Yarosz
to Restless Oaks for more conversation, and when he followed up the
invitation, was surprised by the splendor in which the plainly dressed
Shoemaker lived.[72] Explaining such sources for his chapter in *Pennsylvania
Songs and Legends,* Shoemaker explained to George Korson that he collected the story of the Phantom Pennsylvania Lion:

> Driving down the West Mahantango Creek one beautiful moonlight
> night, and always on the alert for folklore, I noticed the tall, gaunt
> form of Mr. Rau standing in front of his cabin by the stream. I
> stopped the car and with my companion, Mr. J. Herbert Walker,
> Secretary of the Pennsylvania Alpine Club, spoke to the old gentle-
> man who was very friendly and agreeable. He invited us to sit down,
> and in the course of the conversation panthers were discussed, and
> he told us the story of the "Panther of the Foothills," which had
> happened at the village of Penn's Creek, Snyder County, and the
> story is as near as I heard it as I could write it down, except that as
> he did not think that they would be pleased to have their names in
> print, I changed the name of the family from Sampsel to Sanson, but
> otherwise the names of persons and places are as I heard them.
> Further down the creek we paused for a time to admire an immense
> hemlock, on which thousands of fireflies were synchronizing, turning
> their lights on and off in perfect unison.[73]

In pioneering the collecting of folklore in Central Pennsylvania, even if
imperfectly, Shoemaker's amateurish hope was to inspire professionals,
both the "scientific" folklorists and the writers, and eventually "a more
general interest in the Pennsylvania folk-lore can be created."[74] Shoemaker
humbled himself by stating, "While the compiler of these old legends feels
that he might have done better with the rich vein uncovered, yet he is
content in the knowledge that others will finish the work more artistically,
more analytically, more patiently."[75] "No pretense at literary workmanship
is claimed," he told his readers, "and the stories should be read, not as

romances or short stories, but as a by-product of history—the folk-lore, the heart of the Pennsylvania mountain people."[76] Shoemaker believed that the collection would "create a greater local pride and stimulate original research."[77]

The growing sales of his sequels to *Pennsylvania Mountain Stories,* Shoemaker hoped, were indications that this research could lead to a Pennsylvania renaissance that took its artistic inspiration from the poetic soul of the "common folk." "While it has been expensive to bring out these books," he wrote Potter County historian George Donehoo, "I have found that each one has sold better than its predecessor. This points to the fact that there is a growing interest in all writings of this kind. The work I am doing is only a beginning of what could be done later on by abler and more patient writers. Mine are recitals of bare facts, but they can be used as the background for a rich field by some literary artist."[78]

Style and Form in Shoemaker's Narratives

As for their narrative style, Shoemaker's stories fall roughly into three categories. One category is a literary retelling of a legend, usually an "Indian legend" reported from the point of view of the "writer."[79] *Pennsylvania Mountain Stories* (1907), *More Pennsylvania Mountain Stories* (1912), and *Allegheny Episodes* (1922) exemplify this approach. By "Indian legend," Shoemaker meant narratives *about* Indians, usually told by whites in Central Pennsylvania, as well as stories told *by* Indians, and it is often difficult to distinguish between the two in his writings. Legends by and about Indians held a special fascination for him because they gave a glimpse of life before European settlement, a life in commune with nature. To a convention of librarians he said: "The history of the Indian tribes whose members had inhabited our native state for centuries, was in oral form, and handed down by them to the first white settlers, some of whom were adopted or married into the tribes. These pioneers in turn passed them on to their descendants, from generation to generation, with no thought of ever publishing them, until the present day of machinery and rush and roar came on, and interest in quiet moments around the inglenook ceased and many Indian legends found an apotheosis of oblivion."[80] He ended with the collector's call: "Let us hope that this modest inspiration or thought, now expressed, to collect more of our unwritten history of Pennsylvania, will open up new and happy channels of research and indirectly create wider opportunities for the use and benefits of libraries and the able and cultured men and women who direct their destinies!"[81]

Although Shoemaker claimed that his collector's motivation was "to preserve and protect, as well as to popularize," columnist William Allison believed that Shoemaker belied his literary aspirations. Noting that Shoemaker presented legends with "the enthusiasm of an adventurer," Allison asked, "Was it not also because you loved to write, as well as loved the people and the places—because you 'filled up' on them, and 'could contain the stories no longer?' "[82] In Allison's view, Shoemaker was the "ardent lover of nature" who "excavated" rough buried tales, polished them and rendered them artistic and spiritual as the nature from which they came.[83] It was Allison who suggested the title *Juniata Memories,* with the subtitle "Mystical and Mythical Traditions of Indians and Early Settlers," to Shoemaker for his collection from the Juniata Valley.[84]

The "History of Tamarack Swamp" is a good example of Shoemaker's literary hand giving a sense of the mystical and the mythical, as well as the romantic, to stories. He opens with a mysterious find, a discovery of fossil horns of moose and caribou in the Tamarack Swamp, Clinton County, by a pioneer farmer clearing a field. The farmer receives a rational explanation from other pioneer neighbors for traces of animals usually found far to the north: the animals were there in remote antiquity. But an Indian selling medicinal herbs in town had a mythical explanation. He relates a familiar diluvian Indian myth from the Adirondacks about how the "big water," or Atlantic Ocean, overflowed its banks creating a tremendous inland flood. "The Indian people had received advance tidings on the subject from Gitchie Manito, the Great Spirit, which enabled them to save themselves and their chosen animals and birds by ascending to the summit of Tahawus, now Mt. Marcy, the highest peak in the Adirondack Mountains, the only point not submerged [Thompson motif A1022]. All their human enemies, races of gigantic white and yellow men who were constantly at war with them and the huge, serpentine sea and land animals, bat-winged and griffin-clawed, which preyed on them, were drowned." What follows is a later legend, a romance between Ko-wat-go-chee, who travels north to make a historical narration, and the Indian princess Me-shon-nita. They marry and settle on the site of Tamarack Swamp, but she becomes homesick. To appease her, Ko-wat-go-chee arranges to have animals and trees brought from the north. Wanting still more, the princess goes with her husband to the north again and wanders out into a snowstorm in search of her mountain home. "Eternally unhappy" out of her natural element, the princess dies in the storm.[85] Having been placed in a mythical setting, this narrative of a romance between Ko-wat-go-chee and Me-shon-nita takes even more of a mystical quality. It also underscores conservationist themes of the importance of native flora and fauna to one's well-being, and human arrogance in artificially changing the natural order of things.

In presenting his legends in narrative form, Shoemaker refused to render them in dialect or some other replication of oral form. He explained: "One newspaper commented on the fact that the characters used such good English in their dialogues, it seemed strange that backwoodsmen could be such rhetoricians. But there was no need of dialect in these stories, they were preserved as folk lore and not as samples of backwoods talk. It is the quaintness of the tales themselves and not the way in which they were told that warranted their preservation."[86] Despite his protestations that his work lacked "literary workmanship," one can get a feel for Shoemaker's narrative style in this first category by reading the legend of Penn's Cave supposedly "related by Isaac Steele": "Old O-ko-cho's chief pride was centered in his seven stalwart sons, Hum-kin, Ho-ko-lin, Too-chin, Os-tin, Chaw-kee-bin, A-ha-kin, Ko-lo-pa-kin and his Diana-like daughter, Nita-nee. The seven brothers resolved themselves into a guard of honor for their sister, who had many suitors, among whom was the young chief E-Faw, from the adjoining sub-tribe of the A-caw-ko-tahs. But Nita-nee gently, though firmly, repulsed her numerous suitors, until such time as her father would give her in marriage to one worthy of her regal blood."[87]

Shoemaker's literary retellings conveyed a mystique because of the combination of details about the land and the mysteries of events and traditions he seemed to place in every story. "The Original" from *Juniata Memories* (1916), for example, moves clearly in three sentences from a glorified natural site to historic events and lands ultimately in the mysterious realm of tradition. "Kittaning point," the story begins, "is a spot pre-eminent in Pennsylvania song and story. As a pivotal point in history it will always be remembered; as a scenic glory it holds a secure place, for clustered about it are many weird and curious traditions, some of which still linger only in the hearts and minds of the old folks."[88] Shoemaker reveled particularly in telling of "cobwebby personages and places" with surprising twists. One columnist noted: "He quivers with reverence for the unseen, with longing for the unattainable. Even when dealing with the unknowable, he tinges his readers with his sympathetic imagery so that they, too, believe in the reality of the mystical and the mythical, the unprecedented and the weirdsome."[89] The line between legendary and documentary history became blurred because he made exciting "stories" out of dry facts of the past. By romanticizing the surroundings or speculating on the fate of the participants, Shoemaker turns a "true story" of a hunting trip into a legendary exploit,[90] or creates a storied feeling by including in a string of narratives a belief or traditional motif followed by a historical account of life in the woods.

What Shoemaker called "the true story," he told the Story-Telling League, "has the added value that it keeps alive an historical fragment, which some day may be a part of history, and has the possibilities of being the plot of an historical novel, or a stage drama in future years. It is well to have the inventive faculty and the keen imagination, yet true stories are always better than made up ones."[91] An actual battle, murder, or assembly led him to speculate about the human sagas that surrounded them, or an inspiring natural sight led to his imagining a battle, a murder, or an assembly occurring there. He especially displayed flourishes of his romantic imagination when declaring the "first," "last," or "grandest" event in the historical record. It was not always clear what history he was providing and what oral accounts he was recounting, but they made for good reading in any case. The supposedly last raft down the Susquehanna, the last wolf shot, the last Indian in the forest, or the first "Nimrod" to hunt in the mountains became the stuff of adventurous legend. He dwelled on the "grandest" cavern (Penn's Cave), Pennsylvania's "grandest" animal (the mountain lion), or the "king" of Pennsylvania hunters (Bill Long for lions, C. W. Dickinson for wolves).[92]

"Any story which relates to human beings will sooner or later become folklore," Shoemaker broadly declared, and added: "Some are old, as ancient as the old, old forests. Others are of recent making or in formation now. Each one is different, each is full of its own local color."[93] Shoemaker rarely went for comic legend or folk humor; his stories were typically serious or spooky. His "light" stories were romances of historical figures or personal accounts ranging from naming of the forests to dream narratives, and he varied the sequence of "light" historical accounts and more intense spooky legends in his books to "prevent if possible its reading like a monograph." "He is always and forever digging down after 'the beginnings' of his heroes," Allison observed, "and if there be anything on earth that he loves above everything else it is 'a mystery.' "[94]

A second narrative category might be called a travelogue form, in which Shoemaker recounts the sights on a trip through a mountain region. He enters a camp, cabin, or trail and meets one or more unusual characters, who tell him a story, then Shoemaker relates the story in quotation marks as told by the storyteller. In the telling, he describes the scene or context in substantial detail and inserts historical background for the region, character, or event described. He also frequently editorializes about the devastation to the region wrought by industry or the bad treatment of Indians, blacks, or others. Or he might draw attention to the historic contributions of some neglected "races" by having his storyteller take on "typical" Scots-Irish or German ways. Especially noticeable is Shoemaker's fondness for French and Gypsy characters—a sign of Shoemaker's advocacy of French Huguenot ethnicity and his interest in the often overlooked German Gypsy population in Pennsylvania.

In his narrative technique of encounters with backwoods types who have tales to tell, Shoemaker often has raconteurs offer several legends held together loosely by reference to an event or place. *In the Seven Mountains* (1913), to name one book in the Pennsylvania Folklore Series, contains several examples of this narrative technique. Consider the following excerpt from the opening of "The Canoe (A Story of Penn's Creek)":

> "I guess the young man's going to make a die of it," said old David Frantz, the wolf hunter. "I saw the canoe go under the bridge last night." We were leaning over the railing of the old bridge, on a rainy morning in March, gazing at the surging, gray waters of Penn's Creek, when the ancient nimrod began his strange narrative. It was in 1901, and I had come by the morning train to Coburn, hiring a team at a livery, and driving three miles west along the creek to where the old man resided. I had long wanted to meet this quaint character, and fortunately found him in a communicative mood. After a pleasant chat by his stove, we had gone outside, as he wanted to show me where he had seen a pair of Otters during the previous September. Then his conversation turned to local gossip, and the supernatural, each word being interesting. "Every time when a member of the Clawaghter family dies, a canoe, manned by the first settler of that name in this region, goes down the creek at dusk, to goodness alone knows where."[95]

Or take this description of a tale-telling setting from "A Ghost of the Lockin's" in *More Allegheny Episodes* (1924):

> A party of foresters were sitting one stormy evening during the pre-Christmas season in the cozy room back of "Doc" Seylar's drug store, at McConnellsburg, exchanging reminiscences, while the snow and wind beat upon the "window lights" and rattled the sashes. Every one who has been within a thousand miles of the Fulton County "Seat of Justice" knows the Seylar establishment. It is more than a drug store. It is an institution, one of the bulwarks of social Pennsylvania. In the aforementioned "back room," or as it is locally called "soda water parlor," may be found, most any evening, the leading travelers who have chosen McConnellsburg as their domicile over the night. State highway officials, game inspectors, fish wardens, foresters, legislators, high-ranking military officers, commercial travelers, bankers, tourists, all hurry to "Doc's" headquarters as if to a "Club" when supper is over at their hotels. It is the place to go for a happy greeting after a long day's journey over mountain highways, there to find congenial acquaintances and smoke a cigar

and enjoy the pleasant society of the remarkable dynamic Seylar himself. . . .

"Interested in ghosts?" said the "Doc" in his cheery, emphatic Rooseveltian way, for his resemblance to the lamented Colonel is striking and impressive, and soon the group of slush-covered foresters were all attention.[96]

In both these excerpts, Shoemaker gives the impression that rustic surroundings naturally inspire story. In these settings, one hears of past events that are not documented in the annals of history but that nonetheless have great human interest, beyond the locality for the lessons they impart. Although at first glance the stories are offered for entertainment, they frequently take an instructive turn as ghosts recall a way of life that is no longer, as romances suggest the mixing of races on the frontier, or as legends bring to mind the majesty of animals brought to extinction by humans.

In my third category for Shoemaker's narratives are social and natural historical chronicles in which folklore, personal narratives, and oral history are interspersed, and sometimes confused. One can find sections of *Wolf Days in Pennsylvania* (1914) or *Extinct Pennsylvania Animals* (1919), for example, in which narrative clearly plays a part but is difficult to distinguish. These chronicles are even more rambling than his travelogues, and at times Shoemaker ignores paragraph breaks altogether. In such accounts, Shoemaker quotes or refers to narratives, rather than framing them as developed plots. Discussing the history and habitat of the "Pennsylvania Lion or Panther" in a paragraph that lasts for three pages, for example, he offers:

> Some of the first Scotch-Irish frontiersmen regarded the panther's wailing as foretelling a death in the family. It was the "token" or "Banshee" of these sturdy souls. Samuel Stradley, a well-known hunter residing on the Tiadaghton or Pine Creek, in Lycoming County, while watching for deer at a crossing in 1870, fell asleep in the forest. When he awoke he found himself covered with leaves. Crawling out he sat perfectly still until he was rewarded by seeing a huge panther come up, which he shot. It had evidently thought him dead, and buried him in leaves to be eaten on some future occasion. Michael Fetzer, born 1834, an old hunter residing near Yarnell, Centre County, recounts that when he was a boy a panther once came to the kitchen window of the Reese homestead and looked in at the family assembled around the supper table. He was soon chased away by the dogs and disappeared in the forest at the foot of Indian

Grave Hill. Franklin Shreckengast describes panthers concealed in the forest grinding their teeth and snarling while Tom Askey and he cleaned a deer at a big spring near Snow Shoe. He said that it was a disconcerting sound, to say the least. This occurred during the Civil War early one evening. The last panther in the Snow Shoe region of Centre county—the great abode of these beasts in early days—was killed on Rock Run in 1886, by Charles Stewart, of Kylertown, Clearfield county, who collected a bounty on its scalp at Bellefonte.[97]

Some of this last technique also has a bearing on many of his essays promoting conservation causes. These convey an editorial tone but often conclude with narratives to bring across a conservationist point. He explained to one correspondent his technique in *Extinct Pennsylvania Animals:* "I got the book out to give the Altoona Tribune subscribers, thinking that by describing the game which formerly existed in Pennsylvania it might instil in some of them a desire to conserve what is left. I made no effort to produce a scientific work and consequently allowed my fancy full rein with the Ursus Arctos Schwenki story; the old hunters believe the brown bears a separate variety and I have written the book entirely from their point of view, and mostly to please them."[98] He also made no great effort to separate folkloric texts from his natural and social history. Often he would include accounts of untimely death and mysterious destruction to those woodsmen who brutally killed animals and cut trees. The implication from these narratives was clear: revenge will be exacted on humans who harm the environment.

Model Writers and Pioneer Folklorists

Shoemaker's narrative efforts were largely influenced by local historians and local-color writers. He expressed special admiration for Nelson Lloyd (1873–1933), a journalist for the *New York Evening Sun* who produced several novels and feature stories for *Scribner's.* Lloyd attended the Pennsylvania State College (as Penn State University was known then) in Centre County and had some family connections to the area. In such titles as *The Chronic Loafer* (1900), *Soldier of the Valley* (1904), and *Six Stars* (1906), Lloyd used the Nittany Valley and Mountain as backdrops to his vignettes highlighting the rustic life of Central Pennsylvania. He also contributed journalistic descriptions of the sectarian folklife of a Pennsylvania-German plain sect, in "Among the Dunkers" (1901). In *Mountain Minstrelsy*, Shoemaker declares, "Was ever a more charming book written than 'The Soldier of the Valley,' and the pity of it is that it has not been followed up by

others."[99] In a letter to folklore professor Samuel Bayard, Shoemaker wrote
that Lloyd's "spook and witch tales with vivid illustrations, laid in Centre
County, I fancy, may have influenced my boyhood folklore studies. . . .
When Barr Ferree, Secretary of the Pennsylvania Society in New York first
called my attention to Lloyd's tales, he said, 'You know the country he
writes about, why not try to collect such legends?'"[100] Bayard disagreed
with his assessment of Lloyd as a folklorist, but Shoemaker arranged to
honor Lloyd anyway as "a great founder of Pennsylvania Folklore study fifty
years ago" at the Pennsylvania Folklore Society meeting in 1955.[101]

Another writer using folklife sources that influenced Shoemaker was
Frederick Lewis Pattee (1863–1950), a professor of American literature at
Penn State, who Shoemaker also called "one of Pennsylvania's pioneer
folklorists."[102] Pattee did not use the folklorist label, but he featured
Pennsylvania-German folk beliefs in the novel *The House of the Black Ring*
(1905), set in Central Pennsylvania's Seven Mountains region, and gained
praise for his faithful renderings of folkways.[103] Seeking advice from his idol,
Shoemaker wrote: "Several years ago I read with interest your novel
entitled 'The House of the Black Ring.' It was a splendid work and has
become the classic it deserves. I have lately finished a volume of legends,
my sixth, the materials for which were gathered in the Seven Mountains. I
think they are the best that I have gotten together. I have visited most of
the remote little valleys and met most of the old pioneers." Shoemaker
explained: "Like yourself, I have had to confuse names, places and dates,
as I did not want to give offense. Apart from this the legends are exactly as
I heard them from the old people."[104] He must have been heartened by
Pattee's reply: "You have certainly rescued a great deal of romantic material
and the State will not forget you. It is a shame that the legends and traditions
have been so lightly regarded that they have been allowed to perish."[105]
Pattee held special praise for Shoemaker's work on legends of Penn's Cave.
"If Penn's Cave had been in the Trossachs how Scott would have woven his
genius about it and how tourists would now be raving over it," he wrote. He
tried to inspire Shoemaker by adding: "He who seeks out and preserves the
local traditions of a region and casts them into forms of beauty is building a
monument for himself more lasting than stone or metal."[106]

While using the books of local-color writers to model the presentation of
"legends in narrative form," Shoemaker insisted that he recorded folklore
as "unwritten history."[107] He belonged to the boards of several county
historical societies in Central Pennsylvania, was a trustee of the Clinton
County Historical Society, and was president of the Pennsylvania Federation
of Historical Societies. Especially in Pennsylvania, it was common to find
legends and folklife information in county histories.[108] Shoemaker singled
out the histories and legend collections of Schuylkill County by Judge D. C.

Henning (1847–1908) for special attention,[109] crediting him with adding Pennsylvania material to the old legends of New England, the South, and the West included in Charles Skinner's anthologies of American folklore. "But death claimed him before he had half completed the task for which, through deep human sympathy and literary skill, he was pre-eminently fitted," Shoemaker wrote.[110] He used an excerpt from Henning's "Tales of the Blue Mountains" for the frontispiece of his *Tales of the Bald Eagle Mountains* (1912): "It can, therefore, be readily seen that in my early days these mountains were, to the minds of many of those, who then lived there, not only a land of wonderment, but of awe, nor has this feeling entirely passed away, nor do I believe it will ever pass away. Generation after generation will tell the tale with greater or less veneration as they may believe that they once were true or false, as the case may be." Originally appearing in the *Miner's Journal* (Pottsville, Pennsylvania) in 1897, Henning's *Tales* drew Shoemaker's praise as literature akin to Nathaniel Hawthorne's *Twice Told Tales* (1837).

Henning made no such claim, however, and in fact considered himself more of a "dumping ground" than a literary artist. Like Shoemaker, Henning worked from a composite of texts he heard to "round out the complete story."[111] Henning's collection included orally acquired legends of events and figures in addition to recounting documents. He explained, "Pure history is dry, but being intermingled with Indian tragedy and superstition, . . . this would form a good basis for the tradition and folk-lore which they contain."[112] The anthropologically oriented editor of the *Journal of American Folklore*, William Wells Newell, took notice of the work and pointed out cognates of the legends in other cultures. Henning meant his work to be a contribution to history, however, and as Newell realized, local historians had probably paid more attention to legends than folklorists had.[113]

Shoemaker also referred to the folklore interests of local historian and State Librarian George Donehoo, whose predecessor at the State Library, William Egle, was a charter member of the American Folklore Society.[114] From this local history work, the first notices of Pennsylvania folklore by J. G. Owens (1891) and W. J. Hoffman (1888) appeared in the *Journal of American Folklore*, which Shoemaker extracted for his files. Although his books typically did not have bibliographies or analyses, Shoemaker belonged to the American Folklore Society and referred generally to his familiarity with the scholarly "masters of folk-lore," specifically citing such figures as Cecil Sharp (1932), Post Wheeler (1912), and Charles Skinner (1896), and later adding Samuel Bayard (1944) and George Korson (1938).[115]

As a writer presenting regional folklore to a popular audience, Shoemaker was the oldest and most experienced in a group that drew considerable public attention, if not folkloristic acceptance, during the "era of the common man" in the 1930s and 1940s. His narrative style informed the likes of J. Frank Dobie, who promoted the storied color of Texas, Richard Chase, who promoted the southern Appalachians, and Vance Randolph, who wrote of the Ozarks.[116] The best-known of the group was probably Dobie, and the conservationist intentions he shared with Shoemaker showed in his often romanticized stories of animals and hunters.[117] In fact, Dobie's wife was from Pennsylvania and he was impressed "how near to her these [Shoemaker's] stories of the soil came." Using the longhorn and the coyote as emblems, much as Shoemaker had used the wolf and mountain lion, Dobie wrote Shoemaker: "I have been very much interested in a movement to preserve the Texas longhorn from extinction. This historic breed of cattle is as near to extinction as ever the buffalo was."[118] Dobie was more unabashed than Shoemaker when he claimed: "I care next to nothing for the science of folklore, which some scholars reverence and which seems to consist of the tedious process of finding out, through comparisons and analogies, that nothing new exists under the sun."[119] To be fair, at the time the development of legend research lagged behind folktale and folk song work that did have goals of cultural interpretation by making comparisons and analogies. In addition, the vagueness of legend—as a narrative of the past or the personal expression of a belief, to name two confused ideas—was still being worked out in folkloristic definitions.[120]

Dobie took Shoemaker's editorial stance of favoring "amazing" stories that carried the feel of legend and sought his support for a Guggenheim Fellowship application. Dobie looked to him as an older authority on the preservation of "the folky part" of his region's "cultural inheritance" and the promotion of residents' pride "in the features of their own inheritances and environments." Dobie avowed that folklore held a popular interest in that "life and life's romance, vitality, flavor, humanity, humor, gusto, drama, songs with tunes and tales without ends, cowchips and stretching rawhide, Bowie knives and quilt patterns and hundreds of other factors of the land I belong to are inherent in it."[121] Through his leadership of the popular Texas Folklore Society, Dobie encouraged reuse of folklore in new literature, music, and poetry toward the popularization of Texas in American regional romanticism. Echoing Shoemaker, Dobie wrote in an early publication of the Texas Folklore Society: "If the ballads of a nation are as important as its laws, its legends are almost as important as its ballads. Here I must confess a great hope that some man or woman who understands will seize upon these legends and use them as Irving used the legends of the Hudson and the Catskills, as Whittier used the legends of New England."[122]

Beyond the Legend

Although most Pennsylvanians knew Shoemaker primarily for his books of legends, he wrote books in other fields of folklore, particularly folk speech, folk crafts, folk belief, and folk song collections from Central Pennsylvania. In these fields, however, he was more the collector than the writer. He compiled a list of Scots-Irish and English proverbs from the region around the West Branch of the Susquehanna (1927) and *Thirteen Hundred Old Time Words of British, Continental or Aboriginal Origins, Still or Recently in Use Among the Pennsylvania Mountain People* (1930). Bringing together his collecting of oral and material traditions, he also published a list of Pennsylvania-German names for antique household implements (1925).

The study of oral and material traditions is especially apparent in Shoemaker's *Early Potters of Clinton County* (1916). Shoemaker supplied the renowned material culture authority Henry Mercer with tools and crafts for his museum in Doylestown, Pennsylvania. After Shoemaker had provided historic axes, Mercer exclaimed about Shoemaker's domain in Central Pennsylvania: "Here by wonderful chance we find a protected recess in the mountains where the modern whirlwind of change has not swept everything away and we can talk directly with the past, out of ear shot of the house wreckers, bungalow builders and joy riders."[123] As with his collections of legends or forays into Pennsylvania caves, Shoemaker's work in speech, beliefs, and crafts had come from mysterious realms that had rarely if ever been explored. Such finds that he claimed were the vernacular languages of Pennsylvania-German Gypsies and Pennsylvania Huguenots, or the survivals of witchcraft found in Central Pennsylvania.[124]

Particularly compelling for folklorists outside Pennsylvania were the veins of folk songs Shoemaker mined from northern Pennsylvania sources beginning in 1898. His folk song collections are the most cited of his works in folkloristic scholarship, probably because, more than the legends, they capture characteristic and comparative traditions of the region. Shoemaker recognized his folk song volumes as his "most ambitious work."[125] In 1919 he published *North Pennsylvania Minstrelsy*, which had 104 songs, plus photographs of singers, musicians, and their occupational settings, and in 1923 he expanded the work to 137 songs. Almost 200 songs were made available in a 1931 revision he titled *Mountain Minstrelsy of Pennsylvania*. In addition to ballads of British origin that had been standard fare in folk song collections, *Mountain Minstrelsy* earned Shoemaker distinction by offering an abundance of American occupational songs of the lumber camps, hunting cabins, river shanties, and coal fields. The volume also offered more of an ethnic mix than other collections because it included songs of Irish, French, German, and American Indian Pennsylvania residents. *Mountain Minstrelsy* was a faithful record of texts as they were spoken or sung and is easily the best annotated of his published collections. Shoemaker often worded requests for material this way: "As I am gradually getting together material for a new edition of 'North Pennsylvania Minstrelsy,' I would like to have the 'Traveller' in it as sung by yourself. Will you please write it out for me from memory and not from a book and send to me at McElhattan, Pa. at your convenience?"[126]

Chronicling Anglo-American folk song studies, D. K. Wilgus categorized Shoemaker as a "local enthusiast" and complained that his books had "just enough information to madden the critic and cause him to distrust the accuracy of every recording."[127] With each song text, Shoemaker offered the name of the singer, his or her location, and the date of collection, and he often added historical information about the song's contents—although, as Wilgus points out, it is not clear "whether the comments come from Shoemaker or a correspondent." Nonetheless, Wilgus saw value in Shoemaker's "indifference to academic concern" because popular material adapted to oral tradition that the academic editor neglects is preserved by the "local enthusiast." "The great comfort to the critic is that changes made by a local enthusiast are more likely to be folk corrections than editorial 'improvements.' "[128]

To be sure, Shoemaker's goal was not academic. He intended his books for an audience of Pennsylvania readers, but he hoped for scholarly notice of his yeoman efforts.[129] He recorded a traditional legacy in one region to save a romanticized past and to boost appreciation for the region. Yet in *Mountain Minstrelsy* he elaborated more than in his books of legends on his interpretations of folk material collected in Central Pennsylvania. The *Minstrelsy* title suggested the connection of singers and their songs to a romantic view of medieval or classical ballad art and communication persisting in the present day. From the singers he knew, he thought he heard roles "reborn of the Ancient Bards and Minstrels." Although he cited his primary goal of preserving the heritage of a proud people—the Pennsylvania mountaineers—he went on to combine late-nineteenth century evolutionary doctrine and geographic diffusion to explain the primacy and persistence of Pennsylvania's folk songs. "Long after the little log cabins . . . and the black-haired, black-eyed girls, with their white skins and cameo features are an almost 'prehistoric' type," Shoemaker offered, "the music of the Pennsylvania syncopated out of recognition a thousand times will ever evoke deep down in refined hearts, in dignified salons of great cities, odd, wild and savage longings that the restraint of urban life and super-civilization will strive and puzzle to unfathom the source."[130]

Race and Evolution

In 1920, Henry Shoemaker credited British folklorist Andrew Lang, who espoused a cultural evolutionary idea of folklore as racial survivals from an earlier savage era into the civilized present, for providing ideas about the universality of folklore and its response to nature.[131] It was also Lang that supported the extension of folkloristic concern for narratives to legends and stories of personal experience.[132] Describing a story about a wolf killed by a woman who crushed the animal's skull with a borrowed kitchen implement and used the skin to cover her infant, Shoemaker found a striking parallel in Scottish tradition. "The story is probably centuries old," he explained, after quoting Lang's idea that folklore survivals "are very much the same, despite varying climes and creeds." "Similar occurrences have revived its details in the minds of the old people in the Pennsylvania wilds," he added.[133]

The best example of Shoemaker's use during the 1920s of cultural "survivals" similar to a treatment of natural history specimens is *The Origins and Language of Central Pennsylvania Witchcraft* (1927). Earlier cultural evolutionists often used speech and belief to find origins, because they were considered comparative specimens that could reveal a natural history of civilization emerging from multiple racial origins. The connection of natural and cultural history appealed to Shoemaker, and his notion of a Pennsylvania human cultural type, for example, was based on his proposal of a distinctive Pennsylvania mountain lion that had developed from a number of "bloodlines" and the influence of a unique environment. Shoemaker read evolutionary natural history, which typically dwelled on origins and development that became evident in detail-rich specimens and cultural history that relied greatly on the remains of comparative speech for its classifications from savagery through barbarism to civilization. In *The Origins and Language of Central Pennsylvania Witchcraft*, he asserted:

> In order to properly grasp the origins of some of the quaintest of these old world beliefs which reached Pennsylvania from the hordes of Continental Europeans, the Palatines, Alsatians, Huguenots, Waldensians, Moravians, Hebrews, Romanies, German Jews, Spaniards and Portuguese who came to Pennsylvania during the first three-quarters of the 18th century, mostly by way of the seaports of Holland, one must compare them with the language and folk lore of mother countries. The student is amazed at the similarity of some of them to the witch stories of the Portuguese mountain people, one of the many dark races represented in that strange racial blend known today as the "Pennsylvania Dutch."[134]

Shoemaker's unfounded claim about the ethnic roots of Pennsylvania-Germans aside, he applied early evolutionary thinking that folklore preserves survivals of archaic usages of ancient customs drawn from multiple racial origins. He argued that the words used for witchcraft, such as "hechs," come from multiple primitive racial origins and that although much of its original meaning has been lost the word's use persists today in the seclusion of Pennsylvania. "The language of Pennsylvania witchcraft," he asserted, "insures the perpetuation of archaic words that otherwise would perish which link the common people of the Keystone State with quaint, archaic origins overseas." With this vista of the "common people" in mind, Shoemaker offered a cabinet of "witchcraft survivals"—verbatim texts "collected from old people" in McElhattan—that contained vestiges of ancient beliefs in modern narratives. He concluded: "The direct language survivals of these peoples of lost or submerged nationalities remains today to the largest extent in the terminology of the hechicery or witchcraft. The fact that Pennsylvania sorcery will not down is the strongest hope for the future identification by language of the medley of races who flooded Colonial Pennsylvania and has made the State the mother of the composite American."[135]

Also borrowing from evolutionary doctrine, Shoemaker often referred to the "medley of races" in Pennsylvania. In the late nineteenth and early twentieth century, race was the primary social classification identifying a common ancestry based on biological heritage and physical characteristics.[136] It was applied to German, Italian, and Irish immigrants, as well as to Indians and blacks. In its emphasis on biological differences, it implied that heredity—a good "bloodline"—rather than culture determined human capacities and behavior. Andrew Lang, for example, wrote: "Race has a great deal to do with the development of myth, if it be race which confers on a people its national genius, and its capacity of becoming civilised." Cultural borrowing fostered by migrations of races explained similarities of folklore among the world's many "races." Folklore, survivals of the past, collected in the present could be useful, Lang surmised, to uncover ancient layers of racial mixing.[137]

Shoemaker freely, and loosely, used race, as he believed that Pennsylvania dramatically displayed the human story of civilization. He presented a view of many immigrants and natives coming together to form a new hearty "blood" that fostered a distinctive regional character. Representing the story of original settlement, this process in Pennsylvania is at the heart of "Americanism," Shoemaker argued. To this conception he added the effect of the secluded wilderness on the folklife and oral tradition of its inhabitants. "Folk lore, legends, and traditions linger longest in mountainous sections where modern influences are slowest to creep in," he said repeatedly.[138] His migration theory followed Pennsylvanians into the Shenandoah Valley, where southern Appalachian tradition, a vestige of Elizabethan days, arose.

After the 1930s, Shoemaker toned down the evolutionary overlay in his writings. In keeping with the social tone of the "era of the common man" and its glorification of everyday regional life, he developed his folklore collections to show the "inner life history"—indeed, the cultural integrity—of the region and its workers. Although still making analogies between natural and cultural history, he was less concerned with racial origins and comparisons with primitive cultures abroad, and more concerned with the vitality of mountaineer lore. As American regional nationalism grew in response to the plight of land-bound Americans during the Great Depression, Shoemaker returned to earlier themes of the picturesqueness of the folklife of Central Pennsylvanians. He recast some of his earlier conservation themes toward the new regional nationalism that viewed the history and folklore of American regions as the basis of an authentic and distinctive American heritage providing inner strength to Americans through crisis and conflict.[139] Preparing the convocation address on "Pennsylvania Folkways in the Development of an American Culture" at Bucknell University in 1935, Shoemaker declared: "From the simple, the primitive, and the unadorned comes all the beauty and comfort and joy that the culture spreads about us."[140] It was an appealing message during the Great Depression, when many writers stressed that the cultural inheritance of the dispossessed took precedence over materialism. They wrote that American regions represented a "coming together" of groups and ideas into an enduring American model. In the program of the Pennsylvania Folk Festival in 1936, Shoemaker wrote of Pennsylvania as developing a new indigenous folklore out of the social and environmental conditions that settlers found there. It was an old, favorite theme that fit into the hopeful thinking of regional nationalism. Shoemaker offered: "Pennsylvania has been justly regarded as the 'Mother of American Folklore,' as it attracted more different nationalities than any other of the colonies prior to the Revolution. . . . But on Pennsylvania soil, where it first took on a national life, American folklore should be most fittingly commemorated."[141] His presentation of legend and lore glorified the resilience of a gritty American type who triumphed over adversity.

If Appalachia received great attention as the prime example of a poverty-stricken area rich in homespun culture during the era of the common man, Shoemaker made a claim for the trove of songs in the northern Pennsylvania mountains, "among the literary treasures of our State," being equal to if not better than the well-known harvests of material from southern Appalachia.[142] He pointed to the ways in which Pennsylvania folk songs preserved traditions from antiquity, and showed adaptation of the traditions to new occupational settings of oil, lumber, and coal. On the basis of this Pennsylvania folklore collection, Shoemaker made a case for the cultural distinctiveness of the "Pennsylvania mountaineers," who provided sources for the later development of southern Appalachian folklife, and argued that this distinctiveness represented a new American hybrid from "an unparalleled blending of races," such as Scottish, Irish, French, English, Hispanic, Dutch, German, and American Indian, which had "more strains than those of the Southern Appalachians."[143] He fretted, however, that the cohesiveness and utility of the folklore were diminishing as the isolation of the region broke down. For Shoemaker, "The wasteful lumbering of the past half century, the all-engulfing forest fires which the gallant Gifford Pinchot has been endeavoring to stop, and the reckless destruction of wild life, have made the most self-reliant specimens of our mountain people foresake their beloved wilderness for the cities, where they have lost their identity in the maelstrom of industrial life."[144] Saving the folklore of the Pennsylvania mountaineers thus helped restore the region's "soul-spirit," established by "the Bards and the Hunters and the Borderers, and the Indians," living "in harmony and in sympathy" with nature. This spirit, he predicted, would "outlast big Business, Wet and Dry, and Factional Political Leaders as the pattern and the mold."[145]

Expanding on Shoemaker's presentation of Pennsylvania coal-mining songs in *Minstrelsy*, fellow journalist and director of the Pennsylvania Folk Festival George Korson (1899–1967) changed the title of his sequel from *Songs and Ballads of the Anthracite Miner* (1926) to *Minstrels of the Mine Patch* (1938). Korson optimistically wrote Shoemaker: "The South has been pretty well worked to exhaustion in folklore. The future in this field lies with us in Pennsylvania and I think in a short time we can succeed in focusing the attention of folklorists on Pennsylvania."[146] Despite Korson's recognition of the worth of American occupational folk songs in Shoemaker's *Minstrelsy*, other folklorists mostly cited Shoemaker's book for its cognates of British ballads. From West Virginia, folk song scholar John Harrington Cox wrote Shoemaker: "I congratulate you on your collections of ballads gathered in the Pennsylvania mountains. Are you aware that you have secured some of the rarest and finest of the older ballads in the English language?"[147] Another leading folk song authority, Albert Friedman, wrote Shoemaker from Harvard: "I myself own one of [George Lyman] Kittredge's copies of *North Pennsylvania Minstrelsy*, and you would be flattered by the place he gave it on his lists. Be assured that your labors as collector and editor have not been in vain. The copies of your work which I have placed on reserve for my students are well worked over. You and your generation of folklorists have discovered for us the glory of our native songs and have helped give the nation stronger cultural self-confidence."[148]

Typically published by his Pennsylvania newspaper presses, Shoemaker's books attracted a loyal following among Pennsylvania readers but were typically "away from the notice of leading folklorists," not to mention a national audience.[149] As an overture to folklorists, Shoemaker began labeling his books of legends as numbers in a "Pennsylvania Folklore Series" starting with reprints of *Pennsylvania Mountain Stories* (1907) and concluding with *More Allegheny Episodes* (vol. 12, 1924). Shoemaker said the idea had come from Senator Boise Penrose (1881–1921), who told him in 1914:

> My friend, you are doing the only original historical research work in our State today, and you must keep it up, even if you have to bring out twenty volumes. The serious purpose of your work is minimized by the fanciful titles you have given your books, such as "The Indian Steps," "Susquehanna Legends," "Tales of the Bald Eagle Mountains," "Black Forest Souvenirs." To properly identify them as scientific productions, they should be labeled, "Pennsylvania Folklore Series, Vols. I, II, III, IV," and so on, like Campbell's "Popular Tales of the West Highlands," Vols. I, II, III, IV, and as such would have a direct appeal to the students of unwritten history all over the United States.[150]

Indeed, the title page of *Black Forest Souvenirs* (1914) carried a quotation from John Francis Campbell's renowned Scottish folklore book *Popular Tales of the West Highlands* (1860–62): "But as there are quiet spots in the world where drift-wood accumulates undisturbed, so there are quiet spots where popular tales flourish in peace, because no man has interfered with them." Shoemaker admired Campbell's record of "romantic popular tales" that signified the picturesqueness of highland life and the national unity that a common folklore inspires.

Shoemaker's original goal was to come out with ten volumes covering "all the sections of the State where he has made folk-lore studies." He admitted giving less of his attention to Pennsylvania-German areas of Berks, Schuylkill, and Lehigh counties because of his limited knowledge of Pennsylvania-German and the active coverage of the field by others. Still, the series amply demonstrated that "an immense fund of folk-lore exists in Southern Pennsylvania, and is worthy of collecting," if not his popularizing wish: "May the years to come enshrine Pennsylvania as the very fountain-head of legendary lore, through some voice that can speak in tones that all can understand and marvel at."[151]

The Spirit and Source of Folklore

By Shoemaker's own account, he had not intended to keep publishing volumes of folklore, and it is clear that, judging by the sales of the books, profit was not the main motivating factor. He provided free books to subscribers of his newspapers and he sent complimentary copies of his publications to politicians, conservationists, state officials, librarians, historians, and fellow publishers in the state. "It has been better, no doubt, to have had a small circle of interested readers than to have been a *name* to thousands," Shoemaker reflected.[152] Speaking of the need for preservation that kept him going, he said: "Probably the motive that brought into existence the first volume can be urged in extenuation for the eleventh, namely, the desire to preserve the folk-lore of the Pennsylvania Mountains."[153] Elsewhere he harped on the almost-spiritual hold the folklore had on him, and how it represented a glorious bygone era. In *Allegheny Episodes* (1922) he asked, "Are they [narratives] worthy of perpetuation as folklore?" and answered: "Apart from the general idea of preserving legendary matter for future generations, there is the added reason that the heroic lines of some of the characters appealed to [me], and, to save them from the oblivion of the 'forgotten millions,' their careers have been herein recorded." In *More Allegheny Episodes* (1924), he added: "The reality is that it has been a wonderful pleasure and privilege to collect the stories, and to compile them; it has taken the writer into out-of-the-way places when in the mountains, and 'out of himself' when in the big cities. It has given him a storehouse of unique information and a sympathy for the life and struggles of the Pennsylvania highlanders and a picture of bygone days, when the Indians roved our hills, but above all, it has given him a bulwark for his faith as to the life beyond the grave."[154]

Shoemaker elaborated on the "spirit" of folklore in *Susquehanna Legends* (1913): "Viewing the legends deeper, and selecting those that have no association with earlier traditions, they may point to some link with the infinite, with the unseen, towards which all thoughtful persons are struggling. To some primitive souls a peep behind the curtains of eternity may have been revealed, when denied to abler seekers. It is in the forest that voices were first heard, linking us to the beyond. There is always a thrill in the mysterious, the inexplicable." In *In the Seven Mountains* (1913), he added: "Though the forest fires and lumbermen are busy devastating the verdant heights, and the fauna is decreasing, the *story* stands out all the more boldly, as strong and imperishable as the High Top or Tussey Knob. Fortunate indeed is a commonwealth to possess such a pristine wonderland; it will grow in appreciation as the mercenary, mechanical modern life wrecks the altars of the primitive and the picturesque."[155]

Although he could wax poetic about folklore as a reflection of a bygone romantic era, Shoemaker grudgingly recognized that modern civilization produced traditions. He spoke of folklore as an integral part of an ongoing cultural process that adapts to change. He made statements to this effect, such as "Folklore is not a dead sea by any means, and the titanic events of the machine age, the depression, unemployment, and civic and economic readjustments of today will furnish some of the folklore of hundreds of years from now." Even in his first collections of folklore, he admitted that "new conditions produce a new set of traditions, and these may be worthier in every way than the ones herein so imperfectly recorded."[156] Yet his conservation goals led him to overrepresent folklore as the romance of the bygone age, and his sympathies were clearly with the legends of the wilderness. His particular fascination with the untrodden folklore field of Central Pennsylvania, home to generations of his forebears, led him to narrow his collecting there. "In my early 20s," he wrote in a letter to Moritz Jagendorf, "I made a vow to collect no Folklore except in Pennsylvania where no one else had attempted it and I ran into many large varieties of Lore in Kentucky and in some of the Southern and Western States and in Europe and Africa, but I never wrote down a single story I heard there."[157]

Shoemaker was well known in the Central Pennsylvania highlands, achieving even legendary status, and apparently his collecting was warmly received. Homer Rosenberger, who taught school near Shoemaker's McElhattan home, recalled: "The people at Pine Station and at McElhattan and on the mountain were somewhat awed by Shoemaker's official positions and by his extensive land holdings, but scarcely regarded him as being a practical person."[158] Rosenberger offered a revealing anecdote about the way the local people viewed Shoemaker. Before he returned home from his ambassadorial post in Bulgaria, Rosenberger had "heard a great deal about him from folks in the Pine vicinity." "Mrs. Flem Simcox said Shoemaker was away in Europe, 'preaching.' Of course I did not try to correct the statement. She might have been offended had I attempted to explain the nature of Shoemaker's diplomatic post,"[159] Rosenberger wrote.

Rosenberger described Shoemaker as serious, shy, energetic, and a capable if reserved conservationist. Fond of roaming the mountains, he "talked with almost anyone who would tell him about the customs of the mountain people," Rosenberger recalled, and "he was difficult to analyze." "He was somewhat of a gentleman of leisure, but must have kept very busy in order to write a lengthy newspaper column six days per week for thirty-five years. He was affable in a way, and distant, too. He seemed to be very reserved, probably being somewhat aware of his inadequacy as a writer of history. Yet nothing could deter him from writing what he seemed to consider to be a record of the mountain people of Central Pennsylvania. I believe that he felt in his heart that no one knew the mountain people of that area better than he did and that no one could write about those people as well as he himself."[160] Rosenberger implied that Shoemaker's upper-class roots prevented him from really understanding the lower-class lifeways of ordinary mountain folks. He thought of his jaunts around the highlands as viewing the color but not capturing the substance of a marginal existence.

Well-traveled beyond Central Pennsylvania, Shoemaker unabashedly made the claim for the Pennsylvania highlands that "there is no lovelier land that tradition or folk-lore could associate itself. The most beautiful streams and rivers rise in its midst; impressive peaked and castellated mountains, the grandest forests cover much of its area; its farms are fertile, its climate extraordinarily good, its people sprightly, clever, good-hearted, the best product of a mixed stock."[161] He was also fond of boasting that "Pennsylvania with its wide heritage from many lands, has probably the greatest amount of uncollected folklore that exists in any part of the Nation."[162] When Cornell Professor Harold Thompson challenged him on that claim, Shoemaker replied: "I do not think that there is more folklore in Pennsylvania than in New York, except that perhaps we have a larger racial background and our tales are more diverse. But I know that we are behind in collecting these tales, by a great many years, and a young collector like Professor [Samuel] Bayard, you recall, stated in his address, that sources get farther apart every year as the old people die. I recall that when I began collecting it was only a case of going from door to door to obtain what I wanted."[163]

After publishing several volumes, Shoemaker drew attention to the similarities among many of the tales he had gathered. "This shows their common origin," he surmised, elaborating: "Out of a dozen which were brought to the Pennsylvania wilderness by the first settlers have grown a hundred versions, each distinctive to the locality where it is handed down. Even the legends which belong to the present generation have some subconscious tie with the past. The actors in them felt the welling of ancient emotions in their breasts and suited their lives and sorrows to the pathways of their ancestors."[164] He recognized that his texts were related to European folk narrative and New England and the Southern legends, but he claimed for the Pennsylvania legends a distinctiveness that resulted from the higher degree of multiethnic contact than in the South or New England. "The origins of Pennsylvania folk-lore," he wrote, "seem to the writer like a happy blending of Indian and European elements which would have gradually, had backwoods conditions continued, developed into a definitely Pennsylvania mythology."[165]

Tale-Tellers and Bards

Lest he be accused of creating this mythology, Shoemaker often named key contributors to his collection of stories. He cited the oral traditions given by raftsman and hunter John Dyce (or Dice) (1830–1904) of Clinton County, prospector and herbalist Thomas Simcox (1840–1914), "brought up by the Indians on Nichols' Run, in Lycoming County," and Clinton County's legend-

Frontispiece to *Black Forest Souvenirs* (1914), which creates icons of Shoemaker's favorite subjects of the extinct past. Above Shoemaker is a depiction of wild passenger pigeons, and below is rafting down the Susquehanna River. Clockwise from the top right is a mountain lion or panther, a frontier "Nimrod," an "Indian princess," a bison, an elk, an Indian brave, a highland lumberman, and a wolf.

Henry Shoemaker exploring the Pennsylvania highlands along Chatham Run, Clinton County, in one of his many horse-drawn carriages, June 24, 1922. (Pennsylvania State Archives, Department of Forestry Photo Collection)

The opening to Penn's Cave, June 1993, which inspired Shoemaker's legend of "Nita-nee." (Simon Bronner)

"Black Forest Camp Life," in *Black Forest Souvenirs* (1914), or "A 'Shack' in the Black Forest," in *Eldorado Found* (1917). Shoemaker used illustrations like this from the collection of William T. Clarke to convey the rusticity and seclusion—indeed, a connection to the primitive past—of Pennsylvania mountaineers. The original print is dated 1895. (Pennsylvania State Archives, Department of Forestry Photo Collection)

"Ready for the Log Drive, Kettle Creek," from *Allegheny Episodes* (1922). Shoemaker used illustrations like this to display the mass destruction of the forest caused by the lumber industry. In one caption in *Eldorado Found* (1917) he labeled the lumbermen "despoilers."

"Telling a Panther Story," from *Black Forest Souvenirs* (1914). The photograph was probably staged, intended to show the romantic rustic setting of storytelling. The building stood near Hammersley, Pennsylvania, in Potter County. Omitted from the shot are the railroad tracks at the left of the building.

"John Q. Dyce (1830–1904), The Famous Clinton County Hunter Who Killed Three Deer with One Shot," from *Pennsylvania Deer and Their Horns* (1912). Shoemaker cited Dyce (Dice) as a prime source of stories and frequently reprinted his photograph in his books.

Jesse Logan (1809–1916), Seneca Indian who provided Shoemaker with Indian legends, songs, and beliefs. Logan was 106 years old at the time P. C. Hockenberry took this photograph at the Indian tract in Warren County, Pennsylvania. He is showing the old-fashioned bow with which he hunted. From *Captain Logan: Blair County's Indian Chief* (1915).

"Jacob Wren Zimmerman, Premier Pennsylvania Mountain Musician." The photograph was the frontis-piece to *North Pennsylvania Minstrelsy* (1923). A farmer by trade, Zimmerman provided Shoemaker with many local legends, in addition to songs and stories about his father David, a legendary deer-slayer covered in *Stories of Great Pennsylvania Hunters* (1913).

"Seth Iredell Nelson, Round Island, Pennsylvania (1809–1905)," from *Wolf Days in Pennsylvania* (1914). Shoemaker called him "the greatest Pennsylvania hunter of his generation," a legendary figure as well as a gifted storyteller.

"Seth Nelson Jr. After a Good Day's Sport," from *Allegheny Episodes* (1922). Working as a guide in the Pennsylvania wilderness, Nelson gave Shoemaker many stories he had heard from his father and other hunters.

John Churchill French, from *Rafting Days in Pennsylvania* (1922). Formerly a raftsman, French actively collected songs and legends for Shoemaker.

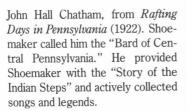

John Hall Chatham, from *Rafting Days in Pennsylvania* (1922). Shoemaker called him the "Bard of Central Pennsylvania." He provided Shoemaker with the "Story of the Indian Steps" and actively collected songs and legends.

Raftsmen's reunion at Camp Shoemaker, 1929. Note the man (probably W. T. Feerar of Jersey Shore, Pennsylvania) in the second row, third from the left, holding an accordion. Shoemaker re-created "lumber-camp entertainment," including accordion-playing, clog-dancing, and storytelling. Shoemaker, far right, also hosted deer hunters' reunions, conservation meetings, and Boy Scouts at the Camp. (Juniata College Archives)

ary hunters Seth Iredell Nelson (1809–1905), his son Seth Jr., and some "splendid old ladies," including Mrs. Anna Stabley (1834–1911) of Wayne Township, Clinton County, for most of the material filling his first few books.[166] Stabley was the wife of a village postmaster and general store-keeper and was in a good position to relate to Shoemaker the old-time stories told around the store's cracker barrel.[167] He credited "probably one-half" of the stories in *Allegheny Episodes* (1922) to another woman, Mrs. W. J. Phillips, also of Clinton County, "who spent some of her girlhood days, many years ago, on the Indian Reservations in Pennsylvania and southwestern New York." To be sure, most of his informants were men, especially hunters, raftsmen, lumbermen, and prospectors, but he made a special effort, so he said, to represent the often forgotten Pennsylvania "heroines" and the "great part that women had formerly played in transportation [and lumbering] in Pennsylvania."[168]

Shoemaker often referred to the songs and stories of "Pennsylvania Indian" Jesse Logan (1809–1916), whose photograph graced the cover of *Pennsylvania Indian Folk-Songs* (1925), and he gave names of other Indian contributors of legends, including Johnny Half-White, Betsey O'Bail (the last surviving granddaughter of Ga-Ni-Di-Euh, or The Cornplanter), Charlie Gordon, and Owen Jacobs (great-grandson of "Captain" Jacobs). He also relied on his relations to Quiggles—such as river pilots Robert (1830–1916) and Jacob (1821–1911), who recounted many legendary episodes of Clinton County lumbering and hunting life reaching back into the eighteenth century. "As a boy," Shoemaker recalled, "noted Indian killer" Peter Pentz made many visits to his father's house, and "this huge frontiersman, with his shock of stiff red hair and big, eloquent mouth, would gather the boys about him at the fireside on winter evenings regaling them for hours with his exploits."[169] He compared these storytellers to "ancient bards" who like the Christians in ancient Rome kept "a faith that belongs to the better, the spiritual side of mankind," keeping alive folklore "in every locality, in cavernous seclusion."[170]

Oft-cited "bards" were John C. French from Potter County and John H. Chatham from Clinton County, to whom he dedicated *Mountain Minstrelsy* (1931). French, born in 1858, had been a primarily oral source, and in 1921 Shoemaker encouraged him to record his memories for a book titled *Rafting Days in Pennsylvania* (1922), edited by J. Herbert Walker. French apparently felt uncomfortable in the role and invited Shoemaker to elaborate on his tales: "I am pleased to know that you like my rafting and lumber tales. It is a fascinating history to contemplate; but to write it 'in spots'—fragments culled at random, or to fit my fancy, over long time and various territory, might not please as would the omitted parts."[171] Shoemaker published the account as it was sent it to him, and introduced the compilation with the wish "May the stories they tell of unbroken forests seventy-five years ago fill us with a greater desire to preserve and conserve something of Pennsylvania for Pennsylvanians who apparently don't want it saved."[172]

Shoemaker admired Chatham's wide narrative repertoire drawing on a "prodigious memory" and called him "the Bard of Pennsylvania" and "the foremost story teller of Pennsylvania." He also boasted that Chatham could have "entertained the members of the Story Telling League 'a thousand and one nights' and never told the same story twice." In addition, Chatham could recite many ballads for Shoemaker and "knew countless proverbs and sayings of the mountain people, and was a storehouse of accurate information on the manners and customs of the Indians and the modes of life followed by the early pioneers." He was particularly adept at handling legendary material, reported Shoemaker: "He loved nothing better than to recount the true, unpublished stories of the frontier, of Indian warfare, of the peculiarities and superstitions of our forefathers along the borderland of civilization." Shoemaker memorialized Chatham (1846–1923) by arranging for the state to name a spring in Clinton County in his honor. "As it flows on its crystalline purity, it will echo and re-echo, forever in its sweet music the thoughts and songs of the old story teller, whose life was typical of a perfect day in the mountains, rich in its sunshine, radiant in the golden hour, glorious in its sunset and twilight," he declared.[173]

A former schoolteacher in Centre County whose family ties had been in the region since the eighteenth century, Chatham was responsible for the legend of the "Indian Steps," out of which Shoemaker got considerable mileage as the title legend of books of both prose and poetry. Chatham had first written Shoemaker on January 12, 1911, after fondly reading his Legend of Penn's Cave, and suggested another story for Shoemaker to develop from his memory of the landscape near his country school in Baileyville. "I think a plot could be designed for another good Indian story at the 'Indian Steps,' " he wrote. He located the tale "just on the line of Centre and Huntingdon County at the head of Spruce Creek, thirteen miles west of Boalsburg and about fifteen miles west of State College."

> Here for some reason the Indians did work, they built a stone road over the Tussy rut. Consisting of a series of steps from the top to the bottom of the Mountain, and the same passage is used by the present inhabitants in crossing the range to Stone valley. . . . I think we could get up an Indian war between the Susquehannox and the Kishocquillis Indians and have the battle ground on the Barrens about two miles from the steps. Then we could people the upper waters of the Susquehanna and Bald Eagle Creek and the vast region between the creek and river to Sumamohining, with the Susquehannox and

the Juniatta Valley and all that region to the Bald Eagle Mts with the Kokoquillis Indians, and there would be ample room for them to fight on the Glades and Barrens of Spruce Creek.[174]

Although Chatham gave the impression that he had totally fabricated the legend, Shoemaker provided the background for the published version of the legend, claiming that "it was told to him [Shoemaker] by the old folks."[175] Shoemaker changed some essential details: "The Lenni-Lanape had swarmed across the Tussey Mountains to give battle to the Susquehannocks from the North. The Lenni-Lanape were completely routed and the bodies of their leaders were thrown into Rock Springs where Spruce Creek makes its head. When Mr. Chatham was at Baileyville the curious stone steps across the mountains which the Indians used were still to be seen. When persons crossed over to Stone Valley they always said they were going over the 'Indian Steps.'"[176] As usual, Shoemaker included a comment on the obliteration of the landscape by industry: "Lumbering operations, which included the skidding of logs off the mountains, have now pretty well obliterated them." He claimed that the battle took place in 1635 and that this year had been verified by historians (he didn't name them), but although standard texts recognize that hostilities existed between the tribes, they dispute the fact that any such decisive battle took place.[177]

Judging from readers' reactions, the facts of the battle mattered less than the way Shoemaker encased the event in romantic sentiment and natural setting. Connecticut's State Ornithologist wrote Shoemaker: "The pretty sentiment that runs through them leaves a very pleasant taste and glow. The sympathetic allusions and descriptions of Nature, and the whole outdoor setting, give the exact setting which appeals to me."[178] George Hess thanked him for "the manner in which you have placed on record very many of the traditions and romantic stories of their region."[179] Journalist Norman Easterbrook, of the *Harrisburg Patriot,* waxed poetically, "When I read your stories the intervening years were rolled away and I was standing on the wind-swept hill again, looking across miles of space to the mystic mountains of boyhood days."[180] Such readers as Katharine Carter Barrow gave Shoemaker poetic license because of his attention to locality away from the "great events" of history. She told him: "The future will thank you even more than we of today—for much of the early history of this locality is fading away—because no historian has saved it as you are saving its traditions and early romantic events."[181] Charlotte Huff spoke for many letter-writers when she said: "It is the personal part—that makes a story—it touches a responsive chord in the reader's heart."[182] Shoemaker's main informant, Chatham, responded: "On the whole the book is certainly right and shows

. . . your descriptions are more vivid than in your first workings." He promised Shoemaker more fragments "from whence stories come."[183]

Of renowned hunter and raftsman Dyce (in a description that applies equally to other backwoods characters, Thomas Simcox, Seth Nelson, "Uncle Charlie" Dickinson, Jim Jacobson, Peter Pentz, and George Gast, on whom Shoemaker relied as informants), Shoemaker fondly recalled "going to the forests ostensibly to hunt, but instead sitting on a log for hours at a time to listen to some Indian story, or to the runs to fish, but instead to rest on the mossy bank to hear a tale of witches or ghosts, with the line trailing down stream."[184] He "was a typical backwoodsman of the best type of sturdy Scotch-Irish ancestry," and "in appearance he was a handsome man, his leonine head, keen blue eyes, clear-cut nose and mouth and flowing beard gave him an almost Roman look of distinction, which was further emphasized by his full six feet of stature. But he was simple and kindly as a child; he drifted along with life's current, and as he grew older he felt more strongly that the old days, the wild days, 'before the railroad came,' as he put it, were by far the best."[185]

And of Seth Nelson, Shoemaker said: "It was a delight to sit with him on summer afternoons on the little board bench which stood between two red maple trees on the bank of the Sinnemahoning—it had not been polluted by the Austin paper mills in those good old days, and flowed as clear as crystal—listening to the old Nimrod tell of his adventures of the chase, his epic as clear and durable as that of the Ancient Bard in 'The Lays of the Deer Forest,' who sang of 'wolves and roes and elks.' Those were halcyon days, for the end of these grand reminiscences was never reached."[186] Shoemaker told George Korson that he began collecting from Nelson as early as 1898, when the senior Nelson, whom he called "one of the last surviving of the famous big game hunters of Pennsylvania," was approaching the age of ninety. After hearing Nelson's legends, such as the story of "Altar Rock" (included in Korson's *Pennsylvania Songs and Legends*), Shoemaker reconstructed the texts from memory "best I could after I got home."[187]

Shoemaker did not have tape recorders on his collecting trips. He wrote down notes or reconstructed items later from memory. From his notes on such people as Dyce and Nelson, he extracted songs, sayings, and beliefs as verbatim folkloric "texts," but legends typically became literary stories explained as part of a regional collection, travelogue, or natural-history treatise. In *Black Forest Souvenirs* (1914), Shoemaker included the names and locations of men and women who had told him legends in the volume, and to underscore the status of these legends as folklore, most of the legends had multiple sources. If this listing helps authenticate the role of the legends in oral tradition, it also suggests that Shoemaker's literary hand was at least evident in forming composite texts for the book. Although the use of composite texts was not uncommon among folklorists of the period, Shoemaker maintained a literary style that often obscured the use of his work for comparative folkloristic purposes. And within the Pennsylvania field, Angus Gillespie complained, "serious scholars of Pennsylvania history and folklore have not relied on his work because it is difficult, if not impossible, to sort out the authentic oral narratives from material that is pure invention." He concluded: "Delightful as these tales are, they have no place in the scientific study of folklore."[188]

Apologies and Boasts

In introductions to his volumes of stories, Shoemaker offered apologies to two audiences: those looking for "scientific" folklore and those seeking literary art. He was defensive about his literary abilities and he worried about "the merit of these chapters as *folklore* [scholarship]."[189] He confessed to columnist William Allison, "I have written too much and in too great a hurry. But you see I have been writing, not for personal glory, but to preserve the old legends as I know that no one else would probably do it. Then again I did not know if in the future I would have the time to do it and felt that I had better do the work quickly and imperfectly than have it left undone and the legends lost."[190] He mentioned consulting the scholarly bookshelf, realizing his work's shortcomings:

> After perusing carefully the various issues of the "Journal of American Folklore" and similar foreign publications, it might look as if the kernel of our stories has been too deeply imbedded in the local color and descriptions which have been woven about the narratives. . . . If the stories had been printed word for word, in the language of the Pennsylvania mountain people who told them to him, then it would be exact, personal, definite folklore. With descriptions and scenery woven about stories, which, when originally related, consisted of a few vivid sentences only, the entire twelve volumes [of his Pennsylvania Folklore Series] might easily have been put under one cover, a bulky volume, it is true, but much condensed from its present form and of far greater value! That perhaps is the great glaring error of the series.[191]

Although recognizing the "errors" of his books as scholarly references, Shoemaker modestly hoped they could be entertaining and informative: "It may be that these chapters, too familiar and too much lacking in literary style or too unscientific to belong to the archives of folklore, may yet season or ripen into something that will be very useful, some thing very valuable, half a century or more from now," he wrote in *More Allegheny Episodes* (1924). "They might find a place then as a picture of frontier life," he continued, "and life in transition from wilderness to civilization, that will cause the volumes to be widely read as references and their compiler's efforts appreciated."[192] Shoemaker consistently pointed out that he was collecting without the advantage of training or precedence in Central Pennsylvania. "Doubtless some one could have done this work more thoroughly or better," he wrote in *Black Forest Souvenirs* (1914), for "it deserved more time, but the truth remains that no one else has tried."[193] Later in his life he told a Clinton County audience, "I believe others more richly gifted like the great folklorists of Ireland, one of the world's richest folk-finders could have done far better than I here."[194] His significant contribution, however, was to record types of folklore before they disappeared and before anyone else did it extensively in Central Pennsylvania, and to encourage others to do so, or to be inspired by what he had found. Aware of more professional efforts in other countries, Shoemaker hoped that "in years to come the folk-lore and traditions of inland Pennsylvania, such as set forth in his several volumes, will rank with the old tales of Scotland, Ireland, France, Germany and Russia, which have been so systematically collected and preserved."[195]

While Shoemaker asserted that "in Ireland, France, Germany, and Italy, folklore still lives on in the same quantities it was near the surface here [Pennsylvania] sixty years ago," he argued that the types of tales and legends he collected in Pennsylvania could not be recovered again. "Why did these quaint stories of which many were a hundred years old fail to pass into the present rising generations?" he asked. "Is it because of increased public information, the spread of newspaper circulation, the moving picture theatres, the radio, television, and the auto? Public interest has moved from the locality to the wide world and events in India and California are as much in the public eye as were the tales of Indians, wolves, wild pigeons, panthers, shooting, rafting, logging and the supernatural sixty years ago."[196] Particularly after World War II, Shoemaker often lamented that "the old people who were rich store-houses of this unwritten information are all dead. All the old folks who entertained me with vivid tales of long ago in the life in which they lived are dead to the last one in most communities. Their descendants who heard these stirring tales often enough have forgotten them, or can't get into the mood of relating them."[197] He called for both preservation and conservation of folklore to keep "alive in an un-ending current the simplest, most kindly, and neighborly continuity of human thought." Further, Shoemaker declared, "Being in itself a picture of a happier past, folklore becomes the pattern of a happier future."[198]

Conservation and Popularization of Regional Tradition

If collecting and archiving folklore represented the preservation of folklore, encouraging its perpetuation by restoring its original settings and applying it to education, entertainment, and literature signified its conservation. Even before he became State Folklorist in 1948, Henry Shoemaker hosted "Raftsman Reunions" at Camp Shoemaker, where he encouraged musical and narrative exchanges. At the 1929 reunion—so one newspaper reported, for example—"The rhythm and beat of old time tunes in the thin but rollicking strains of the accordion, just as rivermen in lumber camps stamped and swayed to them 40 years ago, tales of heroism and hairbreadth escapes 'on the river' and the enthusiastic reunion of the survivors of those heroic days, marked the annual gathering of the lumbermen and raftsmen of this section Saturday afternoon at the pavillion at Camp Shoemaker, McElhattan, when the hundred persons present were entertained by Col. Henry W. Shoemaker, of that place."[199] The camp also served as a Boy Scout center, and Shoemaker held programs for storytelling around the campfire. His Alpine Club outings were also meant to explore and restore the original settings of the wilderness that he believed gave rise to folklore.

Shoemaker promoted the incorporation of folklore by poets, writers, and storytellers in presentations at folklore society meetings and he often arranged for Pennsylvania Folklore Society meetings to be held in conjunction with the Pennsylvania Storytelling League or Poetry Society and organized creative readings based on folklore. At the 1951 Pennsylvania Folklore Society meeting, for example, Blanche Keysner of the Pennsylvania Poetry Society read "two Ballads on Folk Lore subjects: 'The Wedding Gown' and 'Old River Road.' She then presented Mrs. Harry G. Keffer, President of the Story Teller's League of Harrisburg. Mrs. Keffer told a Folktale 'The Walk-Away People.'"[200] Shoemaker had been active in encouraging this kind of literary adaptation well before society meetings of the 1950s. In 1913 he turned John Hall Chatham's "versification" of the Indian Steps legend into a book and in his introduction pointed to the greatness of American literary figures who used folklore as the basis of American letters, such as Longfellow and Hawthorne.

Folk festivals provided another opportunity for Shoemaker to popularize folklore. Meetings and books could build appreciation for the region's cultural inheritance among its residents, but he also wanted to inspire musicians and craftsworkers with the strength of folk tradition. Thus Shoemaker served as chairman of the Pennsylvania Folk Festival and advised the "Americans All" Folk Festival (formerly the Festival of Nations). Bucknell University hosted the Pennsylvania Folk Festival through the 1930s and gave the festival's direction over to folklore collector George Korson. Korson wrote Shoemaker to state his aim to "popularize folklore by means of the folk festival and thus create interest in the subject and build up audiences who will enjoy such interesting works as yours."[201] Always one for pointing out the "usefulness" of public folklore activity, Shoemaker complimented Korson for enabling elderly and retired workers to have a new life as performers. As chairman, Shoemaker helped publicize the festival's goals and activities, and the festival was remarkably successful, attracting as many as 30,000 visitors. Entertainment at the festival was divided into prominent categories of concern during the 1930s era of the common man: "racial" (what would now be called ethnic), "occupational," and "regional."

With the contacts Korson and Shoemaker made, the Pennsylvania Folk Festival presented "authentic" folk artists wherever possible. That was not the case with the "Americans All," or Dauphin County Folk Festival, supported by the Works Progress Administration (WPA). Located in the dignified Forum Auditorium in the Harrisburg Capitol Complex, the festival featured orchestras often backing art singers or revival groups presenting folk music of the nationalities within Dauphin County. The large dance ensembles and singing groups employed many ethnics who were "taught" their traditions. For example, the *Harrisburg Patriot* pointed out in 1936 that separate ensembles of Ukrainian and Romanian folk dancers "were trained by workers in the Dauphin County Division of the WPA recreation bureau." "Several thousand persons" attended regularly, the paper reported, and the governor usually opened and closed the festivities. After the festival, and the WPA, had run its course, Shoemaker arranged for "a certificate of high achievement in folklore" to be awarded to Mary Barnum Bush Hauck, the festival's director, in 1949. Although the goals of Korson's Pennsylvania Folk Festival and Hauck's Americans All Festival seemed to be at odds, Shoemaker supported both as conservation efforts.

With that conservationist mission in mind, Shoemaker established the Pennsylvania Folklore Society and became its first vice-president. "I believe," he wrote fellow officer John Baer Stoudt, "that we are starting what will be a very popular and valuable organization in the literary and historical life of Pennsylvania."[202] The name and purpose of the organization reflected Shoemaker's idea that a new Pennsylvania folklore arose out of the mix of many ethnic cultures. The Pennsylvania Folklore Society promoted a kind of regional nationalism that viewed diverse ethnic traditions leading into a distinct regional type. The society's first president was Bishop James Henry Darlington of Harrisburg, but Shoemaker, as vice-president, guided the organization's direction. Like Shoemaker, Darlington was active in the Alpine Club and various historical societies, as well as in a number of ethnic organizations, such as the Russian Club, the Huguenot Society, and the Italy-American Society. But Darlington was far less of a folklorist. His main claim to folklore work was his references to legends in his poetry, but he offered a steady headquarters for the organization, and considerable prestige.[203] While Darlington offered his home for meetings, Shoemaker set up the society's objective for the "collection and preservation of the folklore of the state of Pennsylvania," including "not only the Anglo-American material which forms such a great part of the folklore of the northeastern section of the United States, but the folklore of other ethnic colonial groups such as the Germans, Swiss, Huguenots, German Jews, and Greeks."[204]

The society's leadership had in mind a grass-roots organization that would share the results of collecting folklore in Pennsylvania, and subsequently popularize the folklore and conserve it, through poets, writers, storytellers, artists, festivals, and schools. Despite its popularizing goals, Shoemaker wanted to maintain ties to the more professional American Folklore Society.[205] Indeed, the Pennsylvania Folklore Society's constitution called for "the encouragement of local folklore research and the publication of the results" but probably was using the maverick Texas Folk-Lore Society, which was building up a reputation for popularizing legends and ballads of the Old West, as an example, rather than one of the regular "local branches" of the American Folklore Society. Like the Pennsylvania Folklore Society, the Texas group, organized in 1909, intended to "interest more Texans in their folk inheritance and to encourage some kind of literary appropriation of its folk-lore findings."[206] The Texas group had a successful publishing program that drew considerable national attention for local-color authors, such as J. Frank Dobie, who built up the legends of the Wild West. With its romantic narrative of Wild West life drawn from folk legend and song, the Texas focus was local, the orientation was popular.

Shoemaker hoped to avoid the mistake of short-lived branch societies that "looked too far afield, often cherishing the exotic values in folklore to the neglect of folk materials closer at hand."[207] He envisioned a network of members collecting folklore in their own localities and contributing their finds to a massive archive for the preservation and reuse of folklore. "The requirements" of the organization, he wrote prospective members, were that "you are interested in preserving Pennsylvania folk tales in which is contained the history of our people. If you would find it possible from time to time to collect these tales concerning our Pennsylvania folk which you must hear, our work will be greatly helped."[208] The connection of the society to history and nature concerns was evident in the organization's council, which was made up of members of the Pennsylvania Historical Commission and the Pennsylvania Alpine Club. At the society's 1928 meeting, the "Pennsylvania Alpine Club Quartet" opened with "a selection of oldtime Pennsylvania mountain folk-tunes." Two papers followed, one by Walker Stephen on Indian legends, the other by H. Beam Piper on the Pennsylvania origin of the "Kentucky" rifle.[209] Shoemaker subsidized the activities of the society and published several of his collections for members from 1925 to 1931.[210] In addition to holding meetings before Alpine Club climbs, the society also hosted politicians at public events. Congressman Charles Esterly arranged for a meeting in September 1929 so that Secretary of War James W. Good could make an appearance in his ancestral home of Lehigh County.[211] The momentum of the society suffered a setback when Darlington died in 1930 and Shoemaker departed for Bulgaria.

In 1935, shortly after Shoemaker returned from his diplomatic post in Europe, the society reorganized at Bucknell University, with one hundred members in attendance. Shoemaker was elected president, an office he held until 1956.[212] Because of the decidedly localized focus of the society's work, its publications, lacking comparative notes or broad contexts, often appeared esoteric to national folklorists—so the editor of the *Journal of American Folklore* complained.[213] Yet among Pennsylvanians, Shoemaker and the reorganized society enjoyed greater visibility during the late 1930s because of connections to the Pennsylvania Folk Festival directed by George Korson (Shoemaker served as "chairman") and the Dauphin County Folk Festival called "Americans All" in Harrisburg organized by Mary Bush Hauck of the Works Progress Administration.[214] The "red-letter day," Shoemaker told the American Folklore Society, "occurred in Lewisburg in 1937 when 30,000 people attended on a fine moonlight night an outdoor session of the Pennsylvania Folk Festival and the Society was acclaimed the founder of the organized movement in the state to collect and compile the folklore of the Keystone State."[215] In a note to Korson, he added: "And the joy and the dignity you have given these people by digging them out of their retirement, and giving them this final opportunity for fame and appreciation, transcends any humanitarian project of the New Deal. If all of these folk activities could have the same recognition, I believe it would result in a spiritual renaissance all over the State."[216] Reflecting Shoemaker's historical interests, the society affiliated with the Pennsylvania Federation of Historical Societies and held annual meetings, usually in Harrisburg or in surrounding cities in Central Pennsylvania.

As State Archivist, Shoemaker pursued the goals of the society. He stated in the *Journal of American Folklore* that "folklore material collected by its members [is] available to scholars and the general public through the Division of Archives, Department of Public Instruction, Harrisburg."[217] One Pennsylvania audience was startled to hear him say that the State Archives, "the most authoritative source of Pennsylvania history, are entirely lacking in human interest," and that "they consist of page after page of cabals of cunning politicians and self seeking soldiers." He continued: "They contain nothing concerning the social, domestic, economic or cultural life of colonial and Revolutionary times. They give us no picture of the home life of the people, of that medley of races who made up colonial Pennsylvania. We soon become tired reading of the rancor, jealousy, and hatred between various military and civilian factions and seek for a new fountain head of history. Therefore it is in the folklore and oral traditions of the people themselves that we must look for the adequate picture of the times."[218]

Such a call for an "adequate picture of the times" based on folk-culture research had more than the usual reception in Pennsylvania because of a growing number of folkloristic efforts related to public history after 1935. Indeed, writer Arthur D. Graeff saw the years after 1935 in Pennsylvania as a renaissance period of interest in culture and lore that drew national attention. Graeff believed that this was at least partly due to American response to Nazi folklore to make a claim for a superior Aryan folk spirit or character.[219] Many writers held up American folklore as a rich trove of democratic society, which showed that, unlike fascist regimes, a national society could be pluralistic, with a special trinity of regional, "racial" or ethnic, and occupational cultures. Benjamin Botkin, for example, offered his *Treasury of American Folklore* against Nazi efforts to speak of folklore "in terms of the 'racial heritage'" or to insist "that a particular folk group or body of tradition is 'superior' or 'pure.'"[220] A familiar call went out for recovering authentic American lore before it disappeared, especially in Pennsylvania where "traditions preserved orally flourished as vigorously as in any North American region."[221] "To rescue it," Penn State professor Samuel Bayard advised during the 1940s, "quick action will be necessary, for to all appearances it will not survive delay. And its disappearance through neglect will be a cultural loss to both the state and the nation."[222]

The fear of cultural loss during the 1930s led to a "search for experience and ways to record it" that led to such documentary classics as *Let Us Now Praise Famous Men* by James Agee and Walker Evans (1941), according to historian Warren Susman.[223] In his assessment, it was as if "the discovery of significant myths, symbols, and images from the culture itself . . . might also serve as a basis of reinforcement or indeed the re-creation or remaking of culture itself."[224] Botkin's *Treasury of American Folklore* bears out that observation when readers saw that folklore represented, in Botkin's words, not only "'Back where I come from' but also 'Where do we go from here?'" Botkin suggested a "healthy provincialism," based on the symbolism of folklore, as a major ingredient of "a well-rounded culture."[225] As consultant to the state guides for the Works Progress Administration from 1938 to 1941, Arthur Graeff similarly had advised including folklore to show the powerful lasting spirit of the common people in American regional life.[226] He cited the formation of the Pennsylvania-German Folklore Society and the outburst of Pennsylvania Dutch folklore studies as significant achievements of documenting and reconstructing regional culture. In addition, Henry and George Landis had organized their "folk museum" near Lancaster, Alfred Shoemaker became the nation's first professor of American folklore at Franklin and Marshall College in Lancaster, Pennsylvania, folk festivals abounded in Lewisburg, Hershey, and Lancaster, and George Korson released recordings of Pennsylvania coal miners for the Library of Congress. [227]

Such achievements aimed at cultural gains came on the heels of the economic losses of the Great Depression. Social attention shifted from the ways that previously poor "foreign elements" would assimilate, to the dignity that native-born workers could muster in the face of Depression poverty. Images of farmers forced off their land and migrants in search of work suggested that the regional map of America was rapidly changing. Passage of immigration restrictions had quieted the debate over the Americanization of ethnic cultures, but reports of foreclosures and natural disasters increased awareness of breaks in regional traditions. As industry suffered and migrations forced by the hunt for economic opportunity spread, a new consciousness of workers and their attachment to place arose. [228] The new realism of documentaries in book, film, and sound during the period voiced questions about generations-long traditions that were being left behind. For many observers, these traditions fostered regional pride and offered dignity to the "common people" that had formed America's rich regional cultures. Reminiscent of Shoemaker's Progressive campaign to "sell Pennsylvania to Pennsylvanians" early in the century, the federally sponsored American Guide Series—set up as state travel manuals featuring sites of historical and folklife interest—were meant to "introduce America to Americans" as a "rich culture."[229] Another indication of regionalism during the period was the American Folkways series edited by novelist Erskine Caldwell. More than twenty regional overviews connecting landscape, people, and culture came into popular circulation at the time. With such titles as *Short Grass Country* (by Stanley Vestal) and *Blue Ridge Country* (by Jean Thomas), writers extolled the virtues of "old-timers" and "unlettered farm workers," especially those in the South and West. [230] Stories of cowboys in the West, sharecroppers in the South, and lumberjacks in the Upper Midwest gave the impression of American ruggedness and persistence in the face of crisis.

In Pennsylvania, the voice of the folk in mines and mills, farms and forests, came across in popular festivals, stories, and songs—many of them government sponsored—to bolster the public spirit. The Pennsylvania installment of the WPA-sponsored American Guide Series opened with a section on history followed by chapters on ethnic groups and their folkways and mine, mill, and factory. In his foreword, S. K. Stevens underscored the connection of this documentation to economic conditions and cultural re-creation and wrote that the guide "should be a contribution to better citizenship through making Pennsylvanians conscious of their traditions and backgrounds. In these troubled times such a work may well aid in the preservation of those fundamental values so essential to the maintenance of our democracy."[231]

Amid this outburst of regional documentary activities stood Henry Shoe-maker, the genial elder statesman of Pennsylvania folklore, whose major claim was more the "popularization" of Pennsylvania's traditions, not the professionalization.[232] As a devoted Progressive, he had tried to conserve *cultural* and natural resources belonging to the "common citizen for the public good." "You were actually the *pioneer* in Pennsylvania Folklore!" Don Yoder wrote Shoemaker.[233] If Shoemaker earned respect for his Progressive efforts, he lacked a flock of professional followers during the New Deal. New workers in the field stressed the realistic depiction of working-class industrial culture and the persistence of ethnic-regional communities. Through the 1940s the growing university system ascended as a source of cultural authority, and young folklore professors in Pennsylvania's public eye, such as Samuel Bayard, Alfred Shoemaker, and Don Yoder, voiced skepticism about the appropriateness of government involvement in the administration of regional heritage. Henry Shoemaker, however, pushed on for a state program for building romantic regionalism around Pennsylvania's history and folklore and quietly defended his stand in the conflicts over Pennsylvania's cultural re-creation: "I think if I can in any way uncover a portion of the magnificently rich lore of Pennsylvania, preserving it for posterity, I shall feel that the time and effort I put into the study has been greatly repaid me. Indeed there is no greater thing that a man can leave to posterity than the fruit of his life's work, knowing it will be preserved and widely used."[234]

Despite his modesty, Henry Shoemaker was for Cornell University's Harold W. Thompson and many others "Mr. Pennsylvania."[235] Thompson straightforwardly told him: "You are now the leading authority on Pennsylva-nia [and] its lore."[236] Shoemaker earned this public reputation as a state official, a writer, and a spokesman. The state, in his opinion, was a historic and cultural region because of its location between the South and New England. As a person involved in state government on the State Forest Commission, the State Historical Commission, and the State Geographic Board, he had served and promoted the integrity—the distinction, he would say—of the state. He had helped give Pennsylvanians a system of state forests and parks with names and legends rooted in the past and in the landscape. He had marked its historic sites for residents and visitors to appreciate the eventful past in Penn's Woods that carried the special spirit of both Pennsylvania and America. Managing forests and parks for a state, even marking historic sites, is a far cry from conserving its intangible culture. To give it shape, to order its diversity, and to show its purpose and potential—all this appeared to be a mighty, if not questionable, task for state government to take on. Yet that was exactly the challenge, and the controversy, that Henry W. Shoemaker, the state's popularizer, took on as his Progressive "real life's work."

3

"Of Service to the Public"

Is the protection of cultural heritage one of the services government should provide for the public good? Henry W. Shoemaker's unequivocal answer, since early in the Progressive years, had been yes, and in his later years he was preoccupied with expanding government's role in managing and promoting the state's folklore and history. He combined his affections for folklore and history under the heading "heritage" and promoted its use to instill civic duty and regional pride. As New Deal writers' projects for state history and folklore came to an end, Shoemaker heard considerable argument about whether such a service was needed beyond the extraordinary conditions of the 1930s. Although much of the impetus during the 1930s for an expanded government role in cultural preservation had come from the federal government, the development of state programs held the greatest promise for extending the work to the local level.

In Pennsylvania, the State Historical Commission, which Shoemaker had formerly chaired and then served as State Archivist, drew attention as the wing of state government to take on the task. To do so, however, the commission needed reorientation. Pennsylvania's historical commission had been a Progressive endeavor to involve government in preserving state historic resources, and it served as a model for other states.[1] The materials it saved were mostly from the state's diplomatic past—its manuscripts, relics, and sites. "As a state agency," Commission Director Brent Glass reflected, "the early Commission showed particular sensitivity to—if not an attempt at the deification of—significant individuals, as well as events, that advanced the interests of the Commonwealth—military regiments, generals and governors." Public history seemed to be more commemorative than interpretive, more selective rather than representative.[2] "What of the heritage of common people, the mountaineers who shaped independence as much as the events in Philadelphia, for example?" Shoemaker asked pointedly.[3] The legacy contained in the people's folklore held the often unrecorded history of the region, and indeed the nation, he argued. Shouldn't the state collect these traditions of the people for the people?

Heritage and Patriotism for the State

While state-sponsored preservation of folklore was not common in the United States, Shoemaker noted that "such work has gone on for over an hundred years in Europe."[4] As early as 1915, Shoemaker informed his audiences that "in some countries it [folklore] is collected under government patronage. England and Ireland have been devoting much time to it of late; Scotland has always made it a part of her national story. France, Germany, Russia, Japan and India would lose much of the picturesqueness of their literature did it not exist."[5] Shoemaker argued that Pennsylvania, particularly, benefited from such collection because of the need for artistic and literary awakening based on regional heritage in the state. He saw benefits of government-sponsored collection for protecting the environment and promoting American patriotism by instilling cultural loyalty to the state.

In America, folklore research in a few states—notably New York and Wisconsin—received support from state historical associations largely because their directors engaged in folkloristic activities.[6] No official positions existed at the level of State Historian, State Archaeologist, and State Archivist found in Pennsylvania, although in Shoemaker's view the study of folklore as part of a state historical commission's conservation activities "gives the common touch more than any other worthwhile activity, and for that reason brings human beings into closer communion."[7] "I had much folklore material collected and I endeavored to publicize Pennsylvania folk lore," Shoemaker wrote the State Archaeologist, "and I endeavored to be in a place where I could be of service to the public interested in the topic."[8]

Shoemaker got a chance to air his views when Governor Edward Martin, who was deeply interested in the preservation of Pennsylvania history as a way to instill civic pride, took office in 1943. Not usually one for adding government programs, and a critic of the New Deal, Martin nonetheless advocated stronger government promotion of state and local heritage to build "loyalty to those ideals and institutions that have fashioned the American way of life."[9] In 1944 he signed a law requiring high schools to teach Pennsylvania history, and making it mandatory for teachers to take college courses in the subject.[10] Known for instigating a new program to erect roadside historical markers and for developing Independence Hall Park, Governor Martin also proposed creating an independent agency to promote the state's heritage. In 1945 he achieved his goal when legislation merged the Historical Commission, the State Archives, and the State Museum into a more active Pennsylvania Historical and Museum Commission with a conservationist mission. The former State Archaeologist, Donald Cadzow, was named the first Executive Director of the new commission, and Sylvester Stevens became State Historian. Both officials were interested in "conserving" the historical heritage of the state.[11] "As the official agency of the Commonwealth for the conservation of Pennsylvania's historical heritage, [the commission] carries on historical, archaeological, archival, and museum activities," they wrote in 1947.[12]

"Heritage" implied a social purpose beyond documenting Pennsylvania's great citizens and battles, and statements of the new commission had an activist ring. Stevens saw his mission as one of preserving "the story of the life of the people" and using that story to provide the public with "a source of inspiration and enlightenment."[13] Echoing patriotic rhetoric used by Shoemaker earlier, Stevens announced: "By arousing pride in what Pennsylvanians have done in the past for the State, for the Nation, and for mankind, the Commission seeks to build up and encourage sound patriotism and true civic feeling."[14]

The patriotic posturing that took place after World War II can be attributed to the climate of political nationalism of the war years. The federal government urged Americans to stand together as a nation and to define themselves patriotically by the democratic ideas and moral values for which the nation stood against evil fascism. A rhetoric of heritage arose to maintain unity as well as to promote a confident spirit.[15] Against this background, American studies dwelled in unprecedented numbers on the ideas behind the unity of the nation and state and renewed the inquiry into American and regional character and the distinctiveness of American culture.[16] Books on distinguishing legacies of America's frontier heritage, its abundance— material and natural—and its vernacular or folk legacy abounded.[17] Americans hung together—and indeed gained prominence—by this narrative of heritage, out of its expansive and equalizing frontier experience. The narrative suggested that the superior government system of democracy was maintained by states and the nation, which managed the country's natural and material riches for the good of all. The image further celebrated a classless society, born of the equalizing impact of the primeval forest, much as—let's say—Robin Hood of English legend brought down sheriffs in Sherwood Forest.[18] According to this thinking, there was a "basic" American—a rough-hewn, ordinary type who influenced the development of democratic ideas because of this folk spirit.

Carrying on the democratic fight against fascism became the main justification for the Pennsylvania commission's work in the postwar years. In the rhetoric of the period, key phrases—such as "the American way of life," "conserving heritage," and "love of country"—recur. The commission's report for 1945–50 declared:

> We need in our Nation and in our Commonwealth, as never before, a new appreciation and understanding of our heritage. The danger of being deprived of the cherished institutions that constitute the American way of life is very real and imminent. Understanding must rest upon a greater diffusion of popular knowledge about our history and the historic roots of our development and progress. A deeper love of our country and appreciation of our heritage should rest upon the firm bedrock of love of state and community. This naturally translates itself into love of country and understanding of all our national ideals and aspirations as Americans.[19]

The civic duty for "bringing history to the people" was a conservation effort and added to the spiritual strength of the state and nation, the report argued, emphasizing that "conserving the raw materials of history is as necessary to the well-being of the Commonwealth as is the conserving of natural resources to its material strength."[20]

The story the new commission planned to present included the patriotic events of the state and the popular story of everyday people. For the latter, folklore and its image of people cooperating in communities entered the picture the commission wanted to promote. Indeed, several directors of state historical societies (especially in Progressive strongholds of New York, Minnesota, and Wisconsin), representing local and family legacies, took the lead in publishing and promoting public folklore as a means of publicizing the "roots" of a distinctive cultural history.[21] Pennsylvania's State Historian Sylvester Stevens argued that if the commission was to present the story of the state's people in various forms, it would need to actively retrieve oral as well as documentary materials for interpretation. He wrote: "I can testify in person to the serious lack of the folklore materials which are badly needed to enrich our understanding and enliven our appreciation of many aspects of our early Pennsylvania history."[22] For the commission, the folklore coming out of "distinctive regional areas, from the occupational groups that comprise the laboring population, and from the numerous nationalities that have Pennsylvania their new home" was especially significant. Shoemaker's work had demonstrated to the commission that folklore was interesting to the public and that including it in traditional historical work could "invest the written record with an imagination and color that reflect the deep-seated, inner forces which lie close to human conduct."[23]

The primary responsibility of the State Archives was to maintain and preserve the written record, but to accomplish the goals of the new commission the structure of the unit needed to be revised. Richard Norris Williams, director of the Historical Society of Pennsylvania and a new member of the commission, headed a committee to review the State Archives. According to Roy Nichols's history of the Pennsylvania Historical and Museum Commission, "the public records committee recommended that the Archivist, Col. Henry W. Shoemaker, who was a former Chairman of the Commission, become head of a folklore division in the State Historian's realm, and that a professional archivist be retained to take over the increasingly complicated task of assembling and establishing control over the records."[24] Shoemaker thus got an opportunity to expand his folklore activities on an official basis, and the state had an opportunity to professionalize its archives operation.[25]

State Folklorist

Outwardly overjoyed, Shoemaker was privately suspicious of the commission's motives for creating the State Folklorist position. He wrote Marion Patterson of the state legislature, "If, as some of my friends feel, that it is politics, to get rid of me and reorganize the Archives, with a new archivist drawing twice the salary I am receiving, and the present appropriation making the proposed folklore division possible, should not be renewed by the legislature of 1949, and the division discontinued, I would be done."[26] He sought assurances that the new division would be safe from legislative cuts. Given the message that he was not being "kicked upstairs and then out," as he put it, Shoemaker welcomed the transfer. "Folk Lore has been a main interest of my life," he wrote Patterson, and added that the position "seemed like official recognition of my life time's effort to collect and preserve Pennsylvania folk lore, and I would receive a salary in keeping with my long services and general training and experience."[27] "It seems to be a beneficial change all around as folklore has been my life's work," Shoemaker underscored in a letter to Michigan archivist Forest Sweet.[28] The title "State Folklorist" especially appealed to him, because it put the conservation of folklore on a par with history, geology, and other subjects represented at the commission.

So strong was his desire for the position of State Folklorist that the usually stretched Shoemaker wrote, "it put all other activities out of my mind in the form of a career."[29] John Witthoft, formerly the State Museum's curator of anthropology, recalled: "Many people in the state wanted folklore represented on the commission. It was a popular subject after the 1940s, and Shoemaker seemed a logical person to do it. He had many friends across the state and he was closely associated with folklore."[30] Dolores Coffey added: "The position of chief or Director of the Folklore Division was a natural for Colonel Shoemaker. He was President of the Pennsylvania Folklore Society, a friend to many of the big folklore writers and collectors such as George Korson."[31]

On October 2, 1947, the Pennsylvania Historical and Museum Commission unanimously adopted the following resolution:

> RESOLVED, That the Historical and Museum Commission hereby authorizes the creation of the position of *State Folklorist;* and
>
> BE IT FURTHER RESOLVED, that *Henry W. Shoemaker,* Senior Archivist, be transferred from the Public Record Division (Archives) to the New Division of Folklore.

Receiving front-page attention from Pennsylvania newspapers, Henry Shoemaker officially began his tenure as America's first State Folklorist in March 1948. After the commission approved the appointment, Shoemaker planned what he would be doing in the position. Most of what he listed revolved around organizing his contributions for public consumption of the storied heritage of the state. "For the first several months I would dictate my notes of years, to be put on cards—legends, ballads, proverbs, etc.—and when that is done make a field trip weekly to collect in regions previously unvisited."[32] He also intended to send out weekly press releases on "the volume of Pennsylvania folklore" and to establish a folklore archives for the state. The new year passed as Cadzow sought to locate Shoemaker in prime office space in the State Museum.

Shoemaker celebrated his sixty-eighth birthday in February 1948 with questions about the restructuring of the State Archives and Historical and Museum Commission hanging about him. Cadzow wrote him on March 5 that because a successor had already been named to the "Public Records Division," "it would be advisable for you to assume your duties as Chief of the Folklore Division of the Commission just as soon as possible."[33] His worry was that "this appointment may give people the wrong idea regarding your status." Cadzow did not want to give the impression that Shoemaker was being forced out of the archives. Shoemaker had delayed the move to the Folklore Division until a deputy could be hired. His goal was to organize the division and upon retirement, turn over the operation to a young deputy. Shoemaker believed it would make sense to bring in someone with expertise in Pennsylvania-German to give coverage that he himself could not provide.[34] The Executive Director approved the deputy position and the assignment of a secretary to the new division. Don Yoder, a freshly minted Ph.D. from the University of Chicago who was at the Union Theological Seminary in New York, offered his services and became Shoemaker's choice.[35] "If we could secure Dr. Yoder," Shoemaker wrote the Executive Director, "he would be the best understudy I have in the State, and if anything happened to me, could step right into my shoes, is a coming man. . . . I would be replaceable after a bit of training to a deputy."[36] Shoemaker wrote Yoder on January 29, 1948, "I know that with your fine training and background you would be a tower of strength to the proposed folklore division," adding, "I know the State needs you, and it will be a pleasure to see you on duty in Harrisburg." But a few days later, Yoder replied that he had accepted a teaching post at Muhlenberg College.[37] After four months of delays after the commission approved the State Folklorist position, Shoemaker was anxious to start up the new division, and once prime office space became available in the State Museum, he agreed to begin his tenure as the nation's first official State Folklorist, without the deputy for the moment.[38]

On March 11, 1948, the commission announced Shoemaker's historic appointment, and the next day the *Harrisburg Patriot* featured on its front-page the news that went out across the state's news wires: "Archivist Gets Folklore Post." "It is an interesting assignment," Shoemaker told the newspaper, for "Pennsylvania has the richest folklore heritage of any state in the union." Cadzow's explanation was that "the Commission decided a fuller use should be made of Colonel Shoemaker's abilities as a folklorist, and the new division was created to give full scope to his talents in this field."[39] In his first day on the job, Shoemaker wrote a friend: "I am taking over a new department in the State Historical Commission, to collect and compile the Pennsylvania Folklore, and I think it is going to be interesting work with considerable time out-of-doors."[40] In addition to continuing his conservationist ends, Shoemaker also espoused social objectives for the position. Encouraging one correspondent to record her great-grandmother's tales, Shoemaker editorialized: "A knowledge of peoples, races, climates and languages provides one with a broad understanding, so much so that anywhere one goes he finds himself upon common ground. Where there is knowledge there is an understanding and where there is understanding there is no prejudice—which is certainly a desirable feature to consider."[41]

The State Folklorist position was essentially created by and for Shoemaker, but Shoemaker indicated that he saw the potential for such positions elsewhere. He planned, he wrote Cadzow, to "correspond with all the American folklore societies" to encourage them to lobby for the State Folklorist positions.[42] "It is amazing how folklore has attracted people all over the country," he observed, and closed on a spiritual note: "It does seem as if, somehow, it is the message for which they have been waiting."[43]

The *Journal of American Folklore* carried an announcement of the position in its fourth issue of 1948, and at the 1949 American Folklore Society meeting in Washington, D.C., Shoemaker's secretary, Victoria Smallzel, delivered a report on the groundbreaking state folklore program.[44] Shoemaker received the warmest response from officers of the New York Folklore Society. Louis C. Jones, editor of *New York Folklore Quarterly* and director of the New York State Historical Association, carried news of the position, and Shoemaker wrote him personally to thank him for acknowledging "the fact that our State of Pennsylvania was the first to have a State Folklorist." Shoemaker excitedly went on to note other developments in the state: "It is not only the one to have the first State Folklorist, but it is also the first to have a chair in folklore in a university, at Franklin and Marshall College; also the Wyomissing Institute of Fine Arts, near Reading, has established a Division of Folklore."[45] Indeed, Shoemaker was witness to a sudden outpouring of folkloristic activities. "It looks as if Pennsylvania folklore," he wrote Arthur D. Graeff, "after a long time in getting started, has taken on real life and there seems to be no end to it and its ramifications and details, which take in every aspect of our daily life."[46]

The "real life" for folklore activities after World War II in Pennsylvania had a strong public, and patriotic, dimension. In 1948, State Historian S. K. Stevens devoted the Pennsylvania Federation of Historical Societies meeting to discussing the role of folklore in the public history movement with Shoemaker as chair of the sessions. "What I am anxious to do," Stevens wrote to Shoemaker, "is to use this as an opportunity to energize the whole movement for preserving Pennsylvania folklore and folk music."[47] As State Folklorist, Shoemaker promised to make collections of the new division "available to the public along the widest front possible."[48] The importance of the term "public" to the civic conception of the position emerged again in the commission's report for 1950. Conceiving of the commission as "an integral, active unit of State Government," Stevens, Cadzow, and Shoemaker emphasized that folklore and history are the mirrors "of our national heritage, and the preservation of that inheritance is the first duty of citizenship."[49] Shoemaker also told a radio audience in 1948 that the study of folklore in the service of history "is a patriotic duty that takes one into all picturesque nooks and corners of our beautiful Commonwealth and enriches the life of the seeker."[50] This patriotic message had been attached to other public presentations of folklore and history in the state. Explaining the Pennsylvania Folk Festival of the 1930s directed by George Korson at Bucknell University, the college president hoped the festival would "interpret our great Commonwealth to us in a manner which will stir within us an increased appreciation of Pennsylvania, its people, and its contribution to civilized life on the Continent. . . . A clear view of it as a whole, as presented by the various phases of the program, should increase our patriotism and pride in Pennsylvania."[51]

Friends and Foes in Pennsylvania Folklore

The director of the Pennsylvania Folk Festival, George Korson (1899–1967) grew in prominence for his work in folklore within the state, and was greatly influenced by Shoemaker. Korson, however, had a more pluralistic conception of folklore than Shoemaker, and sought living rather than historic traditions. He compiled books with field-recorded texts of Pennsylvania miners' lore and envisioned a volume that would promote the lore of many Pennsylvania occupational and "racial" groups. This milestone set of essays in *Pennsylvania Songs and Legends* (1949) was planned as a "practical book, an authoritative book, an entertaining book" relating to efforts to use folklore's revelation of a society's pluralistic roots to build a better future. The first paragraph sounded a call for cultural re-creation: "Within her [Pennsylvania's] borders there is the memory of everything that America has been and the knowledge of what it may become. From the memory of her people great cultural wealth in the form of folklore may be recovered, just as fabulous material wealth has been extracted from her fertile soil and underlying minerals." Korson wrapped up his introduction by asserting: "Our primary appeal is to the reader who welcomes a chance to increase his knowledge of America's past to the end that he may form an intelligent understanding of our country's growth."[52] Chapters covered ethnic, regional, and occupational traditions. The British, Indian, and German inheritance received separate chapters, and wagoners, canallers, railroaders, lumberjacks, coal miners, and oilmen were given their due. Shoemaker contributed a chapter titled "Central Pennsylvania Legends" and commended the volume, for "the field is yet untilled to any great extent and up and coming folklorists need something good and substantial for the starting."[53]

In his official capacity as State Folklorist, Shoemaker arranged a special meeting of the Pennsylvania Folklore Society in Harrisburg to present the contributors in Korson's volume with commendations from the governor. He quoted Louis C. Jones's published comment: "It is fitting that the first state to have an official State Folklorist (Colonel Shoemaker) should produce this handsome, valuable collection."[54] Yet Shoemaker's contribution to the volume seemed out of place. It merely related legends in rambling fashion, rather than saying anything about them. Meanwhile, the younger folklorists, Samuel Bayard and George Korson, were subtly exploring the "functional view of folklore," the "relation between the folk and the lore," and the ways that lore "adjusts itself to changing times and new conditions."[55] While recognizing the great impact of the volume and of Korson's message, folklorist Angus Gillespie called Shoemaker's chapter the "weakest" in the book and cited Korson's misgivings about including it.[56] Korson had rejected Shoemaker's first submission, in which he offered advice on collecting folklore and gave examples from historical legendry. He worried that Shoemaker's use of William Penn narratives would be "severely criticized by both historians and folklorists if we were to publish these legends" and feared that "the line between history and folklore is too finely drawn in these stories of Governor Penn."[57] To be sure, Shoemaker did not draw so fine a line, and he responded that he "would hate not to be represented in your forthcoming anthology as having been the beginner of the collecting of Pennsylvania folklore, it would seem odd to be only represented by my disciples.[58] Korson ended up constructing Shoemaker's chapter from previously published material and notes sent to him in correspondence.[59]

Despite Korson's difficulties with Shoemaker's contribution, the chapter received the most popular response and it was the one chosen by the *Philadelphia Inquirer* for its Sunday supplement on August 28, 1949. Gimbel's department store featured the book in its annual Pennsylvania Week promotion. Each display window of the store featured a chapter of the book. Its lasting contribution was to recognize folkloric responses to new industrial and urban conditions in chapters on songs of an industrial city and traditions of coal miners. As the review in the *New York Times* announced, "The authors have a vital and dynamic conception of folklore. To them it is not primarily antiquarian but a process continuously operative, or ever-renewed adaptations to the forms and pressures of a changing environment."[60] In his speeches and columns, however, Shoemaker still showed much of an antiquarian bent and seemed tainted in 1950 by Professor Richard Dorson's condemnation of literary retellings of folklore as "fakelore."[61]

Korson, who was gaining favor in the national scholarly folklore scene (he was elected a fellow of the American Folklore Society and awarded a Guggenheim Fellowship), remained loyal to Shoemaker and encouraged him. While Korson sensed that Shoemaker's heyday for contributions to folklore studies was well past, he wrote Shoemaker in early 1954: "Your vast collection, in manuscript and published books and pamphlets, constitutes a solid foundation upon which to build a Pennsylvania archive of folklore.

Needless to say, it is an enduring monument to your long service to our state as a distinguished folklorist. These should inspire you to continue with your folklore career as long as you can."[62] Like Shoemaker, Korson had started out as a journalist, and he defended the elder Shoemaker in an article titled "Henry W. Shoemaker: Folklorist" (1957). "Priority is not his only claim to distinction," he wrote, "for he has accomplished a prodigious amount of work in the field. . . . Throughout Shoemaker's writings deep sympathy is expressed for the common people—the folk—who were his informants. In this feeling, the Pennsylvanian heeds the advice of the noted English folklorist, Joseph Jacobs, who wrote, 'In our study of folklore, we should pay attention not alone to the Lore but also to the Folk.' "[63]

Alfred L. Shoemaker, another rising star in Pennsylvania folklore circles, was less kind to his namesake. A native Pennsylvania-German, the brilliant yet cantankerous Alfred had earned a Ph.D. in German and had impressive credentials in folklore studies in Europe as well as the United States. In 1948 he arrived at Franklin and Marshall College in Lancaster, Pennsylvania, as the country's first professor of "American folklore," and he subsequently established both the nation's first Department of Folklore and the Pennsylvania Dutch Folklore Center. While he sought a public role for folklore through publications and festivals sponsored by the center, he adhered to staunchly academic, ethnological principles. He insisted on verbatim texts compiled for comparative purposes in archives, and he carefully classified and annotated his collections. He meticulously sought out "cultural source areas" in Europe for Pennsylvania customs and systematically collected folk traditions through questionnaires and field interview, seeking a comprehensive view of the "total folk culture" including authentic material and social, as well as oral, tradition.[64]

The relationship between Alfred and Henry was cordial at first. Henry supported Alfred's ideas of setting up archives and fieldwork teams along the lines of European folklife centers at the Pennsylvania Historical and Museum Commission, but a lack of funds prevented their implementation. Referring to the relationship between the Folklore Division and the Folklore Center, Henry wrote Alfred: "I only wish that we could cooperate more closely, since we are both starting our new activities simultaneously."[65] But in keeping with the rise of an American folkloristic discipline and the academy as cultural authority during the 1950s, Alfred publicly criticized literary distortions and political uses of folklore and named the State Folklorist's work as a prime example.[66] Dolores Coffey, who served in the commission's Executive Director's office, recalled: "It was a terrible blow to him when Alfred Shoemaker and Don Yoder began to criticize his work, and even more so when the criticism was published in the press. . . . I do know the Commission did not feel it could come to the Colonel's defense which might have been another blow. It was very apparent that this type of criticism had never happened to the Colonel as he was a very gentle person."[67]

Alfred became annoyed at Henry's invitations to writers to elaborate on folklore, and he resisted associations Henry made between the Folklore Society and storytelling leagues and poetry societies. The rift grew when Alfred, who promoted an ethnological folklife approach, publicly ridiculed the superficiality and romanticism of Henry's literary folklore collections. Alfred accordingly announced at one Pennsylvania Folklore Society meeting that to make the distinction between the shallowness of Henry's folklore and the depth of folklife research, "we will drop the term folk lore and substitute 'folk life' and 'folk culture.' "[68] Brandishing his expertise as an experienced publisher and journalist, Henry meanwhile made unflattering remarks about the appearance and contents of Alfred's *Pennsylvania Dutchman* (later replaced by *Pennsylvania Folklife*), which boasted "a larger circulation than all the folklore periodicals in the U.S. lumped together."[69] "As to my personal comments on the 'Dutchman,' " Henry wrote Alfred, "I realized that the Pennsylvania Dutch, a far more valuable culture than New England, deserved a more fitting mouthpiece, on good paper, well illustrated, and ploughing out into new fields rather than repeating the old stories we have known all our lives."[70] This statement reveals Henry Shoemaker's philosophical differences between his literary view of folklore and Alfred's ethnological perspective. Alfred systematically gathered objective data—mostly material and social, such as barns, customs, foods, and crafts—that could be quantified and analyzed. For Alfred, the goal was to record the ordinary and the characteristic lifeways of traditional communities, in their totality, and he demonstrated this goal in the special attention he paid to the "Dutch Country" within America.[71] In Alfred's view, America had a diverse social landscape that underscored the persistence of ethnic-religious cultures, such as the Pennsylvania-Germans. Henry, on the other side, wanted to record lore to inspire the public with imaginative local narratives that recover America as a nation.

Henry Shoemaker's Pennsylvania Folklore Society was an extension of its president. In its publications and meetings, and its support for booster festivals, the Society perpetuated his romantic regionalism. Alfred launched a proposal to reorganize the Society to take it in an ethnological direction. To go along with this direction, which was needed for an accurate and comprehensive survey of Pennsylvania's distinct communities, Alfred called for the professionalization of the Society, placing academics in charge of publications and activities. He argued that the membership was languishing and serving little scholarly purpose under Henry's leadership. Henry's organization was loose, to be sure, but he adhered to its popular principles and fought back. Citing the Society's long-neglected constitution, Henry mobilized supporters at a meeting and defeated Alfred's proposal. "As to Alfred L. Shoemaker," Henry wrote a representative from the American Folklore Society, "his part in my life has not been a pleasant one as with a group of his friends he tried to take possession of the Pennsylvania Folklore Society of which I have been President since 1930. . . . In his way he is doing fine work among the Pennsylvania Dutch but his Folklore and ours do not coincide."[72]

Moritz Jagendorf, who was prominent in the New York Folklore Society and active in popularizing folklore there, may have fueled the fires between the two Shoemakers when he wrote his friend Henry: "I heard all about the argument with Shoemaker and of all the damnable people he is the very worst. I heard how insulting he was and my only regret is that I was not present to tell him what I think of him. He is not fit to be amongst men and if ever you want to see a real Nazi just listen to him."[73] Some jealousy of Alfred's success might have been at play, for Jagendorf continues: "I am very anxious to help all I can, if for no other reason than to show Dr. Shoemaker that we can do something not as flamboyant as he can, but surely as valuable, if not more so." Years later, the feud continued. In 1955, Jagendorf lamented: "It is a tragedy indeed that envy and in a large measure greed and lust for power can do so much harm to your work. But, the man is vicious and I said long ago that he was a typical Nazi-minded human being. He can not be trusted to the extent of the eye of a needle."[74] This followed an earlier plaint that Alfred looked on the organization "with disdain and dislike and nothing would make him happier than to see it go out of existence." "Unless your organization keeps on being active," he continued, "It will give him the chance for which he is looking and I would do everything in the world to prevent this. It is for that reason that it is so important for you to have at least one or two meetings a year. That would take all the ammunition from him and he could not say that here is a dead organization which is being supported for no reason at all."[75]

Alfred Shoemaker's bid for control of the Pennsylvania Folklore Society failed, so together with Don Yoder and J. William Frey he formed the Pennsylvania Folklife Society to eclipse the folklore society and achieve his goals of scholarly folklife studies.[76] In 1952 he began folk-culture seminars during the summer so that "serious students of American folk-life may at last study this folk-culture on an academic plane."[77] In the same year, he claimed that his Kutztown Festival, with its "authentic" performers identified through field research, "has grown, in point of scope and attendance, into the greatest folk-cultural event in the nation."[78] Especially after Alfred Shoemaker left Franklin and Marshall in 1956 to devote himself full-time to the Pennsylvania Folklife Society (until 1963), he took on many of the roles of a state folklorist—promoting festivals, maintaining archives, writing cultural guides to the "Dutch country," and issuing publications devoted to Pennsylvania.

The War Between Popularizers and Professionals

At the time, the feud between Alfred and Henry Shoemaker was reminiscent of a national one shaking the foundations of the American Folklore Society. Outspoken Richard Dorson (1916–81), who taught folklore at Michigan State University and later chaired the Ph.D.-granting Folklore Institute at Indiana University, unleashed a firestorm by discouraging figures he called "popularizers" and "amateurs" from assuming leadership positions in the American Folklore Society.[79] He especially pointed an accusing finger at popularizing activity in New York and Pennsylvania. Representing the academic "purists" calling for professionalization of the Society, Dorson railed against the secretary-treasurer of the American Folklore Society, MacEdward Leach (1896–1967) of the University of Pennsylvania, for defending the "popularizers" from New York, such as Benjamin Botkin (1901–75), Harold Thompson (1891–1964), and Moritz Jagendorf (1888–1981).[80] Dorson wanted to discredit them and preserve the American Folklore Society as a scholarly society.

In Dorson's eyes, popularizers undermined the serious study of folklore, destroyed the integrity of authentic traditions, misrepresented folklore's meaning, and endangered the academic growth of a folkloristic discipline. Dorson never attacked Henry Shoemaker personally, although in promoting his own "Theory for American Folklore" he named Shoemaker as one of the problematic "regional collectors" who "turns into a parochial folklorist, ploughing the same field endlessly, collecting simply to collect."[81] To be sure, Dorson relied on field-collecting directly from the lips of storytellers, but unlike most popularizers, he presented undoctored texts characteristic of certain traditions in an ethnic or regional group. Dorson insisted on high standards of oral transmission for texts to qualify as authentic folklore. To Dorson, the texts were "the basic source, and pure stream, the inviolable document of oral tradition."[82] Literary tampering with the folklorist's texts was akin to desecrating the historian's manuscripts. While Leach thought that the popularizers did a service by keeping folklore interests before a public hungry for colorful regional literature, Dorson damned their efforts as "fakelore."[83] To Dorson, regional folklore needed to be broadly collated and analyzed in terms of the sweep of American history, not amassed as political propaganda or a cabinet of curiosities. Although he praised Leach's scholarship, Dorson criticized his leadership, especially since he represented such a distinguished institution as the University of Pennsylvania.

Dorson expressed his views against the background of rising academic authority in American fields of knowledge generally after World War II and a widening of specialized graduate and professional education. Since the end of the war, universities had grown dramatically, as veterans crammed into college classrooms to take advantage of educational benefits. State universities especially experienced growing pains and responded by increasing public access to the campuses and diversifying the curriculum with American cultural studies, among other subjects closer to home. American studies, for example, were recent additions that represented a turn away from the classical curriculum. A growing number of professors in English and history departments, many of them reflecting the rise of immigrant and working-class backgrounds in the colleges, took up cultural interests such as regional-ethnic studies and folklore.[84] When Dorson received his Ph.D. from Harvard in 1943, he was one of the first Americans to receive a doctorate in American Civilization. Leach was almost twenty years Dorson's senior and had earlier come to folklore through his work in medieval literature.[85]

Henry Shoemaker had known Leach since the 1920s, when he enlisted his aid for the Pennsylvania Historical Commission's state archaeological surveys. "I will do whatever I can to help the Susquehanna Survey," Leach wrote Shoemaker, adding that he shared Shoemaker's concern for recovering hidden traditions along the waterway. "I have done some field work on the lower Susquehanna from Peach Bottom to the mainland opposite Garrett's Island," he said.[86] Henry Shoemaker and the Pennsylvania Folklore Society maintained close ties with the embattled Leach and the New York folklorists through the 1950s. In 1952, Korson and other supporters pushed through Shoemaker's election to the Executive Council of the American Folklore Society and reelected him in 1956.[87] "I appreciate your kind interest in my ambitions," Shoemaker wrote Moritz Jagendorf, "and hope that through Dr. Leach and Dr. [Francis Lee] Utley, I will be represented on the board of Directors of the American Folklore Society in a field where I have been so active for so many years."[88] "In electing you," George Korson wrote Shoemaker, "the Society honors itself in view of your great contributions to the field of American folklore."[89] Leach called on Shoemaker to help recruit members for the Society, and Shoemaker agreed, citing the Society's "good work" for public appreciation of folklore.[90]

Shoemaker expressed special gratitude to B. A. Botkin for "recognizing my folklore researches." Botkin had reprinted two legends from Shoemaker's Pennsylvania Folklore Society publications in the best-seller *Treasury of American Folklore* (1944).[91] In addition, Botkin used Shoemaker's notes on informants to authenticate the stories. "It was a great lift not only for myself but for Pennsylvania folklore in general," he wrote Botkin, "as we have not many active folklorists in this great Commonwealth which is so rich of non-collected legendary lore."[92] But Dorson trashed the book for its "appeal to superficial American nationalism" and the way it "brought within its covers a number of writers who regarded the materials of folklore as subjects for romantic and sentimental treatments."[93]

Dorson expanded his assault to Shoemaker's friend Moritz Jagendorf, an officer of both the New York and Pennsylvania folklore societies, who Dorson called the "shrillest spokesman" for the popularizers.[94] In 1949, Jagendorf published *Upstate Downstate: Folk Stories of the Middle Atlantic States* with a foreword by Henry Shoemaker that labeled the book "among the best in American Folklore." Jagendorf had told Shoemaker that with his publications of the "American folk story"—rewritten legends—he was "following in [his] footsteps."[95] Dorson, however, heatedly charged that Jagendorf's work was "a literary product passed off as folklore, or what I have called fakelore."[96] Referring to Dorson, Jagendorf wrote Shoemaker: "I have just returned from a national folklore meeting and I saw a display there of meanness and viciousness which is incredible and unbelievable amongst men of education. . . . I hope sincerely you are thinking of having a folklore meeting and I will help you to do all the arranging and preparations. That will be a direct slap in the face to that fellow who is doing all these ugly things."[97]

With Dorson trying to disgrace the "popularizers" as undesirable "amateurs," Moritz Jagendorf felt compelled to write Shoemaker to reassure him: "You are entirely wrong when you say that you will have to wait fifty years to have your work appreciated. Your work is appreciated today—right now by folklorists who feel that folklore is—FOR FOLK EVEN AS IT IS FOR SCHOLARS. There has grown up unfortunately a small group of men amongst folklore students who hold that folklore is for study only. A man who bears the same name as you and another one Richard Dorson and a few more of that kind are making a great deal of noise about it but I assure you that the majority of those who are interested and work in the field of folklore feel exactly the same way as I do."[98] Shoemaker replied: "I agree with you that there is a small group of men who say that folklore is for study only. I would not rather do it any other way than I have and the thrill of the stories I collected has fully compensated me all through my life. I would not want to do it any other method even though this group is trying to crowd out folklore tales and replace it with technical statistics. I hope that our form of folklore will be in the end victorious but it will at least show the pleasure it gives."[99]

Shoemaker actually had kind words for Dorson's *Bloodstoppers and Bear-walkers* (1952), and he might have been tweaking Dorson a bit by comparing it with his own work. I "have read it with intense interest," he told Dorson, "especially the part about the werewolf in Canada about which I have so much in the old tales of Pennsylvania," and went on to say: "While I have been collecting and publishing folklore all my life, I never realized the amount that can be concentrated in one volume such as yours, and I congratulate you on giving such a vivid picture of the North. I know that it will be very popular with the members of the Pennsylvania Folklore Society to whose attention I will call it at the next meeting. . . . There is still as much folklore in Pennsylvania to be collected now as there was when I was a boy 40 years ago and like in your case it is a gift which enables one to collect it."[100] Contrary to Shoemaker's conception of "State Folklorist," Dorson believed that collection and analysis properly belonged in the academy, carried out by students trained in a separate discipline of folklore, and he argued against expanding public folklore positions like Shoemaker's.[101] Dorson's barrage helped secure the American Folklore Society as a scholarly society for professionals. Although he could not stop the spread of state folklore programs during the 1970s, he continued to insist on academic training for folklorists working for government and public agencies.

Hopes and Frustrations at the Commission

As the first official State Folklorist, Shoemaker was given great latitude by the Executive Director of the Pennsylvania Historical and Museum Commission to define his responsibilities. His planning for the position began with a two-year plan in which he envisioned supervising three branches to the division: "collection, compilation, publicity." He planned, further, for four "departments" engaging in fieldwork to ensure that the division would have statewide coverage:

> As there are four folk cultures in Pennsylvania, Western, Northern, Southern, and Eastern, four departments, with a collector assigned to each county, as the ultimate aim, equipped with typewriter, recording machine, to range these localities all the year round, gathering up ballads, legends, customs, proverbs, old words, but in next two years if the Division could have four, or even two collectors in the field, one for each locality, all provided with a knowledge of Pennsylvania Dutch, in which form most of the Folklore exists, a beginning could be made. In the home office these collectors would [turn] in their findings monthly, either in shorthand notes or in typed form, where four office assistants would separate as to topics, and file in the most available manner for public use. There should be

a secretary stenographer for each of these helpers, a secretary stenographer for the chief, a secretary stenographer for his assistant, and a messenger. The chief and his assistant would act as general program directors, interview callers, give out interviews, make addresses, write articles, and go out in the field as advisors to the searchers, or on personal quests which seemed [expedient] for them to run down. Once a year the Division should publish an index by topics and localities of all materials collected, under the imprint of the Historical and Museum Commission. For the next two years in order to collect before it is too late, the ranks of old people, for example the old canal boatmen, raftmen, log drivers, charcoal furnace hands, wagoners are thinning, and we know hardly a civil war veteran survives. It would seem essential to have at least two workers in the field, their sustenance, returning to their homes Friday afternoons until Monday A.M., with automobiles etc. provided, by State and (serviced, equipped with typing machines, recorders, etc.) Four compilers in the home office with Secretary stenographers, machines, etc. The Chief with Secretary stenographer, his assistant similarly equipped, and a messenger. This would mean a staff of fifteen including the chief and same [space] as was Division of Archives in 1912. When they were doing a good piece of work, but gradually cut down to four, including the Archives, when became only partly effective. It would seem that the Chief of Folklore should receive $5,000, as he gives the Division the experience of a life time, an energy and enthusiasm which only comes to one who began the work fifty years ago and knows every nook and corner of Pennsylvania, its people, history and folklore, to give him less discourages, especially after his years of research.

The four men in the field should receive $200 each monthly, and keep of selves, car, stationery. The office compilers $40 weekly, the six stationery stenographers, at the current rate of such employment, the messenger on the same basis. The assistant should be paid $3500, in which event would not have lost Prof. Don Yoder, and might still secure a great man like Prof. Sam Bayard. If it should be this level could not be reached, 1949–1951, I would feel that two field men the most important the compilers in the Harrisburg office cut to two, and four secretary stenographers instead of six and keep the messenger. The recapitulation of the reduced force would be, 2 field men, 2 cars, 2 recording machines, 2 office compilers, 4 secretary stenographers, 4 machines, 1 messenger, or 11 in staff. The work would lapse and lag on less. Why not get it off to a good start, or abandon it, single-handed your chief has done his best, but it is like putting him to count the grains of the sands of the ocean. Cutting down from four men in field to two, four office helpers to two, secretary-stenographers to two, I feel some progress could be made yet far out of line to my look ahead of March 13, 1948, yet the growth can only come by the size of staff in the field.[102]

After a year in the job, Henry Shoemaker reported feeling most frustrated by the lack of staff. It forced him, he said, to follow a "conservative path." He outlined a "two fold purpose" for the position: "Not only does it preserve the history of a people according to law, geography and economics, but it preserves the manners, customs, the heart and soul of a people as well."[103] "My instructions from Dr. Cadzow," he continued, "were to make the folklore division a success, and a permanent branch of the Historical and Museum Commission. I am doing this as best I can with one secretary, but folklore expands only with the number of workers put on it, and I have been unable to get more." The Folklore Division was not a high priority for the commission, which was devoted to historical rather than cultural preservation, and there was even speculation that it had been created partly to get the politically connected Shoemaker out of the way of the new professionals in the archives and history divisions.[104]

During his tenure as State Folklorist, Henry Shoemaker prepared monthly reports to the Executive Director which provide a good record of what he accomplished. According to the reports, he went on an average of two to four collecting trips a month, mostly to areas he had not covered during his peak years of collecting before 1930. In addition, he wrote a weekly release on folklore for *Capitol News,* which was distributed to the state's newspapers. He delivered between two and four addresses a month, attended a similar number of organizational meetings, and appeared frequently on radio and television shows. He made appearances at ceremonies and other official functions, including dedications of historical markers, openings of exhibits, and events at inaugurations and Pennsylvania Farm Shows. He answered between 70 and 130 letters a month and received a similar number of visitors at his office. He prepared scrapbooks and card indexes on different topics with clippings, mostly Shoemaker's, on folklore. He distributed mimeographed folklore collections for distribution to members of the Pennsylvania Folklore Society and interested parties.[105] He organized branches of the Pennsylvania Folklore Society, with the goal of placing a branch in every county of the state, "under competent chairmen, who will collect and send to the Folklore Division at Harrisburg, all material collected in their localities."[106] And by 1949 he claimed "a hundred enthusiastic volunteer workers in all the counties throughout the state" who contributed material to the division.[107] To reach these far-flung volunteers, he proposed a number of regional meetings of the Pennsylvania Folklore Society to replace the annual meeting in Harrisburg, and he spoke frequently on "county" folklore, encouraging local historical and folklore societies to collect it.[108] He hoped to compile these results into folklore archives and build a library of folkloristic books. As the states contributed to the nation, so he had in mind encouraging a relationship of counties to the state Common-wealth tradition.

Shoemaker needed help to realize his ambitious plans. During one brief interval, he had paid fieldwork help from Victoria Smallzel, and on occasion he benefited from extra secretarial or archival assistance, but for the most part he worked alone with a secretary. This is the way he described his day:

> I usually arrive at 8:00 A.M. and put out the things that I am planning to work with during the day. At 8:30 the mail begins to arrive, and by 9:00 I am ready to dictate answers to secretary-stenographer who arrives around 8:30. By 11 o'clock I am generally through the mail and have many of the letters answered. Around 11 my secretary goes for my light lunch and often gets her own. On other days, she goes out from 12 to 1 o'clock. Generally visitors do not come in until about 1, and they appear off and on for the rest of the day, some on appointment, others happen in. I have many phone calls, generally asking for information from nine until four thirty. In my spare moments I work on articles for Capitol News, and folk tales from my notes, being typed and filed. Or I work up my notes so as to make stories from them ready for typing. I endeavor to clear my days work by "going home time," and often succeed at this. The scope of folklore is the time put on it. I do about all that is possible with one helper.[109]

Much of his time, especially after the first few years, was spent writing down his memories of stories and beliefs he had not published. With a journalistic bent, he packaged them as brief pamphlets, with titles such as "Pennsylvania Mountain Snakelore" (1951), "Two Tales from the Folklore of the Clinton-Clearfield Border in North Central Pennsylvania" (1951), "Mrs. Ida Doyle Remembers (She vividly recalls the days of the mighty Pennsylvania pineries, rafting, log driving and canals, when Indians, wolves, panthers, wild pigeons and shad abounded all not so very many years ago)" (1952), and "Katie Eisenberger's Spook Stories" (1952). These differed from the "stories" he published forty years earlier in that the State Folklorist productions were more like field reports giving source names and dates. Perhaps in answer to folkloristic criticisms, he circulated his typescripts with archival titles, such as "Two Tales from the Folklore of the Clinton-

Clearfield Border in North Central Pennsylvania, Compiled and Transmitted, 1923, by Miss Helen McGonigal to Henry W. Shoemaker" (1951). Toward the end of his tenure, the pamphlets had less and less cohesion, as he prepared sloppy reports of "Some Currently Collected Bits of Folklore" (1953) and "Ghosts at Random, Bits of the Supernatural Jotted Down From Time to Time, But Never Previously Made Use Of" (1953). One Harrisburg newspaper account of his activity added: "The Colonel gets about a dozen requests for information on historical matters daily and about an equal number of criticisms of things he has written."[110]

Answering criticisms and queries took more time in his job as the years passed. Introduced to a Juniata College audience in 1954, Shoemaker heard the speaker say, "Mr. Shoemaker has a lot of controversies to settle including many of his own folklore tales." In his speech, Shoemaker defended himself as the state official to turn to for innumerable questions the public has about the "facts" of local history and tradition neglected in the universities. He used the tone of a cultural authority for the state when he answered: "I do the best I can to answer the queries so as to set any controversy right without contradicting any local legends. The criticisms I accept philosophically as the lot of an historian."[111]

Early in television's development, Shoemaker, ever the communicator, saw great potential in using the media to spread interest in folklore and gain research outlets. He wrote Cadzow:

> I believe that television would be an ideal means for bringing the facts of Folklore to the public's attention and thereby getting more help from outsiders who know where some of the dying Folklore can be found. I have spoken on radio a number of times and on television two or three times and from the number of letters and phone calls I receive after these talks it seems to me that the public is interested and would be more so if they heard of it oftener. I would think that a publication of a quarterly or even a monthly slip, telling of the progress of the Division would be also helpful in publicizing the work. Probably the best stroke we made was connecting ourselves with Capitol News as these stories go to many newspapers every week and I get very interesting responses from people who know stories that I have not previously heard. As I said before, I feel that the success of this Division is largely in the hands of the Folklorist, whose knowledge and enthusiasm feed the mill and keep up a constant public interest.[112]

Experienced in column-writing, Shoemaker made the most of the weekly news releases to publicize, and popularize, Pennsylvania folklore. Many newspapers in the state were only too glad to pick up the releases carrying the well-known name of Henry Shoemaker, who added lively reading to their pages.

In addition to identifying his affiliation with the folklore division, Shoemaker also promoted the Pennsylvania Folklore Society. While giving public notice about state folklore work, the releases also made many academic folklorists and historians cringe because of the watered-down versions of collections peddled to the public. Responding to the popularity of "Paul Bunyan" as a journalistically developed (or invented) frontier folk hero, Shoemaker quickly offered up a real-life Pennsylvania version in "Cherry Tree Joe McCreery": "his heroic deeds from Cherry Tree to Williamsport being sung in every lumber camp and mountain cabin."[113] The release continued: "His super-human breaking of the log jam at Buttermilk Falls, his calling John L. Sullivan's bluff at a hotel in Renovo, his carrying a raft, single handed, off Geary's Rocks, and floating it, are only a few of his reported exploits. Born on Muncy Creek in 1805, he followed the river for sixty years, every year a memorable one, dying in 1895 at the age of ninety, in the midst of the great river saga."[114] Then there was Peter Grove, "among Pennsylvania's super-men and legendary figures of folklore," who swung a tree limb three hundred and fifty feet to escape the clutches of hostile Indians.[115] Scrambling to come up with fresh material each week, Shoemaker frequently paraphrased the collection of others, as he did in his elaboration of Arthur Graeff's research into the Pennsylvania-German legend of recluse Mountain Mary.[116] Shoemaker's releases especially gained notice when he issued timely columns on the origins and customs of such holidays as Halloween and Christmas. He also issued releases with flashy headlines commemorating anniversaries, especially for the state's ethnic groups. For example, he used the occasion of the 300th anniversary of Jewish settlement in Pennsylvania to briefly trace other "lost colonies" in Pennsylvania, those of Acadians and Waldensians.[117]

Shoemaker expanded on his vision for the State Folklorist position in proposals to the Jansen Foundation and the Pennsylvania Historical and Museum Commission for funding. To the Jansen Foundation, he proposed first the funding of a quarterly publication, "like the one put out by the New York Folklore Society, to publish the doings of the division and of the state and folklore societies, plus the addresses of outstanding folklorists in the state."[118] Second, he proposed supporting the folk festival "Americans All," which had run into financial difficulties. He hoped that the commission would underwrite the costs of hiring a deputy, two field workers, and a secretary. In addition, he asked for a publication fund to produce monographs similar to those published by other divisions. "This has been my unalterable idea from the start," he wrote Executive Director Cadzow, "but I have carried along 'as is' to keep the division alive."[119]

Showing his frustration at his high hopes for the division being dashed, and perhaps weary from his feuds with Alfred Shoemaker, Henry wrote Cadzow in 1951 that he would likely leave his post before 1953 and asked him to find a way to "ease out gracefully."[120] "I saw the chance of my life," he wrote of the State Folklorist position, "but it did not materialize, though I have done my best to beat the drum alone. . . . I am truly grateful to you for bringing me here, and your many acts of consideration, I have enjoyed my work despite limitations, and I dream how it can be made wonderful as here in Pennsylvania is *America's richest vein of folklore.* I am astonished at the amount I have collected, and get more every day."[121] Many times during his tenure as State Folklorist he reiterated in memorandums to the Executive Director the need to collect and conserve folklore: "Folklore is an expanding field to which the only limit is the time the collector and compiler can put on it. . . . I would like very much to pass my methods on to a helper, as I have found my system richly productive, the art of getting people to talk, to impart folklore. I am trying to preserve as many folktales as there is time."[122]

A bright spot in an otherwise dark period for Shoemaker was the honor bestowed on him by the Pennsylvania Federation of Historical Societies in April 1952. In front of a packed meeting, old friends from the Pennsylvania Historical and Museum Commission, the Pennsylvania Poetry Society, the Story-Tellers League, and the Pennsylvania Folklore Society handed him a stunningly beautiful citation. Composed by the Assistant State Historian, the citation read:

> To Colonel Henry W. Shoemaker, dean of Pennsylvania folklore, patron of poetry and inspirer of the art of storytelling. For the leadership and guidance he has given to many societies devoted to these fascinating pursuits and to others concerned with the study and writing of history, the preservation of the scenic beauty of our state, and the dissemination of knowledge in the field of animal lore. For the many informative books, pamphlets and brochures he has published, and for the generous giving of his time as speaker on these subjects to the many groups that have repeatedly availed themselves of his rich store of knowledge. These have been the accomplishments of a man also busily engaged in public life as banker, diplomat, publisher and archivist, and leader in many philanthropic and social service organizations. The Pennsylvania Folklore Society, the Story-Tellers League and the Pennsylvania Federation of Histori-

cal Societies are honored to accord this tribute to one who has displayed throughout the years an amazing versatility, a spirit of helpfulness and an unflagging zeal to promote the best interest of our societies.[123]

In an emotion-filled response, Shoemaker declared: "The love of Pennsylvania is the greatest love of my heart."

Shoemaker's "unflagging zeal" for Pennsylvania was still evident in letters during the 1950s promoting a Pennsylvania mystique coming out of the lore of the land. He wrote one correspondent: "I am more and more delighted with the stories that have had their birth in these same forests and on these hills and mountains, so lovely in the gay fresh garb of spring, so glorious in the tumult of blazing color that clothes them in the fall, so austere, when stripped by the hardy winds of winter in the north of this state."[124] He proposed that, in addition to preserving the record of folklore in the state, the folklore division could be instrumental in awakening Pennsylvanians to their cultural riches and promoting folk tradition as a state resource.

Promoting the expansion of state folklore collection, Henry Shoemaker referred more and more to the "Division" rather than to the "State Folklorist" as the 1950s began. Although the tradition at the commission had been to have a single state official represent a particular field of endeavor, such as archaeology or history, Shoemaker believed, as did State Historian Sylvester Stevens, that referring to a chief of a division allowed for growth within the ranks. Shoemaker stayed on as State Folklorist through 1953—by most accounts because he still hoped that a successor, if not a deputy, could step in and carry on the fight to expand the division. After unsuccessfully trying to convince Samuel Bayard and George Korson to come to the division, Shoemaker approached Charles Steese, a curator at the State Museum who had published on Indian legend and medical folklore—but Steese stayed put.[125] The future of the position seemed to be in doubt. The situation became more critical in 1954, when Shoemaker vigorously opposed a recommendation by the Pennsylvania Economy League to integrate the activities of the State Folklorist into the commission's division of history. Cadzow backed him up, however, and the folklore work continued—for the time being.[126]

The Last Years

During the 1950s, the tone in Shoemaker's letters became more bitter, and he implied that his days on earth were numbered. "I regret it deeply I have not found anybody to act as my successor and take my place," he wrote Moritz Jagendorf in 1955.[127]

> Those who have the ability regard me with jealousy and have no friendly desire to help me in any way. I had hoped when I took over this Folk Lore division I would have an assistant who would in time, succeed me but the only younger men who are interested in the subject have a feeling of rivalry rather than cooperation. The active members of the Pennsylvania Folklore Society are mostly men and women in middle life around my own age and will pass off the scene with me leaving the evil spirit kindled by Dr. Shoemaker to take over and carry on the work. As long as I can keep at it I hope to stay but one never can tell how long one will exist in a political job. If I could find three or four young men and women who would be loyal and interested I would feel content to pass off the scene.[128]

"As to the time I give," Shoemaker told Cadzow, "I might say I live with the Division and am working on its plans and schemes during all my waking hours."[129]

But the schedule was apparently taking its toll on the seventy-five-year-old. Shoemaker's wife expressed concern to friends that his diligence in the position was having ill effects on his health.[130] He had developed a diabetic condition and often had difficulty climbing the stairs to his office. Colleagues reported that at times he acted confused.

In 1955, only the second Democratic governor since 1900, George Leader, was elected. At thirty-four years of age, Leader was the youngest governor the state had ever had, and he ushered in a postwar youth movement. Seeking to eliminate years of political patronage in state government, Governor Leader "upheld high standards for all major state appointments" and derided the old politicos who had been rewarded with cushy state jobs.[131] Shoemaker, who had supported Leader, was optimistic about the future: "I am hoping that when the Commission gets settled under the New Administration a helper can be provided, to undergo training, so as to continue the Division's work for the future."[132] The behavior of the aging Shoemaker, who had long been associated with the patronage of Republican administrations, found disfavor among the new governor's staff.[133] In February 1956 the Governor's Office insisted that Cadzow dismiss Shoemaker, apparently after an embarrassing incident in which the frail Shoemaker relieved himself in an office sink rather than struggle down three flights of stairs. Apparently Cadzow did not have the heart to face his old colleague, so he sent his stern comptroller to deliver the blow. John Witthoft was in Shoemaker's office at the time of the dismissal, and he recalled the comptrol-

Shoemaker giving an address by the Tiadaghton Elm, July 4, 1951, legendary spot of the declaration of independence made by the "Fair Play Settlers" of Clinton County. His address that day emphasized the multiple ethnic roots of the composers of the "Pine Creek Declaration of Independence" and their emergence as Americans. "It showed conclusively the wide scope of the demand for freedom by the colonists, how these settlers of different races and creeds got together, framed a document and signed it—the greatest document in all of the history of Revolution yet still to be rescued from the realms of tradition and folklore and confirmed by markers put up by Governor Fine's Pennsylvania Historical and Museum Commission." Shoemaker was proud of the spot as an example of folklore revealing "unrecorded history." *(Lock Haven Express)*

James Henry Darlington, Episcopal Bishop of Harrisburg and co-founder of the Pennsylvania Folklore Society, 1924.

Alfred Shoemaker, first Professor of American Folklore in the United States, and director of the Pennsylvania Dutch Folklore Center, at the Pennsylvania Dutch Folk Festival he directed, 1951. (Pennsylvania Folklife Society)

Samuel Bayard, Penn State Professor Emeritus of English and Comparative Literature, former president of the American Folklore Society, and eminent collector of Pennsylvania folk tunes, songs, and ballads, May 1987. (Simon Bronner)

"Purists" and "Popularizers" at the American Folklore Society meeting, July 28, 1962, Indiana University. This photograph of the society's Fellows shows many prominent figures in the battle of the two groups that brought into question Henry Shoemaker's contribution to folklore studies. In the bottom row, far left, "popularizer" Benjamin Botkin sits next to his defender MacEdward Leach of the University of Pennsylvania. In the second row, far right, stands Richard M. Dorson of Indiana University, leader of the purists. In the top row stand Pennsylvania folklorists Samuel Bayard (second from left), a vocal critic of Shoemaker's "state folklorist" work, and George Korson (second from right), Shoemaker's successor as president of the Pennsylvania Folklore Society.

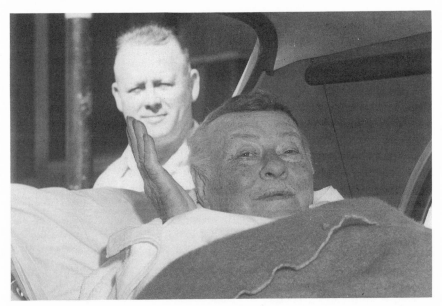

The last public photograph of Henry Shoemaker, October 16, 1957, which appeared in the *Lock Haven Express*. He is leaving Lock Haven Hospital by ambulance to convalesce in his Harrisburg home. *(Lock Haven Express)*

Some of Shoemaker's many sleighs and carriages up for auction at his "museum barn," Restless Oaks, September 28, 1959. *(Lock Haven Express)*

ler unceremoniously ordering Shoemaker out shortly after his seventy-sixth birthday.[134]

After the dismissal, Shoemaker felt understandably "crushed and depressed."[135] His line to friends was that he "was let out for 'age.'"[136] "From a busy writer I have become virtually silent," he moaned. "I guess everything must come to an end, but I was collecting and publishing my unpublished stories at a rate I felt would get them all in print, then the sudden ending of it all! I am trying to figure out some way that I can become busy again, and print my stuff, but thus far can't see a way, and I have so little initiative to write stories that will never be and, have written only three stories since I was 'let out' and they will probably never see the light."[137] He insisted on changing the location of the spring Pennsylvania Folklore Society meeting from the State Museum to another site, and the organization met in April at the Harrisburg Public Library. It was a bittersweet meeting, for while the Society finally managed to get a journal off the ground with the appearance of *Keystone Folklore Quarterly,* edited by Frank Hoffmann at Bucknell, in the spring of 1956, it also became apparent that Shoemaker could no longer lead the Society.[138] According to Angus Gillespie, "Shoemaker, still depressed at the time of the meeting, did attend, but did not have the stamina to preside. The meeting was turned over to Vice President George Korson."[139]

A new phase began for the Pennsylvania Folklore Society in 1957, when Shoemaker stepped aside after more than twenty years at the helm and George Korson became president. Shoemaker was honored with a farewell reception after the spring 1957 meeting and with the publication of a special "Henry Shoemaker" issue of *Keystone Folklore Quarterly* (1957) edited by Frank Hoffmann. As if to rebuff Dorson's criticisms of the popularizers, Korson titled his piece "Henry W. Shoemaker, *Folklorist,*" following a dedication by New York's popularizer Harold Thompson. A strong folklorist-editor's hand was apparent in the selection of Shoemaker's manuscripts that made up the special issue. Included were Pennsylvania versions of recognized British ballads canonized by Harvard's Francis James Child, and local legends containing traditional werewolf and ghost motifs.

During the summer of 1957, Shoemaker returned to his beloved home, Restless Oaks, in McElhattan, but in August he suffered a heart attack, which forced him into the Lock Haven Hospital for seven weeks. In October he returned to Harrisburg, where he convalesced at his riverside home. As the summer of 1958 approached, he longed again for Restless Oaks and insisted that he was well enough to make the trip. Out on the grounds of his home on July 14, he fell victim to another attack. Reportedly he had spent that morning visiting his stable and barn, where his historical collections and books were housed.[140] Rushed to a hospital in Williamsport at 3:00 P.M., he finally gave in to death a half hour into July 15. The next day, the *New York Times* carried a photograph and a full column on his life highlighting his role as diplomat and historian.[141] Pennsylvania newspapers typically dwelled on his newspaper publishing, his public service in Pennsylvania, and his writings on folklore. His local paper, the *Lock Haven Express,* eulogized him as "an individual of small and compact frame who by his presence gave a feeling of solidity and dependability," and "to this external appearance he added a mind that absorbed history and folklore with eager interest and made the past live in his writing." "He was a teller of tales," the paper continued, "a folklorist of the first rank," who "was always interested in the outdoors, and was fascinated with the wildlife of Central Pennsylvania, as well as other parts of the world. Tales of hunting prowess were garnered and treasured by him in his researches into local history, folklore and tradition." The reporter was in awe of Shoemaker's range of activity and his international scope: "He gave to each of these interests a distinction of personal touch that marked him as an individual."[142] Meanwhile, his sister offered this poem in tribute:

> The long voyage ended
> The dream of life suspended,
> A royal welcoming
> From the heavenly King
> In regions unexplored
> Where love and lore are stored
> Waiting for him to come;
> His lyre was never dumb
> His gift to the world was great . . .
> Now he is dwelling in triumphant state
> With God, fulfilled and blest
> In loving and eternal rest.[143]

His funeral took place on February 18, and after an Episcopal service he was buried in Highland Cemetery in Lock Haven. Placed at the highest part of the mountainside cemetery, his stone overlooked his beloved West Branch of the Susquehanna River and the Bald Eagle mountains. It simply and humbly carried his name overlooked by a yew tree, the same kind of tree that inspired many a romantic Arthurian legend.[144]

Henry Shoemaker's wife inherited Restless Oaks and his historical collections housed in the "barn museum." The collections, including his many books, were sold at auction on September 23–24, 1959. The *Lock Haven Express* considered it so newsworthy an event that it gave the auction full-page coverage. The sale notice announced, "Colonel Henry W. Shoemaker

was a noted writer on Penna. Folklore and his Barn Museum was well
known in the northern part of Penna."[145] Scores of carriages and sleighs, a
Conestoga wagon, an "early Indian canoe carved out of a log," "early
woodland plows," brass, pewter, and tinware dating back to colonial days,
stuffed and mounted animals (including fifty mounted deer heads), duck
decoys, rare Sugar Valley pottery, Pennsylvania-German fraktur, Gypsy
baskets, Indian relics, stove plates, a medieval suit of armor, paintings of
landscapes and animals, and finally an enormous number of Currier and Ives
prints that constituted his first artifact collection, went on sale. Some of
those prints, along with his domestic utensils, went up in a "Colonel
Shoemaker Room" for a local restaurant. An article announcing the room
read: "In his memory we dedicate this room for not only was he a collector,
but was a historian, public servant and notable personage as well."[146] In
1964 the Colonel Henry W. Shoemaker Galleries for the exhibition of new
art opened at Juniata College with a gift from Shoemaker's widow.

   Folklorists acknowledged Shoemaker's death in the *Journal of American
Folklore* and *Keystone Folklore Quarterly*. In the *Journal of American Folklore*,
Frank Hoffmann honored Shoemaker as the "dean of Pennsylvania folklorists" and declared that his collections "deserve to be made generally
available to folklore scholars." He particularly praised Shoemaker's pioneer
efforts for Pennsylvania folklore: "At a time when few people realized the
wealth of lore that was there for the asking, he roamed the mountains and
forests of his beloved Central Pennsylvania, listening and writing." As
others would do later, Hoffmann was particularly impressed by Shoemaker's
devotion to the people from whom he collected: ". . . he also collected
hundred of friends, for to him a teller or singer was as important as the tale
or song he possessed. And these friendships formed in lumber camps,
crossroads stores, hunting lodges, and along mountain trails were as
highly cherished as any formed in the capitol buildings of Harrisburg and
Washington or at diplomatic functions in Lisbon, Berlin, or Sofia."[147]

   In the *Keystone Folklore Quarterly*, George Korson offered that "Colonel
Shoemaker was a great collector primarily because he was a great human
being." Restless Oaks, where he first discovered folklore, Korson said, was
symbolic of his life, a life in which "above everything else folklore was
closest to his heart."[148] Most unrestrained in the *Quarterly* was J. Herbert
Walker, Shoemaker's frequent fieldwork companion, who recalled how he
first met him—appropriately, he thought, "on the top of a mountain in
Centre County":

> In retrospect, now that he is gone, I shall always think of Colonel
> Shoemaker as I first saw him that day on the top of a Centre County
> Mountain. He belonged there amid the whispering pines and the

great, gray rocks, a stalwart man, who during all his mature years gathered data to preserve the rich heritage of legend and folklore—tales of Indians, mountaineers, lumberjacks, early settlers, hunters—all tales of enchantment.

From a vantage point in the great Hereafter Colonel Shoemaker can look down on a life devoted to the things of his soul and spirit—the recording of great tales that will become even more important in the years to come.

Certainly the whispering winds in the tall pines of North-Central Pennsylvania—which area he seemed to love best of all—and the chattering trout streams will sing a requiem for all the future for one who gave Pennsylvania a collection of folktales that has never been matched and perhaps never will be surpassed. His books, redolent with the romance and mystery of the outdoors, become collector's items as the years advance. They will be his greatest monument—and that is as he would have wished. [149]

The new crop of professional folklorists was not so kind to Henry Shoemaker's past work. Distinguished Penn State Professor Samuel Preston Bayard, who would later go on to be president of the American Folklore Society, published a stinging criticism after Henry Shoemaker's death in Alfred Shoemaker's widely read *Pennsylvania Folklife*. In the popularizer-professional debates of the 1950s, Bayard flatly considered Henry Shoemaker "as arrant a faker and 'fakelorist' as ever existed." Had Alfred Shoemaker not requested it, Bayard later recalled, "it would doubtless never have been written"—but written and published it was, and it sent noticeable shockwaves through historical and folkloristic circles. [150] It called the damage Henry Shoemaker had done to the cause of collecting English-language folk culture in Pennsylvania "enormous" and "probably irreparable." He accused Shoemaker of being "unable and unwilling to distinguish between folklore, history and romantic fiction," of filling out his collections with "all manner of information, a great deal of it quite irrelevant to the traditions they were supposedly discussing." This condition, he complained, "had the long-run effects of misleading some of the public, alienating others, hampering normal collection and study of the material, and completely destroying the ethnological value of anything published." [151]

In addition to protecting the integrity of the verbatim texts offered by tradition-bearers, Bayard also wanted to authenticate the folklorist's work as a trained specialty. He expressed annoyance that Shoemaker called every naturalist, local colorist, or historian he admired a folklorist. Echoing Dorson's separatism, Bayard suggested that folklorists properly constitute a discipline, if not a science, and that they should be qualified not as historians, naturalists, writers, but indeed as folklorists. He implied that the marriage Shoemaker had arranged between folklore and history in the commission was not desired, because historians were not accustomed to working with living informants and did not comprehend the "special circumstances and implications of this sort of work."[152] He observed that working in the public sector led to temptations to popularize and dilute the potentially great scholarly value of folklore. Popularization for Shoemaker was a beneficial goal, for it promoted the value of the state and encouraged the reuse of folklore, but for Bayard popularization misrepresented reality and tampered with the authenticity of the folk's own literature. Bayard believed that Shoemaker had used folklore for his own political rather than scholarly ends and worried that any connection of heritage to a public agency would result in a distortion of the facts.

Bayard proceeded to destroy Shoemaker's most cherished assumptions. He made a case for understanding folklore in reference to its diffusion from European sources, and not for arising anew out of local conditions and events, as Shoemaker saw it. As for Shoemaker's claim that folklore is unrecorded history, Bayard asserted that "what the historian considers important is usually disregarded and forgotten by bearers of a folk tradition, while legends tend to cluster thickly around happenings that, historically speaking, are quite obscure." Bayard recognized that Shoemaker's purpose was to promote the state's cultural uniqueness, but he suggested that ethnologically collected evidence leads away from the idea of a "state culture." Bayard resented Shoemaker's romantic implication that folklore attaches especially to "picturesque" groups, such as lumbermen, railroaders, and canallers. Yet it is among ordinary farmers in Pennsylvania, Bayard declared, "that the oldest, most enduring, and most enlightening popular lore normally persists." Then Bayard blasted Shoemaker by stating that "this piece of common knowledge to folklorists throughout the western world has never been emphasized by any 'official historian' publicizer of folklore in Pennsylvania."[153] Bayard was right, but he did not recognize the source of Shoemaker's neglect in his self-conscious promotion of the wilderness myth and conservation goals, not to mention his campaign for a literary Americanism based on the romance and picturesqueness of characters from preindustrial life. It was a campaign that owed much to the inspiration of Theodore Roosevelt and Progressivism, and was revised for post–World War II political nationalism.[154]

Even having unleashed these academic salvos, Bayard was not through with his barrage at the popularizer Shoemaker. He went after the sacrosanct assumption that survivals of "three civilizations" of early Pennsylvania (English, Scots-Irish, and German) reflect the development, indeed the greatness, of Pennsylvania folklore. Actually, Shoemaker did not slavishly follow this trinity, as Bayard implied. Shoemaker's view was more "intercultural," in keeping with the rhetoric of the 1940s.[155] He believed that many ethnic strains—some hardly given notice, such as Waldensians, Jews, Gypsies, and French Huguenots—went into Pennsylvania's "medley of races." Departing from the "melting pot" idea, he offered that the mixing of these groups created a new regional type while maintaining "racial" customs into contemporary life. It also differed from Alfred Shoemaker's projection of selective traditions and entire communities persisting, offering alternative lifeways and world views commonly within, but sometimes apart from, a majority culture. Bayard argued that the traditions of the big three, at least, were not so separable, even in Europe, and that more systematic collection was necessary before conclusions could be made about the origins of contemporary folklore.

Shoemaker's work was spotty and selective to suit his purposes, Bayard implied. Why, Bayard asked, was there hardly any mention of as prominent a tradition as the English in Shoemaker's collection? And is it really possible, Bayard inquired, to differentiate from a few current Pennsylvania fragments the character of Scots-Irish and North Irish traditions? As for Shoemaker's long-stated claim that folklore makes historical writing lively, Bayard took issue with the "search for the picturesque in folklore." Its "fatal defect" is that, because of its selectivity and adornment, it is unreliable. It may be lively writing, Bayard admitted, but "it can't be depended upon as an accurate depiction of part of the cultural life of our people." What was needed, he asserted, is "detailed and comprehensive folklore collecting work." It was a call that Alfred Shoemaker and his followers made strongly, and if that call were needed, they were convinced, Henry Shoemaker's picture of the Pennsylvania wilderness as the soul of Pennsylvania would be debunked.

Bayard anticipated the scientific regionalism that was being developed by linguists, cultural geographers, and folklife scholars during the 1950s. It called for mapping regions on the basis of objective data that were subject to variation across space and stability over time—such as dialect words, houses, barns, foods, and town forms.[156] Such data could be counted and mapped much more easily than intangible oral tradition. The result of many such studies was that a "Pennsylvania Culture Region" was identified, but it differed markedly from Henry Shoemaker's subjective portrayal of the heartland in rugged North Central Pennsylvania.[157] The objective map showed a Philadelphia "cultural hearth" fostering a strong Pennsylvania-German imprint on the landscape in central and southeastern Pennsylvania and extending down into western Maryland and Virginia. Out of this farmland "core" a Middle Atlantic region, moving westward toward Pittsburgh, formed.[158] So much for Henry Shoemaker's mystical priority of Pennsylvania's forested wilderness.

Scientific regionalism challenged cherished American myths of the nation's ancestors in other romantic highland "regions" of the southern Appalachians, the Ozarks, the Rockies, and the Adirondacks. Instead, it traced migrations from urban ports of entry on America's eastern seaboard. The romantic regionalism that gave rise to the highland myths was subjective; it was based on the way people narrated themselves—or, rather, the way the narrative was invented and popularized for some national need. Besides projecting the ruggedness of highland existence, as well as the equalizing and renewing effects of the woods, romantic regionalism offered a religious overtone for America's ideals by placing them on the holy mountaintop, close to God and nature. Henry Shoemaker might say that Pennsylvanians have their soul in the highlands and forests because they imagine their values are enshrined in the legends of the fertile wilderness. He would argue that they use those legends to give the "inner meaning" or self-perception of locality and national experience.[159]

Wilbur Zelinsky, probably the most prominent mapper of objective regions and who wrote at Penn State in the midst of Shoemaker's highland paradise, later took up the idea of regional self-perception in proposing "vernacular" regions—the ways Americans describe, if not narrate, themselves.[160] That map varies from the objective one, Zelinsky found repeatedly, and it is far more changeful. One difference is that the objective "Middle Atlantic" region is not recognized by most Americans, who probably do have an idea of where the South, the West, and New England are. Pennsylvanians do not align themselves with any of those vernacular regions. Pennsylvania and New York are vaguely "Eastern" but generally lack regional identity, even more so in Shoemaker's backcountry of western Pennsylvania and southwestern New York State, according to Zelinsky. With the efforts of Henry Shoemaker, Moritz Jagendorf, and Harold Thompson, these states, which are supposedly the least regional, were the setting for the nation's most pronounced popularization of regional romanticism within a state historical and political context. Yet because these settings were not generally associated with clear cultural boundaries, they also allowed for the connection, and maybe invention, of local narratives within these unattached regions to a national one.

Bayard's harshest cut may ultimately have been to Shoemaker's service for Pennsylvania. He assailed Shoemaker's goal of finding the unique traditions of Pennsylvania. This obsession with uniqueness, Bayard opined, must have been influenced by his position as State Folklorist, which serves purposes of publicity and patriotism, not the mission of furthering cultural knowledge. "What a folklore investigator is concerned with in the traditions of a region," Bayard wrote, "is not the distinctive and unique . . . but the characteristic and revealing."[161] Bayard was not even willing to grant Shoemaker the usual credit for blazing new trails for others to follow, because "attempting a synthesis long before the folklore materials for it were available . . . is none the less lamentable," especially since it may have the consequence of inhibiting solid fieldwork. Because Shoemaker gave the impression that folklore constituted a certain bygone romantic type of story—"the empty gesturing of the past," Bayard called it—other genuine traditions that could have been collected have been neglected. Shoemaker's stories, prematurely rushed into print, said Bayard, have a detrimental effect because they raise a mistaken image of authentic Pennsylvania traditions.

Exactly. Shoemaker's conservationist purposes, his mission to "awaken Pennsylvanians," were markedly different from Bayard's analytical goals. For scholarly documentation and analysis, Bayard sought to demystify Shoemaker's image of the Pennsylvania wilderness and recoiled at the "publicity effects resorted to in order to hold the attention of an uninformed public" at festivals and in popular publications. Appreciation for folklore would be best served by scholarship, not by popularization, he concluded. Bayard chastised the Pennsylvania Historical and Museum Commission for taking up Shoemaker's "irresponsible and tiresome cant" that because Pennsylvania is so ethnically diverse, it probably has the richest folk heritage of any state in the Union. Bayard exclaimed that this cant "is a sickening reminder of the past in which the bodies most loudly concerned with folklore activity in Pennsylvania encouraged everything under the sun except the one and only activity that was lacking, and was ever really needed: the field collection of folklore in this commonwealth."[162] On that point Shoemaker probably would have agreed, although he probably would not want to "quit talking about our rich heritage" or present traditions systematically and dispassionately, as did Bayard's folkloristic hero, the little-known but diligent Reverend Thomas R. Brendle (1889–1966), or even Bayard himself.[163] In any case, as far as folklore scholarship was concerned, Bayard's unrebutted charges had the effect of skewering Henry Shoemaker's work.

By the time Henry Shoemaker died, his books had gone out of print and were difficult to obtain. His most lasting monument was the folklore division he created at the Pennsylvania Historical and Museum Commission, and deserving of intellectual attention is his role in promoting conservation, cultural and natural, and Pennsylvania identity—some may even say destiny—through a popularized mythology or narrative mystique.

In addition to promoting a lasting American commitment to the nation's natural environment, Shoemaker is significant for his participation in the intercultural debate of the mid-twentieth century. Shoemaker was a proponent of the idea that multiethnic Pennsylvania, home to Penn's holy experiment of tolerance, offered a more promising original heritage for future generations to build on than the New England Puritan version. Early on, he called for more historical attention in the American story to such groups as women, African-Americans, Pennsylvania-Germans, French Huguenots, Jews, Gypsies, and even Waldensians, and he saw folklore as the unrecorded history that could reveal many of their "forgotten" contributions and customs. His special concern was for the regions, ethnic groups, and occupations that gave America its character and color.

Because history is written from the viewpoint of the elite, Shoemaker also argued, folklore revealed the "inner meaning" of both national and local events. By that he meant that oral tradition recorded the perspectives—a folk commentary, if you will—of different groups on the events around them. Unlike leaders of the present "multicultural" movement, Shoemaker often couched this boosterism in biological and evolutionary terms, believing that a new robust American type can develop from the "medley of races." His interest in the conservation of folklore as a kind of natural resource came out of the Progressive movement and evolutionary doctrine of the early nineteenth century. Nonetheless, he echoes some of current rhetoric that urges a social civility and cultural respect that comes from an appreciation for the persistent traditions and historic achievements of America's many ethnic communities, most of which he claimed were comfortably at home in Pennsylvania. In his eyes, the collection and reuse of folklore was a key to building this appreciation, and he was prophetic in realizing the potential of government involvement in encouraging folkloristic goals.

Folklore for Shoemaker was like the forests, the "people's property" meant for public use. It was a source of imagination and awe, spirituality and unity, and its public and popular application continues in ways that the professional folklorists who abandoned Shoemaker are only now fathoming. In schools, libraries, and communities, folklore narrates identity for children and adults alike. As supposedly materialistic and scientific as American society has become, the demand for an imaginative narration of the past has, if anything, increased. It was to this movement that Shoemaker was devoted. Whatever is made of his successes and failures now, his mission carries lessons of past hopes and future goals. Although Shoemaker believed that it would be at least fifty years after his death before his contributions were appreciated, he wrote Ralph Steele Boggs (founder of America's first collegiate curriculum in folklore at the University of North Carolina) in 1950 that he had been able to witness the ways that "folklore is evolving itself and becoming accepted as an integral part of culture, nationally."[164] That statement was prophetic, considering that now more than forty states have state folklorist positions, an integral element of the "cultural conservation" movement.[165]

Pennsylvania Heritage After Shoemaker

What happened after Shoemaker was dismissed as State Folklorist reveals much about the changing character of the promotion of Pennsylvania heritage from romantic regionalism to social realism. After Shoemaker left the Pennsylvania Historical and Museum Commission, another reorganization took place when Governor Leader appointed Frank Melvin as chair of the seventh historical commission. Sylvester Stevens replaced Cadzow as Executive Director and the divisions were consolidated, thus eliminating the folklore division. That is not to say that folklore interests did not continue—the commission published a sheaf of Pennsylvania folk songs and sponsored summer institutes in folklife at the Landis Valley Museum.[166] Commission Director Stevens even supported the publication of a Pennsylvania Folklore Society miscellany of regional folklore for popular consumption edited by two academically trained scholars.[167] Despite attempts to bring folklorists to the commission within the history division during the 1950s, Stevens failed to restore the State Folklorist position until 1966, when MacEdward Leach, building on Shoemaker's precedent, helped secure funding for a profession-ally sounding "Ethnic Culture Survey" within the commission by an act of the legislature.[168] Its purpose was defined as to "collect, preserve, and make available materials on the cultural and historical contributions of the major ethnic groups which had a part in the making of modern Pennsylvania."[169] In addition to surveying the legacy of colonial settlers, the project planned to give unprecedented coverage to recent industrial and urban immigrants.[170] Shoemaker's old commission colleague, S. K. Stevens, over-saw the project. "Because it is actually another phase of gathering data for Pennsylvania history, the ethnic culture program was made a section of the History Division," he announced.[171]

Stevens intended the job for the elderly Leach, but the revered ballad scholar took ill before the position could be filled. Henry Glassie, a student of Leach and Yoder in the Department of Folklore and Folklife at the University of Pennsylvania, took the State Folklorist job with Leach as adviser to the program, but Leach died shortly after Glassie came to Harrisburg. As State Folklorist, Glassie set up archives, advised festivals, held conferences, and issued publications, much as the position had earlier been defined, but he was more inclined to use Alfred Shoemaker's model of folk-cultural research.[172] According to Glassie, who was not native to the state, the survey stressed "modern concepts of folklore" and planned "to make the public more aware of the richness and diversity of folk culture, to guide the amateur into a more careful study, and to assist the scholar in his work."[173] Unlike Henry Shoemaker, however, Glassie recorded buildings and arts that represented the persistent folklife and material culture of ethnic communities in the state. He held a "Middle States Conference on Folk Culture" and helped spur the creation of similar programs in Maryland, Ohio, and New Jersey, starting a chain reaction of such positions across the United States. Whereas Shoemaker had primarily relied on his network of local historians, folklore enthusiasts, and journalists for support of his work, Glassie, much more successfully than Shoemaker, courted a constituency of professional folklorists and gained wide scholarly notice for the state folklore program.

The new State Folklorist took a leadership role in the Pennsylvania Folklore Society by editing the journal much as Henry Shoemaker had done. After being offered and accepting an academic position, Glassie was succeeded by David Hufford, also a young graduate student at the University of Pennsylvania. In 1969, Hufford published an account of the "History and Work of the Ethnic Culture Survey and State Folklorist Program of the Pennsylvania Historical and Museum Commission," which was notable in its lack of mention of Shoemaker. Hufford knew of Shoemaker's precedent, but he stressed the groundbreaking role of the Ethnic Culture Survey more as a systematic ethnological instrument than as a public agency.[174] Glassie, who had gone on to Indiana University's Folklore Institute, was treated in Hufford's piece as a young pioneer hero. The Ethnic Culture Survey appeared to be the first state folklorist program because it was the first to be staffed by professional folklorists trained in university folklore programs. Shoemaker was viewed as "old" when he began the first state folklore program, so his ideas were seen as out-of-date. As a journalist and a popularizer, he was branded a repulsive "amateur."

Glassie and Hufford, however, looked young and academically credentialed, which gave the new state program the cachet of the modern and the professional. Chronicles of public folklore after Hufford's article appeared failed to mention Shoemaker's innovation.[175] With Glassie crowned as the originator of state folklore programming, an image of continuous professional growth from a propitious beginning could be conveyed to folklorists. The source of public folklore could be placed in academe, and the direction could be mapped away from the amateurs interested in folklore. Professional folklorists, if they were to accept public folklore, needed this narrative to affirm, in the words of Roger Abrahams in 1992, that "the work of public folklorists, then, is not less objective or scientific than that of academic folklorists."[176] As Shoemaker had predicted, his governmental contributions had drifted into obscurity, although he is still well remembered in the highlands as the great Pennsylvania "storyteller."[177]

The Ethnic Culture Survey documented the social traditions of many communities in the state, including their historic folk customs and arts. As objective chroniclers of the realism of modern-day folklore, the State Folklorist also received material that included currently circulating ethnic slurs and bawdy material. Such items were hardly in keeping with the romance of Shoemaker's history, but they were considered essential for evaluating social attitudes, and conflicts, in a society. When *Keystone Folklore Quarterly,* published out of the State Folklorist's office, carried articles with some of the risqué material, it raised concern at the commission about the public's reaction. Executive Director Stevens wrote a commission member: "We are greatly disturbed by its content and especially the article by Thomas Peck on dirty jokes. As you know, I just got through defending Dave Hufford on the Polack issue, and if anyone ever picks up the Summer Issue, they really can cause us some trouble. . . . I have talked to Dave about this, and he is totally innocent of any thought that it might contain objectionable material."[178] Stevens heard criticism from members of the General Assembly and his own board.

After Hufford voluntarily left to teach at Memorial University in New-foundland, Canada, the commission dropped the Ethnic Culture Survey and went in a direction that emphasized historic preservation and social history. Spurred by federal legislation, attention to historic preservation and the documentation of the built environment increased. Chords of national patriotism were not sounded as much as chimes of validating underrepresented social histories. In addition to safeguarding the state's historic treasures, the newly built state museum "demonstrated the usefulness of the visual and physical record as sources of information and interpretation."[179] The oral and traditional record, and the promotion of a unique image, appeared less in the commission's work.

After a hiatus of more than a decade, Governor Dick Thornburgh author-ized a new State Folklorist position in the Ethnic Heritage Affairs Commis-sion (now the Pennsylvania Heritage Affairs Commission) in 1982. Its purpose was "to advocate and encourage the presentation of folk artists and the interpretation of folk cultural traditions in the public forum."[180] Although this sounds close to Shoemaker's precedent—and indeed it loudly sings out the cant of cultural conservation—the new office is assuredly focused more on artistic and ethnological concerns than on the historical and natural goals set by the original State Folklorist position. It voices concerns for the "diversity" of Pennsylvania, rather than the former "unity." Its structure includes forty-nine "ethnic commissioners" representing separate communities, such as Assyrian and Bangladeshi, as well as African-American and Native American. More than half the commissioners come from the Philadelphia and Pittsburgh areas. The Heritage Affairs Commission brandishes such key words as "multicultural," "interethnic," and "cultural heritage"[181] and brings to the fore contemporary industrial and urban folk arts of recent immigrants and migrants much more than the poetic rural roots of Pennsylvania's frontiersmen.[182] These folk arts happen to be in Pennsylvania, rather than being Pennsylvanian; they belong to artists rather than to the romantic "soil" or regional "soul."

The dynamic array of social movement and event in the modern city now seems to epitomize rather than antithesize the character of folkways.[183] You can now hear much more about Philadelphia and Pittsburgh from the Pennsylvania Heritage Affairs Commission than you ever did in Shoemaker's day, and it comes in a way that verifies, if not celebrates, the opportunities and excitements of the varied and fast-paced city. In emphasizing the essential role of folklore in media, industry, and urban life, many contemporary folklorists view their subject as embracing rather than opposing modernity.[184] Folklore appears more ethnographic than historical because of the image of people today constantly reconstituting and adapting tradition for their needs. In this view, folklore is not buried in the past waiting to be dug up; it is at everyone's very doors, waiting to be interpreted for its comment on modern life. Indeed, many have argued, modern conditions give rise to oral traditions, if not traditional cultural processes.[185] Giving validity to the mobility of community traditions in a diverse, teeming metropolis offers a strong political imagery for a changing society based on an unmeltable "cultural pluralism."[186]

There has been a significant shift in state involvement in folklore, from the broad collection of historical folklore to the presentation of contemporary folk arts, and indeed of outstanding individual artists.[187] In keeping with this trend, the National Endowment for the Arts (NEA) and many states, including Pennsylvania, have award programs to recognize individual achievement in mastering creative heritage. Heritage is less hereditary and more behavioral, individualizing the practice of tradition in a mass culture. Instead of being a collective response to the environment, folk arts involve personal skill and adaptive choices suggesting contemporary psychological and social functions.[188] There is much to be said for realizing the ways in which traditions become expressive—artistic, if you will—in a more complex way that takes into account cultural roles as men or women, children and adults, family and community members, and personalities of different stripes. But questions remain about how the historical and organizational dimension to collective lives—indeed, the impact of the nation and state— have affected the functions of tradition.[189]

Popularizing Tradition in New and Old Modes

Tradition in ethnographic studies of folk arts is not preserved in relic form before it disappears; rather, its constant change and aesthetic appeal are celebrated. But much of the historic tradition we knew *is* disappearing. And the human connection to place—the land, the region, the state—and the ways in which they are being preserved to foster tradition, demand attention in order to comprehend the sense of belonging and interrelationship with nature that Americans have. The appeal to action that accompanied federal government programs of the American Folklife Center for applying folklife to land-use policy in the Pine Barrens of New Jersey and for the integration of folklife and historic preservation in Grouse Creek, Utah, as late as the 1980s, underscores an attempt at revision and resurgence of Shoemaker's conservationist mission amid the new urban folk arts model.[190] The programs alerted agencies to the fact that properly integrating the environment with the heritage drawn from it for some public good is a thorny cultural as well as political issue. Statistics show that, since the 1930s, Americans have been moved to visit in ever-increasing numbers both scenic areas and sites of a relic past—while a rising environmental movement questions the exploitation of nature for recreation and tourist activity.[191] In the United States, public agencies have been responsible for marking "sacred" cultural places, guiding the interpretation of the great events (as in battlefield parks) and of just as eventful backwoods areas where Americans lived plainly and nature flourished.

That a new model—more social science than humanistic history, more industrial than natural—seems to have largely pushed aside the unified mythologizing of the American countryside does not mean that a romantic narrative does not still persist or that within agencies competition to produce the narrative does not occur.[192] The new social sensitivity of the urban folk arts model offers a vision, described by Bess Lomax Hawes, former director of the NEA Folk Arts Program: "It is a vision of a confident and open-hearted nation, where differences can be seen as exciting instead of fear-laden, where men of good will, across all manner of racial, linguistic, and historical barriers, can find common ground in understanding solid craftsmanship, virtuoso techniques, and deeply felt expressions."[193] As the Progressives fashioned a response to rapid immigration and industrialization in a popular version of American tradition, so this new model offers an answer to new immigration (much of it from Latin America and Asia) and to mass incorporation. The wilderness is gone from the rhetoric, but the need for a mystique that supports a sense of destiny and identity remains. Its mythology before the public may be less narrated and more "imaged" in art and performance, but it is no less imagined.[194]

The dramatic shift of cultural presentation between the Progressive era and the 1990s matches the chronology historian Michael Kammen has projected for the role of tradition in American culture. Since 1870, he has pointed out, the most significant role involved the deliberate Americanization of folk heritage through collected and presented narrative, speech, and song.[195] Broadly speaking, what followed was an imperfect democratization in regions and occupations, and later pluralization in groupings of ethnicity, race, gender, age, sexuality, appearance, and class, to name some in the ever-growing list. Kammen also noted the influence of tourism on later uses of tradition, and Pennsylvania, with its whopping fifty-one separate tourist agencies, certainly attests to that trend in the state.[196] Even more than attracting tourism, heritage-writing—indeed, a whole heritage industry—is being called on for purposes of "economic development," to promote community pride and image.[197] Judging from the meteoric increase in museums, magazines, and films on heritage during the 1980s and 1990s, and the leveling-off of American studies programs in universities, the production of American heritage knowledge comes increasingly from media and public agencies. If the 1980s reports on higher education are to be believed, the role for public agencies may be heightened by the diminishing cultural authority of the academy.[198] At the same time, American cultural education by many public agencies in the 1990s is a frequent target of conservative criticism in an effort to scale back or re-devise governmental programs.

One might now forecast a period in which American folk tradition is geared toward emotional community-building in order to deal with the role of individuals in a global mass culture, where electronic communication and constant mobility create a need for organizing belonging.[199] That opens up the kinds of traditions—the kinds of communities and organizations, identities and rituals—representing the American memory of the past, the American perception of the present, to a tremendously wide array of possibilities for a mobile and electronically communicating society. Museums, books, films, and schools are scrambling to keep up. It used to be that Americans were preoccupied with the ways in which such institutions and the media reflected society's traditions. Now, and Shoemaker's building of the Pennsylvania mystique is a notable example, Americans have a view in which they see themselves as shaping traditions, or at least as defining what's important. Therefore, history is more than recorded; it is constructed. And folklore is more than collected; it is projected.[200]

In Pennsylvania, much of the mystique-building through folklore and history of the highland paradise seems to have worn off (and probably so has American romantic regionalism generally). Nevertheless, Shoemaker would be heartened to know that Pennsylvanians have retained their woods and their rustic traditions. You can still see them heartily setting out into what they like to call "God's country" in the North Woods every November to hunt and live in the wild.[201] And once there, they often do more storytelling than hunting, recounting the days of yore, although they utter far more folk humor than the sober Shoemaker realized. Men grow backwoods beards, attend to their rough-hewn cabins, and bemoan the loss of the good old wilderness. In other seasons, they tell their stories out fishing in "Big Woods Country," or brandishing muskets and bows in the forests. And they worry that they might be a dying breed in the face of assaults on their traditions by animal rights advocates.

Meanwhile, environmentalists calling for restoring the wilderness are more likely to use ecological arguments than folkloristic arguments. Pennsylvania newspapers still carry a good deal of outdoors talk, but one is more likely to read about state regulations, animal rights protests, and herd statistics than romantic narratives about famed hunters and their game. Much of the industry that once threatened the environment has left the region, taking with them jobs and income. Town meetings discuss building economic opportunities on the bucolic image of the region through cultural and historical tourism, but ironically the most pronounced efforts in this regard have been the *industrial heritage* parks developed by the National Park Service.[202] Interesting collections of folklore from the area have appeared, but they do not have the booster or conservationist impact that Shoemaker's work did, and much more can still be done to document the traditions of this and other areas.[203] The beauty of the highlands can still take your breath away, but I do not hear writers proclaiming that spirituality. In fact, I cannot say that the strong literary outpouring based on this trove of tradition, which Shoemaker hoped for, has grown, although Shoemaker probably played a large part in giving Pennsylvania some due next to the vistas of the Rockies, the Ozarks, and the Appalachians.

Not that it would have helped. In this era of electronic communication, television and film have a more powerful hold on the public imagination—a mass appeal—than the local and regional periodicals of Shoemaker's day. And the popularity of the movie *Witness* and the documentary *People of Preservation* has done a great deal to transfer the old highlands mystique to the Amish in the "garden spot" of Lancaster County and surrounding "Dutchland" areas in southeastern Pennsylvania.[204] Its proximity to the eastern megalopolis and the promise of pastoral splendor have a lot to do with the boom in national knowledge about a small religious sect that is not unique to Pennsylvania. Here folklore and history are again used—and applied even more intensely than during Henry Shoemaker's day—to promote a sense of tradition and a garden ideal in a slice of Americana, even though visitors are more likely to visit retail outlets and amusement parks

than they are to participate in old-time customs or seek out bucolic settings—or for that matter even see the Amish. Ironic, isn't it, that the
country's largest folk festival at Kutztown, which celebrates Pennsylvania-
German and Amish culture, also necessitates one of the area's most massive
parking lots? Meanwhile, the old pastoral settings of Pennsylvania-German
life in Lancaster County have largely been built over in concrete and roadside
attractions. Henry Shoemaker would probably have resisted the tourist gaze
that has been foisted on the Amish, for he wanted, first, for Pennsylvanians
to return to their own traditions and, second, to protect their natural
environments.

Several of Shoemaker's books are now in print again, for local consumption mostly, but how to categorize them gives bibliographers fits.[205] Are
they history, folklore, nature studies, conservation tracts? Maybe they're
what Europeans call "folklorism," or "the presentation of folk culture at
second-hand," often for entertainment, commercial, or political purposes.[206]
But that label obscures the peculiar historicism and romanticization of natural
history that come to be packaged together with folkish narratives as a kind
of regional literature.[207] Lost too is the political purpose of such works in
service of Progressive goals of conservation and managed heritage. I am
not sure the firsthand can be sifted from the secondhand, or that the facts
will ever be sorted out from the fiction, but Henry Shoemaker's works
reveal a man of power and passion, a place of beauty and mystery, a
mythology of imagination and purpose. They signify a man's effort and
thought in composing a mythology in service to conservation and regionalism, and the invention of a mystique that said much about American national
identity and destiny during the early twentieth century. They are, in short,
a sign of their times, or at least the times that leaders in journalism,
business, and Progressive Republican politics shaped for America.

Shoemaker's books are among many by elite cultural brokers who in their
representation of American memory at the time gave testimony to the ways
in which the past is narrated anew for the present. That they tried to
persuade readers through folklore places them in a legacy of America's
often-strained efforts to define its contested cultural heritage apart from
Europe. Is it a long heritage extending to the wilderness and the time of
Indian settlement, or a short one from the founding of a nation? What are
the roles of Asians, African-Americans, religions, women, the West, the
South, the city, in the projected narratives of the legacy? Will they empha-
size a tradition of stabilizing unity from varied sources, or changeful diversity
in a series of conflicts? What stories, what images, represent our identity,
local and national, our destiny, from the past and into the future? Who will
step forward to gather and present this tradition? Will it be the ordinary
people of the soil from whom "roots" material comes, or the often privileged

cultural brokers, who enable the story to be told in a certain way? Will it be the schools, the libraries, the museums, the historical and cultural organizations, the local, state, and national governments? Will it be each of us taking pride in conserving tradition, knowing our history, relating ideas—or will it be a few authorities to whom we refer our questions?

If Shoemaker was a joiner, a part of a Progressive movement, he was also an innovator—indeed, a remarkable individual whose life was full of purpose and drama. Without his determination, the Pennsylvania highlands would probably not have gained notice for its culture or its scenery, alongside the southern Appalachians. Still often overlooked, the Pennsylvania mountain region has not had another writer with the output of Shoemaker, certainly, and probably not any with his crusading mission either. The Progressive impetus for instituting historical and natural conservation at state sites, state forests, and state parks would probably have not been as forceful without him. And I seriously doubt whether the idea of an official state folklore program would have arisen first in Pennsylvania—and maybe nationally—without Henry Shoemaker's original initiative. He created American tradition as much as he was a part of it, and he imagined much that he was not involved in for a receptive regional audience. Especially telling was his conviction that Americans still needed a mythology, a common tradition, to rely on, and to struggle with into the future.

Epilogue

The drive across Pennsylvania Route 220 toward Lock Haven moves quickly. Cars carry colorful Pennsylvania license plates sounding a call to "Conserve Wild Resources." Technology has easily flattened the once-mighty land to make a nice level ride into Clinton County. Although the road's cement surface stretches wide to either side, one can hardly miss nature's sentries through the edges of the windshield. Mountains with thick forested armor stand proudly while forceful rivers cut paths in the landscape. Finished with my search through dusty papers in windowless archives, I'm trekking outdoors after the remnants of Henry Shoemaker's "mystic region." I've moved, as he would have wanted, from the artificial to the natural.

Like Citizen Kane's "Rosebud," the often-uttered "Restless Oaks" holds a vital clue to the meaning of Henry Shoemaker's life. What's left of it? Would it be relegated to the fire along with lost childhood like Rosebud in the great movie about another wealthy newspaper publisher who battled in the governmental arena? As I turned off the highway, I first saw Restless Oaks on a sign advertising a restaurant. Is that it? Has it become part of the commercial interests Shoemaker so often railed about? Shaped into a log cabin, the new place boasts a homey country charm inside. Photographs of the area's old lumber industry fill a wall. Many of them, taken by William T. Clarke during the nineteenth century, were rescued by Henry Shoemaker from a muddy barn for preservation by the state and used in his books to show the beauty of the forest and its devastation by industry. Images of Shoemaker's favorite animals—deer, birds, buffalo—hang on other walls. The people inside are indeed friendly, as Shoemaker used to brag about his hometown, and I ask about him.

"Oh yeah, he's a legend," I hear. "I heard he was born into wealth and died a pauper."

"He was eccentric," another person pipes in. "He used to bring in trees and animals from all over the world into his place. He had wolves there on his estate, and you know what, he owned the reservoir and kept wild animals there. There wasn't much here then but the trees and the mountains, and his place.

"He owned everything around here," the dialogue continued. "He had all kinds of old stuff—carriages from Russia, a Conestoga Wagon. Yep, he had barns full of stuff."

"He wrote books," someone added, "and told stories."

I somehow feel as if I'm in one of the many backwoods stores Shoemaker so often described, where talk and legend abounded. As the coffee poured, a stout fellow in a flannel shirt strode in. Lots of waves greeted him, and it seemed that everyone knew the smiling man.

"He's my brother," the server explained, "and he can tell all the history around here." She beckoned him over and he sat down.

"Shoemaker," he uttered. "You want to know about Shoemaker? Why, I bought his place some years back. It was in the family for two hundred years and then it sold out before me. It was pretty run down by the time I got it."

"This isn't Restless Oaks?" I asked, puzzled.

"It is, but it isn't the original, the real thing," he offered. "People know the whole place, though, as Restless Oaks. It's a legendary name."

We walked outside and I looked around. With traffic noise behind us, I could see signs of new development—an Army Reserve Post, the Clinton County Prison, and an industrial park. Across the road, construction was going up for—of all things—a factory outlet mall. A sign announced a coming housing development called "Linnippi," raising images of Shoemaker's beloved ancestral "Lenape" peculiarly given to such modern buildings. To one side, though, was a quiet pocket of trees and fields.

"Yeah, that's it there," my guide said, nodding, as he saw me looking in the direction of the woods and the Bald Eagle mountains.

Walking up the path, I saw a stately white country house. The shaded latticework porches and surrounding tall trees were inviting in the heat, and I passed through the gate to reach them. A stone in the yard had those magic words "Restless Oaks" engraved in it, and I recalled photographs of Henry Shoemaker sitting on that stone playing with his favorite wolfhound. A Quiggley coat-of-arms with long-past dates had a prominent position on a window toward the top center of the house. Entering, I could imagine Henry enjoying this place, for the house held a peaceful historical charm protected by the trees. But few signs of Shoemaker's interior comfort remained. "The place was gutted, and everything removed," my guide explained. "I fixed it up and it's a bed-and-breakfast now."

In one of the front parlors I see an old photograph showing what the room used to look like. A tall bookcase bulges with reading, and on top mounted panthers and eagles hover over the room. The desk looks out the window

on the tree-lined property, and on it lie the papers for another book or
pamphlet. There's more traffic noise out those windows now than Shoemaker ever heard, and the plush front garden has made way for a Log
Homes outlet, but at night I can take in the symphony of birds, animals, and
insects, and the trees swaying in the wind. The only interruption is the
sound of the train howling as it rolls its cargo to destination.

Walking up the country lane in the morning, I came on Shoemaker's
"museum barn," now a commercial wood chips outlet. The integrity of the
exterior has been retained, however, and freshened-up right down to the
hex signs Shoemaker originally painted on the barn in 1915. Walking farther,
I see that the surrounding woods get thicker and darker. A few peaceful
animals graze. A mountain stream ambles through the property and cools
the air. My eyes glance backward to the white frame, then forward to a
rustic log cabin Shoemaker had brought onto the site. And farther up, I see
a path cut into the forest, which then disappears as my eyes follow the trees
blending into the mountains.

Driving west into the heights, I could see the West Branch of the
Susquehanna River trapping the town of Lock Haven against the mountainside. Signs of lumbering on the landscape can be spotted here and there,
but the scenes are quiet indeed, compared with those captured and hung on
the walls of the restaurant. The roar of engines breaks the silence, however,
as bulldozers push a path for a dike against the riverbank, and construction
creeps up the mountain's steep slope. The construction raised more than its
share of protest here in what brochures call "Unspoiled Pennsylvania"
where "nothing comes close, except the mountains."

Building on this mystique, the state has produced a slick publication that
urges motorists to "Take The Back Roads" to find the "Wonders of Rural
Pennsylvania." It guides the reader through Shoemaker's pet projects: state
forests and parks, historic sites, antiques, clean-water lakes and streams,
and hiking and camping. Also taking a page from Shoemaker's book, the
guide announces: "America starts here." That book has special words of
praise for Centre County, as "home to some of the most breathtaking
scenery you'll see anywhere," not to mention the home of the legend of
Penn's Cave.

On almost every road in these parts, I run into signs urging me to "Visit
Penn's Cave." Penn's Cave is, as the brochure at the Restless Oaks
restaurant told me, "a stunning example of nature's flawless beauty and
color" nestled in "Central Pennsylvania's scenic Lion Country." Closer and
closer I am beckoned to the natural wonder by Lake Nitanee: five miles to
Penn's Cave, three miles to Penn's Cave, one quarter mile to Penn's Cave.
I rush past those picturesque Pennsylvania place names of Snow Shoe,
Pleasant Gap, and Old Fort in Centre County—which is smack in the center

of the state, as the name implies. When I arrive at Penn's Cave, what I first
see isn't natural scenery but a huge flea market amid every conceivable
species of automobile. I get my ticket at the tourist shop and pass through
the store to the cave entrance, but not before seeing the various wares
being hawked. They are commercialized versions of Indian trinkets, frontier
garb, and natural specimens. A mountain lion named "Boomer," a living
reminder of "Pennsylvania's grandest animal," as Shoemaker called it, is
among the first sights as I head down toward the cave. Then I turn past the
"wildlife sanctuary" toward a large signboard holding Shoemaker's "Legend
of Penn's Cave as told by Isaac Steele, an aged Seneca Indian, in 1892"
(seven years after the cave first opened to the public): "Long before
settlements reached beyond Sunbury, Pennsylvania, a young Frenchman
from Lancaster County, Malachi Boyer, set out to explore the wilderness.
He roamed the forests peopled by American Indians, with whom he was
friendly. . . ." Shoemaker's name wasn't anywhere to be found, but the
legend was his. Others join me in reading the sign and make remarks about
the last line that Shoemaker didn't write—how the "world famous Nittany
Lion, located on The Pennsylvania State University campus," was named in
honor of the "beautiful Princess Nita-nee," If I wanted to, I could send a
postcard with this "Legend of the Nittany Lion" alongside an almost religious
portrayal of Nittany Mountain. I could also refer to the legend in brochures
that inform me the legend "has been told around campfires for generations."
Especially at Camp Shoemaker, I think.

The path beyond the sign takes me to a ledge where I could look up at
jagged cliffs or down into a cavern opening and murky water. I have to
descend many steep steps to boats docked by the water's edge. The boat
pushes off and floats into darkness and a strange, somehow disturbing
silence. The guide points out the springs of "unknown origin." Mystery?
Romance? You have to use your imagination, I guess, but it definitely could
inspire legend. The guide doesn't mention Nita-nee's story, but he does
point out the cavern's sights named by Shoemaker long ago with such
imaginative imagery as "Garden of the Gods," "Statue of Liberty," and
"Niagara Falls." Then the boat floats from the cavernous darkness into open
sunshine illuminating a pristine lake called "Nita-nee," a reminder of nature's
background to Indian and frontier days.

Henry Shoemaker's notes rave about the view from Karthaus Mountain
in Clearfield County just west of where the West Branch of the Susquehanna
River flows along the Centre County line. On this mountain my companion's
relation J. P. McGonigal sang for Henry Shoemaker. We walk past homes
that have forms reflecting their Pennsylvania-German, English, and Scots-
Irish origins. Some have been abandoned and are barely visible behind the
thick undergrowth that has reclaimed them. In this tiny hamlet, a historical

marker put up by the Pennsylvania Historical and Museum Commission points to the site of a short-lived iron furnace erected in 1817 by Peter Karthaus. This doesn't interest my companion as much as "her" history— the site of "the store," as it was called, now a residence. Run by her grandparents, the store was the only one in town for groceries and supplies. "Pap Pap" knew all the customers, their stories, and their songs. It's a strenuous walk up the mountain to the store from Mosquito Creek where log rafts floated regularly and inspired talk about the big drives and the hardy characters who worked them. Farther up the mountain from the store, there's a small clearing by the side of the road, where a low marker sits oddly in the shade. The lonely, out-of-place stone reads: "Clara Price Murdered 1889 by Alfred Andrews." "You know, there's a legend about that," my companion tells me.

When we reach the town of Clearfield, I read that an Indian village by the name of Chinklacamoose once stood there. The pioneer settlement of Clearfield, "it is said," got its name from the clearings made by grazing bison along nearby creeks. At nearby Hawk Run, the once-bustling Empire Hotel stands empty. Inside, its keeper, "Uncle Lewis," lies in old age, not wanting to remove anything from the day the place closed decades earlier. The portrait of his Slovak parents takes him back to the nineteenth century and the days when the hotel served streams of loggers, coal miners, and hunters, all with stories to tell, so it seemed. My companion shows me the hole in the back yard where children played and heard the story of "Indian Chief Hide-Behind." "If you uncovered the hole, the ghost of the Indian chief would come up and get you," she explains.

"We have to go to Frenchville," she urges. Coming as she does from Slovak, Hungarian, and Scots-Irish, as well as French, ancestry, Frenchville holds a significant part of her story. It is like many other towns in the highlands, tucked into the slopes beside fertile forestland. French names on the mailboxes, a mountainside nineteenth-century Catholic church, and a relic bake-oven behind the tavern offer clues of a difference here. At the church old-timers recall when just about everyone in town spoke a "pure" French inherited from colonial settlers who established this obscure outpost, but now only a few can even give a "parlez-vous Français?" At the annual Frenchville picnic, many former residents and relatives come back and reminisce about the past. Many old stones high on the cemetery slope mark death in French and announce families from farther down the mountain, such as Leconte, Charbonnet, and Billotte, that had left the original settlement.

Near Frenchville, I drive off the road down an unpaved route. I keep going farther and wonder where this leads. My companion assures me that our goal will shed more light on Shoemaker's world, but as I look in the rear-view mirror I am a bit unnerved by the darkness of the forest closing in behind me. "That's God country," I remember her father telling me about this wilderness, echoing Shoemaker's accolades. The long path finally takes me to a rough-hewn hunting cabin belonging to Frenchville's Richard Rougeux. To continue from here, the car must be left behind. I have to walk, but signs of trodden trails are rare. The flora and fauna are in charge here. The brush comes to my knees, and I can hear the sounds of animal cries in the distance. As night falls, I can barely see the hand in front of my face. It's not a time to wander from the cabin. A few folks back at our base start up a fire, and as a curtain of darkness comes down around us, they tell about the wild animals they have looked in the eye, the hunts they recall from Grandpap's day. So this is where Shoemaker heard about wolf days, about the last elks, some extraordinary deer horns, and the pesky snakes.

By contrast, the State Capitol in Harrisburg is well lit and paved over. Buildings replace the tall trees and look out onto traffic congestion, but on Front Street along the Susquehanna River, windows have an exquisite view over the water and the islands. Riverside Park, for which conservationist Horace McFarland lobbied during the Progressive Era, plays host to strollers who walk by State Street and barely notice the mansions in the background. They're known in the Dauphin County Historical Society guide as the J. Donald Cameron Mansion, the William Maclay Mansion, Bishop's Court, and the old Governor's Mansion (no longer standing). One not mentioned is Henry Shoemaker's sprawling old place between Maclay's mansion and Bishop's Court just up from the old Governor's Mansion. As I view it from the park, it looks much too large for one couple, but I remember Henry's fondness for accumulating books and collections, as well as for hosting dignitaries, and I feel confident that the colonel indeed filled this residence to the brim. I recall Cornell professor Harold Thompson's description of his "spacious house, which *looks* as though it belonged to a great folklorist and archivist, as it does."[1] Late in his life, Shoemaker and his wife moved a few blocks north, still by the river, where he lived in the only residence on the street shaded in by abundant trees. The Capitol Dome, a short distance away, can be seen from either place, and he must have enjoyed recalling that it was dedicated in 1906 by none other than his hero Teddy Roosevelt with his old friend Bishop Darlington at the President's side.

I retrace the steps Shoemaker must have taken to work at the Capitol Complex. He would have been surprised at the changes to his offices at the Pennsylvania Historical and Museum Commission. Once crammed into an antiquated building, the State Museum is now in a huge circular structure commanding the entire side of the block across from the Capitol. The archives are housed in a separate edifice that rises into the sky like a giant file cabinet. These structures stand out in the cityscape, and in their prominence within the Capitol Complex seem to imply the importance of heritage of Pennsylvania's way of doing things. In the Division of History, the professional recording of unwritten history, now called oral history, plays a major part in documentation of the state's story, while across Capitol Park the Office of Folklife Programs maintains records on folk artists in the state and works on "heritage parks." Transcriptions of electronic recordings ensure accuracy of narratives from out-of-the-way communities, extinct industrial pursuits, and all stripes of ethnic and religious groups. There's hardly anyone on Capitol Hill now to recall Henry Shoemaker, but much of his legacy remains there. And I bet the new policemen and janitors still have tales to tell, just like they did in Shoemaker's day.

Much of the talk in the "City on the Move" concerns the mayor's ambitious plans for future progress, and I'm sure Shoemaker would have been moved to issue an editorial on the matter. The mayor has proposed a dam that would enhance the use of the river for recreation and tourism dollars, but environmentalists have opposed it because of the damage it would do to wildlife. In the middle of the river, City Island, which Shoemaker used to be able to see from his window, has already been built over with a stadium, a marina, playgrounds, and parking lots, while an archaeological dig moves quickly to try to recover remnants of Indian settlement on the island before it's too late. In 1992 a picture of a local sycamore with Shoemaker protectively standing beside it appears in the *Harrisburg Patriot-News*. A legend reported by Shoemaker attests to the sacredness of the large old tree. Yet this product of nature is threatened by advancing development in the area, and the newspaper editorializes that the tree should be preserved as a "lesson in Penn's Woods"—"a surviving example of the environment's ongoing battle against economic expediency."[2] The Progressive issues of Shoemaker's day haven't gone away.

The "Battle of Blue Mountain" shapes up to be a classic confrontation for conservation issues in the mid-state. The picturesque spot is one on which Henry Shoemaker bestowed many a sacred legend and invited seekers to behold nature's mythical wonder. A federal court deals with a challenge to an East Pennsboro township ordinance to control commercial development on the mountain, and many municipalities across the nation listen attentively for the outcome to gauge their strategy for fostering prosperity and the environmental "public good." "Protecting the mountain is important," a resident of the township who happens to be a professional football player declares. The local newspaper underscores his words on the image of Pennsylvania at stake: "It's a resource that we have not only in our country, but in our state. That's what Pennsylvania is all about. These hills with these trees on them." On this day, the court rules for the developer, but, with the assistance of the "Governor Pinchot chapter of the Sierra Club," prominent citizens vow to "build a shining example" of progressive tradition with a "strong, loud, informed voice of a newly incorporated organization."[3]

Meanwhile, a historical society officer from Harrisburg calls me to talk about the legend of the city's founder, John Harris.[4] "All the old locals know it here," he declares, but after a pause he added, "or a version of it." "The trader Harris refused some hostile Indians drink, and they tied him up and threatened to burn him. Now, some tell that friendly Indians—the Paxton tribe, for whom Paxton is named—came and rescued him. But others say it was the slave 'Hercules' who brought relief. One even offered that it was a 'manifest evidence of God's merciful interposition.' But I have evidence that the story builds up his courage and faith more than it should. It was more likely that ole Harris ran and hid from the group rather than be captured." He then sighs, "We've got parts of the tree he supposedly was tied to in our collection. I guess we'll never know the fact from the fiction."

I probably surprised him by asking, "Why is that important to you?"

"Why, you hear it in school. That's what people believe and then retell. People love those captivity stories, and it happened right here." Each version told carries more than a hint of editorializing on the figures of the past and the ways of the frontier. Whether the "hard facts" could be found or not, the stories continue as matters of belief within history.

At Penn State Harrisburg, my students locate Pennsylvania on the map by talking about their inherited traditions. The Census tells me that if these students come from Pennsylvania they're likely to stay there, and have several generations back there too. If they come from the state, they're indeed likely to live in rural or suburban environs. What the Census doesn't tell me is how they personalize their surroundings. They may not use "mystique" or "paradise," as Shoemaker liked to do, but they know a narrative of the farmlands, forests, and mountains. They recount a place where all kinds of people dwell and where family roots run deep. They talk about the traditional foods they eat, the houses they live in, the beliefs they hear. They're sure that each epitomizes Pennsylvania apart from the South or New England. It's a varied picture they draw. They tell me about Latvian songs from Lancaster, Pennsylvania-German pig's stomach dinners from Rough and Ready, Slovak customs from Hazleton, Polish music from Pittsburgh, Welsh slatework from Delta, Brethren worship near Mount Joy, coal miners' stories from Mauch Chunk, government workers' photocopied humor from Harrisburg, children's street games from Philadelphia, college student pranks on campus, "urban legends" about computers and microwaves, and teenage ritual trips to haunts outside Columbia. Several come forward and talk to me about what goes on at hunting camp in the forested highlands as folklore. More tell me about reputed horror stories of abduction and mutilation in cities and malls. It strikes me that Shoemaker was wrong in saying that youth don't tell stories anymore. They still have the need to narrate, but it's more likely to happen at slumber parties than at campfires, and it will more likely concern what happened last week than what occurred in Indian and frontier days.

I teach them to record and understand traditions in the context of history and culture. Thanks to new communications technology, we are able to record the sights and sounds of traditions much better than Shoemaker was ever able to, and we still probe their meaning, though using more ethnographic techniques than Shoemaker would have recognized. Despite this professional turn, we still bring up Shoemaker's lesson in discussing the proper "public" and "academic" roles in the interpretation and presentation of heritage. Our archives bulge with results of "fieldwork," and our scholars try to make sense of it all. A Center for Pennsylvania Culture Studies arises to the challenge. It isn't so much in Shoemaker's spirit of promoting the "romance" of history and folklore as it is in the idea of studying the ways in which tradition "works." The center isn't trying to make a case for one regional culture, but rather looks for cultural process in the complex environments fostering tradition within Pennsylvania. A heap of letters come in daily inquiring about "roots" that need to be answered and contemplated as part of a modern-day search for cultural meaning.

Indeed, many citizens, as well as students, are not just locating Pennsylvania on the map in terms of its traditions. They are locating themselves. They ask to recover their heritage from family, ethnic background, religion, occupation, and region. Increasingly mobile yet uneasy about the future, they ask more than I remember years ago about realizing their identities, connecting to communities, facing new experiences with the strength of a "foundation"—indeed, about belonging. Having so many choices for the future in modern America, they ask about their past and their bonds to others as Pennsylvanians and as Americans. More and more, I face restless oaks spreading their branches while their roots run hidden from view. Henry Shoemaker, and others like him, popularized a special and often mystical soil of tradition as a way to steady themselves against the pressures of modern times. Even though their names often go unrecognized in the grounding of the state, their stories, their struggles, and their questions, follow our destinies.

Almost fifty years after Henry Shoemaker realized his Progressive vision of state government taking responsibility for cultural conservation for the sake of the "public good," a new administration dismantled a key agency created to carry out this state function. After Thomas Ridge became Governor in 1995, his administration proposed eliminating the Department of Community

Affairs, in which the Pennsylvania Heritage Affairs Commission resided.
The state administration proposed relocating many agencies from Community Affairs into other departments, but the administration announced plans
to abolish the Commission and its Office of State Folklife Programs by June
30, 1996, and to seek repeal of the Heritage Affairs Act of 1992, which
authorized the Commission to offer cultural conservation activities. The
Ridge administration called for "privatizing" such state services, but it didn't
create a mechanism for privatization. The director of the Commission,
Shalom Staub, resigned in October 1995, and indeed established a private,
nonprofit organization called the Institute for Cultural Partnerships.

The administration's move fit into a Republican promise to reduce state
government, even though Pennsylvania already had the lowest ratio of state
employees to population in the nation, and even though it was a Republican,
former Governor Dick Thornburgh, who had created the Commission to
promote ethnic participation in, and loyalty to, his administration. It may not
have helped the fate of the Heritage Affairs Commission that former
Lieutenant Governor Mark Singel, who ran for Governor against Tom Ridge,
visibly led the Commission for many years.

Although Henry Shoemaker viewed the involvement of state government
in cultural services as a "conservative" program to unite and promote a
state, by the 1990s many vocal conservatives viewed such activities as
divisive or political when the programs promote a multicultural social vision.
More than the size of state government was obviously at stake. At issue in
this political discourse were the "proper" values conserved along with the
records of folklore and history. Shoemaker probably would bristle at the
social vision and ethnological principles of Pennsylvania's state folklife program, although it grew out of his Progressive impulse for state involvement
in conservation of resources, cultural and natural.

The Pennsylvania Historical and Museum Commission that Shoemaker
guided is still intact, although in the 1990s it seeks to refine its mission for
the state as a keeper of the Commonwealth's "memory" and teller of its
"story." The Historical and Museum Commission is active in facilitating
activities at the grass-roots level, where conservation of local and ethnic
heritage signifies a modern-day search for identity within a mass society.
Meanwhile, Shoemaker's Progressive guidelines of managing culture in a
modernizing state, as well as promoting its tradition, have taken a dramatic
turn in the reorganization and privatization of public heritage programs, and
Pennsylvania—indeed, the nation—appears to be controversially entering a
new period of cultural and historical programming for the "public good." The
public debate over government involvement in cultural programming offers
reminders of long-standing emotional conflicts raised by the narratives that
legitimize different social views of the American experience.

Appendix

A Sampler of Shoemaker Stories

I. The Legend of Penn's Cave (from *Pennsylvania Mountain Stories*, 1908)

II. Nita-nee: The Indian Maiden for Whom Nittany Mountain Is Named (from *Juniata Memories*, 1916)

III. The Indian Steps (from *Indian Steps*, 1912)

IV. Wildmannli (from *North Mountain Mementos*, 1920)

I. The Legend of Penn's Cave

In the days when the West Branch Valley was a trackless wilderness of defiant pines and submissive hemlocks, twenty-five years before the first pioneer had attempted a permanent lodgment beyond Sunbury, a young Pennsylvania Frenchman from Lancaster county, named Malachi Boyer, alone and unaided, pierced the jungle to a point where Bellefonte is now located. The history of his travels has never been written, partly because he had no white companion to observe them, and partly because he himself was unable to write. His very identity would now be forgotten were it not for traditions of the Indians, with whose lives he became strangely entangled.

A short stockily built fellow was Malachi Boyer, with unusually prominent black eyes, and black hair that hung in ribbon-like strands over his broad, low forehead. Fearless, yet conciliatory, he escaped a thousand times from Indian cunning and treachery, and as the months went by and he penetrated further into the forests he numbered many redskins among his cherished friends.

Why he explored these boundless wilds he could not explain, for it was not in the interest of science, as he scarcely knew of such a thing as geography, and it was not for trading, as he lived by the way. But on he

forced his path, ever aloof from his own race, on the alert for the strange
scenes which encompassed him day by day.

One beautiful month of April, there is no one who can tell the exact year,
found Malachi Boyer camped on the shores of Spring Creek. Near the
Mammoth Spring was an Indian camp whose occupants maintained a quasi-
intercourse with the pale-face stranger. Sometimes old Chief O-ko-cho
would bring gifts of corn to Malachi, who in turn presented the chieftain
with a hunting knife of truest steel. And in this way Malachi came to spend
more and more of his time about the Indian camps, only keeping his distance
at night and during religious ceremonies.

Old O-ko-cho's chief pride was centered in his seven stalwart sons, Hum-
kin, Ho-ko-lin, Too-chin, Os-tin, Chaw-kee-bin, A-ha-kin, Ko-lo-pa-kin, and
his Diana-like daughter, Nita-nee. The seven brothers resolved themselves
into a guard of honor for their sister, who had many suitors, among whom
was the young chief, E-Faw, from the adjoining sub-tribe of the A-caw-ko-
taws. But Nita-nee gently though firmly repulsed her numerous suitors,
until such time as her father would give her in marriage to one worthy of
her regal blood.

Thus ran the course of Indian life when Malachi Boyer made his bed of
hemlock boughs by the gurgling waters of Spring Creek. And it was the first
sight of her, washing a deer skin in the stream, that led him to prolong his
stay and ingratiate himself with her father's tribe.

Few were the words that passed between Malachi and Nita-nee, many
the glances, and often did the handsome pair meet in the mossy ravines
near the camp grounds. But this was all clandestine love, for friendly as
Indian and white might be in social intercourse, never could a marriage be
tolerated, until—there always is a turning point in romance—the black-
haired wanderer and the beautiful Nita-nee resolved to spend their lives
together, and one moonless night started for the more habitable east. All
night long they threaded their silent way, climbing the mountain ridges,
gliding through the velvet soiled hemlock glades, and wading, hand in hand,
the splashing, resolute torrents. When morning came they breakfasted on
dried meat and huckleberries, and bathed their faces in a mineral spring.
Until—there is always a turning point in romance—seven tall, stealthy
forms, like animated mountain pines, stepped from the gloom and surrounded the eloping couple. Malachi drew a hunting knife, identical with the
one he had given to Chief O-ko-cho, and seizing Nita-nee around the waist,
stabbed right and left at his would-be captors. The first stroke pierced Hum-
kin's heart, and uncomplaining he sank down dying. The six remaining
brothers, although receiving stab wounds, caught Malachi in their combined
grasp and disarmed him; then one brother held sobbing Nita-nee, while the
others dragged fighting Malachi across the mountain. That was the last the

lovers saw of one another. Below the mountain lay a broad valley, from the center of which rose a circular hillock, and it was to this mound the savage brothers led their victim. As they approached a yawning cavern met their eyes, filled with greenish limestone water. There is a ledge at the mouth of the cave, about six feet higher than the water, above which the arched roof rises thirty feet, and it was from here they shoved Malachi Boyer into the tide below. He sank for a moment, but when he rose to the surface, commenced to swim. He approached the ledge, but the brothers beat him back, so he turned and made for some dry land in the rear of the cavern. Two of the brothers ran from the entrance over the ridge to watch where there is another small opening, but though Malachi tried his best, in the impenetrable darkness he could not find this or any other avenue of escape. He swam back to the cave's mouth, but the merciless Indians were still on guard. He climbed up again and again, but was repulsed, and once more retired to the dry cave. Every day for a week he renewed his efforts to escape, but the brothers were never absent. Hunger became unbearable, his strength gave way but he vowed he would not let the redskins see him die, so forcing himself into one of the furthermost labyrinths, Malachi Boyer breathed his last.

Two days afterwards the brothers entered the cave and discovered the body. They touched not the coins in his pockets, but weighted him with stones and dropped him into the deepest part of the greenish limestone water. And after these years those who have heard this legend declare that on the still summer nights an unaccountable echo rings through the cave, which sounds like "Nita-nee," "Nita-nee."

II. Nita-nee: The Indian Maiden for Whom Nittany Mountain Is Named

One of the last Indians to wander through the Juniata Valley, either to revive old memories or merely to hunt and trap, his controlling motive is not certain, was old Jake Faddy. As he was supposed to belong to the Seneca tribe, and spent most of his time on the Coudersport Pike on the border line between Clinton and Potter Counties, it is to be surmised that he never lived permanently on the Juniata, but had hunted there or participated in the bloody wars in the days of his youth. He continued his visits until he reached a very advanced age. Of a younger generation than Shaney John, he was nevertheless well acquainted with that unique old redman, and always spent a couple of weeks with him at his cabin on Saddler's Run.

Old Jake, partly to earn his board and partly to show his superior knowledge, was a gifted story teller. He liked to obtain the chance to spend the night at farmhouses where there were aged people, and his smattering of history would be fully utilized to put the older folks in good humor.

For while the hard-working younger generations fancied that *history* was a waste of time, the old people loved it, and fought against the cruel way in which all local tradition and legend was being snuffed out. If it had not been for a few people carrying it over the past generation, all of it would now be lost in the whirlpool of a commercial, materialistic age. And to those few, unknown to fame, and of obscure life and residence, is due the credit of saving for us the wealth of folklore that the noble mountains, the dark forests, the wars and the Indians, instilled in the minds of the first settlers. And there is no old man or woman living in the wilderness who is without a story that is ready to be imparted, and worthy of preservation. But the question remains, how can these old people all be reached before they pass away? It would take an army of collectors, working simultaneously, as the Grim Reaper is hard at work removing these human landmarks with their untold stories.

Out near the heading of Beaver Dam Run, at the foot of Jack's Mountain, stands a very solid-looking stone farmhouse, a relic of pioneer days. Its earliest inhabitants had run counter to the Indians of the neighborhood for the possession of the beavers whose dens and "cabins" were its most noticeable feature clear to the mouth of the stream, and later for the otters who defied the white annihilators a quarter of a century longer. Beaver trapping had made the stream a favorite rendezvous for the red men, and their campgrounds at the springs near the headwaters were pointed out until a comparatively recent date.

But one by one the aborigines dropped away, until Jake Faddy alone upheld the traditions of the race. There were no beavers to quarrel over in his day, consequently his visits were on a more friendly basis. The old North of Ireland family who occupied the stone farmhouse was closely linked with the history of the Juniata Valley, and they felt the thrill of the vivid past whenever the old Indian appeared at the kitchen door. As he was ever ready to work and, what was better, a very useful man at gardening and flowers, he was always given his meals and lodging for as long as he cared to remain. But that was not very long, as his restless nature was ever goading him on, and he had "many other friends to see," putting it in his own language. He seemed proud to have it known that he was popular with a good class of white people, and his ruling passion may have been to cultivate these associations. On several occasions he brought some of his sons with him, but they did not seem anxious to live up to their father's standards. And after the old man had passed away none of this younger generation ever came to the Juniata Valley.

The past seemed like the present to Jake Faddy, he was so familiar with it. To him it was as if it happened yesterday, the vast formations and changes and epochs. And the Indian race, especially the eastern Indians, seemed to have played the most important part in those titanic days. It seemed so recent and so real to the old redman that his stories were always interesting. The children also were fond of hearing him talk; he had a way of never becoming tiresome. Every young person who heard him remembered what he said. There would have been no break in the "apostolic succession" of Pennsylvania legendary lore if all had been seated at Jake Faddy's knee.

Of all his stories, by odds his favorite one, dealt with the Indian maiden, Nita-nee, for whom the fruitful Nittany Valley and the towering Nittany Mountain are named. This Indian girl was born on the banks of the lovely Juniata, not far from the present town of Newton Hamilton, the daughter of a powerful chief. It was in the early days of the world, when the physical aspect of Nature could be changed over night by a fiat from the Gitchie-Manitto or Great Spirit. It was therefore in the age of great and wonderful things, before a rigid world produced beings whose lives followed grooves as tight and permanent as the gullies and ridges.

During the early life of Nita-nee a great war was waged for the possession of the Juniata Valley. The aggressors were Indians from the South, who longed for the scope and fertility of this earthly Paradise. Though Nita-nee's father and his brave cohorts defended their beloved land to the last extremity, they were driven northward into the Seven Mountains and beyond. Though they found themselves in beautiful valleys, filled with bubbling springs and teeming with game, they missed the Blue Juniata, and were never wholly content. The father of Nita-nee, who was named Chun-Eh-Hoe, felt so humiliated that he only went about after night in his new home. He took up his residence on a broad plain, not far from where State College now stands, and should be the Indian patron of that growing institution, instead of Chief Bald Eagle, who never lived near there and whose good deeds are far outweighed by his crimes.

Chun-Eh-Hoe was an Indian of exact conscience. He did his best in the cruel war, but the southern Indians must have had more sagacious leaders or a better *esprit de corps*. At any rate they conquered. Chun-Eh-Hoe was not an old man at the time of his defeat, but it is related that his raven black locks turned white over night. He was broken in spirit after his downfall and only lived a few years in his new home. His widow, as well as his daughter, Nita-nee, and many other children, were left to mourn him. As Nita-nee was the oldest, she assumed a vicereineship over the tribe until her young brother, Wo-Wi-Na-Pie, should be old enough to rule the councils and go on the warpath.

The defeat on the Juniata, the exile to the northern valleys and the premature death of Chun-Eh-Hoe were to be avenged. Active days were ahead of the tribesmen. Meanwhile if the southern Indians crossed the mountains to still further covet their lands and liberties, who should lead them to battle but Nita-nee. But the Indian vicereine was of a peace-loving disposition. She hoped that the time would never come when she would have to preside over scenes of carnage and slaughter. She wanted to see her late father's tribe become the most cultured and prosperous in the

Indian world, and in that way be revenged on their warlike foes: "Peace hath its victories."

But she was not to be destined to lead a peaceful nation through years of upward growth. In the Juniata Valley the southern Indians had become overpopulated; they sought broader territories, like the Germans of today. They had driven the present occupants of the northern valleys out of the Juniata country, they wanted to again drive them further north.

Nita-nee did not want war, but the time came when she could not prevent it. The southern Indians sought to provoke a conflict by making settlements in the Bare Meadows, and in some fertile patches on Tussey Knob and Bald Top, all of which were countenanced in silence. But when they murdered some peaceable farmers and took possession of plantations at the foot of the mountains in the valley of the Karoondinha, then the mildness of Nita-nee's cohorts came to an end. Meanwhile her mother and brother had died, Nita-nee had been elected queen.

Every man and boy volunteered to fight; a huge army was recruited over night. They swept down to the settlements of the southern Indians, butchering every one of them. They pressed onward to the Bare Meadows, and to the slopes of Bald Top and Tussey Knob. There they gave up the population to fire and sword. Crossing the Seven Mountains, they formed a powerful cordon all along the southerly slope of the Long Mountain. Building block houses and stone fortifications—some of the stonework can be seen to this day—they could not be easily dislodged.

The southern Indians, noticing the flames of the burning plantations, and hearing from the one or two survivors of the completeness of the rout, were slow to start an offensive movement. But as Nita-nee's forces showed no signs of advancing beyond the foot of Long Mountain, they mistook this hesitancy for cowardice, and sent an attacking army. It was completely defeated in the gorge of Laurel Run, above Milroy, and on the slopes of Sample Knob, the right of the northern Indians to the Karoondinha and the adjacent valleys was signed, sealed and delivered in blood. The southern Indians were in turn driven out by other tribes; in fact, every half century or so a different race ruled over the Juniata Valley. But in all those years none of the Juniata rulers sought to question the rights of the northern Indians until 1635, when the Lenni-Lenape invaded the country of the Susquehannocks and were decisively beaten on the plains near Rock Spring, in Spruce Creek Valley, at the Battle of the Indian Steps. (This battle has been described in stirring verse by Central Pennsylvania's bard, John H. Chatham, "The Indian Steps," Altoona, 1913.)

As Nita-nee wanted no territorial accessions, she left the garrisons at her southerly forts intact, and retired her main army to its home valleys, where it was disbanded as quickly as it came together. All were glad to be back to peaceful avocations, none of them craved glory in war. And there were no honors given out, no great generals created. All served as private soldiers under the direct supervision of their queen. It was the theory of this Joan of Arc that by eliminating titles and important posts there would be no military class created, no ulterior motive assisted except *patriotism*. The soldiers serving anonymously, and for their country's need alone, would be ready to end their military duties as soon as their patriotic task was done.

Nita-nee regarded soldiering as a stern necessity, not as an excuse for pleasure or pillage, or personal advancement. Under her there was no nobility, all were on a common level of dignified citizenship. Every Indian in her realm had a task, not one that he was born to follow, but the one which appealed to him mostly, and therefore the task at which he was most successful. Women also had their work, apart from domestic life in this ideal democracy of ancient days. Suffrage was universal to both sexes over twenty years of age, but as there were no official positions, no public trusts, a political class could not come into existence, and the queen, as long as she was cunning and able, had the unanimous support of her people. She was given a great ovation as she modestly walked along the fighting line after the winning battle of Laurel Run. It made her feel not that she was great, but that the democracy of her father and her ancestors was a living force. In those days of pure democracy the rulers walked: the litters and palanquins were a later development.

After the conflict the gentle Nita-nee, at the head of the soon to be disbanded army, marched across the Seven Brothers, and westerly toward her permanent encampment, where State College now stands. As her only trophy she carried a bundle of spears, which her brave henchmen had wrenched from the hands of the southern Indians as they charged the forts along Long Mountain. These were not to deck her own lodge house, nor for vain display, but were to be placed on the grave of her father, the lamented Chun-Eh-Hoe, who had been avenged. In her heart she had hoped for victory, almost as much for his sake as for the comfort of her people. She knew how he had grieved himself to death when he was outgeneraled in the previous war.

In those dimly remote days there was no range of mountains where the Nittany chain now raise their noble summits to the sky. All was a plain, a prairie, clear north to the Bald Eagles, which only recently had come into existence. The tradition was that far older than all the other hills were the Seven Mountains. And geological speculation seems to bear this out. At all seasons of the year cruel and chilling winds blew out of the north, hindering the work of agriculture on the broad plains ruled over by Nita-nee. Only the strong and the brave could cope with these killing blasts, so intense and so different from the calming zephyrs of the Juniata. The seasons for this cause were several weeks shorter than across the Seven Mountains; that is, there was a later spring and an earlier fall. But though the work was harder, the soil being equally rich and broader area, the crops averaged fully as large as those further south. So, taken altogether, the people of Nita-nee could not be said to be an unhappy aggregation.

As the victorious queen was marching along at the head of her troops, she was frequently almost mobbed by women and children, who rushed out from the settlements and made her all manner of gifts. As it was in the early spring, there were no floral garlands, but instead wreaths and festoons of laurel, of ground pine and ground spruce. There were gifts of precious stones and metals, of rare furs, of beautiful specimens of Indian pottery, basketry and the like. These were graciously acknowledged by Nita-nee, who turned them over to her bodyguards to be carried to her permanent abode on the "Barrens." But it was not a "barrens" in those days, but a rich agricultural region, carefully irrigated from the north, and yielding the most bountiful crops of Indian corn. It was only when abandoned by the frugal redmen and grown up with forest which burned over repeatedly through the carelessness of the white settlers that it acquired that disagreeable name. In those days it was known as the "Hills of Plenty."

As Nita-nee neared the scenes of her happy days she was stopped in the middle of the path by an aged Indian couple. Leaning on staffs in order to present a dignified appearance, it was easily seen that age had bent them nearly double. Their weazened, weather-beaten old faces were pitiful to behold. Toothless, and barely able to speak above a whisper, they addressed the gracious queen.

"We are very old," they began, "the winters of more than a century have passed over our heads. Our sons and our grandsons were killed fighting bravely under your immortal sire, Chun-Eh-Hoe. We have had to struggle on by ourselves as best we could ever since. We are about to set out a crop of corn, which we need badly. For the past three years the north wind has destroyed our crop every time it appeared; the seeds which we plan to put in the earth this year are the last we've got. Really we should have kept them for food, but we hoped that the future would treat us more generously. We would like a windbreak built along the northern side of our corn patch; we are too feeble to go to the forests and cut and carry the poles. Will not our most kindly queen have some one assist us?"

Nita-nee smiled on the aged couple, then she looked at her army of able-bodied warriors.

Turning to them she said, "Soldiers, will a hundred of you go to the nearest royal forest, which is in the center of this plain, and cut enough cedar poles with brush on them to build a wind-break for these good people?"

Instantly a roar arose, a perfect babel of voices: it was every soldier trying to volunteer for this philanthropic task.

When quiet was restored, a warrior stepped out from the lines saying,

"Queen, we are very happy to do this, we who have lived in this valley know full well how all suffer from the uncheckable north winds."

The queen escorted the old couple back to their humble cottage, and sat with them until her stalwart braves returned with the green-tipped poles. It looked like another Birnam Wood in process of locomotion. The work was so quickly and so carefully done that it seemed almost like a miracle to the wretched old Indians. They fell on their knees, kissing the hem of their queen's garment and thanking her for her beneficence. She could hardly leave them, so profuse were they in their gratitude. In all but a few hours were consumed in granting what to her was a simple favor, and she was safe and sound within her royal lodge house by dark. Before she left she had promised to return when the corn crop was ripe and partake of a corn roast with the venerable couple. The old people hardly dared hope she would come, but those about her knew that her word was as good as her bond. That night bonfires were lighted to celebrate her return, and there was much Indian music and revelry.

Nita-nee was compelled to address the frenzied mob, and in her speech she told them that while they had won a victory, she hoped it would be the last while she lived; she hated war, but would give her life rather than have her people invaded. All she asked in this world was peace with honor. That expressed the sentiment of her people exactly, and they literally went mad with loyalty and enthusiasm for the balance of the night. Naturally with such an uproar there was no sleep for Nita-nee.

As she lay awake on her couch she thought that far sweeter than victory or earthly fame was the helping of others, the smoothing of rough pathways for the weak or oppressed. She resolved more than ever to dedicate her life to the benefiting of her subjects. No love affair had come into her life, she would use her great love-nature to put brightness into unhappy souls about her. And she got up the next morning much more refreshed than she could have after a night of sleep surcharged with dreams of victory and glory.

As the summer progressed, and the corn crop in the valleys became ripe, the queen sent an orderly to notify the aged couple that she would come to their home alone the next evening for the promised corn roast. It was a wonderful, calm, cloudless night, with the full moon shedding its effulgent smile over the plain. Unaccompanied, except by her orderly, Nita-nee walked to the modest cabin of the aged couple, a distance of about five miles, for the cottage stood not far from the present village of Linden Hall. Evidently the windbreak had been a success, for, bathed in moonlight, the tasseled heads of the cornstalks appeared above the tops of the cedar hedge. Smoke was issuing from the open hearth back of the hut, which showed that the roast was being prepared. The aged couple were delighted to see her, and the evening passed by, bringing innocent and supreme happiness to all. And thus in broad unselfishness and generosity of thought and deed the great queen's life was spent, making her pathway through her realm radiant with sunshine.

And when she came to die, after a full century of life, she requested that her body be laid to rest in the royal forest, in the center of the valley whose people she loved and served so well. Her funeral cortege, which included every person in the plains and valleys, a vast assemblage, shook with a common grief. It would be hard to find a successor like her, a pure soul so deeply animated with true godliness.

And it came to pass that on the night when she was buried beneath a modest mound covered with cedar boughs, and the vast funeral party had dispersed, a terrific storm arose, greater than even the oldest person could remember. The blackness of the night was intense, the roar and rumbling heard made every being fear that the end of the world had come. It was a night of intense terror, of horror. But at dawn, the tempest abated, only a gentle breeze remained, a golden sunlight overspread the scene, and great was the wonder thereof! In the center of the vast plain where Nita-nee had been laid away stood a mound-like mountain, a towering, sylvan giant covered with dense groves of cedar and pine. And as it stood there, eternal, it tempered and broke the breezes from the north, promising a new prosperity, a greater tranquility, to the peaceful dwellers in the newly-created vale that has since been called the Valley of the Karoondinha.

A miracle, a sign of approval from the Great Spirit, had happened during the night to forever keep alive the memory of Nita-nee, who had tempered the winds from the cornpatch of the aged, helpless couple years before. And the dwellers in the valleys adjacent to the now protected Valley of the Karoondinha awoke to a greater pride in themselves, a high ideal must be observed, since they were the special objects of celestial notice.

And the name of Nita-nee was the favorite cognomen for Indian maidens, and has been borne by many of saintly and useful life ever since, and none of these namesakes were more deserving than the Nita-nee who lived centuries later near the mouth of Penn's Cave, the daughter of Chief O-Ko-Cho.

III. The Indian Steps

It was at the foot-races between the Indians south of the Tussey Mountains and the Indians north of these mountains, which took place on the "plains" near what is now Pine Grove, that Silver Eagle, ruler of the Kishoquoquilas, or Southern Indians, saw his cousin, the beautiful Princess Meadow Sweet. He had not laid eyes on her since she was carried away when the Northern Indians, or Susquehanahs, overran the Southern country and killed her father, King Yellow Thistle. She had been a nominal captive since her sixth year, and she was now sixteen. Ironwood, the mighty warrior and King of the Susquehanahs, who invaded the Southern country, had adopted her, and her beauty and intelligence made him lavish on her more affection than on his own children. At his death his eldest son, Pipsisseway, or Prince's Pine, inherited the rulership of the vast domain which included all the territory now known as "northern," "central," and "western" Pennsylvania. He greatly admired his exquisite-looking foster-sister Meadow Sweet, who in turn looked up to him on account of his sterling character, intrepid military skill and giant strength. The young monarch had always called her his "little sister," and looking upon her as such, romantic impulses were not stirred within him as early as they might otherwise have been. When old Ironwood was dying he begged his sons to see that Meadow Sweet received a dowry on her marriage. Pipsisseway promised the expiring ruler that she should have "all the lands which lay east of Spruce Creek, south and west of the Susquehanah and north of Jack's Mountains." There was a smile on the aged chieftain's lips when he heard this, and in another hour he was dead. None mourned him more than his foster-daughter, for there was a deep sympathetic bond between them. Pipsisseway carried out his promise, which made Meadow Sweet possessor of a domain of singular beauty and natural wealth. And this territory became speedily known under the poetic title of "The Land of Meadow Sweet." Thus it was described in Indian oratory and in agreements with distant tribes. There may have been a "love motive" back of Pipsisseway's generous suggestion, as it would seem unusual to present a foster-sister with a territory comprising some of the richest land in what is now Central Pennsylvania. It even included the royal camp-grounds, burial grounds and pottery works which were located in what is now Wayne Township, Clinton County. This beautiful retreat, known to the first white settlers as "Patterson's Town," had been the favorite headquarters for the great chieftains for centuries, and unless Pipsisseway intended marrying Meadow Sweet he would be forced to move the royal lodge-houses and abandon the graves of his ancestors if she became the wife of another. It may have been her extreme youth that prevented his open love-making, or some secret understanding between the girl and himself that the betrothal was not to be announced until some future date. The princess was treated with the greatest deference by Pipsisseway and his three brothers, Checkerberry, Red Pine and Moonseed. Most of her time was spent at the royal encampment by the Susquehanah, where she was attended by a score of maidens, the daughters of noted war-chiefs. Wise men, from beyond the Allegheny Mountains and from the far South, instructed her in all the arts and sciences known to the redmen. She was taught the use of the bow and arrow, and dart. The mysteries of woodcraft were explained by the greatest hunters that could be summoned for that purpose. Her life was a happy one, surrounded by congenial company, and, living in a beautiful region, she had little to wish for. During important religious ceremonials or sporting events she accompanied Pipsisseway to different parts of his domain. It had hitherto been deemed wise not to encourage any athletic competitions with other Indian kingdoms, but the Kishoquoquilas had challenged so repeatedly that the Council of Wise Men, after grave deliberation, advised Pipsisseway to allow it to be accepted. These Wise Men knew that in their realm resided the fleetest runners, jumpers, wrestlers, and weight-throwers, and no challenging party would stand any chance against them. They considered it would be humbling to the pride of their opponents to give them a decisive defeat in the field of sport and make them feel less likely to stir up warfare. This was logic, but they omitted to figure in the effect of the presence of Princess Meadow Sweet, stolen in her early childhood from the Kishoquoquilas, upon the horde of warriors from the South. The great athletic meet took place the latter part of May, when nature was at her loveliest. The "plains" where it occurred were just north of the mountains which formed the boundary between the two rival kingdoms. They had been formed by fires frequently burning the timber, which had eventually fallen down, and the ground pastured smooth by vast herds of buffaloes, elks, moose, and deer. The sports were to continue during four days and at night love feasts were to be held for the visiting redmen to become better acquainted with their neighbors. The greatest precautions were made to have everything pass off pleasantly. Pipsisseway, who was a diplomat as well as a warrior, called all the athletes before him in a private audience, urging them in no case to defeat a Southern Indian by a wide margin. Every finish was to be close, and if it looked as if the Susquehanahs were to roll up a huge score of points against their competitors, some events must be purposely lost. This was a slightly different program from the one advised by the Wise Men, who urged that the Northern athletes give a decisive beating to their rivals. The weather was ideal for the tournament, and the number of Indians present far exceeded anticipations. They came from every direction, marshaled by their chiefs. It was twenty years since the last contest of this kind had taken place. The Susquehanahs had been victorious by a wide margin, and the Kishoquoquilas had returned across the mountains in an ugly frame of mind. On several occasions they had sent expeditions to the North, which, though always repudiated by King Yellow Thistle, inflicted serious damage on unprotected Northern tribes. The direct result of the athletic games had been King Ironwood's great invasion of the South, ending with the killing of Yellow Thistle and the capture of his young daughter. Ten years had passed, and the jealousy of the Kishoquoquilas, while not wholly appeased, was apparently not at a very acute stage. Embassies protesting friendship and laden with gifts had visited Pipsisseway after his father's death. The first challenge for an athletic tournament had been made in a friendly spirit. Had it been accepted at once, the unpleasant features which later clustered about it might have been averted. Pipsisseway was young, and referred the matter to his Council. They voted against it unanimously, so the challenge was rejected. Later when Pipsisseway heard the disagreeable talk occasioned he regretted what had been done. When he discussed it with the Councillors they told him that the previous tournament had brought on a bloody and senseless war. This one would do the same. When a second challenge arrived it was rejected on similar grounds. Had the third challenge been refused, war would undoubtedly have resulted. Pipsisseway said if the meet were held and no ill-feeling resulted, it would show that he was as great a ruler as the greatest of his ancestors. None of them had ever sanctioned an athletic contest with the Kishoquoquilas that had not ended in a war. This was as sure as the sun would rise in the morning. Pipsisseway surely wanted no wars during his reign. He wanted to make an agricultural people out of his subjects; wars and disease had made awful inroads in the Indian population. He would recoup their numbers. He was the first man on the American continent to preach against race suicide. Not that Indians wilfully prevented large families, but the mothers were often ignorant or careless, consequently infant mortality was high. Prizes were offered for large families, and to mothers who were able to raise their children beyond the "dangerous age" where children's diseases were most fatal. Prizes were offered for the largest patches of cleared land, the largest yields of crops, the most substantially built lodges, for the scalps of dangerous animals and the like. Pipsisseway was essentially a "constructive monarch." A description of his personal appearance has come down to us, and is strangely like that of the most constructive American of the present day, Col. Theodore Roosevelt. He was, of course, darker than the Colonel, but like him was of medium height, powerfully built, and with prominent, aggressive teeth. Unlike his modern prototype, he died at an early age, but he ranked as the greatest Indian King Central Pennsylvania ever possessed. He was simple in his habits, being extremely democratic and affable. His subjects, who numbered about fifty thousand souls of different tribal characteristics and residing vast distances apart, all worshiped him, and would have laid down their lives for him without a murmur. When he appeared at the "plains," accompanied by his faithful brothers, and his foster-sister Meadow Sweet, he was greeted with the wildest enthusiasm. As a personal tribute nothing like it was known in Indian annals. Many old men said that the bulk of the vast turnout of people was due to a desire to see the popular monarch rather than to witness the contests. Fewer Indians would have tramped a hundred miles to see races alone. They had come from the headwaters of the Allegheny, the Chemung, the Lycoming, from Chillesquaque, Shamokin and Mahantango, ostensibly to see a magnificent tourney, but in reality to show their loyalty to their King. Unlike other Indian rulers, and some of lesser rank, Pipsisseway did not travel in a litter. He walked every foot of the way from the Susquehanna to the Spruce Creek Valley. His brothers also walked, but insisted that Meadow Sweet ride in a litter. She reluctantly consented, as she had absorbed her foster relatives' democratic spirit. Horses were unknown in those days, but sometimes the priests rode elks and moose in religious pageants. As these animals were only ridden on sacred occasions, races between Indians mounted upon them would have been impossible. The first event was a foot-race from the head of the plains to the Rock Spring and return. Two champion runners, one representing the

Susquehanahs and the other the Kishoquoquilas, started on a signal given by Meadow Sweet, who waved a bunch of heron's feathers. The Susquehanah runner leaped to the front and led his Southern competitor by several hundred yards. There was silence in the Kishoquoquilas camp, and not too much applause among the Susquehanahs, as they had been warned not to display undue enthusiasm lest it anger their rivals. The race seemed like a procession until the last hundred yards, when the Susquehanah runner seemed to tire badly. His Southern rival crept upon him amid the terrifying yells of his cohorts, but the Susquehanah managed to last long enough to win by a foot. The Southern Indians were delighted with the result, but they little knew that the Susquehanah runner had only feigned fatigue, and could have won by several hundred yards, if he wished. The second event was a twenty-mile point-to-point relay race, which the Susquehanahs could have won easily, but they held back and only allowed themselves to win by a narrow margin. The first day's sport ending without ill-feeling of any kind, Pipsisseway felt much encouraged. A magnificent banquet was spread under the white oaks, which was attended by King Silver Eagle, of the Kishoquoquilas, his retinue, as well as Pipsisseway, his brothers, retainers, and the Princess Meadow Sweet. Silver Eagle was presented to the princess, whom, as already stated, he had not seen in many years, since she was carried off by the conquering invader, Ironwood. Although she was his cousin, Silver Eagle fell in love with her instantly. He was very attentive to her all through the evening, but she kept him at a distance, being discreet enough not to want to offend him, but at the same time not caring to arouse Pipsisseway's jealousy. She was woman enough to feel that underneath her foster-brother's calm exterior, there smoldered a deep interest for her. She admired him, and was only waiting for him to say the word, when she would gladly agree to become his wife. Silver Eagle laid great stress on their relationship, and suggested now that the feeling between his tribes and the Susquehanahs were so thoroughly amicable that, accompanied by a proper bodyguard, she be allowed to pay a visit to her old home south of the Tussey Mountains. She told him that she would love to do this *some time,* and felt confident her kingly foster-brother and guardian Pipsisseway would gladly give her permission. At midnight the visitors retired to their quarters, and every one in authority among the Susquehanahs breathed easier. The first day's festivities had come and gone, and everybody was happy. On the next day took place the jumping contests and shooting matches. At high-jumping and broad-jumping the Susquehanahs excelled, but they were careful not to win too easily from the Kishoquoquilas. The shooting was the most interesting part of the entire tournament. There were contests at archery, participated in by trained warriors, by aged warriors, by small boys and by women. In all these classes, Susquehanah prowess prevailed, but only by the narrowest of margins. The Kishoquoquilas were beaten, but not disgraced.

The Indians from the South were still hopeful they might win something before the contest ended, and exhibited no ill-feeling. That night King Pipsisseway dined a select company under the white oaks. The only outsiders were Silver Eagle and his personal suite. He renewed his attentions to Meadow Sweet, painting to her in lurid colors the beauties of the Southern Country, its valleys, its mountains, its rivers, its population so intelligent and handsome compared to those in the North. "They are your people," he said; "you must mingle with them; you will love them as much as they love you. You know how they cheer you every time you appear at the tournament." Meadow Sweet continued her tactfully guarded conduct, and Silver Eagle departed at the midnight hour, in excellent humor. "You are a born diplomatist," said Pipsisseway to her after the distinguished guest had gone. "You were born to rule over vast dominions. The world has never seen your equal in womankind." Meadow Sweet smiled to herself; Silver Eagle's attentions were arousing the latent fire of Pipsisseway. Probably the crowning event of the tournament would be his public announcement of their betrothal. But he hadn't proposed as yet. She knew full well who she was, and how at a word from herself Silver Eagle would demand her restoration to the Kishoquoquilas. But she would remain where she was for two considerations. Being a woman, she had no inheritance beside her rank in her own country; with the Susquehanahs she had inherited a large territory, and had a chance of becoming the Queen of King Pipsisseway, if he proposed. With the third day took place the wrestling matches, the live-bird shoots, the weight-throwing competitions and the grand animal drive. The Susquehanah wrestlers and weight-throwers were the victors, but their rivals apparently put up good fights. Ten thousand live wild pigeons and parrots were shot at in the live-bird competition, the majority of which were killed by the Susquehanahs. Then came the animal drive. A thousand buffaloes, elks, moose, and deer were released one by one from a corral and driven across the plains. The idea was to kill an animal at the first shot. If it did not fall it scored one against the party who held the bow. Out of the thousand animals seven hundred fell at the first bow thrust. Of these, three hundred and forty-nine were killed by the Susquehanah nimrods, so carefully had they measured their skill against their opponents. The Kishoquoquilas had won an event, so were happy. That evening Silver Eagle was again entertained at Pipsisseway's quarters. He was in excellent spirits and monopolized so much of Meadow Sweet's attentions that Pipsisseway almost felt slighted. This was especially so when he began talking to her in his Southern dialect, as if to cut Pipsisseway entirely out of the conversation. Meadow Sweet was glad when he left, and threw herself at full length at Pipsisseway's feet, exclaiming, "Oh, how he tires me." "I'll be glad when this is all over, just to get rid of Silver Eagle," said Pipsisseway. The next day's program consisted of several minor contests, such as a three-legged race, a race for cripples, and a dart-throwing competition. These the Susquehanahs let the Kishoquoquilas win. The score of the tournament stood fifty-five to forty-five; the Susquehanahs had "played their cards well." After these contests, a magnificent barbecue took place, and the beasts slain in the animal drive the day before were served up, deliciously cooked, to the multitude. It was estimated that ten thousand Indians "partook" of the repast, but in what proportion seven hundred animals could go into ten thousand rapacious Indian stomachs is a question for an expert hotel-keeper, and not for an historian. A private repast was served under the white oaks by Pipsisseway, as a parting honor to King Silver Eagle, his retinue, and staff. Antelopes brought from what is now Kentucky were served to these dignitaries, as was green corn and tomatoes preserved in their natural state from the year before. Silver Eagle was crouched close to Meadow Sweet while the feast was in progress, and whispering compliments in her ears. After the meal was over he contrived to edge her into a quiet corner, where he could talk to her undisturbed. "I love you, fairest cousin," he expostulated, "I can keep back these words no longer. Come with me to-night; we shall be married with great pomp, and you shall rule with me over my dominions. You belong to our people by birth; you are an alien among the Susquehanahs." Meadow Sweet fully expected this outcome, and was prepared to meet it. It was a trying position, as to give an excuse that would not insult her admirer took considerable tact. "I am honored by your proposal, famous cousin," she replied, "but you are aware that I am a captive, though a willing one, of Pipsisseway; I am also very young; my power of choice is vested in him as my guardian. Ask his permission; I shall be guided by his noble sense of fairness." Silver Eagle could not tell whether it was "yes" or "no," but was not displeased. He took the maiden's hand in his and kissed it. "We will go at once to your worthy guardian, Pipsisseway, who is not the man to hinder a cause like true love." Pipsisseway had been pretending to be holding a conversation with some of his chiefs while this little talk was in progress, but he had been watching the two actors carefully. He was especially anxious to note any sign in Meadow Sweet's face indicating that she possessed a lurking interest for her cousin. Being impressed by her lack of concern, he was determined to outwit the wily interloper. Of course, he could not be sure that Silver Eagle had been proposing, but it looked very much that way. When the Southern monarch and Meadow Sweet approached, and the retainers fell back leaving the trio together, he was prepared for any emergency. "Worthy King, I have come to ask your foster-sister's hand in holy marriage," said Silver Eagle. "Gracious ruler, I much regret to say that I have promised her in marriage to *myself*," replied Pipsisseway. This was a stinging blow to Silver Eagle's hope and pride; his black eyes snapped angrily; he staggered like a drunken man. When he recovered himself he said, "Is this true, fairest cousin?" Meadow Sweet, while Pipsisseway had never proposed to her, would have taken him any time if he had, was only too glad to answer, "It *is* the truth." "Then, why didn't you tell me so a few minutes ago, and save me this humiliation?" said Silver Eagle with renewed anger. "I am, great king, as you are aware, only a captive of Pipsisseway's; I could not answer for myself. But I can truthfully say that I love him with all my heart." Pipsisseway smiled at this clever rejoinder, and held out his hand in a friendly manner to Silver Eagle. The Southern monarch put his own hand behind his back, and edged away from him, muttering to himself. Pipsisseway walked after him, but he refused to notice him. The four days' festivities had wound up in a quarrel after all. There was no use trying to pacify Silver Eagle; he had probably been mad all along over the almost continuous victories of the Susquehanahs in the tournament, but now had come "the unkindest cut of all." Early in the morning it was reported that Silver Eagle had broken camp at dawn, and withdrawn across the Tussey Mountains. There were a number of unpleasant incidents between the Kishoquoquilas and the Susquehanahs over the breaking up of camp; several unprovoked murders were committed by the Southern Indians, and threats of all kinds passed. Their King's disappointment, though unknown to them, was evidently telegraphed to them in some form of unrest, and all the ugliness in their natures came to the surface on "moving day." Nothing further was said about the marriage of Pipsisseway and Meadow Sweet until they had returned to the royal camping-grounds on the Susquehanna. There the betrothal was publicly announced, and fleet runners sent to all quarters of the realm to acquaint the various tribes of the gladsome news. This, coming so soon after the signal victory over the Kishoquoquilas in the athletic tournament, stirred the Susquehanahs into a white heat of patriotism. It would have been a good time to go to war; every one was in a mood to fight for his country. The wedding took place "two moons" after the betrothal was announced, being attended by fully five thousand Indians, as many Susquehanahs who had witnessed the athletic tournament. Ambassadors were present from all the neighboring kingdoms, with the one notable exception of the Kishoquoquilas. This was accounted extraordinary, as Meadow Sweet, being a Kishoquoquilas princess, the daughter of their late King Yellow Thistle, should have married in the presence of some of her own countrymen. A brief honeymoon was taken to Lewis' Lake, a spot sacred to the Indians as having been once the entrance to the Underworld, or realm of spirits. Upon their return, the Council of Wise Men had what they considered bad tidings to relate. Hunters had reported that a vast force of Kishoquoquilas were building a flight of stone steps in Stone Valley, from the foot of the Tussey Mountains to the summit.

Why this was being built was a mystery, except that it would enable the Kishoquoquilas Indians, in case they invaded the Northern Country, to cross the mountains with greater rapidity. They could make a "flying attack," as it were. Pipsisseway looked grave when he heard this. "Not only that," he said, "but I believe those steps are being built because they feel certain they will conquer us after their invasion, and they want to minimize nature's barriers. After they imagine they have conquered us, they will expect to finish the steps down the northern slope of the mountain." Pipsisseway's abilities as a strategist were confirmed by spies whom he caused to be sent out. They returned, saying that Silver Eagle was assembling a vast army in the Southern valleys. He was drafting warriors from as far South as what is now Maryland and Virginia. From talk they had heard six or seven thousand braves were under arms. The purpose of the steps was now established. This vast force of Indians was at present spread out through the valleys. When the time arrived they could be marshaled quickly and sent across into Spruce Creek Valley on a run. They would appear in this valley so suddenly that there would be no time to resist. Sweeping northward, they would pillage and capture everything in sight until they reached the royal encampment by the Susquehanna. The buildings would be burnt, Pipsisseway and his brothers surprised and murdered, while the beautiful Princess Meadow Sweet would be carried off to her old home in the South. Pipsisseway and his brothers dead, a marriage could be arranged between the young widow and Silver Eagle, who would rule over the largest domain on the eastern slope of the Alleghenies. The Indian Steps would be a recognized gateway of travel between the South and North. The most trustworthy and intelligent chiefs were summoned for conference with Pipsisseway and his Council. Fifty chieftains answered the call. It was decided by them that every male Indian fit for service should be moved in the direction of the Tussey Mountains. That was to be the ultimate destination, but they should tarry at all the frequented mountain passes where ingress from the South was afforded. But the rallying point was to be at the northern side of the "Indian Steps." Every brave was to start separately; no two men should travel together. It could not be said that a vast "body" of Indians was moving to the South; they would go as individuals. The chiefs returned to their homes, and ere long the advance began. Among them were Indians from the Chillesquaque country, led by Chief Hidden River; Indians from the Loyalsock region under Chief Mountain Ash; Indians from Nippenose Valley, led by Chief Lock-and-Bar; Indians from the region north of the royal encampment, in what is now Wayne Township, Clinton County, led by Chief Hazelwood; Indians from the Monsey Town Flats, as the country around what is now Lock Haven was called, commanded by Chief Gold Thread; Indians from the Sinnemahoning region, led by Chief Sonicle; Indians from the Bald Eagle Valley, under Chief Mountain Lion; Indians from Penn's Valley, led by Chief Panther Fangs, the grandfather, by the way, of the celebrated Indian Red Panther; Indians from the Black Forest, famed for their skill with bow and arrow and spear, led by Chief Tiadaghton; the Indians residing in Spruce Creek Valley, under Chief Golden Hour;—all moving in a common direction by different routes, each as an individual, silent, loyal, determined. It was subject of some discussion among Pipsisseway and his brothers if Meadow Sweet be allowed to accompany them. She pleaded so hard, and Pipsisseway relied so much on her judgment, that she went with the royal party. This consisted of King Pipsisseway, his brothers, the council of Fifty Wise Men, the royal bodyguard, and household. Queen Meadow Sweet was attended by a single maiden. The rest of her retinue remained in the beautiful retreat by the Susquehanna, watched by one hundred picked Indians of the home-guard. The regal camp-ground looked deserted when they were gone; it seemed a pity to leave such an ideal spot. Arriving in the Southern country the various tribesmen of the Susquehanahs camped out as individuals and waited. Spies who visited Stone Valley and adjoining valleys under cover of darkness reported that the main bodies of the Southern Indians, or Kishoquoquilas, were camping along what are now known as Shaver's Run, Globe Run, and Garner's Run. This showed that the line of attack was to be by way of the Steps. It was to be the sudden rush of a vast horde of warriors, whose combined strength would sweep everything before. When this information was thoroughly verified, the Indians that were posted near the various points of ingress to the Susquehanah kingdom were concentrated in Spruce Creek Valley. All were ordered to remain in the forests, and it would be impossible to have imagined army lurking at the foot of the Tussey Mountains. Undoubtedly the Kishoquoquilas sent out spies, but not finding any connected bodies of warriors, would imagine that the ones they saw were hunters or fishermen. The Steps were completed in the early winter, and the invasion was expected to follow. The army of the defense was on the alert, but nothing seemed to happen. Days and weeks passed. The forests were banked with snow. The waiting force became restless, hungry, and unhappy. They begged to be allowed to visit their homes and help their families. Permission was granted in rotation, and when an Indian left on a week's furlough, another would return from his trip the same day. Evidently the Kishoquoquilas finally received some intimation that a strong force awaited them, and were trying tactics of delay in order to reduce the numbers of their enemies. Some day when the defense was disorganized they would sweep over the mountain and the domain of Pipsisseway would be theirs. But the same dissatisfaction which had reigned among the Susquehanahs broke out among the Kishoquoquilas. It was an outrage to keep them so long without sign of a battle. Being encamped in compact bodies it was impossible to grant furloughs wholesale. In consequence there were threats of mutiny and desertion from some of the warriors from below the Potomac. An advance must be made, or the force could not be held together, was the advice given repeatedly to Silver Eagle by his aides. He would try to show them that the longer it was postponed the better the chance of finding their adversaries scattered and unprepared. "Your great mistake, sire," said Dangleberry, one of his oldest warriors, "was in assembling your force before the completion of the Steps. You should have waited until a year after they were finished; then you would have found our enemies completely off their guard." "It's too late now," replied Silver Eagle, ruefully; "we must do the best we can." The reports of dissatisfaction were so overwhelming that one snowy morning at daybreak the advance, at double quick, was ordered. The force, numbering some five thousand braves, trooped up the Steps, over the summit, and down the rough mountain sides, coming on the level at the "plains." As they emerged into the open country a terrific fusillade of arrows, darts, and spears assailed them from the forests on either side. Some of the more mercenary quickly retreated into the woods and up the mountain, but the majority, goaded on by their chiefs, kept advancing across the plain. The casualties in Pickett's Charge at Gettysburg were trifles compared to the harvest of death in this invasion of Spruce Creek Valley by the Kishoquoquilas. Before they were halfway across the open space, panic began seizing the entire body, and they ran from side to side, under the merciless rain of arrows. Many dropped into the snow from sheer fright and lay as dead. It is related that the entire invading army did not shoot five hundred arrows. They were overcome with terror too quickly. All they could do was stagger about, waiting to be killed. Out of the five thousand who appeared on the plains, scarcely a thousand reached the forest on the northern edge of it in safety. These, when they came face to face with their enemies, felt renewed courage, and drawing their knives and tomahawks fought desperately. In a few minutes a thousand hand to hand conflicts of the bloodiest character were in progress. Silver Eagle was one of those lucky enough to cross the plain safely, and fought with diabolical bravery. He hacked his way through a mass of Susquehanahs, swearing that he'd reach the headquarters of Pipsisseway, the location of which he seemed to know, if he had to kill a thousand tribesmen on the way. He probably slew a score of Indians before he was free to run forward unhampered. In the distance, through the spaces between the trunks of the giant white oaks, he could make out a substantial lodge house built of logs. It stood a hundred yards from the Rock Spring, the source of Spruce Creek. "That's Pipsisseway's house; I'll kill him, I'll kill him; Meadow Sweet will yet be mine!" As he neared the door he saw the beautiful Queen emerge, looking weary and anxious. He waved to her, roaring, "I've killed your cursed husband; fly with me and be mine," and redoubled his pace through the wet snow. Just then a powerful voice rang out, "Not so fast, ambitious king, not so fast; I'm far from dead." He looked around and beheld his arch-enemy, Pipsisseway. He had not time to raise his tomahawk, for the King of the Susquehanahs had punctuated his greeting by cleaving his skull. He fell in a limp mass in the slush, his brains spattering about like a fox's entrails. Silver Eagle being dead, Pipsisseway rushed back into the thick of the conflict, and helped despatch some of the few remaining Kishoquoquilas. The slaughter continued all day long, and when night fell it was safe to say that there wasn't a living Kishoquoquilas north of Tussey Mountains. Even those who had fallen, panic-stricken, in the snow on the plains were butchered later when they attempted to sneak away. The order went out, "Kill every Kishoquoquilas; take no prisoners." As Pipsisseway, reeking with blood, tramped back to his lodge-house that night his mind evolved a fiendish revenge on his enemies. "I'll have Silver Eagle's body thrown into the Rock Spring, and every other corpse of his followers of high rank that we can identify. Rock Spring is the source of Spruce Creek, and Spruce Creek flows into the Juniata, that runs through the richest territory of the Kishoquoquilas. The putrifying carcasses of their king and the pick of their warriors shall taint the water that they drink." Next morning this scheme was put into effect; over a hundred scalped and mutilated corpses being dumped into the Spring. For a full year the Indians who lived at the mouth of the creek said that the water smelled rancid even there. It was deemed unwholesome, and for years the redmen had an idea it was not fit to drink. But what was pollution then adds to its purity now. Just as sugar is strained through bones, the crystalline source at Rock Spring flows through bones, the bones of warriors which time has left unsullied, and bubbles into the bowl of the spring limpid and sweet as dew. After the great conflict, which was called "The Battle of the Indian Steps," the Kishoquoquilas went on the decline. They split up into small tribes, and were constantly at war with one another. Pipsisseway did not follow up his victory, but returned to his beautiful retreat by the Susquehanna, where he died the following autumn of chills and fever. Besides his widow he left a son, named War Bonnet, who ultimately came to rule over his possessions. The Susquehanah kingdom enjoyed marked prosperity for nearly a hundred years after the great battle, only falling into a state of civil war during the last years of the Seventeenth Century. King Merciless and King Golden Treasure were two rival rulers of a later date, whose factional fights did much to disrupt the old kingdom. It seemed a shame that the passing of the redmen should have practically obliterated the Story of the Indian Steps and the resultant battle. But it is only one of the many historical legends that are fading away.

IV. Wildmannli

It was a gala Saturday night in the Forest King Hotel, in the palmy days of
Jamison City. A traveling mountebank had braved the snows and ice and had
come to the hostelry to give his simple performance in the lobby. He was a
shabby, thick-set individual, low-browed, with a convict hair-cut and a clean
shaven face, a face sunk in depravity and showing he marks of surrender to
every passion, natural and otherwise, that was the whim of his uncharted
nature. But his songs and antics were highly pleasing to the men from the
camps, the sled-drivers, the skidway men, the hardwood crews, the cooks
and hangers-on. They applauded and shouted over such inanities as the song
which began, "I was born in the City of Norfolk, city of women and war
talk," and when the battered derby hat was passed around, there were put
into it over ten dollars in bills and silver to reward the ill-favored performer.

After the show all hands adjourned to the bar, got all they wanted, then
with hands tucked in the change pockets of their trousers, the loggers
swaggered out the side doors into the frosty night and started up the gorge
in the direction of the camps. A few who were not "boozers" remained in
the lobby, their stiff chairs tilted against the walls, discussing bits of the
day's work, politics and local gossip, poor, disjointed efforts at conversation
without purpose and without result. "Some of those lads were pretty well

'corned,' " said old Mike Gleason, as he slipped a fresh quid of tobacco under his heavy mustache. "They'll be seeing ghosts as they go up the gorge."

Another elderly man against the opposite wall, Jason Hall, nodded his acquiescence. "That is," he added, "if the ghosts remained after the timber was taken out, which I doubt very much."

The younger men present now became all attention. They liked to hear the older men talk, but the veterans were generally reticent about the strange, wild, romantic days before the railroad and the loggers came.

"I mind," said old Hall, "when I was 'baching it' in Morgan's Gap, near the Panther's Path, over in Clinton County. I worked one winter on a pine job in the Narrows between Penn's Valley and Brush Valley, that's just across the Centre County line. It was before the pike was built, and there was no lonelier spot on earth than the Elk Creek Narrows. We occasionally heard wolves howl at night on the 'Dog Back.' They had a crossing in the Brush Mountain near our camp, where they traveled back and forth from the Seven Mountains.

"When we pitched camp we soon heard that the Narrows were haunted by the ghost of a wild man—that is, a poor fellow who went crazy and lived for several years in a cave before they found him frozen to death. He had been badly treated by his friends in life. After death he sought to work out his grudge against mankind in general. In those days there was a good deal of hauling in the winter time between Brush Valley and Millheim. Some of the sleds, loaded with corn and lumber, came from as far as Wolf's Store and Stover's, and often they did not get started back much before dark.

"There was one part of the Narrows at the foot of the Dog Back where the road ran very close to the creek, and where the water was very deep. Once some roystering teamsters going back to Kreamersville saw the wild man taking a moonlight bath in the pool, and had shot at him, wounding him badly. It was from the result of that wound that he ultimately died, it is said, for it weakened his system, made him more liable to exposure.

"After he had been dead a few years the belated sled-drivers reported that his ghost had taken to haunting that particular part of the Narrows and wreaking vengeance against the traveling public. It was queer he did not become a 'hant' right away, but there is no accounting for ghosts.

"On dark nights the spook could not be seen at all, but on moonlight nights it was clearly apparent. There would be no warning, but as the sleds came opposite to the pool, even when it was coated with ice, transparent form of the wild man, his flowing beard shining like foxfire, rose out of the ice and sailed straight for the sleds. With a bound it would land in the box just behind the driver's seat; then the trouble would begin. The horses could not pull the sled with the ghost on board. The drivers would order it to get off, strike at it with their cruel sjamboks, or blacksnake whips, shoot at it with the rifles they always carried, swear and curse and shout, but the wild man's ghost would not budge until cockcrow; then it would dart away as quickly and quietly as it came.

"As the sleds were usually empty, except for a few groceries on the homeward journeys, it seemed all the more incomprehensible that the horses could not haul the ghost. A number of horses caught cold by the exposure; some died, and not a few drivers were laid up with various ailments for weeks. The teamsters sought to combine their forces, but the ghost always stopped the foremost team, leaving it and jumping in the next sled if one of those in the convoy sought to pass the one that was stalled.

"The staid, church-going business men of Millheim were interested, but none of the doubters cared to make the journey and investigate, so that the matter was never 'scientifically explained.' Many's the night that I have worked over a balky, lathery team, trying to get them started for home, to help the panic-stricken drivers, with all the while that ghost like a ball of foxfire squatting in the wagon-box.

"One old driver, a Dutchman, told us that he heard his grandmother, who had been born in the old country, tell him when he was a boy that a certain prince was riding through the forest near his castle when he saw a pretty little baby lying by the roadside. He ordered one of his attendants to dismount and pick up the child. It was so heavy he could not lift it. Then one dozen stalwart orderlies tried, but could not raise it; it seemed to weigh a ton. The prince ordered the imp to be left where it was, and rode post haste homeward, praying like a sky-pilot.

"The wild man's ghost had to be laid or else sledding between the two valleys would have to be abandoned. It was a fine open winter, and such a course would have been a great loss to the farmers living in remote sections of Brush Valley. Old Daniel Karstetter, the panther hunter, was on one of the sleds when it was stuck; he had had considerable experience with ghosts in his younger days; his advice was to consult a witch, or, as the Dutch called it, a 'hex.' All the best known witches were dead, but there were some few pretenders to the gift who might be requisitioned.

"These would-be exponents of the black art all tried their various charms—I won't repeat what they were, because they were no good. They had evidently never seen the Black Book, and the ghost still held up traffic. It kept up all winter, stopping every belated sled or sleigh, so that a daylight schedule had to be instituted.

"It was just as malevolent in summer, although there was never much hauling at that time of the year. Most of the bark went north to Lock Haven. It was long before the L. & T. was built in the valley of the Karoondinha.

"About the beginning of the second winter before the sledding became really good, the man who had shot and wounded the wild man was found dead in his bed at the first log cabin east of Kreamersville when driving from the Narrows. His face was so distorted that the undertaker would not let the friends view the remains. Some children who had been out gathering kindling wood in the back pastures earlier in that evening said that they saw the wild man standing at the edge of the woods. It made their parents mighty mad, as they knew that the wretch had been dead at least five years. But in the morning, when the man who had shot at him was found dead in his four-poster, they averred that the little folks knew a thing or two.

"That ended the wild man's ghost in the Narrows. He had evened the score, probably scared his would-be slayer to death by looking in his window."

There was a pause when old Hall finished his narrative, then some remarks of approval. The old clock above the desk was just striking eleven.

"One more story before we part," said Hall. "Can't you tell us one that happened around here?" he asked, addressing old Mike Gleason.

"I'd like to," said Gleason, "but the only appropriate story I know is familiar to so many of you; I guess that you even know it, Jason, and you're a comparative stranger here."

"I never had the whole story," replied Hall. "I want to get it from you, so that I can have it straight."

"All right; you shall have it, and straight; but I will not mention names, because there might be some of you who will turn newspaper men and get me into a lot of trouble. It happened, you know, as late as Civil War times."

Most of those present recollected the story, having heard it before, but were anxious to listen to it again with names left out.

"This story," began Gleason, "relates to a wild man who only appeared about here once, but that was enough. I have heard of other wild men; the old man of the Storm, who, like Goffe, the Regicide Judge at Hadley, appeared late one winter's night at a lumber camp on Mosquito Creek, in Clearfield County, not many years ago, warning the loggers of a blizzard, and after being warmed and fed, he went out into the tempest and was never seen again. Then there was the one that the pipe-line walker saw near Trout Run, all whiskered and wild looking, standing by the edge of the path, eating a raw rabbit. None of these were as terrible as the wild man who appeared one snowy night on the trail at the head of the gorge, up where our 'buddies' from the camps are climbing tonight.

"I knew the fellow well who was the wild man's victim—went to school with him at Benton. Never saw much of him after that, as he always thought himself better than me. His father had some money besides I went to war and he stayed home to raise the devil—and get it. At the school we attended, the little red school house just on the edge of the town, was a very pretty little black-eyed girl—you know who I mean. She was very fond of the rich man's son, and he certainly admired her. If he had married her, I do believe that he would have made a decent man, but he thought himself too good for her, just as he felt too good to go to war. I calculate that he would have been a leader of the Benton Copperheads if the devil had not gotten him. He hung around the girl until it came to a point where he had to say the word or else back out. He backed out and she was sick a whole winter—a broken heart, I guess.

"But she recovered, began to take notice again, and married one of the finest young fellows on the top of the North Mountain. He was such a good fellow that he went to war, leaving the young wife in a nice cottage along the road which leads from the gorge to Ganoga. She didn't mind living alone; she could shoot like a man; she's the girl who killed the bear in her pig-pen. She had the courage of a dozen men.

"It was not long after the young husband went to the front that those who had occasion to be out after dark noticed a horse and sleigh driving in the direction of the Mountain Road almost every night. The bells had been taken off. One man, all huddled up in buffalo robes, was the sole occupant of the cutter. It seemed very mysterious. Those who sat up with the sick said that it returned never before three or four o'clock in the morning. Some of the boys thought of going out and stopping the outfit, but they did not quite have the courage. I was in the Army of the Potomac at the time on the Peninsula, but the folks fore I would have had time to do so the matter came wrote it all to me. Some ——— of a ——— who hasn't the courage to enlist, I concluded; then it dawned on me who it was, though I did not write it home. Before long the affair came to a climax, and all parties where shown up and disgraced, as sinners always are. The story was just this way:

"As soon as the young bride's husband had shouldered his musket and gone off to fight, the rich man's son took it into his head to take a moonlight sleighride up the creek and to the top of the mountain. The road wasn't even broken; the white pine had not been cut as yet, so there was no sledding, but he got through somehow. He felt cold, and his horse was tired, and, seeing a light in a window, he stopped and went in. It happened to be the home of his former sweetheart, the love of his school days, now the wife of the young soldier.

"The friendship was speedily renewed around the warm ten-plate stove, while the steaming, blanketed horse rested his tired limbs in the shed. The evening passed so pleasantly that it was extended until almost daybreak. It was repeated almost every night for nearly three months. It was a scandal and an outrage, but what was to be done? Nobody could prove it was the rich fellow who drove up the gorge every night, and those who suspected did not like to write to the poor volunteer off soldiering in Virginia. Some busybodies did drop a word or two to the girl's parents to put them on their guard, but it did not seem to do any good. It was the chief topic of my mother's and sisters' letters to me, so I guess that it was pretty much all that was being talked about along the creek at the time.

"In one of my mother's letters she said: 'This thing ought to be stopped.' In her next letter she told me just how a wild man, an avenging ghost or something, stepped in and stopped it.

"About the last of February there was an unusually severe blizzard. It snowed steadily for three days and nights. It seemed as if the entire valley of Fishing Creek was to be buried from sight. Few went out; the farmers could not get their horses out of their barns. It was hard enough to get to the barns to feed the stock. But the moneyed chap from Benton went out every night just the same. On the last night of the storm, it was the most severe; a terrific wind accompanied the snowfall, causing high drifts everywhere. All went well with the opulent youth until he had almost gotten to the top of the pass. Then the wind blew out of the timber at a velocity that seemed unprecedented for forested country. He shook and shivered as the frigid blasts literally 'went through him.' He urged his already jaded beast, but the wind almost overturned sleigh, horse and all. At the Big Spring, where the camps were built later when the pine was taken out, he noticed what looked like a huge glittering stalagmite icicle by the edge of the trail. As he approached he could see that it was a huge, white-bearded man, glistening like silver, though there was no moon, and even if there had been, its rays could not have shown through the dense forest which overhung the road. When he came abreast of it, the icy monster leaped into the cutter beside him, throwing its long, cold arms about the rich man's neck, squeezing the breath out of his throat in a vice-like grasp. The youth struggled and sputtered, but the wild man only held him the tighter, sinking his freezing nails into the soft flesh of his neck. With self-protection uppermost, the rich man grappled with the weird intruder, though his strong arms seemed to be encircling thin air.

As they grappled the youth dropped the lines, and the blooded horse, released from restraint, careened forward like a mad thing. Somewhere it struck a rock in the road, and, overturning the light cutter, flung driver and the ice fiend out into a snow-bank, where the rich youth almost smothered to death before he could extricate himself. When he got on his feet his foe was gone, the horse and sleigh were nowhere to be seen. It was almost daylight, and he plowed his way along the road, so weak that he had to sit down in the snow to rest every hundred yards or so. It was broad daylight—ten o'clock in the morning—when he arrived at his beloved's cabin at the head of the gorge.

"The young woman was distracted waiting for him. He had a number of terriffie chills after he entered the kitchen, so she put him to bed. The woman did not want her nearest neighbor, who lived a mile further up the road, to know about her visitor, so she attempted to nurse him out of his illness. He grew steadily worse, pneumonia set in and, despite all her poulticing and home-made remedies, the fellow passed away on the third day.

"Soon after his arrival he had told her the story of his attack, showing the bloody marks on his throat where the wild man had gripped him. He declared that it could not have been a ghost, as no spectre would have such sharp nails or be strong enough to throw him out of the sleigh—he, the stoutest young man along the whole creek from the Big Flats to Catawissa.

"His death was an awful one; he screamed and shrieked, and seemed to be battling with the wild man in his last moments. Like all immoral men, he was an infidel, so his end was particularly hideous. Like the Kreamersville man, his features were so distorted as to make him unrecognizable.

"After he was dead the girl had to tell the neighbors, and so the whole story came out. His parents were notified, and they had the body brought down to Benton after night. The preachers were shy about performing the last rites for such a vile wretch, but finally one was persuaded to officiate, but he confined himself to the general topic of the man who dies in sin, making the significant remark that such enter into a partnership with his Satanic Majesty, and, being thus favored, occupy the choice seats next the stove.

"A search was made for the runaway horse and cutter. They were found fifteen miles away, in Davidson Township. The horse had gotten entangled in a rhododendron thicket, having been pursued by a pack of wolves, fallen and been devoured by the rapacious creatures. Only the skeleton of the horse was found in the harness, which the wolves also tried to devour. As it was, they ripped and tore the buffalo robes to pieces.

"Somehow or other, when the husband received the news of the tragedy, he got discharged from the army and slipped back by way of Tunkhannock and got his wife and took her west. They were living a few years ago in Western Kansas.

"That was the only time that a wild man was actually seen in the gorge, though there have been some few very queer happenings there before and since that time. We lay them all to the wild man, though he appeared only once—but that was enough. His memory is sufficient to keep some folks straight who might have gone crooked but for fear of him.

"Soon after the horse ran away, a pack of wolves had scented him. They were scarce in these parts at that time, but they probably came in from Tioga or Potter Counties, famished, and their tracks followed the horse for seven miles until they brought him to bay in the rhododendron jungle, where they finished him.

"The undertaker who brought the dead man's body down to Benton, said that he stopped his team at the Big Spring and examined the snow very carefully. He declared that he saw some very large footprints, bigger than could have been made by the corpse with his wild cat skin moccasins. But they were not hoofprints like the devil makes. We concluded that the wild man, whatever he is, is a power for good, and no devil. He has done one or two helpful turns before and since, as I have said. If we are ever in real trouble, let's hope that his influence will be felt again."

The clock on the wall back of the desk was striking twelve, the landlord was shifting on his feet uneasily and opening and closing his registry book.

"That's a wonderful story," said Jason Hall. "That's a better wild man than they had over in Centre County."

"Yes," concluded old Gleason. "I hope that if our wild man meets that gang of boozing hicks who were here tonight he will steer them back to their camps on the summit in safety."

Abbreviations

AH   Annie Halenbake Ross Library, Lock Haven, Pennsylvania
HC   Huntingdon County Historical Society, Huntingdon, Pennsylvania
HWS   Henry W. Shoemaker
JC   Juniata College, Archives, Huntingdon, Pennsylvania
LH   *Lock Haven Express* Offices, Lock Haven, Pennsylvania
LC   Lycoming County Historical Society, Williamsport
MU   Millersville University, Special Collections, Millersville, Pennsylvania
PC   Private Collection, South Williamsport, Pennsylvania
PHMC   Pennsylvania Historical and Museum Commission
PS   Pennsylvania State University, University Park, Historical Collections and Labor Archives
RB   Pennsylvania State University, University Park, Rare Book Room
SA   Pennsylvania State Archives, Harrisburg
SL   State Library of Pennsylvania, Harrisburg

Notes

Introduction

1. Staub 1994, "Cultural Conservation and Economic Recovery Planning," p. 232.
2. Clebsch 1979, "America's 'Mythique' as Redeemer Nation," p. 79.

Chapter 1

1. Jost 1953, "Sunday Patriot News Salutes: Henry W. Shoemaker."
2. See "Introducing Our Personality of the Week" 1936, *Lock Haven Express*, p. 2; Shearer 1920, "Pennsylvania Folklore: The Life-Work of Colonel Henry W. Shoemaker"; Dickey 1955, "Henry W. Shoemaker: Pennsylvania Folklorist"; HWS, n.d., "Sketch of Henry W. Shoemaker" (Typescript, SA).
3. Allison 1915, *Henry W. Shoemaker: An Appreciation*, p. 30.
4. Churchill 1970, *The Upper Crust*, pp. 141–50.
5. "H. W. Shoemaker, Ex-Diplomat, Dies," 1958.
6. Fosdick 1956, *John D. Rockefeller, Jr.*, p. 22.
7. Although many accounts of Shoemaker's life give 1882 as the year of his birth, his death certificate, passport application, and private papers say 1880. The earlier year is the one inscribed on his tombstone in Highland Cemetery, Lock Haven, and in the genealogy prepared by his uncle James Quiggle (James Quiggle to HWS, 3/17/10, PS).
8. For background on the Pennsylvania Society of New York City, see Cupper 1993, "Ninety-Five Years of the Pennsylvania Society."
9. HWS 1923, *True Stories of the Pennsylvania Mountains*, p. 2.
10. HWS to Florence Watts, 8/28/40, AH.
11. HWS 1931, *Mountain Minstrelsy of Pennsylvania*, p. 101.
12. HWS to Stuart Kinser, 9/11/14, PC.
13. See Green 1986, *Fit for America*, pp. 128–36.
14. James Quiggle to HWS, 3/17/10, PS.
15. Ibid.
16. "Prof. Plumley Dead," HWS Scrapbook, PC.
17. HWS 1912, *The Indian Steps*, pp. 361–67.
18. HWS, n.d., "An Introduction to Pennsylvania Primitive Art."
19. Ruskin 1869, *The Queen of the Air*; Merrill 1989, *The Romance of Victorian Natural History*, pp. 145–62.
20. Ruskin 1869, *Queen of the Air*, p. vii.
21. See ibid., p. vi.
22. HWS 1920, *North Mountain Mementos*, pp. 22–23; Evans 1988, "Folklore as Utopia."
23. Wagstaff 1918, *Narcissus and Other Poems*; Wagstaff 1930, *Mortality and Other Poems*; *Who's Who of American Women*, 1958, vol. 1, pp. 1319–20. A clipping in one of Henry Shoemaker's

scrapbooks, dated April 23, 1913, from *Club Fellow,* comments on the relationship between the two Shoemakers' poetry. Henry Shoemaker, it reports, "has openly disapproved of the kind of poetry that his sister writes, but his disapproval has had no effect on the poet. It was Blanche's poetry and the erotic ravings of the girls who flocked about her that made Henry Shoemaker decide that he would never marry a New York girl." Henry must have mellowed his opinion in his later years, for he frequently encouraged her in correspondence. His sister wrote back in 1930: "We are not more widely recognized because we are sincere and erudite artists" (n.d., PC). Although she criticized his *Pennsylvania Mountain Stories* as unpolished, by 1920 she was telling him: "You show a greater grasp in your theme and handle it with more dexterity. Your English is more polished, the style more flexible. I like best the Sylvania tales for their human interest, but doubtless the fairy lore is more picturesque. Their perusal gave me uninhibited enjoyment especially as the advance on your other stories is *so apparent.* Do continue your good work, it is justifiable that I am full of pride in it!" (n.d., PC).

24. Her entry in *Who's Who of American Women* lists her study of ballet (debuting in 1907 at the Metropolitan Club), her receipt of numerous poetry prizes, her writing for *Golf Illustrated* as well as for many poetry magazines, her presidency of the Society of Pennsylvania Women, and her work for the U. S. Army as a plane-spotter, for which she received Army service citations. Her vita further lists her as an "ardent angler and upland game shot" and "one of the first women to follow aviation." She and her brother both shared a strenuous and busy life, as her vita attests: "Youth passed in outdoor sports and intensive reading of classics. School basket-ball team, daily golf, long distance swimming, bareback riding, sailing knockabout in races, canoeing, chess, track athletics, motor-cycling many years."

25. Blanche Shoemaker Wagstaff to HWS, n.d., PC.

26. Henry Francis Shoemaker to HWS, 10/25/08, PC. The letter was written from Hot Springs, Virginia.

27. Blanche Shoemaker Wagstaff to HWS, 1/10/25, PS.

28. See Merrill 1989, *The Romance of Victorian Natural History,* p. 260.

29. HWS 1924, *More Allegheny Episodes,* p. 11.

30. HWS 1917, *Pennsylvania Folk Lore,* p. 6.

31. HWS 1913, *In the Seven Mountains,* p. 99.

32. "Introducing Our Personality of the Week," 1936, *Lock Haven Express;* see also HWS 1951, "Currier and Ives: A Retrospect."

33. See HWS 1925, *Pennsylvania German and Huguenot Antiques;* HWS 1926, *Pure Bred Stallions at "Restless Oaks";* HWS 1927, *A Catalogue of Early Pennsylvania and Other Firearms and Edged Weapons at "Restless Oaks."*

34. See Bronner 1989, "Object Lessons: The Work of Ethnological Museums and Collections."

35. Merrill 1989, *The Romance of Victorian Natural History,* p. 260.

36. Thoms 1965, "Folklore" (originally published 1846), p. 6.

37. Annan 1966, "The Strands of Unbelief," p. 151.

38. See Beard 1881, *American Nervousness;* Lears 1981, *No Place of Grace,* pp. 47–58.

39. Cordelia Quiggle to HWS, 7/18/10, PC.

40. HWS 1916, *Juniata Memories,* p. 187.

41. Ibid., p. 187.

42. HWS 1913, *In the Seven Mountains,* p. 168.

43. See Zipes 1987, *Victorian Fairy Tales;* Zipes 1988, *The Brothers Grimm;* Zipes 1991, *Spells of Enchantment;* Schenda 1986, "Telling Tales—Spreading Tales"; Cocchiara 1981, *History of Folklore in Europe.*

44. See Dorson 1968, *The British Folklorists;* Bronner 1986, *American Folklore Studies,* pp. 1–38; Zipes 1979, *Breaking the Magic Spell;* Lears 1981, *No Place of Grace;* Fernandez 1986, "Folklorists as Agents of Nationalism."

45. Thoms 1965, "Folklore," p. 5.

46. Roosevelt 1926, *Literary Essays,* p. 131.

47. Ibid., p. 334.

48. Ibid., p. 336.

49. See Dorson 1972, "How Shall We Rewrite Charles M. Skinner Today?"; Bealle 1994, "Another Look at Charles M. Skinner."

50. Newell 1888, "On the Field and Work of a Journal of American Folklore."

51. Nye 1966, *This Almost Chosen People*, pp. 256–304.

52. Merrill 1989, *The Romance of Victorian Natural History*, p. 53.

53. Price 1990, *Captain Sir Richard Francis Burton*.

54. HWS 1896, "Careless Gunners," p. 1.

55. HWS 1898, "The Porter's Tale," p. 9.

56. *Argyle News*, May 1898, p. 1.

57. HWS, n.d., "Extracts from Lancaster to Clearfield."

58. Ibid.; HWS, n.d., "Excerpts from the Later Chapters of 'From Lancaster to Clearfield.'"

59. HWS 1912, *Elizabethan Days*, p. 69.

60. Ibid., p. 41. See also HWS 1898, *Argyle Verse;* HWS 1898, *Immaterial Verses.*

61. HWS 1917, *The Pennsylvania Lion or Panther*, p. 61.

62. HWS 1917, *Pennsylvania Folk Lore*, p. 6.

63. "Introducing Our Personality of the Week," 1936, *Lock Haven Express*, p. 2.

64. HWS Scrapbook, 1901, PC.

65. HWS to Percival Wharton, 7/25/14, PC.

66. HWS 1914, *Black Forest Souvenirs*, pp. xiii–xiv.

67. HWS 1917, *Pennsylvania Folk Lore*, p. 7.

68. HWS 1931, *Mountain Minstrelsy*, p. 31. See also Allen 1891, *Flute and Violin, and Other Kentucky Tales;* Fox 1897, *"Hell fer Sartain" and Other Stories;* Fox 1898, *The Kentuckians;* McNeil 1989, *Appalachian Images in Folk and Popular Culture;* Goode 1989, "Appalachian Literature."

69. HWS 1931, *Mountain Minstrelsy*, p. 9.

70. HWS 1917, "The Abuse of Wealth," p. 3.

71. Roosevelt 1926, *State Papers as Governor and President*, p. 90.

72. Ibid., p. 173. See also Roosevelt 1926, "Social Evolution," in *American Ideals*, pp. 233–41.

73. Roosevelt 1926, *State Papers as Governor and President*, p. 443.

74. Ibid.

75. For discussion of other keywords of Progressivism, including "interests," "utility," and "common good," see Rodgers 1987, *Contested Truths.*

76. Roosevelt 1993, "Preservation of the Forests."

77. Hofstadter 1960, *The Age of Reform*, p. 5.

78. See ibid.; Bowers 1932, *Beveridge and the Progressive Era;* Link 1954, *Woodrow Wilson and the Progressive Era;* Cashman 1988, *America in the Age of Titans.*

79. Roosevelt 1926, *American Ideals*, pp. 500–505; Fausold 1961, *Gifford Pinchot*, pp. 128–50.

80. Hays 1959, *Conservation and the Gospel of Efficiency;* Nash 1968, *The American Environment.*

81. Rodgers 1987, *Contested Truths*, p. 183.

82. Ibid.

83. HWS 1917, "The Abuse of Wealth," p. 2.

84. Ibid., p. 6.

85. Ibid., p. 3.

86. HWS, n.d., "Fairbanks Sentiment in Pennsylvania."

87. HWS to J. Arbuckle, 11/11/16, PC. Republicans dominated Pennsylvania state politics from the Civil War into the late twentieth century. Indeed, Republicans controlled the Governor's Mansion continuously from 1895 until 1935, and again from 1939 through 1955. In many editorials for his newspapers, Shoemaker backed the Progressive Republican politics and conservation movement of Theodore Roosevelt and Gifford Pinchot against industrialist "organization" Republican forces that backed William Atterbury, doughty president of the Pennsylvania Railroad. In 1913,

Shoemaker wrote the editor of the *Altoona Tribune:* "I feel that I am loyal to the party at all times and am only showing my loyalty when from time to time I have attacked its selfish leaders in my editorials" (HWS, to W. H. Schwartz, 12/18/13, PS). Later in life, Shoemaker nonetheless downplayed his support of Republican politics and claimed he was driven by issues of conservation and government management, in a letter to Miriam Dickey, who was devoting her master's thesis to him, on February 15, 1955: "As to my politics, Governor Fisher, when he recommended me to Governor Earle, described me as a fairly good Republican and that is about as far as I ever got with Party Politics and would prefer not to be listed as a 'strong Republican,' as I never was, although most of my votes have been cast for that Party. In the last Election, like many others, I was pretty well disgusted with the quarrels between the leaders and voted a straight Democratic ticket. Consequently, I would rather not be lauded as a 'first class Republican,' a title I do not deserve" (SA).

88. HWS, n.d., "Fairbanks Sentiment in Pennsylvania."

89. HWS 1916, *Wasting the State's Money.* For Cashman, see *America in the Age of the Titans,* p. 46.

90. Bishop James Henry Darlington to HWS, 3/8/12, PC.

91. John Wesley Johnson to HWS, 11/23/09, PC.

92. Ibid.

93. HWS, n.d., "Henry Shoemaker's Convictions"; HWS, n.d., "Fairbanks Sentiment in Pennsylvania."

94. Roosevelt 1926, *Literary Essays,* p. 238.

95. HWS 1917, "The Abuse of Wealth," p. 8.

96. HWS to Blanche Quiggle Shoemaker, 10/23/04, PS.

97. HWS to Charles Fairbanks, 12/3/12, PC. As the letter to Fairbanks indicates, Shoemaker sought to return to diplomatic service in 1912 and tried again when the war broke out in 1914.

98. HWS scrapbook, 8/23/07, PS.

99. HWS to Charles Fairbanks, 12/3/12, PC.

100. Henry F. Shoemaker to HWS, 9/15/08, PC

101. Henry Allen Foote to HWS, 9/20/10, PC.

102. HWS to Frank Lawrence, 1/2/13, PC.

103. Schlereth in *Victorian America* (1991) reports that by 1915 the United States had the highest divorce rate in the world (pp. 280–81). Cashman, in *America in the Age of Titans* (1988), compares the divorce rate of 1 in every 21 marriages in 1880 with 1 in 10 by 1909 (p. 253). According to Cashman, "The Episcopal church was generally opposed to divorce and William Croswell Doone, bishop of Albany, was its most outspoken moral advocate. He would have preferred prohibiting divorce altogether and was absolutely opposed to allowing even the innocent party in an adultery suit to remarry after divorce" (p. 254). The press appeared staunchly opposed to divorce, but relented by the 1920s as accounts of the brutalizing sexual indignities in some marriages were attacked by the new women's movement of the day. Reform of divorce law to make it less stigmatized and more uniform across the states became part of many Progressive platforms. William L. O'Neill observed: "Conservatives could, therefore, more easily resign themselves to other, more extravagant, demonstrations of the changing moral order." Seen broadly, the debate over divorce and the coverage Shoemaker received was part of what O'Neill called a "vast social upheaval" that was "part of the complex transformation of moral values and sexual customs which was to help give the 1920s their bizarre flavor." See his *Divorce in the Progressive Era* (1967).

104. Lille Crawford to HWS, 1/4/13, PC.

105. HWS scrapbook, 4/23/13, PC.

106. "Gives Son a $250,000 House," 1913.

107. Shoemaker kept two scrapbooks on his sister's social activities. In 1904, she had a debutante ball in which she vied for New York newspaper attention with Gladys Vanderbilt, Mildred Barclay, and Beatrice Morgan. "Blanche Shoemaker's tea was the largest and most popular for Mrs. Henry F. Shoemaker baited her hook delightfully with invitations for dinner," one clipped article reported. Clippings of appearances at operas, cotillions, and dog and horse shows include

references to the social competitiveness. One report of the New York dog show carries the headline "Mrs. Reginal C. Vanderbilt, Mrs. Havemeyer, Miss Shoemaker and Mrs. M. Roosevelt Win Prizes." Most of all, the reception of New York society in Europe had an impact back home. An article taken from *Club Fellow* dated June 14, 1905, reports: "New York will not be big enough to hold Miss Blanche Shoemaker when she returns from abroad. Her progress through the Continent has been as spectacular as that of the young king of Spain. Aided and abetted by her doting father Henry Shoemaker, Miss Blanche has motored to every accessible spot in France and Italy. . . . Then she was presented at Court along with the Mills' twins and Mrs. John Jacob Astor. She has assuredly striven 'way ahead of her fellow buds, for out of the thirty or more presented to New York society during the past winter, she is the only one favored by a trip abroad and a peek at London society."

108. HWS to W. L. Taylor, 4/1/13, PC.

109. J. Arbuckle to HWS, 11/15/16, PC.

110. Ibid.

111. HWS to Stuart L. B. Kinzer, 9/11/14, PC.

112. "Millionaire Has Written Legends of Susquehanna," 1913.

113. Dorson 1946, *Jonathan Draws the Long Bow;* Dorson 1971, *American Folklore and the Historian,* pp. 173–85; Dorson 1972, "The Use of Printed Sources."

114. "Millionaire Has Written Legends of Susquehanna," 1913.

115. HWS to W. H. Schwartz, 11/26/13, PC.

116. Allison 1915, *Henry W. Shoemaker,* p. 39.

117. HWS 1917, "The Abuse of Wealth," p. 7.

118. Allison 1915, *Henry W. Shoemaker,* p. 15.

119. Ibid.

120. Ibid., pp. 31, 17.

121. Ibid., p. 30

122. Newland, Tarlton & Co. to HWS, 12/31/10, PS.

123. HWS 1912, *More Pennsylvania Mountain Stories,* p. 19. See also Roosevelt 1926, *American Ideals,* pp. 319–31.

124. See Moore 1957, *The Frontier Mind.*

125. See Dorson 1973, *America in Legend,* pp. 60–98; Boorstin 1965, *The Americans,* pp. 327–37; Greeley 1951, *Forests and Men,* pp. 30–38.

126. HWS to Walter Blair, 12/1/55, SA. See also Abbott 1874, *David Crockett;* Filson 1966, *The Discovery and Settlement of Kentucke* (originally published 1784).

127. HWS 1915, *A Pennsylvania Bison Hunt,* pp. 50–60; HWS 1951, "Some Wild Life Folklore of the Allegheny and Susquehanna." Despite Shoemaker's plaint about the extinction of buffalo in Pennsylvania, some writers are skeptical that the species ever roamed in the state; see Zebrowski 1989, "Debunking a Myth—Were There Really Buffalo in Pennsylvania?" For more discussion of the legend cycles surrounding Mike Fink and other western heroes, see Dorson 1973, *America in Legend,* pp. 80–92.

128. HWS, n.d., "Sketch of Henry W. Shoemaker."

129. Charles E. Dorworth to Governor Fisher, 12/5/28, SA; HWS to F. L. Abbott, 1/14/24, PC.

130. Cyrus Fox to HWS, 5/5/21, PS.

131. HWS, n.d., "Martin G. Brumbaugh, Naturalist Governor"; Martin Brumbaugh to HWS, 9/30/24, PS.

132. Martin Brumbaugh to HWS, 12/6/16, PC.

133. Horace McFarland to HWS, 12/28/14, PC.

134. Horace McFarland to HWS, 1/7/15, PC. See also Hays 1959, *Conservation and the Gospel of Efficiency;* Nash 1968, *The American Environment.*

135. HWS to Horace McFarland, 1/8/15, PC.

136. HWS, n.d., "Sketch of Henry W. Shoemaker."

137. HWS 1914, *Wolf Days in Pennsylvania,* pp. 9–12; HWS, n.d., "Wild Life Conservation."

138. Stephen, n.d., *The Girl, the Parson, the Wolf.*

139. HWS to J. T. Rothrock, 12/18/13, PS.

140. "Col. Henry W. Shoemaker: A Pennsylvania Parks Association Executive," 1941, p. 50.

141. HWS 1917, *Pennsylvania Folk Lore,* p. 7.

142. HWS 1916, *Local Patriotism,* p. 3.

143. HWS 1922, "The Folk Lore and Legends of Clinton County."

144. HWS to Donehoo, 9/29/13, PS.

145. HWS 1927, *The Origins and Language of Central Pennsylvania Witchcraft.*

146. Walker 1967, *Life in the Age of Enterprise,* p. 175. See also Schlereth 1991, *Victorian America.*

147. Fausold 1961, *Gifford Pinchot,* pp. 134–50.

148. Schlereth 1991, *Victorian America,* pp. 182–87.

149. HWS to J. Horace McFarland, 1/6/15, PC.

150. Ibid.

151. HWS 1923, *True Stories of the Pennsylvania Mountains,* p. 2. See also Stephen 1929, "Legend of Hairy John"; Stephen, n.d., *The Girl, the Parson, the Wolf.*

152. HWS 1923, *True Stories of the Pennsylvania Mountains,* p. 2.

153. HWS 1926, *Marking the Historic Sites of Early Pennsylvania* p. 2.

154. Beckwith 1931, *Folklore in America,* p. 54.

155. HWS 1925, *Pennsylvania German and Huguenot Antiques.*

156. Pinkett 1970, *Gifford Pinchot.*

157. Pinchot 1910, *The Fight for Conservation.*

158. Ibid., p. 26.

159. Ibid., p. 23.

160. McGeary 1960, *Gifford Pinchot,* p. 242.

161. Pinchot 1910, *The Fight for Conservation,* p. 19.

162. Pinchot 1993, *Fishing Talk.*

163. The Republican State Committee distributed 100,000 copies of the pamphlet.

164. HWS 1922, *Gifford Pinchot: The Man Who Made Good,* p. 7. After the election, however, Shoemaker was upset that "Gifford Pinchot, in order to pass his dry [prohibition] bills, traded off all of his proposed labor legislation" (HWS to Governor Fisher, 9/30/30, SA). In the same letter he complained that Pinchot turned away from the Progressives who brought him to prominence: "You will recall that after Mr. Pinchot was elected in 1922, he became a very different man. In fact he got so close to the organization, that it was his friends like you, myself, and his pre-nomination supporters whom he overlooked. In fact, he kept in office hosts of organization men, named others, and slighted his real supporters."

165. HWS 1922, *Gifford Pinchot: The Man Who Made Good,* p. 12.

166. Ibid., p. 15.

167. Ibid., p. 13.

168. McNeil 1980, "A History of American Folklore Scholarship," pp. 817–27; Clements 1986, *Native American Folklore in Nineteenth-Century Periodicals,* pp. 187–99; Grinnell 1961, *Pawnee Hero Stories and Folk-Tales;* Grinnell 1962, *Blackfoot Lodge Tales;* Grinnell 1971, *By Cheyenne Campfires;* Grinnell 1976, *Beyond the Old Frontier.*

169. Charles Bird Grinnell to HWS, 3/12/25, PS.

170. Charles Bird Grinnell to HWS, 3/18/25, PS.

171. HWS to Charles Bird Grinnell, 3/19/25, PS.

172. HWS to Ernest Thompson Seton, 3/15/20, PS.

173. Seton 1918, *Lives of the Hunted,* p. 12. See also Wiley 1962, *Ernest Thompson Seton's America;* HWS 1917, *The Pennsylvania Lion or Panther.* Applying Freudian analysis, Jay Mechling has speculated that Seton's fixation on and identification with the wolf suggests that the wolf symbolized his father and had a connection with the development of collecting and anality in Seton's Boy Scouts. See Mechling 1984, "High Kybo Floater"; Mechling 1989, "The Collecting Self and American Youth Movements," p. 283.

174. HWS to Ernest Thompson Seton, 7/22/20, PS.

175. HWS 1939, "Vanished Game"; Seton 1939, "The Rocky Mountain Goat."

176. HWS 1939, "Vanished Game," p. 15.

177. Ibid.

178. HWS to Ernest Thompson Seton, 10/15/25, PS.

179. Dorson 1972, "How Shall we Rewrite Charles W. Skinner Today?"; Bealle 1994, "Another Look at Charles M. Skinner."

180. Skinner 1903, *American Myths and Legends.*

181. Skinner 1911, *Myths and Legends of Flowers, Trees, Fruits, and Plants,* p. 9. See HWS, n.d., "Pennsylvania Folklore."

182. Skinner 1903, *American Myths and Legends,* p. 6.

183. Leach 1966, "Folklore in American Regional Literature."

184. HWS to Robert W. L. Moyer, 11/19/13, PS.

185. HWS 1916, *Wasting the State's Money.*

186. HWS, n.d., "Wild Life Conservation."

187. HWS to A. B. Farquhar, 12/29/13, PS.

188. See HWS 1920, *The Pennsylvania Forestry Problem;* HWS 1939, "Vanished Game"; HWS 1953, "Neighbors."

189. HWS 1939, "Vanished Game," p. 31.

190. HWS to W. H. Schwartz, 11/19/13, PS.

191. HWS 1918, *The Seneca Philosophy,* p. 11.

192. Allison 1915, *Henry W. Shoemaker,* p. 18.

193. HWS 1918, *The Seneca Philosophy,* p. 11.

194. Ibid.

195. HWS to W. H. Schwartz, 12/24/13, PS.

196. See Stevens 1964, *Pennsylvania,* p. 278; "Col. Henry W. Shoemaker: A Pennsylvania Parks Association Executive," 1941.

197. HWS 1927, *The Career of Forestry,* p. 2.

198. HWS to Ellwood B. Chapman, 2/26/32, PS. See also Cupper 1994, "A Century of Conservation."

199. Illick 1928, *Pennsylvania Trees;* HWS and Illick 1928, *In Penn's Woods.*

200. HWS to Governor Fisher, 9/30/30, SA.

201. HWS, n.d., "The Work of the Pennsylvania Historical Commission."

202. "Meet the Former State Historian," 1945, p. 4. See also HWS 1926, *Marking the Historic Sites of Early Pennsylvania;* Beyer 1991, *Guide to the State Historical Markers of Pennsylvania.*

203. HWS to C. Hale Sipe, 6/20/47, SA. In another letter to State Historian S. K. Stevens, he said: "I was distressed at your putting up new signs at the entrances to Altoona, without the courtesy of consulting me. . . . I worked out the wording of four thousand state highway signs, most of which, I think, have stood the test of time" (HWS to S. K. Stevens, 9/25/47, PC).

204. HWS to Albert Cook Myers, 5/12/24, PS.

205. Beyer 1991, *Guide to the State Historical Markers,* p. 3.

206. "Dedication of Monument to Captain John Hansom Steelman," program booklet, 11/29/24, PS.

207. See HWS 1917, *Pennsylvania Folk Lore,* p. 5; Bierly 1928, "Thrilling Story of Capt. Brady"; Brady Dedication, 1928.

208. Beyer 1991, *Guide to the State Historical Markers,* p. 169; HWS to Hon. Michael Donohoe, 5/22/25, PS; HWS 1920, *Some Historic Trees;* Tozier 1974, "The Tiadaghton Elm."

209. Wolf 1969, *The Fair Play Settlers.*

210. Roosevelt 1926, *American Ideals,* p. 24.

211. HWS 1951, "The Tiadaghton or Pine Creek Declaration of Independence."

212. Ibid.

213. Charles Snyder to HWS, 8/22/20, PS.

214. Frederic Lewis Pattee to HWS, 10/17/13, PS.

215. HWS 1917, *Eldorado Found*, p. 7.

216. Frederic A. Godcharles, State Librarian, to HWS, 4/22/29, PS.

217. HWS 1917, *Eldorado Found*, p. 7.

218. Ibid., p. 5. See also Getz 1985, "The Great Escape"; Green 1986, *Fit for America*, pp. 128–36; Merrill 1989, *The Romance of Victorian Natural History*.

219. HWS and Illick 1928, *In Penn's Woods*, pp. 7–8.

220. See Smith 1950, *Virgin Land*; Bowden 1992, "The Invention of American Tradition"; Dorson 1973, *America in Legend*, pp. 57–93.

221. HWS 1935, "There Should Be a Primitive Area Preserved in Pennsylvania," p. 8. See also Grant 1994, "The Inalienable Land"; Oelschlaeger 1991, *The Idea of Wilderness*; Nash 1967, *Wilderness and the American Mind*; Evans 1904, "The Wilderness"; Roosevelt 1926, *The Wilderness Hunter*, pp. 3–17.

222. HWS and Illick 1928, *In Penn's Woods*, p. 3.

223. Ibid.

224. HWS 1922, *A Forgotten People*, pp. 3–4, 8.

225. HWS 1931, *Mountain Minstrelsy*, p. 33.

226. HWS and Illick 1928, *In Penn's Woods*, p. 12.

227. Smith 1950, *Virgin Land*; Bowden 1992, "The Invention of American Tradition."

228. HWS 1916, *Juniata Memories*, pp. 151–65; HWS 1913, *Susquehanna Legends*, pp. 374–87.

229. HWS 1922, *Allegheny Episodes*, pp. 135–46.

230. HWS 1912, *More Pennsylvania Mountain Stories*, pp. xv, 62.

231. HWS and Illick 1928, *In Penn's Woods*, p. 14.

232. Ibid., p. 9.

233. Marx 1964, *The Machine in the Garden*.

234. Beyer 1991, *Guide to the State Historical Markers*, p. 40.

235. See Patterson 1989, "From Battle Ground to Pleasure Ground."

236. "Col. Henry W. Shoemaker: A Pennsylvania Parks Association Executive," 1941, p. 49.

237. See HWS 1916, *Local Patriotism*; HWS 1923, *Place Names and Altitudes of Pennsylvania Mountains*. See also Clebsch 1979, "America's 'Mythique' as Redeemer Nation."

238. Raven 1966, "Man and Nature," p. 175.

239. HWS 1917, *Eldorado Found*, p. 6.

240. Nye 1966, *This Almost Chosen People*, p. 259.

241. Ibid., p. 277.

242. Ibid., pp. 1–42.

243. HWS 1912, *More Pennsylvania Mountain Stories*, p. 358.

244. Nye 1966, *This Almost Chosen People*, p. 293.

245. HWS and Illick 1928, *In Penn's Woods*, p. 5. See also Stroud 1985, *National Leaders of American Conservation*, pp. 21, 306–7; Nye 1966, *This Almost Chosen People*, pp. 293–98.

246. HWS 1923, *True Stories of the Pennsylvania Mountains*, p. 6.

247. Ibid., p. 7.

248. Ibid., p. 2.

249. HWS 1917, *Western Pennsylvania Indian Folk Lore*, p. 13.

250. Ibid., pp. 12–13.

251. Ibid., p. 13.

252. Donehoo 1921, *The Changing of Historic Place Names*; HWS 1923, *Place Names and Altitudes of Pennsylvania Mountains*.

253. HWS 1921, "Introduction."

254. HWS 1923, *Place Names and Altitudes of Pennsylvania Mountains*.

255. Ibid., p. 2.

256. HWS 1924, *More Allegheny Episodes*, pp. 247–48.

257. HWS 1926, "Red Panther's Funeral Pyre."

258. HWS to Thomas Lloyd, 3/19/25, PS.

259. HWS 1924, *More Allegheny Episodes,* pp. 261–62.

260. Donehoo 1921, *The Changing of Historic Place Names,* p. 14.

261. Allison 1915, *Henry W. Shoemaker,* p. 7.

262. HWS scrapbook, 1925, PS.

263. "Secretary of War James W. Good," 1929.

264. HWS to Charles S. Diller, 9/23/41, MU.

265. HWS 1939, *Conserving Pennsylvania's Historic Past,* p. 7.

266. See Glass 1989, "Expanding a Vision."

267. Amerilia Hauck Gross to HWS, 5/1/24, PS.

268. HWS 1922, *The Importance of Collecting Indian Legends,* pp. 6, 4.

269. Sarah Burnett Torbert to HWS, 1910, PS.

270. HWS 1929, "The Romance of Pennsylvania History."

271. HWS to Professor Henry W. Popp, 3/26/29, PS. See also HWS 1929, *The Legends of the Caverns of Centre County.*

272. HWS to H. B. Douglas, General Manager, Clearfield Bituminous Coal Co., 2/10/20, PS.

273. Brumbaugh 1915, *Address.*

274. HWS, "The Ascent of the Mahanoy," pp. 5–6.

275. HWS 1917, *Eldorado Found,* pp. 110–11.

276. Ibid., pp. 111–12.

277. HWS 1917, "Pennsylvania Alpine Club," April 23, 1917.

278. Hoffmann 1956, "The Pennsylvania Folklore Society."

279. See Stoudt 1915, *The Folklore of the Pennsylvania-German;* Reichard 1944, "John Baer Stoudt."

280. HWS to Stoudt, 7/19/21, PS.

281. Pennsylvania Federation 1925, *Year Book,* p. 110.

282. Ferree 1912, *Year Book;* Cupper 1993, "Ninety-Five Years of the Pennsylvania Society"; HWS 1914, "Report of the Library Committee," p. 92.

283. Ferree 1914, *Year Book,* p. 253.

284. HWS 1916, *The Dutchman on the Pennsylvania Frontier.*

285. Rothrock 1979, *The Huguenots;* Shenk 1932, *Encyclopedia of Pennsylvania,* p. 265.

286. See Klein and Hoogenboom 1980, *A History of Pennsylvania,* p. 46; Baird 1966, *History of Huguenot Emigration,* p. 170.

287. HWS to Walter Blair, 12/1/55, SA.

288. HWS 1950, "Some Forgotten Pennsylvania Huguenots."

289. HWS 1920, *A Tour in Huguenot Countries.*

290. HWS 1919, *Address.*

291. HWS to Dr. Hubert Work, 12/29/28, PC.

292. HWS to Gov. Fisher, 12/29/28, SA.

293. Fisher to Hubert Work, 11/16/28, SA.

294. Fisher to HWS 9/20/29, SA.

295. HWS 1950, "Bulgaria in the Memory of a Former American Envoy," p. 5. See also Groueff, *Crown of Thorns,* 1987.

296. HWS, n.d., "Bulgaria."

297. HWS 1950, "Bulgaria in the Memory of a Former American Envoy," p. 5.

298. Ibid.

299. HWS to Estella Callahan, 12/23/31, PS.

300. Ibid.

301. HWS 1950,"Bulgaria in the Memory of a Former American Envoy," p. 5.

302. "Introducing Our Personality of the Week," 1936, p. 2.

303. Ibid.

304. See Minkov 1992, "The Ethnographic Institute"; Minkov 1989, "Fieldwork in Bulgarian Ethnographic Museums."

305. Nicoloff 1979, *Bulgarian Folktales*, pp. xx–xxi.

306. Edward and Elisabeth Haskell, Bulgarian Folk School, to HWS, 8/1/33, PC.

307. HWS to Judge H. T. Hall, 12/28/32, PC.

308. HWS to Hilda Hauri, 3/31/32, PS.

309. Dolores Coffey to Simon Bronner, 12/17/92.

310. Blanche [Shoemaker] Carr to HWS, 11/13/32, PS.

311. HWS to Ted Arter, 9/11/44, PC.

312. "Introducing Our Personality of the Week," 1936, p. 2.

313. Department of State Press Report (typescript), 7/27/33, PC.

314. Edward and Elisabeth Haskell, Bulgarian Folk School, 8/1/33, PC.

315. Department of State Press Report (typescript), 8/4/33, PC.

316. Theodore Arter to HWS, 11/20/35, PC.

317. HWS 1931, *Some Stories of Old Deserted Houses;* HWS 1932, *Tales of the Pennsylvania Highways.*

318. HWS 1932, *Tales of the Pennsylvania Highways.*

319. Ibid., pp. 3–4.

320. Ibid., pp. 2, 4.

321. HWS to Ellwood Chapman, 2/26/32, PS; HWS, n.d., "Martin G. Brumbaugh."

322. HWS to Paul D. Wright, 10/13/24, PS.

323. J. Horace McFarland to HWS, 4/28/29, PS.

324. HWS to Rung, 5/6/36, HC.

325. Botkin to HWS, 5/12/48, SA. See also Botkin 1939, "WPA and Folklore Research"; Botkin 1946, "Living Lore on the New York City Writer's Project"; Hirsch 1987, "Folklore in the Making"; Hirsch 1988, "Cultural Pluralism and Applied Folklore."

Chapter 2

1. Shearer 1920, "Pennsylvania Folklore," November 14, sec. 6, p. 2.

2. HWS 1922, *Allegheny Episodes*, p. 5; HWS 1924, *More Allegheny Episodes*, p. 11.

3. Allison 1915, *Henry W. Shoemaker*, p. 1.

4. HWS 1916, *Penn's Grandest Cavern*, p. 30.

5. Ibid., p. 32.

6. Ibid., pp. 80–94.

7. Donehoo 1928, *The Changing of Historic Place Names*, p. 130.

8. Brault 1979, "Who Remembers Poor Malachi Boyer?" p. 21.

9. HWS 1953, "Reasons for Collecting Pennsylvania Folklore."

10. See Green 1975, "Traits of Indian Character"; Green 1990, "The Pochahontas Perplex"; and Barden 1991, *Virginia Folk Legends*, p. 150, for narratives about Indians by whites. For stories collected from Senecas, see Parker 1923, *Seneca Myths and Folk Tales;* Curtin and Hewitt 1910–1911, "Seneca Fiction, Legends, and Myths."

11. Despite Thompson's neglect generally of legendary narrative and specifically of American regional collectors such as Henry Shoemaker, J. Frank Dobie, and Vance Randolph, his index contains several motifs that relate to Shoemaker's legend of Penn's Cave: C162 Eloping with king's daughter; C162.3 Tabu: marrying outside of group; R315.1 Cave as Eloping lovers' refuge. Ernest Baughman in his *Type and Motif Index of the Folktales of England and North America* (1966) included Shoemaker's collection of werewolf tales as folklore (1951).

12. Yoder 1990, *Discovering American Folklife*, p. 194; Brault 1979, "Who Remembers Poor Malachi Boyer?" p. 21.

13. Yoder 1982, "Folklife in Pennsylvania," p. 15; Yoder 1990, *Discovering American Folklife*, p. 194.

14. Leroy Keefer to HWS, 8/16/20, PS.

15. HWS 1953, "Reasons for Collecting Pennsylvania Folklore," pp. 1–2.

16. HWS 1916, *Penn's Grandest Cavern*, p. 8.

17. See Deardorff 1972, *Chief Cornplanter.*

18. HWS 1953, "Reasons for Collecting Pennsylvania Folklore," p. 2.

19. HWS 1922, *Allegheny Episodes,* pp. 135, 143, 144, 146.

20. HWS 1953, "Reasons for Collecting Pennsylvania Folklore," p. 3.

21. HWS, n.d., "Clinton County Folklore," p. 2.

22. HWS 1953, "Reasons for Collecting Pennsylvania Folklore," p. 3.

23. HWS to S. W. Pennypacker, 9/11/14, PC.

24. HWS 1931, *Some Stories of Old Deserted Houses,* pp. 65–68.

25. HWS 1950, "Blackbeard's Treasure Cave." See also LaBar 1984, "Noah Parker's Treasure," pp. 20–23.

26. LeBar 1984, "Noah Parker's Treasure," pp. 31–32.

27. HWS 1912, *More Pennsylvania Mountain Stories,* pp. v–xv.

28. HWS 1922, "The Folk Lore and Legends of Clinton County," pp. 2–3.

29. HWS 1912, *Tales of the Bald Eagle Mountains,* p. xvii.

30. Ibid., pp. xvii–xviii, xvi.

31. See Beckwith 1931, *Folklore in America;* Rourke 1959, *American Humor* (originally published 1931); Dorson 1971, *American Folklore and the Historian,* pp. 78–93; Dorson 1973, *America in Legend;* Rubin 1980, *Constance Rourke and American Culture;* Bronner 1992, "Martha Warren Beckwith."

32. See HWS 1913, *Stories of Great Pennsylvania Hunters;* HWS 1922, *Allegheny Episodes;* HWS 1924, *More Allegheny Episodes.*

33. HWS 1915, *Pennsylvania Deer and Their Horns,* p. 49.

34. HWS 1912, *The Indian Steps,* p. vi.

35. HWS 1912, *More Pennsylvania Mountain Stories,* p. x.

36. Interview with William Wewer, former Executive Director of the PHMC, 12/14/92.

37. HWS 1912, *The Indian Steps,* p. vi.

38. HWS 1922, *Allegheny Episodes,* pp. 3–6; HWS 1912, *Tales of the Bald Eagle Mountains,* pp. xiii–xx; HWS 1913, *In the Seven Mountains.* See Grant 1994, "The Inalienable Land," for more discussion of the sacredness of the wilderness in American culture.

39. HWS 1913, *Susquehanna Legends.*

40. Ibid., p. xvi.

41. HWS 1919, *Extinct Pennsylvania Animals Part II,* p. 9.

42. HWS 1914, *Black Forest Souvenirs,* p. xvi.

43. HWS 1917, *Pennsylvania Folk Lore,* p. 8.

44. Ibid., pp. 10, 9.

45. Rung 1977, *Rung's Chronicles,* p. v.

46. HWS 1950, "Early Jewish Pioneers in Dauphin County."

47. HWS to Rung, 2/15/36, HC.

48. HWS 1915, *A Pennsylvania Bison Hunt;* HWS 1929, *The Wild Animals of Clinton County.*

49. Zebrowski 1989, "Debunking a Myth—Were There Really Buffalo in Pennsylvania?" pp. 13, 22.

50. Dorson 1972, *American Folklore and the Historian,* p. 144. Dorson made the argument that "oral traditional history," if it doesn't capture fact, does record the "truthfulness" of attitudes, prejudices, and stereotypes. It strengthens prevailing concepts of symbol, myth, and image and provides data on groups that are not in the historical spotlight, such as ethnic and regional groups.

51. HWS 1922, *Allegheny Episodes,* p. 5.

52. Rosenberger 1971, *Adventures and Philosophy of a Pennsylvania Dutchman,* pp. 278–79. See also Rosenberger 1974, *Mountain Folks.*

53. HWS 1907, *Pennsylvania Mountain Stories,* p. xiii.

54. HWS 1913, *In the Seven Mountains,* pp. xvi–xvii.

55. HWS 1924, *More Allegheny Episodes,* p. 11.

56. HWS 1920, *North Mountain Mementos,* p. 8.

57. Ibid., pp. 7–8.
58. HWS 1917, *Pennsylvania Folk Lore,* p. 12.
59. HWS 1917, *Eldorado Found,* pp. 5–6.
60. HWS 1917, *Western Pennsylvania Indian Folk Lore.*
61. HWS to Philip Nordell, 5/16/25, PS.
62. HWS to Philip Nordell, 5/7/25, PS.
63. HWS to Charles Mardt, 5/20/24, PS.
64. HWS to Harold Thompson, 10/7/47, PC.
65. HWS to J. T. Rothrock, 12/31/14, PC.
66. HWS 1925, *Pennsylvania Indian Folk-Songs,* p. 4.
67. HWS 1917, *Pennsylvania Folk Lore,* p. 12.
68. HWS 1922, *Allegheny Episodes,* p. 7.
69. HWS, n.d., "Clinton County Folklore," p. 1.
70. HWS 1920, *South Mountain Sketches,* p. 8.
71. Walker 1958, "Colonel Henry W. Shoemaker," p. 46.
72. Interview with Ben Yarosz, Williamsport, Pennsylvania, 3/6/94.
73. HWS to George Korson, 4/8/47, PC.
74. HWS 1922, *Allegheny Episodes,* p. 7.
75. HWS 1913, *Susquehanna Legends,* p. xvii.
76. HWS 1922, *Allegheny Episodes,* p. 7.
77. HWS to Rev. George P. Donehoo, 10/3/13, PS.
78. Ibid.
79. See HWS 1922, *The Importance of Collecting Indian Legends.*
80. Ibid., p. 3.
81. Ibid., p. 7.
82. Allison 1915, *Henry W. Shoemaker,* p. 45.
83. William Allison to HWS, 12/30/14, PC.
84. William Allison to HWS, 2/10/15, PC.
85. HWS 1912, *More Pennsylvania Mountain Stories,* pp. 323–38.
86. HWS 1914, *Black Forest Souvenirs,* p. xvii.
87. HWS 1916, *Penn's Grandest Cavern,* p. 29.
88. HWS 1916, *Juniata Memories,* p. 151.
89. Allison 1915, *Henry W. Shoemaker,* pp. 26–27.
90. See "The Last Pack" in HWS 1912, *More Pennsylvania Mountain Stories,* pp. 75–83.
91. HWS 1923, *True Stories of the Pennsylvania Mountains,* p. 1.
92. See HWS 1914, *The Pennsylvania Lion or Panther;* HWS 1914, *Wolf Days in Pennsylvania;* HWS 1916, *Penn's Grandest Cavern.*
93. HWS 1912, *The Indian Steps,* p. vi.
94. Allison 1915, *Henry W. Shoemaker,* pp. 27, 30.
95. HWS 1913, *In the Seven Mountains,* p. 97.
96. HWS 1924, *More Allegheny Episodes,* pp. 223–24.
97. HWS 1917, *The Pennsylvania Lion or Panther,* pp. 56–57.
98. HWS to S. N. Rhoads, 12/16/13, PS.
99. HWS 1931, *Mountain Minstrelsy,* p. 31.
100. HWS to Samuel Bayard, 12/2/49, SA.
101. HWS to Donald Cadzow, Executive Director of PHMC, report, 12/20/55, SA.
102. HWS to Jansen Foundation, 3/1/50, SA.
103. See HWS 1913, *In the Seven Mountains;* Yoder 1990, *Discovering American Folklife,* p. 193.
104. HWS to Frederic Lewis Pattee, 10/3/13, PS. See also HWS 1913, *In the Seven Mountains,* p. xvii.
105. Frederic Lewis Pattee to HWS, 10/17/13, PS.
106. Frederic Lewis Pattee to HWS, 11/1/16, PC.

107. HWS, n.d., "The Value of Folklore and Witchcraft Beliefs in Pennsylvania History."

108. See Bronner 1989, "Folklife Starts Here."

109. HWS 1913, *Susquehanna Legends*, p. xiv; HWS 1914, *A Week in the Blue Mountains*, p. 6. See also Henning 1911, *Tales of the Blue Mountains;* Henning and Schalck 1907, *History of Schuylkill County.*

110. HWS 1913, *Susquehanna Legends*, p. xiv.

111. Henning 1911, *Tales of the Blue Mountains*, p. 7.

112. Ibid., p. 10.

113. Ibid., pp. 8–10; Newell, Review of *Tales of the Blue Mountains.*

114. See Bronner 1984, "William Henry Egle"; Egle 1883, *History of the Counties of Dauphin and Lebanon;* HWS 1922, "The Folk Lore and Legends of Clinton County," p.4.

115.. References to "Masters of folk-lore" appear in HWS 1913, *Susquehanna Legends*, p. xiv; see also HWS 1917, *Pennsylvania Folklore;* HWS 1931, *Mountain Minstrelsy.* By the 1940s, Shoemaker had apparently amassed an impressive reference library of folklore. He wrote Donald Cadzow, Executive Director of the PHMC, about his plans "to assemble an international library of folklore": "I have a collection of 300 volumes, including a few of my own. I would turn over for a nominal figure of say $500, but are worth $5 each because of their rarity, and arrange to receive the folklore journals, and correspond with all the American folklore societies, with a secretary and typist, capable to assist researchers, writers, storytellers" (HWS to Cadzow, Memorandum, 11/20/47, SA). Shoemaker's collection did not stay together, however. His books were dispersed at auction in 1959.

116. See Davidson 1951, *A Guide to American Folklore*, p. vii; Dorson 1971, *American Folklore and the Historian*, p. 23; Cochran 1985, *Vance Randolph.*

117. See Dobie 1930, *Man, Bird, and Beast;* Abernethy 1967, *J. Frank Dobie;* Bode 1968, *J. Frank Dobie;* Tinkle 1978, *An American Original.*

118. Dobie to HWS, 11/7/26, PS. See also Dobie 1941, *The Longhorns.*

119. Dobie 1943, "Twenty Years an Editor," p. viii.

120. See Dorson 1971, *American Folklore and the Historian*, pp. 157–72; Georges 1972, "The General Concept of Legend."

121. Dobie 1943, "Twenty Years an Editor," p. viii.

122. Dobie 1924, *Legends of Texas*, p. iv. See also Abernethy 1992, *The Texas Folklore Society.*

123. Henry Mercer to HWS, 1/13/24, PS.

124. See HWS 1925, *Tree Language of the Pennsylvania German Gypsies;* HWS 1926, "The Language of the Pennsylvania German Gypsies"; HWS 1927, *The Origins and Language of Central Pennsylvania Witchcraft;* HWS 1952, "Neighbors."

125. HWS to J. Horace McFarland, 10/25/44, PC.

126. HWS to J. W. Zimmerman, 3/9/25, PS.

127. Wilgus 1959, *Anglo-American Folksong Scholarship*, p. 166.

128. Ibid., pp. 166–67.

129. He was greatly upset, for example, by Samuel Bayard's omission of his books in the bibliography to *Hill Country Tunes* (1944) (HWS to Harold Thompson, 10/7/47, PC).

130. HWS 1923, *The Music and Musical Instruments of the Pennsylvania Mountaineers*, p. 9.

131. HWS 1920, *North Mountain Mementos*, p. 15. See also Lang 1898, *Custom and Myth.*

132. Montenyohl 1988, "Andrew Lang's Contributions," p. 282.

133. HWS 1920, *North Mountain Mementos*, p. 15.

134. HWS 1927, *The Origins and Language of Central Pennsylvania Witchcraft*, pp. 8–9.

135. Ibid., p. 16.

136. Winthrop 1991, *Dictionary of Concepts*, pp. 227–32; Barzun 1965, *Race;* Kautsky 1926, *Are the Jews a Race?*

137. Lang 1898, *Custom and Myth*, pp. 26–28.

138. HWS 1922, "The Folk Lore and Legends of Clinton County."

139. See Botkin 1936, "Regionalism, Cult or Culture?"; Botkin 1937, "Regionalism and Culture"; Halpert 1947, "American Regional Folklore"; Hirsch 1988, "Cultural Pluralism and Applied Folklore."

140. HWS 1935, "Pennsylvania Folkways in the Development of an American Culture" (typescript), PC.

141. HWS 1936, "Pennsylvania Folklore."

142. For discussions of the lure of Appalachia for folk song collectors, see Wilgus 1959, *Anglo-American Folksong Scholarship;* McNeil 1989, *Appalachian Images;* Bronner 1989, "Collectors."

143. HWS 1931, *Mountain Minstrelsy,* p. 23. See also Dunaway 1930, *The French Racial Strain in Colonial Pennsylvania.*

144. HWS 1931, *Mountain Minstrelsy,* p. 29. See also Sajna 1993, "Storyteller."

145. Ibid., pp. 18–19.

146. George Korson to HWS, 9/10/35, PC.

147. HWS 1931, *Mountain Minstrelsy,* p. 26.

148. Albert Friedman to HWS, 7/8/55, SA.

149. HWS 1924, *More Allegheny Episodes,* p. 10.

150. Ibid., pp. 7–8.

151. HWS 1920, *South Mountain Sketches,* pp. 7, 9, 10.

152. HWS 1924, *More Allegheny Episodes,* p. 13.

153. HWS 1922, *Allegheny Episodes,* p. 5.

154. Ibid., p. 6; HWS 1924, *More Allegheny Episodes,* p. 12.

155. HWS 1913, *Susquehanna Legends,* pp. xv–xvi; HWS 1913, *In the Seven Mountains,* p. xix.

156. HWS 1980, "Folk Lore, the Maker of Americans" (originally written 1939), p. 2; HWS 1910, *Pennsylvania Mountain Stories,* p. 5.

157. HWS to Moritz Jagendorf, 2/8/55, SA.

158. Rosenberger 1971, *Adventures and Philosophy,* p. 278.

159. Ibid.

160. Ibid., p. 281. Rosenberger produced his perspective on the folkways of the Pennsylvania highlands in *Mountain Folks* (1974).

161. HWS 1913, *Susquehanna Legends,* p. xvii.

162. HWS 1948, "Rotary Hour," p. 1.

163. HWS to Harold Thompson, 5/25/48, SA.

164. HWS 1913, *Susquehanna Legends,* p. xv.

165. HWS 1922, *Allegheny Episodes.* For his references to how texts are related to European narrative, see HWS 1912, *Tales of the Bald Eagle Mountains,* p. xviii; HWS 1917, *Pennsylvania Folk Lore,* p. 7; HWS 1920, *North Mountain Mementos,* pp. 14–23. For reference to New England and Southern legends, see HWS 1914, *Black Forest Souvenirs,* pp. xviii.

166. HWS 1920, *North Mountain Mementos,* pp. 10–14.

167. Press release, 1/8/54, SA.

168. See HWS 1922, *Some Forgotten Pennsylvania Heroines;* HWS 1930, *Two Old Christmas Stories;* HWS, n.d., "Women's Part in Pennsylvania Lumbering Days."

169. HWS 1912, *More Pennsylvania Mountain Stories,* p. xiii.

170. HWS 1920, *North American Mementos,* p. 10.

171. John French to HWS, 11/24/21, PS.

172. Walker 1922, *Rafting Days,* p. 3.

173. HWS 1923, *True Stories of the Pennsylvania Mountains,* pp. 8, 9.

174. John Chatham to HWS, 1/12/11, PS.

175. HWS 1913, *Story of the Indian Steps,* p. 7.

176. Ibid.

177. See Hanna 1911, *The Wilderness Trail;* Wallace 1961, *Indians in Pennsylvania;* Brinton 1972, *The Lenape and Their Legends* (originally published 1884); Kent 1984, *Susquehanna's Indians;* Hunt 1940, *The Wars of the Iroquois;* Sipe 1931, *The Indian Wars;* Jennings 1984, *The Ambiguous Iroquois Empire;* Richter 1992, *The Ordeal of the Longhouse;* Tooker 1984, "The Demise of the Susquehannocks."

178. Herbert K. Job to HWS, 10/14/12, PC.

179. George Hess to HWS, 1/20/15, PC.
180. Norman Easterbrook to HWS, 1/11/15, PC.
181. Katherine Carter Barrow to HWS, 9/19/12, PC.
182. Charlotte Huff to HWS, 9/16/12, PC.
183. John Chatham to HWS, 9/9/12, PC.
184. HWS 1917, *Pennsylvania Folk Lore*, p. 5. See also HWS 1912, *More Pennsylvania Mountain Stories*, pp. xii–xv; HWS 1913, *Stories of Great Pennsylvania Hunters*, pp. 21–23, 44–46.
185. HWS 1920, *North Mountain Mementos*, p. 11. See also HWS 1955, "Memories of Elimsport."
186. HWS 1920, *North Mountain Mementos*, pp. 2–13; HWS 1913, *Stories of Great Pennsylvania Hunters*, pp. 32–34.
187. HWS to George Korson, 4/8/47, PC.
188. Gillespie 1980, *Folklorist of the Coal Fields*, p. 117.
189. HWS 1924, *More Allegheny Episodes*, p. 8.
190. HWS to William Allison, 1/29/15, PC.
191. HWS 1924, *More Allegheny Episodes*, p. 9.
192. Ibid., p. 12.
193. HWS 1914, *Black Forest Souvenirs*, p. xviii.
194. HWS, n.d., "Clinton County Folklore," p. 1.
195. HWS 1914, *Black Forest Souvenirs*, p. xix.
196. HWS, n.d., "Clinton County Folklore," p. 1.
197. Ibid.
198. HWS 1939, *Conserving Pennsylvania's Historic Past*, p. 1.
199. HWS scrapbook, 1929, JC.
200. Minutes of 1951 Pennsylvania Folklore Society Meeting, PC.
201. George Korson to HWS, 11/23/35, PC.
202. HWS to John Baer Stoudt, 6/13/24, PS.
203. Darlington 1925, *Verses by the Way*, pp. 70–71, 79, 90–91.
204. HWS 1943, "Pennsylvania Folklore Society."
205. HWS to Frank G. Speck, University of Pennsylvania, 6/13/24, PS; HWS to John Baer Stoudt, 6/13/24, PS.
206. Dwyer-Schick 1979, "The American Folklore Society," pp. 132–40. See also Abernethy 1992, *The Texas Folklore Society*.
207. Hand 1946, "North American Folklore Societies," p. 478.
208. HWS to Charles F. Snyder, Sunbury, Pennsylvania, 7/26/49, SA.
209. HWS 1928, *Report of Henry W. Shoemaker*.
210. See HWS 1925, *Pennsylvania German and Huguenot Antiques;* HWS 1927, *Scotch-Irish and English Proverbs and Sayings;* HWS 1928, *Two Pennsylvania Mountain Legends;* HWS 1931, *Scotch-Irish and English Proverbs from Central Pennsylvania*.
211. Congressman Charles J. Esterly to HWS, 8/9/29, PS.
212. Gillespie 1980, *Folklorist of the Coal Fields*, p. 116.
213. Hand 1946, "North American Folklore Societies," p. 480.
214. See HWS 1943, "Pennsylvania Folklore Society," p. 181; Gillespie 1980, *Folklorist of the Coal Fields*, pp. 44–55.
215. HWS 1943, "Pennsylvania Folklore Society," p. 181.
216. Gillespie 1980, *Folklorist of the Coal Fields*, p. 45.
217. HWS 1943, "Pennsylvania Folklore Society," p. 181.
218. HWS, n.d., "The Value of Folklore and Witchcraft Beliefs."
219. Graeff 1955, "Renascence of History." See also James 1948, "Folklore and Propaganda"; Gerndt 1987, *Volkskunde und Nationalsozialismus;* Dow and Lixfeld 1994, *The Nazification of an Academic Discipline*.
220. Botkin 1944, *A Treasury of American Folklore*, p. xxvi.

221. Bayard 1945, "Unrecorded Folk Traditions," p. 1.
222. Ibid., p. 14.
223. Susman 1984, *Culture as History,* p. 178.
224. Ibid.
225. Botkin 1944, *A Treasury of American Folklore,* pp. xxii, xxvi.
226. Graeff 1955, "Renascence of History," p. 37. See also Federal Writers' Project 1936, *Three Hikes Through Wissahickon;* Federal Writers' Project 1939, *Northampton County Guide;* Writers Program of the WPA 1940, *Pennsylvania.*
227. Graeff 1955, "Renascence of History," p. 37. See also Bronner 1989, "Folklife Starts Here"; Bronner 1991, "A Prophetic Vision"; Cary 1989, "The Mercer Museum and the Landis Valley Farm Museum"; Frey 1946, "An Upswing of Pa. Deitsch Activities"; Gillespie 1980, *Folklorist of the Coal Fields,* pp. 97–104.
228. See Susman 1984, *Culture as History,* pp. 150–83; Green 1992, *The Uncertainty of Everyday Life.*
229. Hirsch 1988, "Cultural Pluralism and Applied Folklore," p. 54.
230. See Nixon 1946, *Lower Piedmont Country,* p. 1.
231. Writers Program 1940 of the WPA, *Pennsylvania,* p. vii.
232. See HWS 1953, "Reasons for Collecting Pennsylvania Folklore."
233. Don Yoder to HWS, 5/12/48, SA.
234. HWS to Victoria Smallzell, 3/22/50, SA.
235. Thompson, "Colonel Henry W. Shoemaker," p. 1.
236. Harold Thompson to HWS, 10/24/52, PC.

Chapter 3

1. See Historical Commission 1915, *First Report;* Nichols 1967, *The PHMC;* Glass 1989, "Expanding a Vision."
2. Glass 1989, "Expanding a Vision," p. 26.
3. HWS 1951, "The Tiadaghton or Pine Creek Declaration of Independence."
4. HWS 1948, "Rotary Hour."
5. Allison 1915, *Henry W. Shoemaker,* pp. 19–20.
6. Halpert 1985, "A Note on Charles E. Brown"; Jones 1950, "Folk Culture and the Historical Society."
7. HWS 1980, "Folk Lore, the Maker of Americans" (originally prepared in 1939).
8. HWS to Donald Cadzow, n.d. (probably 1945), SA.
9. PHMC 1950, "The PHMC, 1945–50," p. 24.
10. Graeff 1955, "Renascence of History," p. 38.
11. See Cadzow 1936, *Archaeological Studies;* Stevens and Kent 1947, *Conserving Pennsylvania's Historical Heritage;* PHMC 1950, "The PHMC, 1945–50"; Stevens 1964, *Pennsylvania;* Stevens 1968, "Foreword."
12. Stevens and Kent 1947, *Conserving Pennsylvania's Historical Heritage,* p. 61.
13. Ibid.
14. Ibid., p. 5.
15. See James 1948, "Folklore and Propaganda."
16. See Gleason 1984, "World War II and the Development of American Studies."
17. See ibid.; Botkin 1944, *A Treasury of American Folklore;* Smith 1950, *Virgin Land;* Potter 1954, *People of Plenty;* Dorson 1959, *American Folklore;* Kouwenhoven 1967, *The Arts in Modern American Civilization.*
18. Indeed, mythological woods figures Robin Hood and an American cognate in James Fenimore Cooper's "Hawkeye" were very evident in American popular culture during the 1920s and 1930s in the movies and in growing legends of Pretty Boy Floyd. J. C. Holt in *Robin Hood* (1989) sees in the transformation of the Robin Hood of the forest legend "an expression of present-day social malaise

or discontent," and more interpretation of the Hawkeye figure in the American media during the twentieth century is eruditely provided by Richard Slotkin in *Gunfighter Nation* (1992). Shoemaker's essay "Pennsylvania's Last Frontier" (n.d.) has a special bearing in this regard because of its suggestion that the forested wilderness was an equalizing factor in American culture and its invocation of Robin Hood (in the guise of Robber Lewis) and other noble woodsmen figures.

19. PHMC 1950, "The PHMC, 1945–50," p. 1.

20. Ibid., p. 11.

21. Jordan 1946, "Toward a New Folklore"; Jones 1950, "Folk Culture and the Historical Society"; Halpert 1985, "A Note on Charles E. Brown."

22. Stevens 1965, "An Historian Looks at Folklore," p. xi.

23. PHMC 1950, "The PHMC, 1945–50," p. 15.

24. Nichols 1967, *The PHMC*, p. 27.

25. Dolores Coffey to Simon Bronner, 12/17/92; interview with Martha Simonetti, Harrisburg, Pennsylvania, 12/7/92; interview with William Wewer, Camp Hill, Pennsylvania, 12/1/92.

26. HWS to Marion Patterson, 11/24/47, PC.

27. Ibid.

28. HWS to Forest Sweet, 9/11/49, SA.

29. HWS to Miriam Dickey, 2/16/55, JC.

30. Interview with John Witthoft, West Chester, Pennsylvania, 12/9/92.

31. Dolores Coffey to Simon Bronner, 12/17/92.

32. HWS to Donald Cadzow, 11/20/47, SA.

33. Donald Cadzow to HWS, 3/5/48, PC.

34. HWS to Donald Cadzow, Memorandum, 4/15/48, SA.

35. Don Yoder to HWS, 1/7/48, SA.

36. HWS to Donald Cadzow, Memorandum, 12/30/47, SA.

37. HWS to Don Yoder, 1/29/48, SA; Yoder to HWS, 2/2/48, SA.

38. HWS to D. Cadzow, Memorandum, 3/6/48, SA.

39. "Archivist Gets Folklore Post," 1948, pp. 1, 15.

40. HWS to J. Herbert Walker, 3/12/48, SA.

41. HWS to Mrs. Harry A. Feather, 6/22/49, JC.

42. HWS to D. Cadzow, Memorandum, 11/20/47, SA.

43. HWS to Dorothy M. Lehman, 8/24/49, PC.

44. Pennsylvania Folklore 1948, p. 396; HWS to D. Cadzow, Memorandum, 12/7/49, SA.

45. Jones 1949, "Editor's Page"; HWS to Louis C. Jones, 10/28/49, SA. See also Bronner 1989, "Folklife Starts Here."

46. HWS to Arthur Graeff, 5/12/58, SA.

47. S. K. Stevens to HWS, 1/22/48, PC.

48. HWS to David Judson Haykin, Library of Congress, 1948, PC.

49. PHMC 1950, "The PHMC, 1945–50," p. 24

50. HWS 1948, "Rotary Hour."

51. Arnaud C. Marts 1936 (July 30), program booklet, welcoming letter, *Pennsylvania Folk Festival*, p. 5.

52. Korson 1949, *Pennsylvania Songs and Legends*, pp. 16, 1.

53. HWS to George Korson, 6/27/49, SA.

54. Jones 1949, "Editor's Page."

55. Korson 1949, *Pennsylvania Songs and Legends*, pp. 15–16.

56. Gillespie 1980, *Folklorist of the Coal Fields*, pp. 107–8; Frank Hoffmann to Simon Bronner, 2/28/93.

57. George Korson to HWS, 3/13/47, PC.

58. HWS to George Korson, 3/14/47, PC.

59. George Korson to HWS, 4/8/47, PC.

60. Gillespie 1980, *Folklorist of the Coal Fields*, p. 108.

238 Notes

61. Dorson 1971, *American Folklore and the Historian,* pp. 1–14.
62. George Korson to HWS, 1/11/54, SA.
63. Korson 1957, "Henry W. Shoemaker," p. 4. The quote of Jacobs comes from "The Folk" (1893). For more discussion of Joseph Jacobs, see Fine 1987, "Joseph Jacobs: A Sociological Folklorist"; Dorson 1968, *The British Folklorists,* pp. 266–67.
64. See Bronner 1991, "A Prophetic Vision of Public and Academic Folklife."
65. HWS to Alfred Shoemaker, 4/1/48, SA.
66. Interview with Don Yoder, Middletown, Pennsylvania, 12/9/92; Dolores Coffey to Simon Bronner, 1/21/93.
67. Dolores Coffey to Simon Bronner, 1/21/93.
68. Minutes of Pennsylvania Folklore Society Meeting, 1951, LC.
69. Ibid.
70. HWS to Alfred Shoemaker, 5/4/50, SA.
71. See Alfred Shoemaker 1949, "Pennsylvania Dutch Folklore"; Alfred Shoemaker 1954, *In the Pennsylvania Dutch Country;* Alfred Shoemaker 1959, *Christmas in Pennsylvania.*
72. HWS to Margaret Bryant, 5/12/55, SA.
73. Moritz Jagendorf to HWS, 4/27/51, PS.
74. Moritz Jagendorf to HWS, 8/16/55, SA.
75. Moritz Jagendorf to HWS, 8/1/55, SA.
76. See Yoder 1982, "Folklife in Pennsylvania."
77. Seminars 1952, p. 1.
78. *Third Annual Pennsylvania Dutch Folk Festival,* 1952 (program booklet), p. 1.
79. See Dorson 1976, *Folklore and Fakelore,* pp. 5–8; Baron 1992, "Postwar Public Folklore."
80. Dorson 1971, *American Folklore and the Historian,* pp. 12–13.
81. Ibid., pp. 23–24.
82. Dorson 1968, *Buying the Wind,* p. 1.
83. See Leach 1966, "Folklore in American Regional Literature"; Dorson 1971, *American Folklore and the Historian,* pp. 1–14.
84. Jordan 1946, "Toward a New Folklore"; McDowell 1958, *American Studies;* Dorson 1976, *The Birth of American Studies;* Wise 1979, "Paradigm Dramas."
85. Greenway 1968, *MacEdward Leach Memorial Issue.* See also Beck 1967, "MacEdward Leach"; Zumwalt, *American Folklore Scholarship,* pp. 63–64.
86. HWS 1926, "President's Address to Pennsylvania Federation," p. 8.
87. George Korson to Francis Lee Utley, 5/2/51, PS; HWS to Moritz Jagendorf, 3/28/52, SA.
88. HWS to Moritz Jagendorf, 3/7/52, SA.
89. George Korson to HWS, 1/4/56, SA.
90. MacEdward Leach to HWS, 5/25/55, SA.
91. Botkin 1944, *A Treasury of American Folklore,* pp. 690–92, 750–58; HWS 1928, *Two Pennsylvania Mountain Legends.*
92. HWS to B. A. Botkin, 4/30/48, SA.
93. Dorson 1971, *American Folklore and the Historian,* p. 6.
94. Ibid., p. 26.
95. Moritz Jagendorf to HWS, 10/5/50, SA.
96. Dorson 1976, *Folklore and Fakelore,* pp. 27–28.
97. Moritz Jagendorf to HWS, 1/9/52, SA.
98. Moritz Jagendorf to HWS, 2/3/54, SA.
99. HWS to Moritz Jagendorf, 2/4/54, SA.
100. HWS to Richard Dorson, 6/29/53, SA.
101. Dorson 1971, "Applied Folklore," pp. 40–42; Abrahams 1993, "Phantoms of Romantic Nationalism," pp. 382–84.
102. HWS 1948, "A Two Years Look Ahead."
103. Minutes of Pennsylvania Folklore Society, 5/15/48, SA.

104. Interview with Martha Simonetti, Harrisburg, Pennsylvania, 12/7/92.

105. See HWS 1951, "Pennsylvania Mountain Snakelore"; HWS 1951, "Two Tales"; HWS 1952, "Katie Eisenberger's Spook Stories"; HWS 1952, "Mrs. Ida Doyle Remembers."

106. HWS to D. Cadzow, report, 2/27/50, SA.

107. HWS to D. Cadzow, report, 8/23/49, SA.

108. Pennsylvania Folklore Society, program booklet, 10/16/52, LC; HWS 1950, "The Folklore of Dauphin County"; HWS, n.d., "Clinton County Folklore."

109. HWS to D. Cadzow, report, 3/22/55, SA.

110. Jost 1953, "Patriot News Salutes Shoemaker."

111. Adele Moyer Allison (typescript), 8/17/54, JC.

112. HWS to Cadzow, memorandum, 1/25/55, SA.

113. Press release, 1/12/50, SA. See also Daniel Hoffman 1952, *Paul Bunyan;* Dorson 1976, *Folklore and Fakelore,* pp. 291–336; Rogers 1993, *Paul Bunyan.*

114. Press release, 1/12/50, SA.

115. Press release, 2/27/50, SA.

116. Press release, 10/10/50, SA. See also Wollenweber 1974, *Mountain Mary.*

117. Press release, 12/17/54, SA. See also HWS 1950, "Early Jewish Pioneers."

118. HWS to Jansen Foundation, 3/1/50, SA.

119. HWS to D. Cadzow, memorandum, 7/31/51, SA.

120. Ibid.

121. Ibid.

122. HWS to D. Cadzow, memorandum, 1/25/55, SA; HWS to D. Cadzow, report, 1/24/55, SA.

123. Beaver 1952, "Col. H. W. Shoemaker Honored."

124. HWS to Mrs. J. R. Mellinger, 5/24/51, PS.

125. Shoemaker wrote Samuel Bayard on December 2, 1949, "It has been my cherished hope that you take over this division when I retire" (SA), but Bayard was steadily employed at Penn State and critical of public folklore programs generally and of Shoemaker specifically. "[Shoemaker] was as arrant a faker and 'fakelorist' as ever existed. . . . I was certainly not interested in doing anything in association with the Col.," Bayard wrote much later (Samuel Bayard to Simon Bronner, 4/21/93). Shoemaker considered George Korson but said his salary demands would be too high for the commission (HWS to D. Cadzow, memorandum, 3/6/48, SA). Approaching Charles Steese, Shoemaker worried about his lack of credentials in folklore (HWS to D. Cadzow, memorandum, 7/31/51, SA).

126. HWS to D. Cadzow, memorandum, 10/7/54, SA.

127. HWS to Moritz Jagendorf, 8/3/55, SA.

128. Ibid.

129. HWS to D. Cadzow, memorandum, 1/25/55, SA.

130. Dolores Coffey to Simon Bronner, 12/17/92.

131. Stevens 1964, *Pennsylvania,* p. 294.

132. HWS to D. Cadzow, report, 1/24/55, SA.

133. Dolores Coffey to Simon Bronner, 12/17/92; interview with John Witthoft, West Chester, Pennsylvania, 12/9/92; interview with William Wewer, Camp Hill, Pennsylvania, 12/14/92; interview with Sybil Jane Worden, Harrisburg, Pennsylvania, 12/7/92.

134. Interview with John Witthoft, West Chester, Pennsylvania, 12/9/92.

135. Gillespie 1980, *Folklorist of the Coal Fields,* p. 118.

136. HWS to Miriam Dickey, 5/15/56, JC.

137. Ibid.

138. Frank Hoffmann to Simon Bronner, 2/28/93.

139. Gillespie 1980, *Folklorist of the Coal Fields,* p. 118.

140. Col. Henry Shoemaker Dies, 1958.

141. H. W. Shoemaker, 1958.

142. Col. Henry Shoemaker Dies, 1958.

143. Blanche Shoemaker Carr to State Archives, 8/8/58, SA.

144. Skinner 1911, *Myths and Legends of Flowers, Trees*, pp. 299–300.

145. See Highlights of Auction Sale, 1959; Ancient Conestoga Wagon, 1959.

146. Colonel Shoemaker Room, 1960.

147. Frank A. Hoffmann 1958, "Henry W. Shoemaker," p. 346.

148. Korson 1958, "From the President's Desk," p. 29.

149. Walker 1958, "Colonel Henry W. Shoemaker," p. 46.

150. Samuel Bayard to Simon Bronner, 4/21/93; Samuel Bayard to Simon Bronner, 5/7/93.

151. Bayard 1959, "English-Language Folk Culture," p. 11.

152. Bayard elaborated on this point when he wrote me: "Some among the historians would cite the Welsh in Pennsylvania as likely sources for an investigation into traditions. This simply showed that these scholars had no real understanding of the nature of any folklore work. Phil Jack's and my experience of the Pennsylvania Welsh demonstrated that they were among the unlikeliest group of any in the commonwealth to throw any light on oral folk culture: their pietistic way of life and their early loss of the Welsh language made it useless to work with them, in general. . . . But if matters had been left wholly in the hands of the historians and anthropologists, we should have no collectanea at all worth speaking of and what was undertaken would have ended up in being merely a series of publicity stunts" (Samuel Bayard to Simon Bronner, 5/7/93).

153. Bayard 1959, "English-Language Folk Culture," p. 11.

154. See Slotkin 1981, "Nostalgia and Progress"; Oliver 1989, "Theodore Roosevelt, Brander Matthews, and the Campaign for Literary Americanism."

155. See Gleason 1991, "Minorities (Almost) All."

156. See Jensen 1965 [1951], *Regionalism in America;* Glassie 1968, *Pattern in the Material Folk Culture;* Lewis 1983, "Learning from Looking."

157. See Glass 1986, *The Pennsylvania Culture Region.*

158. See Glassie 1968, *Pattern in the Material Folk Culture;* Zelinsky 1973, *The Cultural Geography of the United States;* Gastil 1975, Cultural Regions of the United States.

159. HWS, n.d., "Pennsylvania's Last Frontier"; Wollenweber 1974, *Mountain Mary,* pp. 9–19.

160. Zelinsky 1974, "Selfward Bound?"; Zelinsky 1980, "North America's Vernacular Regions"; Zelinsky 1992, "The Changing Character of North American Culture Areas."

161. Bayard 1959, "English-Language Folk Culture," p. 12.

162. Ibid., p. 13.

163. See Brendle and Lick 1927, *Plant Names and Plant Lore;* Brendle and Unger 1970, *Folk Medicine of the Pennsylvania Germans;* Beam 1980, "The Thomas Royce Brendle Collection"; Bayard 1982, *Dance to the Fiddle, March to the Fife.* Although Brendle received special praise in Bayard's 1959 article, Bayard added other suitable models of collecting in a letter to me dated May 7, 1993. Besides mentioning Walter Boyer, Phil Jack, and Don Yoder, he offered that "actually the most methodical and thorough collecting of any was done among the miners by George Korson, who managed to put together a series of excellent studies in all aspects of mining life, and gratifyingly, received some decent credit for doing so, in to the bargain. . . . I must not forget Albert Buffington, of this university [Penn State], who made a most worthwhile collection of the 'Dutch' spirituals." Bayard's opinions of Shoemaker had not softened even almost twenty-five years after his criticism was published. On April 21, 1993, he wrote me, "My feelings about him have certainly not changed."

164. HWS to Ralph Steele Boggs, 2/9/50, SA.

165. See Loomis 1983, *Cultural Conservation;* Feintuch 1988, *Conservation of Culture.*

166. See Richman and Myers 1962, *Some Pennsylvania Folksongs;* Biennal Report, 1956–58, SA.

167. Stevens 1965, "A Historian Looks at Folklore."

168. Interview with William Wewer, Camp Hill, Pennsylvania, 12/14/92; Interview with David Hufford, Logan, Utah, 6/11/94; Dolores Coffey to Simon Bronner, 12/14/92; Glassie 1966, "Annual Meeting"; Glassie 1967, *Ethnic Culture Survey Report;* Hufford 1969, "History and Work of the Ethnic Culture Survey."

169. PHMC, report, 7/1/66–6/30/68, SL.

References

Abbott, John S. C. 1874. *David Crockett: His Life and Adventures.* New York: Dodd, Mead and Co.

Abernethy, Francis Edward. 1967. *J. Frank Dobie.* Austin: Steck-Vaughn.

———. 1992. *The Texas Folklore Society, 1909–1943. Volume 1.* Denton: University of North Texas Press.

Abrahams, Roger D. 1992. "The Public, the Folklorist, and the Public Folklorist." In *Public Folklore,* ed. Robert Baron and Nicholas R. Spitzer, pp. 17–28. Washington, D.C.: Smithsonian Institution Press.

———. 1993. "After New Perspectives: Folklore Study in the Late Twentieth Century." *Western Folklore* 52:379–400.

———. 1993. "Phantoms of Romantic Nationalism." *Journal of American Folklore* 106:3–37.

Abrahams, Roger D., and Susan Kalick. 1978. "Folklore and Cultural Pluralism." In *Folklore in the Modern World,* ed. Richard M. Dorson, pp. 233–36. The Hague: Mouton.

Allen, James Lane. 1891. *Flute and Violin, and Other Kentucky Tales and Romances.* New York: Harper and Brothers.

Allison, William M., Jr. 1915. *Henry W. Shoemaker: An Appreciation.* (Reprinted from the *Mount Union Times.*) Altoona: Times Tribune.

"Ancient Conestoga Wagon Goes Back to Conestoga." 1959. *Lock Haven Express,* September 24, pp. 1, 8.

Annan, Noel. 1966. "The Strands of Unbelief." In *Ideas and Beliefs of the Victorians: An Historic Revaluation of the Victorian Age,* ed. Harman Grisewood, pp. 150–56. New York: E. P. Dutton.

"Archivist Gets Folklore Post: Col. Henry Shoemaker Is Assigned to Collect Tales of State's Heritage." 1948. *Harrisburg Patriot,* March 12, pp. 1, 15.

Baird, Charles W. 1966 [1885]. *History of the Huguenot Emigration to America.* 2 vols. Reprint. Baltimore: Regional Publishing Company.

Barden, Thomas E. 1991. *Virginia Folk Legends.* Charlottesville: University Press of Virginia.

Baron, Robert. 1992. "Postwar Public Folklore and the Professionalization of Folklore Studies." In *Public Folklore,* ed. Robert Baron and Nicholas R. Spitzer, pp. 307–38. Washington, D.C.: Smithsonian Institution Press.

Baron, Robert, and Nicholas R. Spitzer, eds. 1992. *Public Folklore.* Washington, D.C.: Smithsonian Institution Press.

Barrick, Mac E. 1964. "Blue Mountain Tales." *Keystone Folklore Quarterly* 9:74–76.

——. 1994. "Lewis the Robber in Life and Legend." *Midwestern Folklore* 20:69–138.

Barton, Michael. 1983. *Life by the Moving Road: An Illustrated History of Greater Harrisburg*. Woodland Hills, Calif.: Windsor Publications.

Barzun, Jacques. 1965. *Race: A Study in Superstition*. Rev. ed. New York: Harper and Row.

Baughman, Ernest W. 1966. *Type and Motif Index of the Folktales of England and North America*. The Hague: Mouton.

Bausinger, Hermann. 1986. "Toward a Critique of Folklorism Criticism." In *German Volkskunde: A Decade of Theoretical Confrontation, Debate, and Reorientation (1967–1977)*, ed. and trans. James R. Dow and Hannjost Lixfelt, pp. 113–23. Bloomington: Indiana University Press.

Bayard, Samuel. 1944. *Hill Country Tunes: Instrumental Folk Tunes in Pennsylvania*. Philadelphia: American Folklore Society.

——. 1945. "Unrecorded Folk Traditions in Pennsylvania." *Pennsylvania History* 12:1–13.

——. 1959. "English-Language Folk Culture in Pennsylvania." *Pennsylvania Folklife* 10(2):11–13.

Bayard, Samuel, ed. 1982. *Dance to the Fiddle, March to the Fife: Instrumental Folk Tunes in Pennsylvania*. University Park: The Pennsylvania State University Press.

Bealle, John. 1994. "Another Look at Charles M. Skinner." *Western Folklore* 53:99–123.

Beam, C. Richard. 1980. "The Thomas Royce Brendle Collection of Pennsylvania German Folklore: A Preliminary Report." In *Sprache und Brauchtum: Bernhard Martin zum 90. Geburtstag*, ed. Reiner Hildebrandt and Hans Friebertschäuser, pp. 443–58. Marburg: N. G. Elwert.

Beard, George Miller. 1881. *American Nervousness: Its Causes and Consequences*. New York: G. P. Putnam's Sons.

Beaver, Kenneth. 1952. "Col. H. W. Shoemaker Honored for State Historical Work." *Harrisburg Patriot-News*, April 27, p. 11.

Beck, Horace P. 1967. "MacEdward Leach, 1896–1967." *Keystone Folklore Quarterly* 12:193–98.

Becker, Jane S., and Barbara Franco, eds. 1988. *Folk Roots, New Roots: Folklore in American Life*. Lexington, Mass.: Museum of Our National Heritage.

Beckwith, Martha Warren. 1931. *Folklore in America: Its Scope and Method*. Poughkeepsie, N. Y.: Vassar College, Folklore Foundation.

Bellah, Robert N., Richard Madsen, William M. Sullivan, Ann Swidler, and Steven M. Tipton. 1985. *Habits of the Heart: Individualism and Commitment in American Life*. New York: Harper and Row.

Benson, Susan Porter, Stephen Brier, and Roy Rosenzweig, eds. 1986. *Presenting the Past: Essays on History and the Public*. Philadelphia: Temple University Press.

Beyer, George R. 1991. *Guide to the State Historical Markers of Pennsylvania*. Harrisburg: Pennsylvania Historical and Museum Commission.

Bierly, Willis Reed. 1928. "Thrilling Story of Capt. Brady." *Lewisburg Saturday News*, September 22, pp. 1, 4.

Bloom, Allan. 1987. *The Closing of the American Mind*. New York: Simon and Schuster.

Bluestein, Gene. 1994. *Poplore: Folk and Pop in American Culture*. Amherst: University of Massachusetts Press.

Bode, Winston. 1968. *J. Frank Dobie: A Portrait of Pancho.* Austin, Tex.: Steck-Vaughn.

Bodnar, John. 1992. *Remaking America: Public Memory, Commemoration, and Patriotism in the Twentieth Century.* Princeton: Princeton University Press.

Boorstin, Daniel J. 1965. *The Americans: The National Experience.* New York: Vintage.

Botkin, B. A. 1936. "Regionalism, Cult or Culture?" *English Journal* 25:181–85.

———. 1937. "Regionalism and Culture." In *The Writer in a Changing World,* ed. Henry Hart, pp. 140–57. New York: Equinox Cooperative Press.

———. 1939. "WPA and Folklore Research: 'Bread and Song.'" *Southern Folklore Quarterly* 3:7–14.

———. 1946. "Living Lore on the New York City Writer's Project." *New York Folklore Quarterly* 2:252–63.

Botkin, B. A., ed. 1944. *A Treasury of American Folklore.* New York: Crown.

Bowden, M. J. 1992. "The Invention of American Tradition." *Journal of Historical Geography* 18:3–26.

Bowers, Claude G. 1932. *Beveridge and the Progressive Era.* Cambridge, Mass.: Riverside Press / Houghton Mifflin.

Boyer, Ernest L. 1987. *College: The Undergraduate Experience in America.* New York: Harper and Row.

Brady Dedication. 1928. *The Miltonian,* September 27, pp. 1, 8.

Brault, Gerard J. 1979. "Who Remembers Poor Malachi Boyer?" *Liberal Arts Faculty Newsletter* (The Pennsylvania State University), no. 4, pp. 20–21.

Brendle, Thomas R., and David E. Lick. 1927. *Plant Names and Plant Lore Among the Pennsylvania Germans.* Lancaster, Pa.: Pennsylvania-German Society.

Brendle, Thomas R., and Claude W. Unger. 1970. *Folk Medicine of the Pennsylvania Germans: The Non-Occult Cures.* New York: A. M. Kelley.

Brinton, Daniel G. 1972 [1884]. *The Lenape and Their Legends.* Reprint. St. Clair Shores, Mich.: Scholarly Press.

Bronner, Simon J. 1982. "Historical Methodology in Folkloristics: Introduction." *Western Folklore* 41:28–29,

———. 1982. "Malaise or Revelation? Observations on the 'American Folklore' Polemic." *Western Folklore* 41:52–61.

———. 1984. "William Henry Egle." *American Folklore Society Newsletter* 13 (December): 3.

———. 1986. *American Folklore Studies: An Intellectual History.* Lawrence: University Press of Kansas.

———. 1986. *Grasping Things: Folk Material Culture and Mass Society in America.* Lexington: University Press of Kentucky.

———. 1988. "Art, Performance, and Praxis: The Rhetoric of Contemporary Folklore Studies." *Western Folklore* 47:75–101.

———. 1989. "Collectors." In *Encyclopedia of Southern Culture,* ed. Charles Reagan Wilson and William Ferris, pp. 468–70. Chapel Hill: University of North Carolina Press.

———. 1989. "Folklife Starts Here: The Background of Material Culture Scholarship in Pennsylvania." In *The Old Traditional Way of Life: Essays in Honor of Warren E. Roberts,* ed. Robert E. Walls and George H. Schoemaker, pp. 283–96. Bloomington, Ind.: Trickster Press.

———. 1989. "Object Lessons: The Work of Ethnological Museums and Collections."

In *Consuming Visions: Accumulation and Display of Goods in America, 1880–1920,* ed. Simon J. Bronner, pp. 217–54. New York: W. W. Norton.

——. 1991. "A Prophetic Vision of Public and Academic Folklife: Alfred Shoemaker and America's First Department of Folklore." *Folklore Historian* 8:38–55.

——. 1992. "Martha Warren Beckwith, America's First Chair of Folklore." *Folklore Historian* 9:5–53.

——. 1993. "Exploring American Traditions: A Survey of Folklore and Folklife Research in American Studies." *American Studies International* 31:4–36.

——. 1993. "Folk Art on Display: America's Conflict of Traditions." *American Quarterly* 45:128–50.

Brumbaugh, Martin Grove. 1915. *Address by Governor Martin Grove Brumbaugh at Valley Forge, July Fourth, 1915.* Philadelphia: Hoskins Press for the Independence Day Commission.

Bulger, Peggy A. 1980. "Defining Folk Arts for the Working Folklorist." *Kentucky Folklore Record* 26:62–66.

Burton, Richard Francis. 1863. *Wanderings in West Africa From Liverpool to Fernando Po,* 2 vols. London: Tinsley Bros.

Cadzow, Donald A. 1936. *Archaeological Studies of the Susquehannock Indians of Pennsylvania.* Harrisburg: Publications of the Pennsylvania Historical Commission.

Campbell, John Francis. 1890 [1860–62]. *Popular Tales of the West Highlands,* 4 vols. Reprint. London: A. Gardner.

Cantwell, Robert. 1991. "Conjuring Culture: Ideology and Magic in the Festival of American Folklife." *Journal of American Folklore* 104:148–63.

Carter, Thomas, and Carl Fleischhauer. 1988. *The Grouse Creek Cultural Survey: Integrating Folklife and Historic Preservation Field Research.* Washington, D.C.: American Folklife Center, Library of Congress.

Cary, Ruth Anna. 1989. "The Mercer Museum and the Landis Valley Farm Museum: Exhibitions of Typology and Ethnicity in Pennsylvania." *Folklore Historian* 6:38–75.

Cashman, Sean Dennis. 1988. *America in the Age of the Titans: The Progressive Era and World War I.* New York: New York University Press.

Chase, Richard. 1943. *The Jack Tales.* Cambridge, Mass.: Houghton Mifflin.

Churchill, Allen. 1970. *The Upper Crust: An Informal History of New York's Highest Society.* Englewood Cliffs, N. J.: Prentice-Hall.

Clebsch, William A. 1979. "America's 'Mythique' as Redeemer Nation." In *Prospects: An Annual of American Cultural Studies,* vol. 4, ed. Jack Salzman, pp. 79–94. New York: Burt Franklin.

Clements, William M., ed. 1986. *Native American Folklore in Nineteenth-Century Periodicals.* Athens, Ohio: Swallow Press / Ohio University Press.

Cocchiara, Guiseppe. 1981. *The History of Folklore in Europe.* Trans. John N. McDaniel. Philadelphia: Institute for the Study of Human Issues.

Cochran, Robert. 1985. *Vance Randolph: An Ozark Life.* Urbana: University of Illinois Press.

"Col. Henry Shoemaker Dies, Had Heart Attack." 1958. *Lock Haven Express,* July 15, p. 1.

"Col. Henry W. Shoemaker: A Pennsylvania Parks Association Executive." 1941. *Pennsylvania Park News,* September, pp. 49–50.

"Col. Shoemaker, in Colorful and Busy Life, Maintained Interest in War Against Tuberculosis." [1958?] (Offprint, Pennsylvania State Archives, Harrisburg)

" 'Colonel Shoemaker Room' at the Locks Announces Opening." 1960. *Lock Haven Express,* January 12.

Cupper, Dan. 1993. "Ninety-Five Years of the Pennsylvania Society: A 'Who's Who' of Business and Politics." *Pennsylvania Heritage* 19:32–37.

———. 1994. "A Century of Conservation: The Story of Pennsylvania's State Parks." *Pennsylvania Heritage* 20:23–27.

Curtin, Jeremiah, and J. N. B. Hewitt. 1910–11. "Seneca Fiction, Legends, and Myths." *Annual Report of the Bureau of American Ethnology* 32:37–813.

Darlington, James Henry. 1925. *Verses by the Way.* New York: Brentano's.

Davidson, Levette J. 1951. *A Guide to American Folklore.* Denver, Colo.: University of Denver Press.

Deardorff, Merle H. 1972. *Chief Cornplanter.* Historic Pennsylvania Leaflet No. 32. Harrisburg: Pennsylvania Historical and Museum Commission.

Dickey, Miriam E. 1955. "Henry W. Shoemaker: Pennsylvania Folklorist." M. A. thesis, Western Reserve University.

Dobie, J. Frank, ed. 1924. *Legends of Texas.* Publications of the Texas Folklore Society III. Austin: University of Texas Press.

———. 1930. *Man, Bird, and Beast.* Austin: Texas Folk-Lore Society.

———. 1941. *The Longhorns.* Boston: Little, Brown, 1941.

———. 1943. "Twenty Years an Editor." In *Backwoods to Border,* ed. Mody C. Boatright, pp. v–ix. Austin: Texas Folklore Society.

Donehoo, George P. 1921. *The Changing of Historic Place Names, With an Introduction and Glossary of Some Historic Names Changed or Misspelled in Pennsylvania, By Henry W. Shoemaker.* Altoona, Pa.: Tribune Press.

———. 1928. *Indian Villages and Place Names in Pennsylvania.* Harrisburg: Telegraph Press.

Dorson, Richard M. 1946. *Jonathan Draws the Long Bow.* Cambridge: Harvard University Press.

———. 1952. *Bloodstoppers and Bearwalkers: Folk Traditions of the Upper Peninsula.* Cambridge: Harvard University Press.

———. 1959. *American Folklore.* Chicago: University of Chicago Press.

———. 1968. *The British Folklorists: A History.* Chicago: University of Chicago Press.

———. 1968. *Buying the Wind: Regional Folklore in the United States.* Chicago: University of Chicago Press.

———. 1971. *American Folklore and the Historian.* Chicago: University of Chicago Press.

———. 1971. "Applied Folklore." In *Papers on Applied Folklore,* ed. Dick Sweterlitsch, pp. 40–42. Bibliographic and Special Series, no. 8, *Folklore Forum.*

———. 1972. *Folklore: Selected Essays.* Bloomington: Indiana University Press.

———. 1972. "How Shall We Rewrite Charles M. Skinner Today?" In *American Folk Legend: A Symposium,* ed. Wayland D. Hand, pp. 69–96. Berkeley and Los Angeles: University of California Press.

———. 1972. "The Use of Printed Sources." In *Folklore and Folklife: An Introduction,* ed. Richard M. Dorson, pp. 465–77. Chicago: University of Chicago Press.

———. 1973. *America in Legend: Folklore from the Colonial Period to the Present.* New York: Pantheon.

————. 1976. *The Birth of American Studies*. Inaugural Address Delivered at the Opening of the American Studies Center, Warsaw University, October 5, 1976. Bloomington: Indiana University.

————. 1976. *Folklore and Fakelore. Essays Toward a Discipline of Folk Studies*. Cambridge: Harvard University Press.

————. 1978. "Folklore in the Modern World." In *Folklore in the Modern World,* ed. Richard M. Dorson, pp. 11–54. The Hague: Mouton.

Dow, James R., and Hannjost Lixfeld, eds. 1994. *The Nazification of an Academic Discipline: Folklore in the Third Reich*. Bloomington: Indiana University Press.

Dunaway, Wayland Fuller. 1930. *The French Racial Strain in Colonial Pennsylvania*. Volume 9, Proceedings of the Huguenot Society of Pennsylvania.

Dwyer-Schick, Susan Adair. 1979. "The American Folklore Society and Folklore Research in America, 1888–1940." Ph.D. diss., University of Pennsylvania.

Egle, William Henry. 1883. *History of the Counties of Dauphin and Lebanon*. Philadelphia: Everts and Peck.

Evans, George S. 1904. "The Wilderness." *Overland Monthly* 43:31–33.

Evans, Timothy H. 1988. "Folklore as Utopia: English Medievalists and the Ideology of Revivalism." *Western Folklore* 47:245–68.

Fausold, Martin L. 1961. *Gifford Pinchot: Bull Moose Progressive*. Syracuse, N.Y.: Syracuse University Press.

Federal Writers' Project, Works Progress Administration. 1936. *Three Hikes Through Wissahickon*. Philadelphia.

————. 1939. *Northampton County Guide*. Bethlehem, Pa.: Bethlehem Times.

Feintuch, Burt, ed. 1988. *The Conservation of Culture: Folklorists and the Public Sector*. Lexington: University Press of Kentucky.

Fernandez, James W. 1986. "Folklorists as Agents of Nationalism: Asturian Legends and the Problem of Identity." In *Fairy Tales and Society: Illusion, Allusion, and Paradigm,* ed. Ruth B. Bottigheimer, pp. 133–48. Philadelphia: University of Pennsylvania Press.

Ferree, Barr, ed. 1912. *Year Book of the Pennsylvania Society, 1912*. New York: Pennsylvania Society.

————. 1914. *Year Book of the Pennsylvania Society, 1914*. New York: Pennsylvania Society.

Filson, John. 1966 [1784]. *The Discovery and Settlement of Kentucke*. Reprint. Ann Arbor, Mich.: University Microfilms.

Fine, Gary Alan. 1987. "Joseph Jacobs: A Sociological Folklorist." *Folklore* 98:183–93.

Fosdick, Raymond B. 1956. *John D. Rockefeller, Jr.: A Portrait*. New York: Harper and Brothers.

Fox, John, Jr., 1897. *"Hell fer Sartain" and Other Stories*. New York: Harper and Brothers.

————. 1898. *The Kentuckians, a Novel*. New York: Harper and Brothers.

Frey, J. William. 1946. "An Upswing of Pa. Deitsch Activities." *Der Pennsylvaanisch Deitsch Eileschpieggel,* nos. 5–6, pp. 2–4.

"Gains $2,000,000 by Change of Name." 1913. *New York Times,* May 24, p. 1.

Gastil, Raymond D. 1975. *Cultural Regions of the United States*. Seattle: University of Washington Press.

Georges, Robert A. 1972. "The General Concept of Legend: Some Assumptions to Be

Reexamined and Reassessed." In *American Folk Legend: A Symposium,* ed. Wayland Hand, pp. 1–19. Berkeley and Los Angeles: University of California Press.

Gerndt, Helge, ed. 1987. *Volkskunde und Nationalsozialismus.* Munich: Vereinigung für Volkskunde.

Getz, Gail M. 1985. "The Great Escape: Camping in the Nineteenth Century." *Pennsylvania Heritage* 11(3):18–25.

Gillespie, Angus K. 1980. *Folklorist of the Coal Fields: George Korson's Life and Work.* University Park: The Pennsylvania State University Press.

"Gives Son a $250,000 House." 1913. *New York Times,* April 22, p. 13.

Glass, Brent D. 1989. "Expanding a Vision: Seventy-Five Years of Public History." *Pennsylvania Heritage,* 15(1):26–31.

Glass, Joseph W. 1986. *The Pennsylvania Culture Region: A View from the Barn.* Ann Arbor, Mich.: UMI Research Press.

Glassberg, David. 1990. *American Historical Pageantry: The Uses of Tradition in the Early Twentieth Century.* Chapel Hill: University of North Carolina Press.

Glassie, Henry. 1966. "Annual Meeting, April 15, in Harrisburg." *Keystone Folklore Quarterly* 14:275–76.

———. 1967. *The Ethnic Culture Survey Report of the Middle States Conference on Folk Culture.* Harrisburg: Pennsylvania Historical and Museum Commission.

———. 1968. *Pattern in the Material Folk Culture of the Eastern United States.* Philadelphia: University of Pennsylvania Press.

Gleason, Philip. 1984. "World War II and the Development of American Studies." *American Quarterly* 36:343–58.

———. 1991. "Minorities (Almost) All: The Minority Concept in American Social Thought." *American Quarterly* 43:392–424.

Glimm, James York: 1983. *Flatlanders and Ridgerunners: Folktales from the Mountains of Northern Pennsylvania.* Pittsburgh: University of Pittsburgh Press.

———. 1991. *Snake-Bite: Lives and Legends of Central Pennsylvania.* Pittsburgh: University of Pittsburgh Press.

Goode, James B. 1989. "Appalachian Literature." *Encyclopedia of Southern Culture,* ed. Charles Reagan Wilson and William Ferris, pp. 845–47. Chapel Hill: University of North Carolina Press.

Graeff, Arthur D. 1955. "Renascence of History." *Pennsylvania Folklife* 6(5):36–38.

Grant, William E. 1994. "The Inalienable Land: American Wilderness as Sacred Symbol." *Journal of American Culture* 17:79–86.

Greeley, William B. 1951. *Forests and Men.* Garden City, N.Y.: Doubleday.

Green, Harvey. 1986. *Fit for America: Health, Fitness, Sport, and American Society.* Baltimore: Johns Hopkins University Press.

———. 1992. *The Uncertainty of Everyday Life, 1915–1945.* New York: Harper Perennial.

Green, Rayna D. 1975. "Traits of Indian Character: The 'Indian' Anecdote in American Vernacular Tradition." *Southern Folklore Quarterly* 39:233–62.

———. 1990. "The Pocahontas Perplex: The Image of Indian Women in American Culture." In *Unequal Sisters: A Multicultural Reader in United States Women's History,* ed. Ellen Carol DuBois and Vicki L. Ruiz. New York: Routledge.

Greenway, John, ed. 1968. *MacEdward Leach Memorial Issue, Journal of American Folklore* 81:97–120.

Grinnell, George Bird. 1961 [1889]. *Pawnee Hero Stories and Folk-Tales.* Reprint. Lincoln: University of Nebraska Press.

———. 1962 [1892]. *Blackfoot Lodge Tales: The Story of a Prairie People.* Reprint. Lincoln: University of Nebraska Press.

———. 1971 [1926]. *By Cheyenne Campfires.* Reprint. Lincoln: University of Nebraska Press.

———. 1976. *Beyond the Old Frontier: Adventures of Indian-Fighters, Hunters, and Fur Traders.* Williamstown, Mass.: Corner House.

Groueff, Stephane. 1987. *Crown of Thorns: The Reign of King Boris III of Bulgaria, 1918–1943.* Lanham, Md.: Madison Books.

Halpert, Herbert. 1947. "American Regional Folklore." *Journal of American Folklore* 60 (1947): 355–60.

———. 1985. "A Note on Charles E. Brown and Wisconsin Folklore." *Midwestern Journal of Language and Folklore* 11:54–59.

Hand, Wayland D., comp. 1943. "North American Folklore Societies." *Journal of American Folklore* 56:161–91.

———, comp. 1946. "North American Folklore Societies. A Supplement." *Journal of American Folklore* 59:477–80.

Hand, Wayland D., ed. 1972. *American Folk Legend: A Symposium.* Berkeley and Los Angeles: University of California Press.

Hanna, Charles A. 1902. *The Scotch-Irish.* 2 vols. New York: G. P. Putnam's Sons.

———. 1911. *The Wilderness Trail, or The Ventures and Adventurers of the Pennsylvania Traders on the Allegheny Path.* 2 vols. New York: G. P. Putnam's Sons.

Hawes, Bess Lomax. 1992. "Happy Birthday, Dear American Folklore Society: Reflections on the Work and Mission of Folklorists." In *Public Folklore,* ed. Robert Baron and Nicholas R. Spitzer, pp. 65–73. Washington, D.C.: Smithsonian Institution Press.

———. 1992. "Introduction." In *American Folk Masters: The National Heritage Fellows,* by Steve Siporin, pp. 14–21. New York: Harry N. Abrams.

Hawthorne, Nathaniel. 1960 [1837]. *Twice-Told Tales and Other Short Stories.* Reprint. New York: Washington Square Press.

Hays, Samuel. 1959. *Conservation and the Gospel of Efficiency: The Progressive Conservation Movement, 1890–1920.* Cambridge: Harvard University Press.

Henning, David C. 1911. *Tales of the Blue Mountains.* Pottsville, Pa.: Publications of the Historical Society of Schuylkill County, vol. 3.

Henning, David C., and Adolf W. Schalck, eds. 1907. *History of Schuylkill County, Pennsylvania.* Madison, Wis.: State Historical Association.

"Highlights of Auction Sale at Shoemaker Museum." 1959. *Lock Haven Express,* September 28, p. 8.

Hirsch, Jerrold. 1987. "Folklore in the Making: B. A. Botkin." *Journal of American Folklore* 100:3–38.

———. 1988. "Cultural Pluralism and Applied Folklore: The New Deal Precedent." In *The Conservation of Culture: Folklorists and the Public Sector,* ed. Burt Feintuch, pp. 46–70. Lexington: University Press of Kentucky.

Historical Commission of Pennsylvania. 1915. *First Report of the Historical Commission of Pennsylvania.* Lancaster, Pa.: New Era Printing.

Hobsbawn, Eric, and Terence Ranger, eds. 1983. *The Invention of Tradition.* Cambridge: Cambridge University Press.

Hoffman, Daniel. 1952. *Paul Bunyan: Last of the Frontier Demigods*. Philadelphia: University of Pennsylvania.

Hoffman, W. J. 1888. "Folk-Lore of the Pennsylvania Germans." *Journal of American Folklore* 1:125–35.

Hoffman, William N. 1989. *Going Dutch: A Visitor's Guide to the Pennsylvania Dutch Country*. New Rochelle, N. Y.: Spring Garden Publications.

Hoffmann, Frank A. 1956. "The Pennsylvania Folklore Society." *Keystone Folklore Quarterly* 1:1.

————. 1958. "Henry W. Shoemaker, 1882–1958." *Journal of American Folklore* 72:345–46.

Hofstadter, Richard. 1960. *The Age of Reform: From Bryan to F. D. R.* New York: Vintage.

Holt, J. C. 1989. *Robin Hood*. London: Thames and Hudson.

Hufford, David. 1969. "History and the Work of the Ethnic Culture Survey and the State Folklorist Program of the Pennsylvania Historical and Museum Commission." *Keystone Folklore Quarterly* 14:166–75.

Hufford, Mary. 1986. *One Space, Many Places: Folklife and Land Use in New Jersey's Pinelands National Reserve*. Washington, D. C.: American Folklife Center, Library of Congress.

Hunt, George T. 1940. *The Wars of the Iroquois: A Study in Intertribal Relations*. Madison: University of Wisconsin Press.

"H. W. Shoemaker, Ex-Diplomat, Dies." 1958. *New York Times*, July 16, p. 29.

Illick, Joseph S. 1928. *Pennsylvania Trees*. Harrisburg: Pennsylvania Department of Forests and Waters.

"Introducing Our Personality of the Week. 1936." *Lock Haven Express*, December 5, pp. 1–2.

Jacobs, Joseph. 1893. "The Folk." *Folklore* 4:233–38.

Jagendorf, M. 1949. *Upstate Downstate: Folk Stories of the Middle Atlantic States*. New York: Vanguard Press.

James, Thelma. 1948. "Folklore and Propaganda." *Journal of American Folklore* 6:311.

Jennings, Francis. 1984. *The Ambiguous Iroquois Empire*. New York: W. W. Norton.

Jensen, Merrill, ed. 1965 [1951]. *Regionalism in America*. Reprint. Madison: University of Wisconsin Press.

Jones, Louis C. 1949. "Editor's Page." *New York Folklore Quarterly* 5:174.

————. 1950. "Folk Culture and the Historical Society." *Minnesota History* 31:11–17.

Jones, Michael Owen. 1982. "Another America: Toward a Behavioral History Based on Folkloristics." *Western Folklore* 41:43–51.

————. 1991. "Why Folklore and Organization(s)?" *Western Folklore* 50:29–41.

————. 1994. "Applying Folklore Studies: An Introduction." In *Putting Folklore to Use*, ed. Michael Owen Jones, pp. 1–41. Lexington: University Press of Kentucky.

Jones, Michael Owen, Michael Dane Moore, and Richard Christopher Snyder, eds. 1988. *Inside Organizations: Understanding the Human Dimension*. Newbury Park, Calif.: Sage Publications.

Jordan, Philip D. 1946. "Toward a New Folklore." *Minnesota History* 27:273–80.

Jost, Gordon. 1953. "Sunday Patriot News Salutes: Henry W. Shoemaker." *Harrisburg Sunday Patriot News*, December 6, p. 22.

Kammen, Michael. 1991. *Mystic Chords of Memory: The Transformation of Tradition in American Culture*. New York: Alfred A. Knopf.

Kautsky, Karl. 1926. *Are the Jews a Race?* New York: International Publishers.

Kent, Barry. 1984. *Susquehanna's Indians.* Harrisburg: Pennsylvania Historical and Museum Commission.

Kessler-Harris, Alice. 1992. "Cultural Locations: Positioning American Studies in the Great Debate." *American Quarterly* 44:299–312.

Kiner, Deb. 1992. "Tree's Size Poses Knot for Hopeful Officials." *Harrisburg Evening News,* Metro East Section, April 7, pp. 1, 7.

Kirschenblatt-Gimblett, Barbara. 1983. "The Future of Folklore Studies in America: The Urban Frontier." *Folklore Forum* 16:175–234.

Klein, Philip, and Ari Hoogenboom. 1980. *A History of Pennsylvania.* Second and enlarged edition. University Park: The Pennsylvania State University Press.

Kodish, Debora. 1992. "On Folklore and Multiculturalism." *Philadelphia Folklore Project Works in Progress* 5(2):8–9.

Korson, George. 1926. *Songs and Ballads of the Anthracite Miner: A Seam of Folklore Which Once Ran Through Life in the Hard Coal Fields of Pennsylvania.* New York: Frederick H. Hitchcock, Grafton Press.

———. 1938. *Minstrels of the Mine Patch.* Philadelphia: University of Pennsylvania Press.

———. 1957. "Henry W. Shoemaker: Folklorist." *Keystone Folklore Quarterly* 2:2–4.

———. 1958. "From the President's Desk." *Keystone Folklore Quarterly* 3:29

Korson, George, ed. 1949. *Pennsylvania Songs and Legends.* Philadelphia: University of Pennsylvania.

Kouwenhoven, John A. 1967 [1948]. *The Arts in Modern American Civilization.* Reprint. New York: W. W. Norton.

Kraybill, Donald B. 1989. *The Riddle of Amish Culture.* Baltimore: Johns Hopkins University Press.

Kulik, Gary, ed. 1993. "Special Issue on Multiculturalism." *American Quarterly* 45, no. 2 (June).

LaBar, Robert J. 1984. "Noah Parker's Treasure: Fact or Fantasy?" Paper delivered at the Society for Pennsylvania Archeology, State College, Pennsylvania, May 12.

Lang, Andrew. 1898. *Custom and Myth.* New edition. New York: Longmans, Green, and Company.

Leach, MacEdward. 1965. " 'King Arthur's Tomb' and 'The Devil's Barn': Two Pennsylvania Folktales Told by Hiram Cranmer." In *Two Penny Ballads and Four Dollar Whiskey: A Pennsylvania Folklore Miscellany,* ed. Kenneth S. Goldstein and Robert H. Byington, pp. 71–80. Hatboro, Pa.: Folklore Associates.

———. 1966. "Folklore in American Regional Literature." *Journal of the Folklore Institute* 3:376–97.

Leach, MacEdward, and Henry Glassie. 1968. *A Guide for Collectors of Oral Traditions and Folk Cultural Material in Pennsylvania.* Harrisburg: Pennsylvania Historical and Museum Commission.

Lears, T. J. Jackson. 1981. *No Place of Grace: Antimodernism and the Transformation of American Culture, 1880–1920.* New York: Pantheon.

"A Lesson in Penn's Woods." 1993. *Harrisburg Patriot-News,* August 20, p. A16.

Levin, Doron. 1982. "Besides Its Amish, Pennsylvania Boasts Croats, Serbs, etc., So State Appoints a Folklorist, Shalom Staub, to Study 'Forgotten' Ethnic Groups." *Wall Street Journal,* November 17, pp. 1, 27.

Lewis, Peirce. 1983. "Learning from Looking: Geographic and Other Writing About the American Cultural Landscape." *American Quarterly* 35:242–61.

Link, Arthur S. 1954. *Woodrow Wilson and the Progressive Era, 1910–1917*. New York: Harper and Row.

Lloyd, Nelson. 1900. *The Chronic Loafer*. New York: J. F. Taylor.

———. 1901. "Among the Dunkers." *Scribner's* 30:513–28.

———. 1904. *Soldier of the Valley*. New York: Scribner's.

———. 1906. *Six Stars*. New York: Scribner's.

Loomis, Ormond H. 1983. *Cultural Conservation: The Protection of Cultural Heritage in the United States*. Washington, D.C.: Library of Congress.

Lowenthal, David. 1985. *The Past Is a Foreign Country*. Cambridge: Cambridge University Press.

———. 1993. *Holistic Heritage: Promises and Problems for Pennsylvania*. Harrisburg: Pennsylvania Heritage Affairs Commission.

Marx, Leo. 1964. *The Machine in the Garden: Technology and the Pastoral Ideal in America*. New York: Oxford University Press.

McDowell, Tremaine. 1958. *American Studies*. Minneapolis: University of Minnesota Press.

McGaw, Jeff. 1994. "Save-the-Mountain Group to Incorporate." *Harrisburg Patriot* December 31, pp. B1, B12.

McGeary, M. Nelson. 1960. *Gifford Pinchot: Forester, Politician*. Princeton: Princeton University Press.

McNeil, W. K. 1980. "A History of American Folklore Scholarship Before 1908." Ph.D. diss., Indiana University.

———. 1982. "History in American Folklore: A Historical Perspective." *Western Folklore* 41:30–35.

McNeil, W. K., ed. 1989. *Appalachian Images in Folk and Popular Culture*. Ann Arbor, Mich.: UMI Research Press.

Mechling, Jay. 1984. "High Kybo Floater: Food and Faeces in the Speech Play at a Boy Scout Camp." *Journal of Psychoanalytic Anthropology* 7:256–68.

———. 1989. "The Collecting Self and American Youth Movements." In *Consuming Visions: Accumulation and Display of Goods in America, 1880–1920*, ed. Simon J. Bronner, pp. 255–86. New York: W. W. Norton.

———. 1993. "On Sharing Folklore and American Identity in a Multicultural Society." *Western Folklore* 52: 271–90.

"Meet the Former State Historian." 1945. *Pennsylvania Park News*, December, p. 4.

Merrill, Lynn L. 1989. *The Romance of Victorian Natural History*. New York: Oxford University Press.

"Millionaire Has Written Legends of Susquehanna." 1913. *Altoona Tribune*, November 12.

Minkov, Ignat. 1989. "The Ethnographic Institute with Museum of the Bulgarian Academy of Sciences." In *Bulgaria: Tradition and Beauty*, ed. Elizabeth I. Kwasnik, pp. 12–13. Liverpool: National Museums and Galleries on Merseyside.

———. 1992. "Fieldwork in Bulgarian Ethnographic Museums." In *British and Bulgarian Ethnography*, ed. Elizabeth I. Kwasnik, pp. 12–17. Liverpool: National Museums and Galleries on Merseyside.

Montenyohl, Eric L. 1988. "Andrew Lang's Contributions to English Folk Narrative Scholarship: A Reevaluation." *Western Folklore* 47:269–84.

Moonsammy, Rita Zorn, David Steven Cohen, and Lorraine E. Williams, eds. 1987. *Pinelands Folklife*. New Brunswick, N.J.: Rutgers for the New Jersey State Council on the Arts, New Jersey Historical Commission, and New Jersey State Museum.

Moore, Arthur K. 1957. *The Frontier Mind: A Cultural Analysis of the Kentucky Frontiersman*. Lexington: University of Kentucky Press.

Moser, Hans. 1964. "Der Folklorismus als Forschungsproblem." *Hessische Blätter für Volkskunde* 55:9–57.

Nash, Roderick. 1967. *Wilderness and the American Mind*. New Haven: Yale University Press.

Nash, Roderick, ed. 1968. *The American Environment: Readings in the History of Conservation*. Reading, Mass.: Addison-Wesley.

Newall, Venetia J. 1987. "The Adaptation of Folklore and Tradition (Folklorismus)." *Folklore* 98:131–51.

Newell, William Wells. 1888. "On the Field and Work of a Journal of American Folklore." *Journal of American Folklore* 1:3–7.

———. 1898. Review of *Tales of the Blue Mountains in Pennsylvania* by D. C. Henning. *Journal of American Folklore* 11:76–78.

Nichols, Roy F. 1967. *The Pennsylvania Historical and Museum Commission: A History*. Harrisburg: Pennsylvania Historical and Museum Commission.

Nicoloff, Assen, ed. and trans. 1979. *Bulgarian Folktales*. Cleveland, Ohio: Assen Nicoloff.

Nixon, H. C. 1946. *Lower Piedmont Country*. New York: Duell, Sloan, and Pearce.

Nye, Russel B. 1966. *This Almost Chosen People: Essays in the History of American Ideas*. East Lansing: Michigan State University Press.

Oelschlaeger, Max. 1991. *The Idea of Wilderness*. New Haven: Yale University Press.

Oliver, Lawrence J. 1989. "Theodore Roosevelt, Brander Matthews, and the Campaign for Literary Americanism." *American Quarterly* 41:93–111.

O'Neill, William L. 1967. *Divorce in the Progressive Era*. New Haven: Yale University Press.

Owens, J. G. 1891. "Folk-Lore from Buffalo Valley, Central Pennsylvania." *Journal of American Folklore* 4:115–28.

Parker, Arthur C. 1923. *Seneca Myths and Folk Tales*, Buffalo, N.Y.: Buffalo Historical Society.

Pattee, Fred Lewis. 1905. *The House of the Black Ring*. New York: Henry Holt.

Patterson, John S. 1989. "From Battle Ground to Pleasure Ground: Gettysburg as a Historic Site." In *History Museums in the United States: A Critical Assessment*, ed. Warren Leon and Roy Rosenzweig, pp. 128–57. Urbana: University of Illinois Press.

Penn's Cave Inc. 1988. *Penn's Cave*. Centre Hall, Pa.: Penn's Cave.

Pennsylvania Federation of Historical Societies. 1925. *Year Book of the Pennsylvania Federation of Historical Societies, 1924*. Altoona, Pa.: Altoona Times Tribune.

"Pennsylvania Folklore." 1948. *Journal of American Folklore* 61:396.

Pennsylvania Historical and Museum Commission. 1950. "The Pennsylvania Historical and Museum Commission 1945–1950." Typescript, State Library of Pennsylvania, Harrisburg.

Perin, Constance. 1988. *Belonging in America: Reading Between the Lines*. Madison: University of Wisconsin Press.

Pinchot, Gifford. 1910. *The Fight for Conservation.* New York: Doubleday, Page.

———. 1928. *The Power Monopoly: Its Make-Up and Its Menace.* Milford, Pa.: Privately printed.

———. 1947. *Breaking New Ground.* New York: Harcourt, Brace and Company.

———. 1993 [1936]. *Fishing Talk.* Reprint. Harrisburg, Pa.: Stackpole Books.

Pinkett, Harold T. 1970. *Gifford Pinchot: Private and Public Forester.* Urbana: University of Illinois Press.

Potter, David M. 1954. *People of Plenty: Economic Abundance and the American Character.* Chicago: University of Chicago Press.

Price, Edward. 1990. *Captain Sir Richard Francis Burton.* New York: Scribner's.

Raven, Canon C. E. 1966. "Man and Nature." In *Ideas and Beliefs of the Victorians: An Historic Revaluation of the Victorian Age,* ed. Harman Grisewood, pp. 173–79. New York: E. P. Dutton.

Reichard, Harry Hess. 1944. "John Baer Stoudt, D. D.: An Appreciation." *Pennsylvania German Folklore Society Publications.* Vol. 9, pp. 221–29. Allentown, Pa.: Schlechter's.

Richman, Vivien, and Richard Myers, comps., and Donald Kent, ed. 1962. *Some Pennsylvania Folksongs* (Pennsylvania Folklore leaflet). Harrisburg: Pennsylvania Historical and Museum Commission.

Richter, Daniel K. 1992. *The Ordeal of the Longhouse: The Peoples of the Iroquois League in the Era of European Civilization.* Chapel Hill: University of North Carolina Press.

Rodgers, Daniel T. 1987. *Contested Truths: Keywords in American Politics Since Independence.* New York: Basic Books.

Rogers, D. Laurence. 1993. *Paul Bunyan: How a Terrible Feller Became a Legend.* Bay City, Mich.: Historical Press.

Roosevelt, Theodore. 1926. *American Ideals, the Strenuous Life, Realizable Ideals.* New York: Charles Scribner's Sons.

———. 1926. *State Papers as Governor and President, 1899–1909.* New York: Charles Scribner's Sons.

———. 1926. *Literary Essays.* New York: Charles Scribner's Sons.

———. 1926. *The Wilderness Hunter: Outdoor Pastimes of an American Hunter.* New York: Charles Scribner's Sons.

———. 1986. *Wilderness Writings,* ed. Paul Schullery. Salt Lake City, Utah: Gibbs M. Smith.

———. 1993. "Preservation of the Forests." In *Great American Speeches,* ed. Gregory R. Suriano, pp. 127–31. New York: Gramercy Books.

Rosenberger, Homer Tope. 1971. *Adventurers and Philosophy of a Pennsylvania Dutchman: An Autobiography in a Broad Setting.* Bellefonte: Pennsylvania Heritage.

———. 1974. *Mountain Folks: Fragments of Central Pennsylvania Lore.* Lock Haven, Pa.: Annie Halenbake Ross Library.

Rothrock, G. A. 1979. *The Huguenots: A Biography of a Minority.* Chicago: Nelson-Hall.

Rourke, Constance. 1959 [1931]. *American Humor: A Study of the National Character.* Reprint. New York: Harcourt Brace Jovanovich.

Rubin, Joan Shelley. 1980. *Constance Rourke and American Culture.* Chapel Hill: University of North Carolina Press.

Rung, Albert M. 1977. *Rung's Chronicles of Pennsylvania History.* Huntingdon, Pa.: Huntingdon County Historical Society.

Ruskin, John. 1869. *The Queen of the Air: Being a Study of the Greek Myths of Cloud and Storm*. Second edition. New York: Merrill and Baker.

Sajna, Mike. 1990. *Buck Fever: The Deer Hunting Tradition in Pennsylvania*. Pittsburgh: University of Pittsburgh Press.

———. 1993. "Storyteller [Henry Shoemaker]." *Pennsylvania Game News* 64:14–18.

Schenda, Rudolf. 1986. "Telling Tales, Spreading Tales: Change in the Communicative Forms of a Popular Genre." In *Fairy Tales and Society: Illusion, Allusion, and Paradigm*, ed. Ruth B. Bottigheimer, pp. 75–93. Philadelphia: University of Pennsylvania Press.

Schlereth, Thomas J. 1991. *Victorian America: Transformations in Everyday Life*. New York: Harper Collins.

Schlesinger, Arthur M., Jr. 1992. *The Disuniting of America: Reflections on a Multicultural Society*. New York: W. W. Norton.

"Secretary of War James W. Good." *Reading (Pa.) Eagle*. September 8, 1929, p. 1.

"Seminars on the Folk Culture of the Pennsylvania Dutch Country." 1952. *Pennsylvania Dutchman*, May, p. 1.

Seton, Ernest Thompson. 1918. *Lives of the Hunted*. New York: Charles Scribner's Sons.

———. 1939. "The Rocky Mountain Goat: Description and Distribution." In *North American Big Game*, comp. Boone & Crockett Club, pp. 319–25. New York: Charles Scribner's Sons.

Sharp, Cecil. 1932. *English Folk Songs from the Southern Appalachians*. Ed. Maud Karpeles. 2 vols. London: Oxford University Press.

Shearer, William L. 1920. "Pennsylvania Folklore: The Life-Work of Colonel Henry W. Shoemaker." *Philadelphia North-American*, November 14, sec. 6, p. 2.

Shenk, Hiram H., ed. 1932. *Encyclopedia of Pennsylvania*. Harrisburg, Pa.: National Historical Association.

Shoemaker, Alfred L. 1949. "Pennsylvania Dutch Folklore." *Pennsylvania Dutchman*, May 5, p. 1.

———. 1959. *Christmas in Pennsylvania: A Folk Cultural Study*. Kutztown: Pennsylvania Folklife Society.

Shoemaker, Alfred, ed. 1954. *In the Pennsylvania Dutch Country*. Lancaster: Pennsylvania Dutch Folklore Center.

Shoemaker, Henry W. n.d. "The Ascent of the Mahanoy: An Account of the First Expedition of the Pennsylvania Alpine Club." (Typescript, PC)

———. n.d. "Bulgaria: A Picture of Future Pennsylvania?" (Typescript, LC)

———. n.d. "Clinton County Folklore, Its Rise, Its Fall, and Reasons, Therefore." (Typescript, LC)

———. n.d. "Excerpts from the Later Chapters of 'From Lancaster to Clearfield,' As Recalled from Memory by Henry W. Shoemaker." (Typescript, HC)

———. n.d. "Extracts from Lancaster to Clearfield: H. W. Shoemaker's First Prose Volume." (Typescript, SA)

———. n.d. "Fairbanks Sentiment in Pennsylvania, Ever-Increasing Demand for the Prosperity Candidate." (Typescript, PC)

———. n.d. "Henry Shoemaker's Convictions." (Typescript, PC)

———. n.d. "An Introduction to Pennsylvania Primitive Art or American Gothic, the Genius of Stettinius, Slagle and Other Masters." (Typescript, MU)

———. n.d. "Martin G. Brumbaugh, Naturalist Governor." (Typescript, HC)

———. n.d. "Pennsylvania Folklore." (Typescript, LC)

———. n.d. "Pennsylvania's Last Frontier." (Typescript, PC)

———. n.d. "Sketch of Henry W. Shoemaker." (Typescript, SA)

———. n.d. "Some Folklore of a Pennsylvania Eeler." (Typescript, JC)

———. n.d. "The Value of Folklore and Witchcraft Beliefs in Pennsylvania History." (Typescript, LC)

———. n.d. "Wild Life Conservation." (Manuscript, LC)

———. n.d. "Women's Part in Pennsylvania Lumbering Days." (Typescript, PC)

———. n.d. "The Work of the Pennsylvania Historical Commission." (Typescript, SA)

———. 1896. "Careless Gunners." *Argyle News* 1:1.

———. 1898. *Argyle Verse*. New York: Composite Printing Company.

———. 1898. *Immaterial Verses*. New York: Composite Printing Company.

———. 1898. "The Porter's Tale." *Argyle News,* May, p. 9.

———. 1900. *From Lancaster to Clearfield, or Scenes on the By-Ways of Pennsylvania*. New York: Composite Printing Company.

———. 1903. *Wild Life in Western Pennsylvania*. New York: Composite Printing Company.

———. 1907. *Pennsylvania Mountain Stories*. Reading, Pa.: Bright Printing Company.

———. 1908. *Pennsylvania Mountain Stories*. Bradford, Pa.: Bradford Record Publishing.

———. 1910. *Pennsylvania Mountain Stories*. Reading, Pa.: Reading Times.

———. 1912. *Elizabethan Days*. Reading, Pa.: Bright Printing Company.

———. 1912. *The Indian Steps and Other Pennsylvania Mountain Stories*. Reading, Pa.: Bright Printing Company.

———. 1912. *More Pennsylvania Mountain Stories*. Reading, Pa.: Bright Printing Company.

———. 1912. *Tales of the Bald Eagle Mountains*. Pennsylvania Folklore Series, vol. 4. Reading, Pa.: Bright Printing Company.

———. 1913. *In the Seven Mountains: Legends Collected in Central Pennsylvania*. Reading, Pa.: Bright Printing Company.

———. 1913. *Stories of Great Pennsylvania Hunters*. Altoona, Pa.: Tribune

———. 1913. *Story of the Indian Steps*. Versified by John H. Chatham. Altoona, Pa.: Tribune.

———. 1913. *Susquehanna Legends Collected in Central Pennsylvania*. Reading, Pa.: Bright Printing Company.

———. 1914. *Black Forest Souvenirs, Collected in Northern Pennsylvania. Legends of the West Branch of the Susquehanna*. Reading, Pa.: Bright-Faust.

———. 1914. *The Pennsylvania Lion or Panther: A Narrative of Our Grandest Animal*. Altoona, Pa.: Altoona Tribune.

———. 1914. Report of the Library Committee. In *Year Book of the Pennsylvania Society, 1914,* ed. Barr Ferree, pp. 91–92. New York: Pennsylvania Society.

———. 1914. *A Week in the Blue Mountains*. Altoona, Pa.: Tribune.

———. 1914. *Wolf Days in Pennsylvania*. Altoona, Pa.: Tribune.

———. 1915. *Captain Logan: Blair County's Indian Chief*. Altoona, Pa.: Tribune.

———. 1915. *A Pennsylvania Bison Hunt*. Middleburg, Pa.: Middleburg Post Press.

———. 1915. *Pennsylvania Deer and Their Horns*. Reading, Pa.: Faust Printing.

———. 1916. *The Dutchman on the Pennsylvania Frontier*. Address at the Banquet of the Netherlands Society of Philadelphia, January 22, 1916. Altoona, Pa.: Tribune Press.

———. 1916. *Early Potters of Clinton County.* Altoona, Pa.: Tribune.

———. 1916. *Juniata Memories: Legends Collected in Central Pennsylvania.* Philadelphia: J. J. McVey.

———. 1916. *Local Patriotism.* Address to Historical Society of Berks County, February 12. Reading, Pa.: Historical Society.

———. 1916. *Penn's Grandest Cavern: The History, Legends, and Description of Penn's Cave in Centre County, Pennsylvania.* Rev. ed. Altoona, Pa.: Tribune.

———. 1916. *Wasting the State's Money.* Altoona, Pa.: Tribune.

———. 1917. *The Abuse of Wealth.* Address to Ministerial Association of Williamsport, Pennsylvania, April 16, 1917. Altoona, Pa.: Altoona Tribune Press.

———. 1917. *Eldorado Found: The Central Pennsylvania Highlands, A Tourist's Survey.* Altoona, Pa.: Altoona Tribune.

———. 1917. "Pennsylvania Alpine Club." April 23 (Typescript, PS)

———. 1917. *Pennsylvania Folk Lore: Its Origin and Preservation.* An address delivered before the members of the Walking Club, Wellsboro, Pennsylvania, June 4, 1917. Altoona, Pa.: Times Tribune.

———. 1917. *The Pennsylvania Lion or Panther, Extinct Pennsylvania Animals Part I. The Panther and Wolf.* Altoona, Pa.: Tribune.

———. 1917. *Western Pennsylvania Indian Folk Lore.* Address to Ohio Valley Historical Association, Pittsburgh, Pennsylvania, November 30, 1917. Altoona, Pa.: Tribune Press.

———. 1918. *The Seneca Philosophy.* An Address Delivered Before the Young Men's Christian Association, Harrisburg, Pennsylvania, May 2, 1918. Altoona, Pa.: Altoona Tribune.

———. 1919, *Address of Henry W. Shoemaker, Litt. D., on His Induction as President of the Huguenot Society of Pennsylvania at the Second Reformed Church, Reading, Pennsylvania, June 17, 1919.* Altoona, Pa.: Altoona Tribune.

———. 1919. *Extinct Pennsylvania Animals, Part II: Black Moose, Elk, Bison, Beaver, Pine Marten, Fisher, Glutton, Canada Lynx.* Altoona, Pa.: Tribune.

———. 1919. *North Pennsylvania Minstrelsy.* Altoona, Pa.: Altoona Tribune.

———. 1920. *North Mountain Mementos: Legends and Traditions Gathered in Northern Pennsylvania.* Altoona, Pa.: Times Tribune.

———. 1920. *The Pennsylvania Forestry Problem.* Address to Garden Club of Williamsport, Pennsylvania, September 15, 1920. Altoona, Pa.: Times Tribune.

———. 1920. *Some Historic Trees of the West Branch Valley.* Altoona, Pa.: Times Tribune.

———. 1920. *South Mountain Sketches: Folk Tales and Legends Collected in the Mountains of Southern Pennsylvania.* Altoona, Pa.: Times Tribune.

———. 1920. *A Tour in Huguenot Countries.* Address delivered at a Meeting of the Executive Committee of the Huguenot Society of Pennsylvania, Reading, July 8, 1920. Altoona, Pa.: Times Tribune.

———. 1921. *The Black Bear of Pennsylvania.* Altoona, Pa.: Times Tribune.

———. 1921. "Introduction." In *The Changing of Historic Place Names,* by George P. Donehoo, p. 2. Altoona, Pa.: Tribune Press.

———. 1922. *Allegheny Episodes: Folk Lore and Legends Collected in Northern and Western Pennsylvania.* Altoona, Pa.: Altoona Tribune.

———. 1922. "The Folk Lore and Legends of Clinton County." Address to Clinton County Historical Society, Lock Haven, Pennsylvania, March 15, 1922. (Typescript, AH)

———. 1922. *A Forgotten People: The Pennsylvania Mountaineers.* Address to Women's Club, Bellefonte, Pennsylvania, April 24, 1922. Altoona, Pa.: Tribune Press.

———. 1922. *The Importance of Collecting Indian Legends.* Address before the Twenty-second Annual Convention of the Keystone State Library Association at Altoona, Pennsylvania, October 25, 1922. Altoona, Pa.: Tribune Press.

———. 1922. *Gifford Pinchot: The Man Who Made Good, a Character Sketch of the People's Governor.* Altoona, Pa.: Times Tribune.

———. 1922. *Some Forgotten Pennsylvania Heroines.* Altoona, Pa.: Times Tribune.

———. 1923. "Convictions of H.W.S. for Private Information." (Typescript, PC)

———. 1923. *The Music and Musical Instruments of the Pennsylvania Mountaineers.* Address to the Travelers Club, Smethport, McKean County, October 20, 1923. Altoona, Pa.: Mountain City Press, Times Tribune.

———. 1923. *North Pennsylvania Minstrelsy: As Sung in the Backwoods Settlements, Hunting Cabins, and Lumber Camps in the "Black Forest" of Pennsylvania, 1840–1923.* Second edition. Altoona, Pa.: Times Tribune.

———. 1923. *Place Names and Altitudes of Pennsylvania Mountains.* Altoona, Pa.: Times Tribune

———. 1923. *True Stories of the Pennsylvania Mountains.* Address to the Story Telling League, Girl's High School, Reading, Pennsylvania, May 2, 1923. Altoona, Pa.: Tribune Press.

———. 1924. *More Allegheny Episodes: Legends and Traditions, Old and New Gathered Among the Pennsylvania Mountains.* Altoona, Pa.: Mountain City Press, Times Tribune.

———. 1925. *Pennsylvania German and Huguenot Antiques.* Prepared by Walker Lewis Stephen. Second edition, revised. Publications of the Pennsylvania Folklore Society, vol. 1, no. 1. Reading, Pa.: Reading Eagle Press.

———. 1925. *Pennsylvania Indian Folk-Songs.* An Address Before the College Club, Williamsport, Penna., November 24, 1925. Privately printed.

———. 1925. *The Tree Language of the Pennsylvania German Gypsies.* Reading, Pa.: Reading Eagle Press.

———. 1926. "The Language of the Pennsylvania German Gypsies." *American Speech* 1:584–86.

———. 1926. *Marking the Historic Sites of Early Pennsylvania.* Fourth report of the Pennsylvania Historical Commission. Harrisburg.

———. 1926. "President's Address to Pennsylvania Federation of Historical Societies," January 14, 1926 (Typescript, PC)

———. 1926. *Pure Bred Stallions at "Restless Oaks," McElhattan, Clinton County, Pennsylvania.* Privately printed.

———. 1926. "Red Panthers Funeral Pyre." *Centre Hall Reporter.* August 19. (Scrapbook, JC)

———. 1927. *The Career of Forestry.* Address at Dedication of the New Building at Mont Alto Forestry School, March 10, 1927. Privately Printed.

———. 1927. *A Catalogue of Early Pennsylvania and Other Firearms and Edged Weapons at "Restless Oaks," McElhattan, Pennsylvania.* Altoona, Pa.: Times Tribune.

———. 1927. *Indian Folk Songs of Pennsylvania.* Ardmore, Pa.: N. F. McGirr.

———. 1927. *The Origins and Language of Central Pennsylvania Witchcraft.* Address to Woman's Study Club, Montgomery, Pennsylvania, April 8, 1927. Privately printed.

———. 1927. *Scotch-Irish and English Proverbs and Sayings of the West Branch Valley of Central Pennsylvania.* Publications of the Pennsylvania Folklore Society, no. 3. Reading, Pa.: Reading Eagle Press.

———. 1928. *In Penn's Woods. See* Shoemaker and Illick, 1928.

———. 1928. *Report of Henry W. Shoemaker, Chairman, Committee on Historical Activities at Annual Meeting, Pennsylvania Federation of Historical Societies.* Privately printed.

———. 1928. *Two Pennsylvania Mountain Legends.* Publications of the Pennsylvania Folklore Society, vol. 1., no. 4. Reading, Pa.: Reading Eagle Press.

———. 1929. *The Legends of the Caverns of Centre County, Pennsylvania.* Address to Science Club, State College, Pennsylvania, May 2, 1929. Reading, Pa.: Reading Eagle.

———. 1929. "The Romance of Pennsylvania History." Address to Lycoming County Historical Society. (Typescript, LC)

———. 1929. *The Wild Animals of Clinton County, Pennsylvania.* Compiled by Henry W. Shoemaker from Conversations and Notes of John H. Chatham, John Q. Dyce . . . and Other Clinton County Naturalists and Hunters. Altoona, Pa.: Times Tribune.

———. 1930. *Penn's Cave, Pennsylvania's Grandest Cavern.* Altoona, Pa.: Times Tribune.

———. 1930. *Thirteen Hundred Old Time Words of British, Continental or Aboriginal Origins, Still or Recently in Use Among the Pennsylvania Mountain People.* Altoona, Pa.: Times Tribune.

———. 1930. *Two Old Christmas Stories of the Great North Road Now Known as the "Susquehanna Trail" (Pennsylvania Highway Route No. 11).* Published for the Pennsylvania Folklore Society, Pamphlet 10. Altoona, Pa.: Times-Tribune Press.

———. 1931. *Mountain Minstrelsy of Pennsylvania.* Rev. ed. Philadelphia: Newman F. McGirr.

———. 1931. *Scotch-Irish and English Proverbs from Central Pennsylvania.* Publications of the Pennsylvania Folklore Society, no. 13. Reading, Pa.: Reading Eagle.

———. 1931. *Some Stories of Old Deserted Houses in the Central Pennsylvania Mountains.* Publications of the Pennsylvania Folklore Society, no. 13. Altoona, Pa.: Times Tribune.

———. 1932. *Tales of the Pennsylvania Highways; Folklore and Legends Collected Along a Number of Well-Known Routes in the Keystone State.* Altoona, Pa.: Times Tribune Press.

———. 1932. *Transplants in Pennsylvania Forests: Stories of Persons from Other Lands and States Whose Lives Are Interwoven in Pennsylvania Mountain Folk Lore.* Reading, Pa.: Reading Eagle.

———. 1935. "Pennsylvania Folkways in the Development of an American Culture." Convocation Address at Bucknell University. (Manuscript, PC)

———. 1935. "There Should be a Primitive Area Preserved in Pennsylvania." *Pennsylvania Park News,* no. 5 (June): 8–9.

———. 1936. "Pennsylvania Folklore." In *Pennsylvania Folk Festival,* ed. George Korson. Lewisburg, Pa.: Pennsylvania Folk Festival.

———. 1939. *Conserving Pennsylvania's Historic Past.* Harrisburg: Pennsylvania Historical Commission.

———. 1939. "Vanished Game." In *North American Big Game,* comp. Boone & Crockett Club, pp. 15–34. New York: Charles Scribner's Sons.

———. 1943. "Pennsylvania Folklore Society." *Journal of American Folklore* 56:180–81.

———. 1948. "Rotary Hour." Radio address, April 15. (Typescript, SA)

———. 1948. "A Two Years Look Ahead by the Folklore Division." August 23. (Memorandum, SA)

———. 1949. "Central Pennsylvania Legends." In *Pennsylvania Songs and Legends,* ed. George Korson, pp. 195–212. Philadelphia: University of Pennsylvania Press, 1949. Reprinted as "Pennsylvania Tall Tales" in *Philadelphia Inquirer,* Sunday Supplement, August 28, 1949.

———. 1950. "Blackbeard's Treasure Cave Is McKean County Mystery." *Capitol News,* May 29, 1950.

———. 1950. "Bulgaria in the Memory of a Former American Envoy." *Pennsylvania Park News,* April–May, p. 5.

———. 1950. "Early Jewish Pioneers in Dauphin County, Pennsylvania." Address to the Jewish Women's Club, Harrisburg, Pennsylvania, May, 1950. (Typescript, SA)

———. 1950. "Peter Grove, Legendary Indian Fighter." Weekly News Report, February 27, Pennsylvania State Archives, Harrisburg.

———. 1950. "Some Forgotten Pennsylvania Huguenots." Address to Huguenot Society at Bethlehem, Pennsylvania, May 6, 1950. (Typescript, SA)

———. 1951. "Currier and Ives: A Retrospect." (Typescript, RB)

———. 1951. "Neighbors. The Werewolf in Pennsylvania." *New York Folklore Quarterly* 7:145–55.

———. 1951. "Pennsylvania Mountain Snakelore." (Typescript, JC)

———. 1951. "Some Wild Life Folklore of the Allegheny and Susquehanna, Wherein Are Quotations of Mike Fink, John Drerbarrow, Dr. Friant, J. S. Wertz, Dr. Herbert H. Beck, and other Authorities." (Manuscript, LC)

———. 1951. "The Tiadaghton or Pine Creek Declaration of Independence" [July 4, 1951]. (Typescript, LC)

———. 1951. "Two Tales from the Folklore of the Clinton-Clearfield Border in North Central Pennsylvania. Compiled and Transmitted, 1923 by Miss Helen McGonigal to Henry W. Shoemaker." Harrisburg. (Typescript, MU)

———. 1952. "Katie Eisenberger's Spook Stories." (Typescript, JC)

———. 1952. "Mrs. Ida Doyle Remembers: She Vividly Recalls the Days of the Mighty Pennsylvania Pineries, Rafting, Log Driving and Canals, When Indians, Wolves, Panthers, Wild Pigeons and Shad Abounded, All Not So Very Many Years Ago." Harrisburg. (Typescript, SA)

———. 1953. "Ghosts at Random, Bits of the Supernatural Jotted Down From Time to Time, But Never Previously Made Use Of." (Typescript, SA) Published as "Ghosts at Random," *Keystone Folklore Quarterly* 2 (1957): 14–19.

———. 1953. "Neighbors. 'May Paulet Le Vieux Charlot,' A Pennsylvania-Huguenot Tale." *New York Folklore Quarterly* 9:307–13.

———. 1953. "The Pigeons of Capitol Hill, Some Memories of Old Time Harrisburg." (Typescript, SA)

————. 1953. "Reasons for Collecting Pennsylvania Folklore." Speech delivered in Annville, Pennsylvania. (Typescript, MU)

————. 1953. "Some Currently Collected Bits of Folklore." December 9, 1953. (Typescript, JC)

————. 1954. "Deeds of Captain Sam Brady." Weekly News Release, August 13, Pennsylvania State Archives, Harrisburg.

————. 1954. "A Strange Story of the Ghost of Lund's Lane." Weekly News Report, December 10, Pennsylvania State Archives, Harrisburg.

————. 1954. "Weather Beliefs." Weekly News Release, September 17, Pennsylvania State Archives, Harrisburg.

————. 1955. "Memories of Elimsport and North White Deer Mountain, John Q. Dyce Tells of a Night Among the Wolves." (Typescript, SA)

————. 1956. "The Two Corblies." *Keystone Folklore Quarterly* 1:3–4.

————. 1957. "Ballads and Songs." *Keystone Folklore Quarterly* 2:20–28.

————. 1980 [1939]. "Folk Lore, the Maker of Americans and Enricher of Life." *Journal of the Lycoming County Historical Society* 16:20–27. (From typescript of speech, March 6, 1939)

————. 1991 [1914]. *Black Forest Souvenirs: Collected in Northern Pennsylvania*. Reprint. Baltimore: Gateway Press for the Pine Creek Historian.

————. 1992. [1915] *Pennsylvania Deer And Their Horns*. Baltimore: Gateway Press for the Lycoming Historical Society.

————. 1992. [1915]. *Tales of the Bald Eagle Mountains in Central Pennsylvania*. Reprint. Baltimore: Gateway Press for the Lycoming County Historical Society.

Shoemaker, Henry W., and Joseph S. Illick. 1928. *In Penn's Woods: A Guide to Recreational Opportunities in the State Forests of Pennsylvania*. Harrisburg, Pa.: Department of Forests and Waters.

Sipe, C. Hale. 1931. *The Indian Wars of Pennsylvania*. Harrisburg, Pa.: Telegraph Press.

Siporin, Steve. 1992. *American Folk Masters: The National Heritage Fellows*. New York: Harry N. Abrams.

Skinner, Charles W. 1896. *Myths and Legends of Our Own Land*. 2 vols. Philadelphia: J. B. Lippincott.

————. 1903. *American Myths and Legends*. Philadelphia: J.B. Lippincott.

————. 1911. *Myths and Legends of Flowers, Trees, Fruits, and Plants in All Ages and in All Climes*. Philadelphia: J. B. Lippincott.

Slotkin, Richard. 1981. "Nostalgia and Progress: Theodore Roosevelt's Myth of the Frontier." *American Quarterly* 33: 608–38.

————. 1992. *Gunfighter Nation: The Myth of the Frontier in Twentieth Century America*. New York: Harper Perennial.

Smith, Henry Nash. 1950. *Virgin Land: The American West as Symbol and Myth*. Cambridge: Harvard University Press, 1950.

Sollors, Werner, ed. 1989. *The Invention of Ethnicity*. New York: Oxford University Press.

Sommers, Laurie Kay. 1991. "Inventing Latinismo: The Creation of 'Hispanic' Panethnicity in the United States." *Journal of American Folklore* 104:32–53.

Sorrells, Niels C. 1993. "Tourism Agencies Could be Halved." *Harrisburg Patriot,* July 1, p. 5.

Speke, John Hanning. 1863. *Journal of the Discovery of the Source of the Nile*. London: William Blackwood & Sons.

Staub, Shalom. 1982. "The Work of the Office of State Folklife Programs." *Keystone Folklore*, n.s., 1:1–7.

———. 1994. "Cultural Conservation and Economic Recovery Planning: The Pennsylvania Heritage Parks Program." In *Conserving Culture: A New Discourse on Heritage*, ed. Mary Hufford, pp. 229–44. Urbana: University of Illinois Press.

Staub, Shalom, ed. 1988. *Craft and Community: Traditional Arts in Contemporary Society*. Philadelphia: Balch Institute for Ethnic Studies and the Pennsylvania Heritage Affairs Commission.

———, ed. 1990. *Governor's Conference on Ethnicity: A Conference to Explore the Impact of Pennsylvania's Cultural Diversity on Public Policy*. Harrisburg: Pennsylvania Heritage Affairs Commission.

Stearns, Peter N. 1993. *Meaning over Memory: Recasting the Teaching of Culture and History*. Chapel Hill: University of North Carolina Press.

Steese, Charles M. 1952. "The Necklace War: An Indian Tale of Buffalo Valley (Union County)." Harrisburg: Pennsylvania Folklore Society. (Typescript, SL)

———. 1953. *Medical Folklore*. Harrisburg: Publication of the Pennsylvania Folklore Society, no. 26.

Steinberg, Stephen. 1981. *The Ethnic Myth: Race, Ethnicity, and Class in America*. New York: Atheneum.

Stephen, Walker Lewis. n.d. *The Girl, the Parson, the Wolf: A Story of the Alleghenies Many Years Ago*. Reading, Pa.: Reading Eagle Press.

———. 1929. "Legend of Hairy John and His Park; Man's Spirit Abides in Chestnut Tree." *Reading Eagle*, August 18. (Scrapbook, JC)

Stevens, Sylvester K. 1964. *Pennsylvania: Birthplace of a Nation*. New York: Random House.

———. 1965. "An Historian Looks at Folklore." In *Two Penny Ballads and Four Dollar Whiskey: A Pennsylvania Folklore Miscellany*, ed. Kenneth S. Goldstein and Robert H. Byington, pp. ix–xi. Hatboro, Pa.: Folklore Associates.

———. 1968. "Foreword." In *A Guide for Collectors of Oral Traditions and Folk Cultural Material in Pennsylvania*, by MacEdward Leach and Henry Glassie, pp. iii–iv. Harrisburg: Pennsylvania Historical and Museum Commission.

Stevens, Sylvester K., and Donald H. Kent. 1947. *Conserving Pennsylvania's Historical Heritage*. Harrisburg: Publications of the Pennsylvania Historical and Museum Commission.

Stoudt, Rev. John Baer. 1915. *The Folklore of the Pennsylvania-German*. Paper read before the Pennsylvania-German Society, York, Pennsylvania, October 14, 1910, supplement to vol. 23 of the Proceedings. Lancaster: Pennsylvania-German Society.

Stroud, Richard H., ed. 1985. *National Leaders of American Conservation*. Washington, D.C.: Smithsonian Institution Press.

Susman, Warren I. 1984. *Culture as History: The Transformation of American Society in the Twentieth Century*. New York: Pantheon.

Sweterlitsch, Dick. 1971. "Applied Folklore: The Debate Goes On." *Folklore Forum* 4:15–18.

Sweterlitsch, Dick, ed. 1971. *Papers on Applied Folklore*. Folklore Forum Bibliographic and Special Series, no. 8.

Teske, Robert T. 1988. "State Folk Art Exhibitions: Review and Preview." In *The

Conservation of Culture: Folklorists and the Public Sector, ed. Burt Feintuch, pp. 109–17. Lexington: University Press of Kentucky.

Thompson, Harold W. 1957. "Colonel Henry W. Shoemaker." *Keystone Folklore Quarterly* 2:1.

Thompson, Stith. 1975 [1955]. *Motif-Index of Folk-Literature,* 6 vols. Reprint. Revised and enlarged edition. Bloomington: Indiana University Press.

Thoms, William. 1965 [1846]. "Folklore." In *The Study of Folklore,* ed. Alan Dundes. Englewood Cliffs, N. J.: Prentice-Hall.

Tinkle, Lon. 1978. *An American Original: A Biography of J. Frank Dobie.* Boston: Little, Brown.

Tooker, Elizabeth. 1984. The Demise of the Susquehannocks: A 17th Century Mystery. *Pennsylvania Archaeologist* 54:1–10.

Toulmin, Stephen, and June Goodfield. 1965. *The Discovery of Time.* New York: Harper and Row.

Tozier, Gladys. 1974. "The Tiadaghton Elm." *Journal of the Lycoming County Historical Society* 10:14–15.

Voight, Vilmos. 1978. "Folklore and 'Folklorism' Today." In *Folklore Studies in the Twentieth Century,* ed. Venetia J. Newall, pp. 419–24. Suffolk: D. S. Brewer.

Wagstaff, Blanche Shoemaker. 1918. *Narcissus and Other Poems.* New York: J. T. White.

———. 1930. *Mortality and Other Poems.* Boston: Four Seas.

Walker, J. Herbert, ed. 1922. *Rafting Days in Pennsylvania.* Foreword by Henry W. Shoemaker. Altoona, Pa.: Times Tribune.

———. 1958. "Colonel Henry W. Shoemaker: A Biographical Sketch and a Tribute." *Keystone Folklore Quarterly* 3:46–48.

Walker, Robert H. 1967. *Life in the Age of Enterprise, 1865–1900.* New York: Paragon.

Wallace, Paul A. W. 1961. *Indians in Pennsylvania.* Harrisburg: Pennsylvania Historical and Museum Commission.

Wheeler, Post. 1912. *Russian Wonder Tales.* London: A. & C. Black.

Whisnant, David E. 1983. *All That Is Native and Fine: The Politics of Culture in an American Region.* Chapel Hill: University of North Carolina Press.

Who's Who of American Women. 1958. Volume I (1958–59). Chicago: A. N. Marquis.

Wiley, Farida A., ed. 1955. *Theodore Roosevelt's America.* New York: Devin-Adair.

———. 1962. *Ernest Thompson Seton's America.* New York: Devin-Adair.

Wilgus, D. K. 1959. *Anglo-American Folksong Scholarship Since 1898.* New Brunswick, N. J.: Rutgers University Press.

Willett, Henry. 1980. "Re-Thinking the State Folk Arts Program (Or Alternatives to the Festival)." *Kentucky Folklore Record* 26:12–15.

Winthrop, Robert H. 1991. *Dictionary of Concepts in Cultural Anthropology.* New York: Greenwood Press.

Wise, Gene. 1979. " 'Paradigm Dramas' in American Studies: A Cultural and Institutional History of the Movement." *American Quarterly* 31:293–337.

Wolf, George D. 1969. *The Fair Play Settlers of the West Branch Valley, 1769–1784: A Study of Frontier Ethnography.* Harrisburg: Pennsylvania Historical and Museum Commission.

Wollenweber, Ludwig August. 1974. *Mountain Mary: An Historical Tale of Early Pennsylvania.* Trans. and introd. John Joseph Stoudt. York, Pa.: Liberty Cap Books.

Writers Program of the Works Progress Administration in the State of Pennsylvania. 1940. *Pennsylvania: A Guide to the Keystone State*. New York: Oxford University Press.

Yoder, Don. 1982. "Folklife in Pennsylvania: An Historical Survey." *Keystone Folklore,* n.s. 1:8–20.

———. 1990. *Discovering American Folklife*. Ann Arbor, Mich.: UMI Research Press.

Zebrowski, Stephanie R. 1989. "Debunking a Myth—Were There Really Buffalo in Pennsylvania?" *Journal of the Lycoming County Historical Society* 23:11–23.

Zelinsky, Wilbur. 1973. *The Cultural Geography of the United States*. Englewood Cliffs, N. J.: Prentice-Hall.

———. 1974. "Selfward Bound? Personal Preference Patterns and the Changing Map of American Society." *Economic Geography* 50:144–79.

———. 1980. "North America's Vernacular Regions." *Annals of the Association of American Geographers* 70:1–16.

———. 1990. "Nationalistic Pilgrimages in the United States." In *Pilgrimage in the United States,* ed. G. Rinschede and S. M. Bhardwaj, pp. 253–67. Berlin: Dietrich Reimer Verlag.

———. 1992. "The Changing Character of North American Culture Areas." In *Regional Studies: The Interplay of Land and People,* ed. Glen E. Lich, pp. 113–35. College Station: Texas A&M University Press.

Zipes, Jack. 1979. *Breaking the Magic Spell: Radical Theories of Folk and Fairy Tales*. Austin: University of Texas Press.

———. 1988. *The Brothers Grimm: From Enchanted Forests to the Modern World*. New York: Routledge.

———. 1991. *Spells of Enchantment: The Wondrous Fairy Tales of Western Culture*. New York: Penguin.

Zipes, Jack, ed. 1987. *Victorian Fairy Tales: The Revolt of the Fairies and Elves*. Austin: University of Texas Press.

Zumwalt, Rosemary. 1988. *American Folklore Scholarship: A Dialogue of Dissent*. Bloomington: Indiana University Press.

Index

Also by Simon J. Bronner

Piled Higher and Deeper: The Folklore of Campus Life

American Children's Folklore

Old-Time Music Makers of New York State

Grasping Things: Folk Material Culture and Mass Society in America

American Folklore Studies: An Intellectual History

Chain Carvers: Old Men Crafting Meaning